THE AFTERLIFE OF APULEIUS

BULLETIN OF THE INSTITUTE OF CLASSICAL STUDIES SUPPLEMENT 140
DIRECTOR & EDITOR: GREG WOOLF

THE AFTERLIFE
OF APULEIUS

EDITED BY
FLORENCE BISTAGNE,
CAROLE BOIDIN,
AND RAPHAËLE MOUREN

INSTITUTE OF CLASSICAL STUDIES

SCHOOL OF ADVANCED STUDY
UNIVERSITY OF LONDON PRESS

2021

The cover image shows an initial letter from a manuscript in the Vatican Library: Vat. Lat. 2194, p. 65 v. Used with permission.

ISBN 978-1-905670-88-8 (paperback)
ISBN 978-1-905670-95-6 (PDF)
ISBN 978-1-905670-96-3 (epub)

Designed and typeset at the Institute of Classical Studies, University of London.

CONTENTS

NOTES ON CONTRIBUTORS

Florence Bistagne is Maître de conférences-HDR in Italian and Latin Language and Literature at Université d'Avignon, and member of the Institut universitaire de France. Her research combines a philological approach to Renaissance Latin and Italian texts with a socio-cultural study of European linguistic practices, from vernacular prose and verse to Latin treatises and diplomatic documents, with a special interest in national constructions involving linguistic references to antiquity. She has published multiple editions and translations of ancient and early Modern literary works, including Giovanni Pontano's *De Sermone* and several papers on the classical tradition and history of translation in the Kingdom of Naples.

Carole Boidin is Associate Professor (*Maître de conférences*) in Comparative Literature at Université Paris Nanterre. Her research focuses on comparing narrative and poetical practices from the Greek, Latin, and Arabic traditions. She has published several papers on Apuleius'*Golden Ass* and *The Arabian Nights,* as well as on their reception through time, especially in terms of ideological appropriations. She also has a keen interest in early modern knowledge and representation of Arabic poetics and North-African identities.

Igor Candido is Assistant Professor of Italian at Trinity College Dublin. In 2013-14 he was the recipient of the Alexander von Humboldt Fellowship at Freie Universität Berlin. He has lectured and taught in Italy, the US, Germany, and Ireland, and has written on Dante, Petrarch, Boccaccio, Poliziano, Emerson, and Longfellow. He has provided the critical edition of Ralph Waldo Emerson's translation of Dante's *Vita nuova* (Aragno 2012) and a monograph on Boccaccio as reader and imitator of Apuleius of Madauros (*Boccaccio umanista. Studi su Boccaccio e Apuleio*, Longo, 2014). He has edited a volume entitled *Petrarch and Boccaccio. The Unity of Knowledge in the Pre-modern World* (De Gruyter 2018) and is currently working on a new commented edition of Petrarch's *De vita solitaria* (Toronto UP). He is one of the editors of *Lettere italiane, Griseldaonline, Archivio Novellistico Italiano*; and he collaborates with Italian and American journals (*L'Indice dei libri del mese* and *MLN*).

Robert H. F. Carver is an Associate Professor of Renaissance Literature in the Department of English Studies at Durham University. His publications include *The Protean Ass: The 'Metamorphoses' of Apuleius from Antiquity to the Renaissance* (Oxford 2007); articles on Sir Philip Sidney and the reception of Heliodorus and Pierio Valeriano; the chapter on 'English Fiction and the Ancient Novel' in the first volume of the *Oxford History of the Novel in English*, ed. Thomas Keymer (Oxford 2017); and translations from the Latin writings of a twelfth-century mystic, *Hildegard of Bingen: An Anthology* (London 1990). He is currently investigating the relationship between ancient prose fiction and the so-called 'rise of the novel'.

Julia Haig Gaisser is Eugenia Chase Guild Professor Emeritus in the Humanities, Bryn Mawr College. She is principally interested in Latin poetry, Renaissance humanism, and the reception and transmission of classical texts. She is the author of the article on Catullus in *Catalogus Translationum et Commentariorum* 7 (1992). Her books include *Catullus and His Renaissance Readers* (1993), *The Fortunes of Apuleius and the Golden Ass* (2008), and *Catullus* (2009); she is also the editor and translator of *Pierio Valeriano on the Ill Fortune of Learned Men* (1999), Giovanni Pontano's *Dialogues: Charon and Antonius* (2012), and Giovanni Pontano's *Dialogues:Actius, Aegidius, and Asinus* (forthcoming).

Stephen Harrison is Fellow and Tutor in Classics at Corpus Christi College, Oxford and Professor of Latin Literature in the University of Oxford. He is author of *Apuleius: A Latin Sophist* (Oxford 2000) and of *Framing the Ass: Literary Form in Apuleius' Metamorphoses* (Oxford 2013), has worked in the Groningen Commentaries on Apuleius group for the volumes on Cupid and Psyche (2004) and the Isis book (2015), and is currently working with Regine May on a monograph on the reception of the Cupid and Psyche story in Western Europe since 1650 (a co-edited conference book on the same topic will appear in 2020 with De Gruyter).

Ahuvia Kahane is Regius Professor of Greek and A.G. Leventis Professor of Greek Culture at Trinity College Dublin. He previously taught at Royal Holloway, University of London, where he was Director of the Humanities and Arts Research Centre; at Northwestern University; and in Oxford. He is interested in evolutionary genealogies of consciousness, values and historical traditions, in questions of time, stochastic movement and emergence in discourse and in the ethics of form, and is completing books on orality and complexity in archaic verse (de Gruyter) and on epic, the ancient novel and perceptions of the temporal progress of antiquity (Bloomsbury).

Andrew Laird is John Rowe Workman Distinguished Professor of Classics and Humanities at Brown University, Rhode Island. Previously he was Professor of Classical Literature at Warwick University in the United Kingdom, where he held a Leverhulme Major Research Fellowship from 2008–11. Much of his research has been devoted to classical literature, but he has also published extensively on Latin humanism in Renaissance Europe, as well as in colonial Spanish America and Brazil. His self-authored and collaborative publications include *Powers of Expression, Expressions of Power* (1999), *Ancient Literary Criticism* (2006), *The Epic of America* (2006), *Italy and the Classical Tradition: Language, Thought, and Poetry 1300–1600* (2009), *The Role of Latin in the Early Modern World: Linguistic Identity and Nationalism 1350–1800* (2012), *Antiquities and Classical Traditions in Latin America* (2018), and *A Companion to the Prologue of Apuleius' Metamorphoses* (2001), co-edited with Ahuvia Kahane.

Françoise Lavocat is a professor and the chair of comparative literature at the Université Sorbonne Nouvelle—Paris 3. She was a former fellow at the Wissenschaftkolleg zu Berlin (2014–15), and is currently a member of the Institut Universitaire de France (2015–20). She has been a member of the European Academy since 2018, and president of the International Society for fiction and fictionality studies since 2019. She specializes in theories of fiction (fact and fiction, possible worlds, characters), early modern literature, and narratives of catastrophes. She has written *Arcadies malheureuses, aux origines du roman moderne* (Champion, 1997); *La Syrinx au bûcher, Pan et les satyres à la renaissance et à l'âge baroque* (Droz 2005); *Usages et théories de la fiction, la théorie contemporaine à l'épreuve des textes anciens* (ed. Presses Universitaires de Rennes 2004); *La théorie littéraire des mondes possibles* (éd. CNRS, 2010); *Fait et fiction: pour une frontière* (Seuil, 2016).

Clementina Marsico is a researcher at the Ludwig Boltzmann Institute for Neo-Latin Studies in Innsbruck. She is a member of the Italian *Edizione Nazionale delle Opere di Lorenzo Valla*. Much of her work has been on Italian humanism, the legacy of Latin classics between the Middle Ages and the Renaissance, the history of education, humanist preaching, as well as Medieval and Renaissance linguistics. Her publications include the critical editions of Lorenzo Valla's *Emendationes* to Alexander de Villadei's *Doctrinale* (2009), the fifth book of the *Elegantie lingue latine* (2013), and the *Sermo de mysterio eucharistie* (2019). She has co-edited several volumes, among which *Giovanni Tortelli primo bibliotecario della Vaticana. Miscellanea di studi* (2016).

Loreto Núñez worked from 2004 to 2018 at the University of Lausanne, first as Latin assistant, then in comparative literature as assistant, lecturer, and finally as deputy assistant professor at the CLE-Centre (Comparing Literatures in European languages). She was visiting-researcher at the University of Wales-Swansea, the Swiss Institute in Rome, and the Scuola Normale Superiore di Pisa. Her research focuses largely on narrative (ancient, especially the ancient novel; Renaissance; contemporary) and fairy tales, as well as on adaptation and translation for children. In 2018, she was appointed director of the French-speaking part of the Swiss Institute for Children's and Youth Media, an organization active in the field of literature and other media for children and young people and responsible for reading promotion.

Regine May is Associate Professor in Latin Language and Literature at the University of Leeds and the author of three books on Apuleius: *Apuleius and Drama. The Ass on Stage* (Oxford 2006), Apuleius. *Metamorphoses Book 1. With an Introduction, Translation and Notes* (Oxford 2013), and *Apuleius. The Story of Cupid and Psyche. With Translation, Introduction and Notes* (Manchester 2019). She has also written numerous articles on drama, women, and characterization in the novels, especially Apuleius. *Cupid and Psyche. The Reception of Apuleius' Love Story since 1650*, edited together with S.J. Harrison, will appear with de Gruyter for their Trends in Classics: Pathways of Reception series in 2020, and currently both authors are collaborating on a monograph on the reception of Cupid and Psyche in western literature.

Raphaële Mouren is Reader in the History of the Book and History of Libraries and Librarian of the Warburg Institute, University of London and deputy director, Centre Gabriel Naudé. Her main interests are the history of scholarship and the transmission of classics in the Renaissance; the Republic of Letters; the history of the book and the relationship between humanists and publishers, mainly in Italy, France, and the European humanist printers; the cultural history of Florence and Rome in the sixteenth century; and the history of private libraries in the modern period. She is author of *Biographie et éloges funèbres de Piero Vettori: entre rhétorique et histoire* (Paris 2014). She has curated books including *Bibliothèques et lecteurs dans l'Europe moderne* (Geneva 2016), *Auteur, collaborateur, traducteur, imprimeur ... que écrit?* (Paris 2013), and published articles and chapters in her fields of interest.

Andrea Severi is senior Assistant Professor (RtdB) in Italian Literature in the Department of Classical and Italian Studies of the University of Bologna, where he teaches Italian Renaissance Literature. He studies in particular the Bologna Renaissance in the fifteenth and sixteenth centuries, and the reception of classics and intertextuality in Renaissance works. He edited Mantuan's *eglogues*, Leon Battista Alberti's satirical works and Antonio Codro's

Sermones. Among his monographs are: *Filippo Beroaldo il Vecchio un maestro per l'Europa. Da commentatore di classici a classico europeo* (Bologna 2015); *Leggere i moderni con gli antichi e gli antichi coi moderni. Petrarca, Valla, Beroaldo,* (Bologna 2017). He edited with Scott Blanchard *Renaissance Encyclopaedism. Studies in Curiosity and Ambition* (Toronto 2018).

PREFACE AND ACKNOWLEDGEMENTS

FLORENCE BISTAGNE, CAROLE BOIDIN, AND RAPHAËLE MOUREN

This collection of articles on the 'Afterlife of Apuleius' is the result of a two-day international conference held at the Warburg Institute in London on 3 and 4 March 2016. The conference was jointly organized by the Warburg Institute, the Institut Universitaire de France, and the Institute of Classical Studies. It formed part of a series of conferences on the 'afterlife' of ancient authors (following a long tradition of *Nachleben* investigations at the Warburg Institute), the proceedings of which are published as supplements to the *Bulletin of the Institute of Classical Studies*. We wish to thank the editors of the *Bulletin* for accepting the present volume as part of this series.

The fortunes of Apuleius' *Metamorphoses* owe a great deal to the negative judgement of Macrobius and his position in favour of philosophy over recreational literature in late antiquity.[1] As a result, Apuleius' narrative writings suffered the same fate as various other discredited forms of escapist literature; late antiquity and the Middle Ages were only able to save Apuleius the philosopher and the fable of Cupid and Psyche, an isolated episode which allowed for an allegorical interpretation of the sort that was popular at the time. The first manuscript to restore the antique tradition was the *Mediceus alter* (Laur. 68.2), stamped F, which was to become the source for the whole medieval tradition, and includes the *Apologia*, the *Metamorphoses*, and *Florida*. Thanks to Boccaccio, transmission of Apuleius' *Opera omnia* began once again.

An important change can be noticed here: Apuleius was no longer only considered to be some distant and mute philosopher, or a strange magician, but rather a literary and stylistic genius.[2] The central role of the literary and rhetorical works in the material history of Apuleian texts has long been studied by philologists, mostly specialized in Renaissance textual traditions.[3] However, this volume of the 'Afterlife' series deliberately focuses on the medieval and early modern periods, down to the eighteenth century, in order to try to shed a new light on the philological and historical conditions of the appreciation of Apuleius, as well as on the literary and linguistic productivity of this reception. The project was guided by the will to gather together various approaches and to provide an interdisciplinary investigation of the evolution of the image of Apuleius and his texts through time, and of the literary

---

[1] Macr., *Somn.* 1.2.8: 'Auditum mulcent uel comoediae, quales Menander eiusue imitatores agendas dederunt, uel argumenta fictis casibus amatorum referta, quibus uel multum se Arbiter exercuit uel Apuleium non numquam lusisse miramur. Hoc totum fabularum genus, quod solas aurium delicias profitetur, a sacrario suo in nutricum cunas sapientias eliminat ed. M. Armisen-Marchetti, Collection des Universités de France (Paris 2003).

[2] On the construction of the literary value of Apuleius' works in modern scholarship, see S. Harrison, 'Constructing Apuleius: the emergence of a literary artist', *Ancient Narrative* 2 (2002) 143–171.

[3] See, for example, M. A. Acocella, '*L'asino d'oro' nel Rinascimento. Dai volgarizzamenti alle raffigurazioni pittoriche* (Ravenna 2001); R. H. F. Carver, *The Protean Ass: The 'Metamorphoses' of Apuleius from Antiquity to the Renaissance* (Oxford-New York 2007); J. H. Gaisser, *The Fortunes of Apuleius and the 'Golden Ass'. A Study in Transmission and Reception* (Princeton-Oxford 2008).

appropriations to which this renewed image gave birth. This early modern panorama is, thus, a contribution to the history of the reception of Apuleius, set within an enlarged historical frame and explored through the use of a range of methodological procedures. In addition, it also offers new perspectives by widening the geographical scope of interest to take in Latin American and Near Eastern receptions.[4]

The philological study of the material transmission of Apuleian texts leads directly to literary considerations, not only in terms of aesthetic influence but also because of the inscription of this influence within literary milieux. The literary debates about and polemics concerning these texts reveal the evolution of tastes, norms, and licences, with the growing circulation of manuscript and printed versions drawing ever-wider circles of readers into these discussions. The Italian connection played a major and multidimensional role in this regard. When we look at the manuscripts that Boccaccio possessed, annotated, or copied, we can see the definite influence of the narrator Apuleius not only on Boccaccio's early work but also on his *Decameron*. This is true especially for the manuscript, now known as *Laurentianus* 29.2 (φ), that was copied sometime around the year 1200: Boccaccio had access to this manuscript in Naples in 1339-1341, and he both read and annotated it.[5] Petrarch also owned a manuscript of a work by Apuleius, now the *Vaticanus latinus* 2193, which he annotated at some point between 1340 and 1343.[6] We therefore know that Apuleius' works were circulating a long time before the publication of the *editio princeps* of 1469 by Sweynheim and Pannartz in the edition established by Giovanni Andrea Bussi (one of the first ten books they published, predating even Virgil and Cicero's epistles). Later, in Bologna, Filippo Beroaldo the Elder's *Commentarii in asinum aureum* were published by Benedetto d'Ettore Faelli in 1500, and then again in 1501 by Aldus in Venice.[7] Printed in more than 1200 copies, then reprinted in numerous editions in Italy and beyond, Apuleius benefitted from the popularity of the current fashion for anything 'Egyptian' and became, once more, a key text.

One of the decisive moments in Apuleius' subsequent voyages throughout Western culture was at the court of the Estes in Ferrara during the quattrocento. Here, between 1469 and 1479, Matteo Maria Boiardo prepared his translation as a '*volgarizzamento*', with the work finally being printed some forty years later in 1518. In the final book, Boiardo includes the epilogue of Lucian's *Loukios or the Ass*, the history of which has always been linked to that of Apuleius.[8] The court of Isabella d'Este was also the place where the fable of Cupid and Psyche began to circulate as an autonomous text. There, Niccolò da Correggio composed a long Latin poem, *Fabula Psiches et Cupidinis*, on the subject towards 1490, and it also became a pictorial theme. Long after Fulgentius' allegorical reading of this story within the story, Psyche would become the subject of a renewed interest.[9] In nearby Mantua, Giulio

[4] Wider investigations of this sort, looking beyond the European context, have also been presented, primarily with regard to the ancient period, in *Apuleius and Africa*, eds B. T. Lee, E. Finkelpearl, and L. Graverini (New York 2014).

[5] See G. F. Gianotti, 'Da Montecassino a Firenze: la riscoperta di Apuleio', in *Il 'Decameron' nella letteratura europea*, ed. C. Allasia (Rome 2006) 9–46 and I. Candido, *Boccaccio umanista: studi su Boccaccio e Apuleio* (Ravenna 2014).

[6] See C. Tristano, 'Le postille del Petrarca nel ms. Vat. Lat. 2193 (Apuleio, Frontino, Vegezio, Palladio)', *Italia medioevale e umanistica* 17 (1974) 365–468.

[7] See *Filippo Beroaldo l'Ancien. Un passeur d'humanités / Filippo Beroaldo il Vecchio. Un umanista ad limina*, eds S. Fabrizio-Costa and F. La Brasca (Bern 2005).

[8] See E. Fumagalli, *Matteo Maria Boiardo volgarizzatore dell''Asino d'oro'. Contributo allo studio della fortuna di Apuleio nell'Umanesimo*, Medioevo e Umanesimo 70 (Padova 1988).

[9] On the fortunes of the story of Cupid and Psyche, see S. Cavicchioli, *Le metamorfosi di Psiche. La fortuna della*

Romano also devoted a whole cycle of paintings in the Palazzo del Te to the myth. With the great Aldine editions of 1501, the Apuleian text began to circulate more widely and was to have an incredible success in vernacular literature in sixteenth-century Spain, seventeenth-century England, and in France in 1669, when Jean de la Fontaine took advantage of the current taste for both oriental matters and the *roman à clefs* by setting his *Les Amours de Psyché et de Cupidon* in Versailles.

The international conference on *The Afterlife of Apuleius* brought together a number of the most knowledgeable scholars working on various aspects of the reception of Apuleius, from late antiquity to the modern period and beyond. This volume gathers together papers which include the results of the multiple discussions that were held during the conference. The order in which they are presented here is not only chronological but, rather, reflects the diversity of methodological choices in the papers, from diachronic analysis to micro-historical studies. This diversity opens up new perspectives on the early modern reception of Apuleius' work. The first group of contributions offers a global vision of Apuleius' historical and geographical diffusion, with various selected focuses. Robert Carver draws new conclusions concerning the High Medieval transmission and reception of the *Metamorphoses* in Europe, whereas Andrew Laird presents the means and consequences of the circulation and appropriations of the book in New Spain after the first European incursions. Carole Boidin suggests a complementary approach by considering the multifarious influence of Apuleius and the *Metamorphoses* in Europe and the way in which it was unexpectedly framed by ideological discussions concerning the African origin of the author, and by the supposedly oriental taste of the novel. Two sections are then devoted to the famous fable of Cupid and Psyche. The first focuses on the reception of the fable in the Middle Ages, with Julia Gaisser retracing its genealogy while Igor Candido examines how the tale was used by Petrarch and Boccaccio. The second section considers two English readings and adaptations of the fable, with studies of theatrical and poetic versions by Thomas Heywood in 1634 (Stephen Harrison) and Mary Tighe in 1805 (Regine May). Once again, the aim in these chapters is to combine historical case studies with a literary approach, insisting on the creative effects of the intellectual polemics and of the artistic genres in which the Apuleian material was used and reshaped. The *Metamorphoses* are also the subject of a more diachronic section concerning the evolution of specific formal devices and the variation of literary values. Ahuvia Kahane, Françoise Lavocat, and Loreto Nuñez demonstrate how the device of the embedded narrative illustrated in the *Metamorphoses* became generalized as a fictional model, and how the book made its way into the Western literary canon, from late antiquity to the Italian Renaissance and the Spanish *Siglo de Oro*. In a final section on lexicography, the focus shifts from the reception of the book to the appreciation of Apuleius' language and style. This section shows how, during the quattrocento in Italy and the early sixteenth century in Paris, Apuleius and his vocabulary and syntax became a major issue in contemporary discussions not only on the purity of the Latin language of Ancient Rome (Clementina Marsico) but also concerning the role of grammar and, leading on from this, the new philological methods of the humanists (Andrea Severi). It is no coincidence that we find in Giovanni Pontano's dialogue *Asinus* (1491) a satire of both clerics and politicians, in the form of what is almost a comedy in five acts, in which the greatest source of expressiveness is in fact the very language that is used.

---

favola di Apuleio nei secoli (Venice 2002); V. Gély, *L'Invention d'un mythe : Psyché, Allégorie et fiction, du siècle de Platon au temps de La Fontaine* (Paris 2006).

This is not Ciceronian written Latin but the mimetic Latin of the oral tradition, the variety that is the most able to reproduce the vividness of the spoken word, the Latin of Plautus and Apuleius. The donkey, used here as a symbol of ingratitude (a political event having sparked off the dialogue), subsequently becomes a pretext for a deeper excursus on the nature of language, in which dialogue is impossible unless all the available resources of the lexicon are used. Far from being a conservative exercise, imitation becomes a model for modernity. And this is precisely what this conference set out to prove: the modernity, in every sense of the term, that an 'ancient' author can have, and the necessity of taking an interdisciplinary approach when studying the culture of the early modern period.

We wish to thank the co-organizers of the conference, Greg Woolf and Olivier Pédeflous, for their scientific expertise, as well as Jane Ferguson for her efficient practical assistance and warm welcome. Thanks are also due to Elizabeth Potter, Publications Manager at the Institute of Classical Studies, and Paul Scade for their help during the publication process.

THE MEDIEVAL ASS:
RE-EVALUATING THE RECEPTION OF APULEIUS
IN THE HIGH MIDDLE AGES

ROBERT H. F. CARVER

What do we know for certain about the medieval transmission and reception of *The Golden Ass* or *Metamorphoses* of Apuleius? Our firmest evidence is codicological. The traditional stemma (fig. 1) shows some key moments, beginning, in the 1050s–80s, with the creation, at Monte Cassino, of F (Florence, Biblioteca Laurenziana 68.2), a manuscript containing the *Metamorphoses*, the *Apologia*, and the *Florida*.[1]

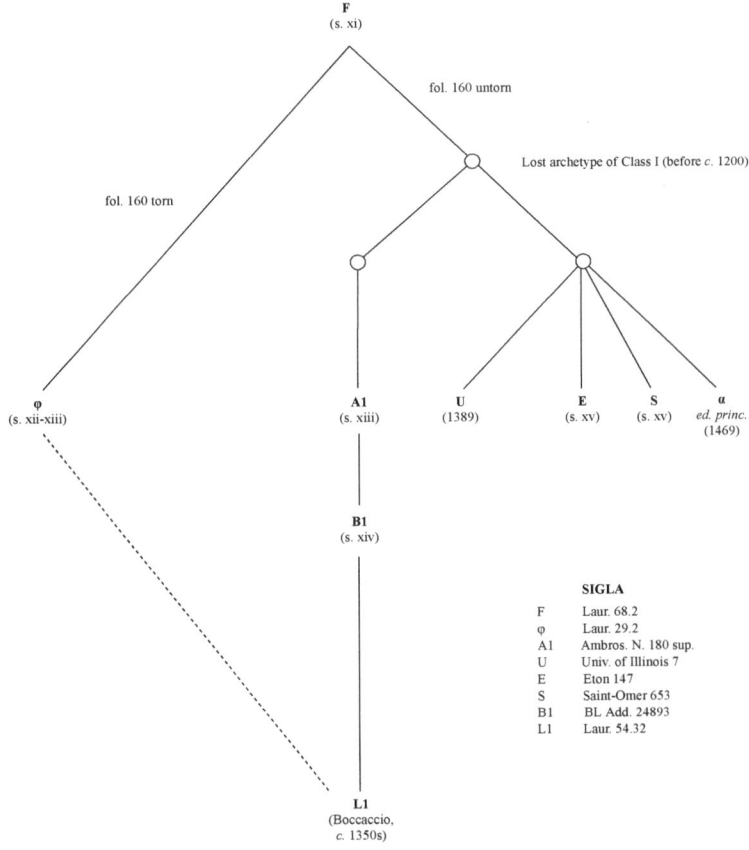

Figure 1. Traditional stemma.

[1] The stemma is reproduced from R. H. F. Carver, *The Protean Ass: The 'Metamorphoses' of Apuleius from Antiquity to the Renaissance* (Oxford 2007) 66.

The ink started to flake quite quickly from the flesh side of the parchment, and, around 1200, a copy of F was made which we call φ (Florence, Biblioteca Medicea Laurenziana, *Laurentianus* 29.2). Towards the end of the eleventh century (before 1086), Guaiferius, monk of Monte Cassino, makes undeniable use of the *Florida*, producing an almost cento-like effect. He also seems to extract details from Lucius' vision of Isis' mantle in *The Golden Ass* ('palla [...] nodulis fimbriarum', Apul. *Met.* 11.3), the 'threads of the mantle' which, despite being 'surrounded by ashes', have somehow remained 'intact' ('palle fimbrie cineribus involute sed integre').[2]

After Guaiferius and φ, however, the trail of Apuleian influence goes very cold indeed. One potential factor inhibiting the diffusion of manuscripts from Monte Cassino is the supposed difficulty of Beneventan ('Lombardic') script compared with Caroline minuscule. For a long time, it was believed that *The Golden Ass* only 'escaped' from the confines of Monte Cassino sometime around 1350, when Boccaccio or Zanobi da Strada 'rescued' the text. That myth has been exposed by scholarly analysis, but speculation about the availability of *The Golden Ass* has been hampered by a continuing fetishization of the roles of Monte Cassino and F. The logic, even of the traditional stemmatic model established by D. S. Robertson, demands that at least one copy of F (the lost ancestor of Class-1 manuscripts) had been made before folio 160 of F suffered a rent (that is to say, between 1050 or 1080 and the copying of φ around 1200).[3]

In recent decades, the date for diffusion outside Monte Cassino has been pushed back to the 1330s (Boccaccio's earliest works), the 1320s (Benzo of Alessandria), and (as I argued in 2007) the late 1310s (if we accept the internal dating of 1319 for Albertino Mussato's Latin poem describing a metamorphic journey).[4] The recent redating of A1 (Milan, Biblioteca Ambrosiana N180 sup.) from the early fourteenth century[5] to the late thirteenth century[6] takes us into very interesting territory, but it still leaves a significant gap in the fossil record.

There have been various attempts to fill this gap, but none of them has been entirely convincing.[7] The most compelling counter-evidence is the absence of a decisive mention of *The Golden Ass* in the places we would most expect to find it—monastic catalogues, medieval encyclopaedias, and learned commentaries, particularly relating to that notable exploiter and imitator of Apuleius, Martianus Capella.

If we *can* fill that gap, or find one or more of the 'missing links', it will have profound, indeed, radical implications for our understanding of the history of Western literature. The mid-twelfth to the mid-thirteenth century is a seminal epoch for imaginative fiction: it sees the revival of classical modes, epic, and comedy; the emergence of new modes, such as medieval

[2]   Carver, *Protean Ass* (n. 1, above) 63–65, citing O. Limone, 'L'opera agiografica di Guaiferio di Montecassino', in *Monastica III. Scritti raccolti in memoria del XV centenario della nascita di S. Benedetto (480–1980)*, Miscellanea Cassinese 47 (Monte Cassino 1983) 77–130 (104).

[3]   Carver, *Protean Ass* (n. 1, above) 67, extrapolating from D. S. Robertson, 'The manuscripts of the *Metamorphoses* of Apuleius', *CQ* 18 (1924) 27–42 and 85–99.

[4]   Carver, *Protean Ass* (n. 1, above) 121–22.

[5]   Robertson, 'The manuscripts' (n. 3, above) 29.

[6]   J. H. Gaisser, *The Fortunes of Apuleius and the 'Golden Ass': A Study in Transmission and Reception* (Princeton-Oxford 2008) 93 and 309.

[7]   *E.g.* D. Rollo, 'From Apuleius' Psyche to Chrétien's *Erec and Enide*', in *The Search for the Ancient Novel*, ed. J. Tatum (Baltimore 1994) 347–69; P. Dronke, 'Metamorphoses: allegory in early medieval commentaries on Ovid and Apuleius', *Journal of the Warburg and Courtauld Institutes* 72 (2009) 21–39; J. Fumo, 'Romancing the rose: Apuleius, Guillaume de Lorris, and moral horticulture', *Modern Philology* 107.3 (2010) 343–79. For a critical survey of the claims up until 2006, see Carver, *Protean Ass* (n. 1, above) 73–107. Neither the *Speculum stultorum* nor the *Asinarius* was considered in that monograph.

romance; the Celtic or 'Breton' *lai* with its fabulous (or 'fairy-tale'-like) content; and the fabliaux, those bawdy verse narratives which feed directly into the comic achievement of Boccaccio and Chaucer, while also exhibiting (whether as a result of convergent evolution or actual filiation) some uncanny affinities with Milesian tales. If *The Golden Ass* was available to readers and writers at this time, it may have played a significant part in this efflorescence of fiction.

Our focus in this preliminary re-evaluation of the medieval reception of *The Golden Ass* will be two Latin poems whose protagonists share some significant features with Apuleius' hero-narrator: they both manifest a mind that is human (or nearly human) in a body that (for all or most of the work) is fully asinine.

Case-study 1: 'Speculum stultorum'

The *Speculum stultorum* ('The mirror of fools') is a Latin satirical poem of 3,900 lines, composed (perhaps between November 1179 and March 1180) by an English monk, 'Nigellus', variously identified as Nigel de Longchamps, Nigel Wireker (or Whiteacre), or Nigel of Canterbury.[8] In the introduction to his English translation, Graydon W. Regenos observes, in passing, that 'The means by which Nigellus wishes to convey his message is imitative of the method used by Apuleius in his *Golden Ass*'. However, the claim is neither substantiated nor developed.[9]

The *Speculum* owes an obvious debt to Avianus' fable of 'The Ass in the Lion's Skin'.[10] But Apuleius' Lucius and Nigel's Burnellus share many characteristics, most notably a love of novelty ('nouitas') and forbidden things, and a desire for transformation. While Lucius travels to Thessaly in search of magic, Galienus sends Burnellus to Salerno (a centre of medical learning, and strongly connected with Monte Cassino) to purchase the requisites for a longer tail (619–20; R 51).[11] Galienus makes explicit the link between medicine and the divine: 'Sed deus est medicus nomine reque simul' ('God is doctor both in name and deed' (128; R 33). The tale ('narratio') that Galienus tells about Brunetta and Bicornis in order 'to turn the ass away from his foolishness' (205–594; R 36–50) has a structural affinity with Byrrhena's attempts to save Lucius from the consequences of his misplaced *curiositas* (Apul. *Met*. 2.5). And, like Apuleius, Nigel makes use of intercalated tales as a way of shortening a journey:

Simul iugi quod insurgimus aspritudinem fabularum lepida iucunditas levigabit.

---

[8] A. G. Rigg, 'Canterbury, Nigel of [Nigel Wireker or Whiteacre (*c*. 1135–1198?)', *ODNB*.

[9] G. W. Regenos, trans., *The Book of Daun Burnel the Ass: Nigellus Wireker's 'Speculum stultorum'* (Austin 1959) 9. For a narrative summary of the *Speculum stultorum*, see J. Mann, *From Aesop to Reynard: Beast Literature in Medieval Britain* (Oxford 2009) 312–13 (Appendix 2).

[10] Avianus, *Fab*. 5.17–18, in *Minor Latin Poets*, eds and trans J. W. Duff and A. M. Duff, 2 vols (London 1934) II 680–749 (= Perry 358). *Cf. Speculum* 61–62: 'Pelle leonina tectum detexit asellum / Fastus et excedens Gloria vana modum' ('Vainglory and excessive pride betray / The ass, though he be decked in lion's skin' (trans. Regenos 31). All references are to the Latin text (cited by line numbers) given in Nigel de Longchamps, *Speculum stultorum*, eds J. H. Mozley and R. R. Raymo (Berkeley 1960), and to Regenos' English translation (n. 9, above), which will subsequently be cited in abbreviated form (*e.g.* 'R 31').

[11] Burnellus' desire for a longer tail ('De asino qui voluit caudam suam longiorem fieri', 81; R 32) and his grief at losing half his existing tail (847–48 and 861; R 62) contrast with Lucius' relief at finally losing the asinine attribute: 'quae me potissimum cruciabat ante, cauda nusquam' (Apul. *Met*. 11.13). J. N. Adams, *The Latin Sexual Vocabulary* (London 1982) 36, notes that '*Cauda* = "penis" is securely attested only in Horace (*Serm*. 1.2.45, 2.7.49)' (*cf*. 35, 37, 221).

Besides, the charming delight of some stories will smooth out the ruggedness of the hill we are climbing.[12]
(Apul. *Met.* 1.2)

[…] et quod ingressui primum fuerit stabulum prandio participabo.

[…] and I will invite you to share dinner with me at the first inn after we come into town.[13]
(Apul. *Met.* 1.4)

Talia cum pariter gradientes plura referrent,
   Parisius subeunt hospitiumque petunt.

Conversing thus together as they walked,
   They came to Paris and they found an inn.
(1503–04; R 84)

Burnellus' inability to learn anything in Paris besides 'hy ha' might be compared with Lucius' inability to say anything but 'O':

Cum nihil ex toto, quodcunque docente magistro
   Aut socio, potuit discere praeter hy ha.

Yet absolutely nothing had he learned
   Of what his master taught except 'heehaw!'
(1545–46; R 85)

[…] sed viduatum ceteris syllabis ac litteris processit 'O' tantum […]

[…] but all that came out was 'He […]', missing all the other syllables and letters.
(Apul. *Met.* 8.29)

There is also a general similarity between the 'monstrous sharp-toothed hounds' ('immensos mordaci dente molossos') that Fromundus (one of the White Monks) sets on Burnellus as he crosses the fields (833; R 61), and the 'fierce, monstrous farm- and sheep-dogs' ('canes pastoricios villaticos feros atque immanes') that attack the boundary markers at the instigation of Apuleius' bloodthirsty landowner (Apul. *Met.* 9.36).

   There are also some tantalizing moments where one might suspect that Nigel is using the geography of southern Italy ('Apulia') to play on the 'Apuleian' characteristics of his protagonist (a foolish ass with a misplaced yearning for philosophy and transformation).[14] Reproaching himself for the 'follies' of his 'wasted youth' ('ineptae' / 'Damna juventutis',

---

[12]   All quotations from Apuleius are based on the Loeb edition, *Apuleius: Metamorphoses*, ed. and trans. J. A. Hanson, 2 vols (Cambridge, MA 1989).

[13]   Lucius fails to fulfil this pledge to Aristomenes when they reach Hypata at Apul. *Met.* 1.20–21.

[14]   On the representation of Frederick II (1194–1250) as the 'puer Apuliae' ('child of Apulia') and 'stupor mundi' ('wonder of the world'), see E. H. Kantorowicz's mythologizing biography, *Frederick the Second 1194–1250*, trans. E. O. Lorimer (London 1931).

571–72; R 86),[15] Burnellus wishes that he had never 'scaled the Alps' to visit 'the Paris schools':

> Appulus[16] huc veni, sed Gallicus ecce revertor.
>   Burnellus tamen qui fuit ante manet.

> Apulian came I here, a Gaul I leave,
>   Brunellus stays, however, just the same.
> (1585–86; R 86–87)

A safe default position might be that *The Golden Ass* was known *about*, but not actually *known* first-hand at this point; desired but not possessed. Yet some features of the poem may make us question that assumption:

> Mitra caput nostrum sine munere pontificali
>   Nulla deaurabit, auxiliante Deo.

> The miter shall not gild this head of mine
>   Without the bishop's powers, so help me God!
> (1681–82; R 90)

Of all the metaphors available to him to describe the placing of a bishop's mitre on the head of a donkey, why does Nigel choose 'gilding' ('deaurabit')? The immediate answer might be that 'gilding' conveys effectively the gap between semblance and substance—between the superficial pomp of office and actual ecclesiastical impotence.[17] But if we loosen the shackles of that negative ('nulla') and relax the 'bit' of that future simple ('deaurabit'), Burnellus becomes, if only for the most fleeting of moments, a 'golden ass', at least from the neck up. This is an illusion, of course—the thinnest layer of gold leaf—but it may also, just possibly, be an allusion to the title of Apuleius' work (*De asino aureo*) as transmitted by Augustine (*De civitate dei* 18.18).

We might consider, finally, Burnellus' escape from the blows of his master, Bernardus, and the brief idyll that he enjoys in his flight:

> **Aestus erat, <u>lassus</u> que fui voluique sub umbra**
>   Ilicis optato **membra <u>fovere</u> toro.**
> Carmina quae nuper me composuisse juvabat

---

[15] *Cf.* Apul. *Met.* 11.15: 'sed lubrico virentis aetatulae ad serviles delapsus voluptates, curiositatis improsperae sinistrum praemium reportasti' ('but on the slippery path of headstrong youth you plunged into slavish pleasures and reaped the perverse reward of your ill-starred curiosity').

[16] Manuscript D (Dublin, Trinity College, ms 440; mid-fifteenth century; owned by Peter Lee, monk of Durham, student of Oxford [1511], and Bursar [1514], then Prior [1523] of Durham College, Oxford) reads *Anglicus* ('[As] an Englishman') for 'Appulus'. See *Speculum stultorum*, eds Mozley and Raymo (n. 10, above), 9–10 and 134. The variant may reflect the satirical tradition ('caudatus Anglicus') of Englishmen having tails, explored by A. G. Miller, '"Tails" of masculinity: knights, clerics, and the mutilation of horses in medieval England', *Speculum* 88.4 (Oct. 2013) 958–95 (960–61). *Cf.* 'Arnold's Story about the Priest's Son and the Little Chick': 'Contigit Apuliae celebri res digna relatu, / Tempore Willelmi principis hujus avi' ('Apulia saw a strange event take place / When William ruled, the present duke's grandsire', 1255–56; R 75).

[17] Note the discussion of sterility and genitalia in the lines that follow: Burnellus wants to be a horse and not a mule. There seems to be a sideways swipe at the Church's hypocrisy regarding clerical celibacy: Arnoldus (1251ff.; R 75ff.) tells the tale of Gundulfus, the priest's son.

Scribere conabar tutus ab hoste meo.
Et locus et tempus, studio nimis apta, volentem
    Scribere cogebant improbitate sua.
Venter erat plenus, pes lassus, pagina prompta
    Excerptura nova carmina digna nota.
Cumque manus calamum ferrumque teneret acutum
    Exciperetque novos pellis ovina tonos,
Nescio quem prope me ramos super ilicis altae
    Audio garritum percipioque sonum.[18]

'Twas summer, I was tired, I chose to stretch
    On pleasant turf beneath a shady oak.
A poem which I had just composed I tried
    To put in writing; safe was I from foe.
Both time and place for study were just right,
    And since I wished to write, they urged me on. [132]
My stomach was well filled, my feet were tired,
    The page was ready to record my song.
And as I took my slender iron-tipped pen,
    And on the parchment was about to write,
I heard nearby some kind of chattering,
    I heard the sound beneath the lofty oak.
(2891–902; R 131–32)

The debt to Ovid's evocation of an erotic siesta in *Amores* 1.5.1–2 is obvious:

Aestus erat, mediamque dies exegerat horam;
    adposui medio **membra** levanda **toro**.

But there are also some interesting parallels with Lucius' flight from Corinth at the end of Book 10, and the moment of peace that he experiences as he stretches out beside the water before his vision of the goddess Isis (beginning at Apul. *Met.* 11.1). We note the elements in common: a donkey escaping from a town (2875–76: 'Nuper cum profugus fugerem festinus ab urbe, / Bernardum fugiens'); the hero's concern about being attacked by his master's animals (the wild beasts expected to devour the condemned woman while she mates with Lucius in the spectacle organized by Thiasus, see Apul. *Met.* 10.23, 10.29, and 10.34; the dogs accompanying Bernardus in his hunt for the fugitive Burnellus, 2879–80); a lying down to rest in a safe place (compare Apul. *Met.* 10.35, '**lassum** corpus porrectus **refoveo**', with Nigel's 'lassus […] fovere', 2891-92); a vision, theophany, or epiphany of some kind.

The medieval convention would be for Burnellus to fall asleep at this point and have a dream vision—which is exactly the convention that Chaucer follows when he adapts the avian epiphany in his *Parlement of foules*. But Burnellus' vision of speaking birds occurs while he is awake, and it supplants the 'noteworthy new poems' ('nova carmina digna nota', 2898) of his own composition that he was intending to inscribe on parchment ('pellis ovina') with the 'slender iron-tipped pen' that he manages (despite his asinine form) to 'hold' in his 'hand' ('manus […] teneret'). At the end of 'Cupid and Psyche' (Apul. *Met.* 6.25), the asinine

---

[18] *Garritus-us* (m.) (Late Latin): Sidonius, *Ep.* 3.6 (med.).

Lucius laments that he does not have to hand 'tablets and stilus' ('pugillares et stylum') with which to 'note down such a pretty little tale' ('tam bellam fabellam praenotarem').

There is, of course, a huge amount in the *Speculum* that is not Apuleian at all, and there is no single detail that proves, decisively, direct acquaintance with a text of Apuleius' *Metamorphoses*. But the number of correspondences that we have detected allows us, at the very least, to conclude that the poem emerges out of—and, in turn, functions within—a cultural milieu and a system of signification in which the idea of a 'golden ass' (a noted philosopher turned into a donkey) means *something*.

Case-study 2: Anon., 'Asinarius'

Our second case-study, the anonymous *Asinarius*, is a much shorter work—a mere 404 lines (also in elegiac couplets)—composed, it is generally thought, around 1200, and usually associated with Frederick II (1194–1250) of the House of Hohenstaufen, Holy Roman Emperor and King of Sicily. The poem circulated widely in manuscript in France, Germany, and Italy (fourteen copies survive).[19] In his *Registrum multorum auctorum* (*c.* 1280), Hugo von Trimberg numbers it among the Latin 'comedies' popular 'within the schools' ('in scholis').[20] However, the basic plot is best known today because the Brothers Grimm used the Latin work as the sole basis for their concocted folk-tale, *Das Eselein* ('The little donkey'), first published in 1815.[21]

In this heavily pared-down folk-tale version, the plot may look barely Apuleian at all: instead of a man turning into a donkey for twelve months (as happens to Lucius), a donkey turns into a man on a nightly basis, and is only forced to stay permanently in human form by the Western King's expedient of burning the donkey's hide that his son-in-law has been taking off and then putting back on at dawn. The same device of asinine hide-burning is found in a Sanskrit tale (of doubtful date and origin) which supplies at least an analogue to the Western plot.[22]

In 1983, the poem's most recent editor, Simona Rizzardi, noted certain superficial resemblances between the *Asinarius* and the story of Cupid and Psyche.[23] But even six years after the appearance of Detlev Fehling's iconoclastic monograph,[24] Rizzardi (still under the influence of the taxonomic tradition exemplified by Antti Aarne and Stith Thompson)[25] favoured the 'universalist' explanation of folk-tale studies: the Mysterious or Monster

---

[19]   Anon., *Asinarius*, ed. S. Rizzardi, in *Commedie latine del XII e XIII secolo*, 8 vols (Genoa 1983) IV 137–251 (173–86). *Cf.* S. Praet, 'The Trojan ass: *Asinarius* as mock epic', *Viator* 44.3 (2013) 157–73 (159).

[20]   *Asinarius*, ed. Rizzardi (n. 19, above) 147–48.

[21]   J. and W. Grimm, *Kinder- und Hausmärchen*, 2 vols (Berlin 2015) II no. 58.

[22]   For a discussion connecting *Asinarius* to *The Story of Vikramaditya's Birth*, see J. M. Ziolkowski, *Fairy Tales from before Fairy Tales: The Medieval Latin Past of Wonderful Lies* (Ann Arbor 2007) 219–25.

[23]   *Asinarius*, ed. Rizzardi (n. 19, above) XX. *Cf.* Praet, 'The Trojan ass' (n. 19, above) 166 n. 35: 'I shall not discuss the possibility of the *Asinarius* author having known Apuleius' *Metamorphoses* here. While mainstream scholarship assumes the text was not well known at the time, Carver [*Protean Ass* (n. 1, above) 78] does discern a vague influence in 12th-c.y romance literature'.

[24]   D. Fehling, *Amor und Psyche: Die Schöpfung des Apuleius und ihre Einwirkung auf das Märchen, eine Kritik der romantischen Märchentheorie* (Mainz 1977) 79–88.

[25]   S. Thompson, *Motif-Index of Folk-Literature: A Classification of Narrative Elements in Folk-Tales, Ballads, Myths, Fables, Mediaeval Romances, Exempla, Fabliaux, Jest-Books, and Local Legends*, 6 vols (Helsinki 1932–36); J.-Ö. Swahn, *The Tale of Cupid and Psyche (Aarne-Thompson 425 & 428)* (Lund 1955); A. Scobie, *Apuleius and Folklore: Toward a History of ML3045, AaTh567, 449A* (London 1983).

Husband; the curious onlooker; the flight (or *attempted* flight) of the husband after the violation of a taboo. That folkloric bias explains her decision to choose the reading of *fabula* over *pagina* in the second line of the poem (a tendency followed by Jan Ziolkowski—*fabula* better supports his 'Once upon a time' translation of the opening).[26]

Inevitably, perhaps, I favour *pagina*: too much emphasis on the supposedly 'folk-tale' or 'fairy tale' elements obscures the fundamentally ludic nature of the text. The *Asinarius* seems to me to be, above all, the work of a learned mind at play: it is funny, titillating, allusive, and highly performative. But if we choose to gaze intently, with Apuleian eyes, on the medieval Latin poem, we will also find, I believe, a pattern of close correspondence, in theme and function, sequence and structure, not merely with some version of the tale of Cupid and Psyche, but with the novel more widely. My hypothesis (and, indeed, my conclusion) is that the *Asinarius* is the work of a poet with an intimate knowledge of the totality of *The Golden Ass*, and a sophisticated understanding of how the parts of Apuleius' work interconnect. The poet chooses to collapse the diegetic shells that separate those parts: he focuses on the embedded tale, 'Cupid and Psyche', which forms Apuleius' centre-piece (*Met.* 4–6), but he maps onto it the asinine narrative as a whole (the *cornice*), recasting the secret husband Cupid (who has been depicted by the oracle, and by Psyche's jealous sisters, as a serpent-monster) as a Lucius-like donkey-monster—a handsome young man hidden within the hide of a hideous beast. (The *asellus* is also a Psyche figure when he wants to return home.) In turn, the Western King's daughter functions mainly as Psyche, but also, in part, as Photis (the slave-girl who initiates Lucius into the art of love-making); as the libidinous *matrona* of Corinth (the Pasiphae-figure of Book Ten); and, finally, as Isis (the salvific deity of Book Eleven who engineers his return to human form).[27]

Is such an argumentative kite even worth flying? There is no objection in purely theoretical terms. The date usually assigned to the poem (*c.* 1200) coincides precisely with the production, at Monte Cassino, of φ, an apograph (or exact copy) of F, and our second-oldest extant manuscript of the *Metamorphoses*, the *Apologia*, and the *Florida*. The Hohenstaufen are well placed to facilitate the diffusion of such texts, given the long and intimate association of the German royal houses with the Abbey.[28] And, as we have noted above, even before the copying of φ (*c.* 1200), at least one copy of F (the ancestor of Class-1 manuscripts) existed outside the confines of Monte Cassino.[29]

---

[26]   J. M. Ziolkowski, 'The beast and the beauty: the reorientation of "The Donkey" from the Middle Ages to the Brothers Grimm', *The Journal of Medieval Latin* 5 (1995) 53–94 (58); Ziolkowski, *Fairy Tales* (n. 22, above) 341. All subsequent quotations in English from the *Asinarius* are taken from the translation that Ziolkowski appends to these two publications.

[27]   On the inter-relatedness of these female characters, see R. H. F. Carver, 'Between Photis and Isis: fiction, reality, and the ideal in *The Golden Ass* of Apuleius', in *The Construction of the Real and the Ideal in the Ancient Novel*, eds M. Paschalis and S. Panayotakis (Groningen 2013) 243–74.

[28]   The German Richerius owed his appointment in 1038 as abbot of Monte Cassino to Conrad II, Holy Roman Emperor (and member of the Salian dynasty). On the occupation of the abbey by Hohenstaufen troops between 1239 and 1266, H. Bloch, *Montecassino in the Middle Ages: Volume II (Parts III–V)* (Rome 1986) 1005 n. 2, quotes *Regesti Bernardi I Abbatis Casinensis fragmenta*, ed. A. M. Caplet O.S.B. (Rome 1890), 145 no. 364: 'Fredericus quondam Romanorum Imperator et post eum duo filii eius, Conradus videlicet et Manfredus […] speluncam latronum de templo Domini facientes, viginti et sex fere annis ante ingressum nostrum in arcem dampnabiliter tenuerunt' ('for almost twenty-six years before our entry into the citadel, Frederick, the former Emperor of the Romans, and, after him, his two sons, namely, Conrad and Manfred, occupied [it] in damnable fashion, making a den of thieves of the temple of the Lord').

[29]   Carver, *Protean Ass* (n. 1, above) 67. On the possibility that Class-1 MSS represent a tradition older than F, see O. Pecere, 'Qualche riflessione sulla tradizione di Apuleio a Montecassino', in *Le strade del testo*, Studi e commenti

The opening of the poem is suggestive of Apuleian influence, but not decisive:

Rex erat ignotae quondam regionis et **urbis**,
  Et nomen regis fabula[30] [**pagina**] nulla tenet.
Is sibi consortem regni thalamique sodalem
  Sortitus fuerat nobilitate parem.

Once upon a time there was a king of an unknown region and city,
and, what is more, no tale [page] tells the king's name.
This king had acquired for himself as consort of his realm and
companion of his bedchamber a woman who was his peer in nobility.
(1–4)

Compare Apul. *Met.* 4.28:

Erant in **quadam civitate rex** et regina.

Once upon a time in a certain city there lived a king and queen.

We notice some overlap (king, queen, unspecified city), but these elements are also found in Fulgentius' *Mitologiae* (a work certainly known in the Middle Ages):

Apuleius in libris metamorphoseon hanc fabulam planissime designauit: dicens esse in quadam **ciuitate regem** & reginam [...]

Apuleius traced out this tale most clearly in [his] books of *Metamorphoses*, saying that there were, in a certain city, a king and queen [...]
(Fulgentius, *Mitologiae* 3)

If we move to the two love-scenes near the end of the poem, we have more striking correspondences, particularly in the account of the wedding night of the 'fearless little donkey'. Some of the lineaments of 'Cupid and Psyche' appear to have been changed in order to accommodate an asinine spouse, but the response of the new bride to 'the noble body of a handsome man' (311) echoes Apuleius' passage (*Met.* 5.22), where the light of the lamp transforms the monstrous serpent of Psyche's expectations into 'the mildest and sweetest beast of all wild creatures', Cupid himself. Moreover, the erotic details of the *Asinarius* are resonant of Apuleius' accounts of Lucius' lovemaking (as man and as donkey) with (respectively) Photis and the Corinthian *matrona*:

Virginis intrepidus thalamum tunc intrat asellus,
  Ut sponse tenerum mulceat ipse sinum.
Ergo subit thalamum dilecte virginis, in quo
  Lumina sunt posita rege iubente duo.
Ut videat, quid agant hic asellus et hec domicella,[31] [305]
  Sub velo servus nocte locatus erat.
Omnibus egressis cum nullus adesse putatur,

5, ed. G. Cavallo (Bari 1987) 99–124.

[30] Thus manuscripts B, E, and G.

[31] *Cf.* Apul. *Met.* 10.20 (Corinthian *matrona*): 'At intus cerei praeclara micantes luce nocturnas nobis tenebras inalbabanti'.

Munitur vectis obice valva domus.[32]
 Extimplo sponsus asininum ponit amictum,[33]
  Exposita veteri pelle **novus fit homo**. [310]
Virgo videns hominis formosi nobile corpus,
 Cuius iam pridem turpis imago fuit,[34]
Mox **incredibilem sponsi mirata decorum**
 In laqueum Veneris precipitata ruit.
Tunc **simul ambo**[35] suis stringunt sua **colla lacertis**[36]
 Et sua concedunt oribus ora suis.
Protinus in lectum salit hic sequiturque puella.
 Quod sequitur, norunt novit et ipse thorus.
Nec reor omnino latitantem posse latere,
 Qui qualesve ioci nocte gerantur ea. [320]
Ille cupidineum pro tempore temperat estum
 Uxoris vices exhibet illa viro.
Dumque redit pulsis rutilans Aurora tenebris,
 E gremio sponse prosilit ille sue.[37]
Inde revestitur asinino rursus amictu
 Et **fit asellus** item, **sicut et ante fuit**.

Then the fearless little donkey enters the maiden's bedchamber
 so that he may caress the tender breast of his bride.
Therefore he enters the bedchamber of the beloved maiden, in which
 two lights have been placed at the king's bidding.
So that he may see what this little donkey and this little lady do,
 a servant is present, having been placed by night behind a wall hanging.
When everyone has stepped outside, when no one is thought to be present,
 the house door is barred and bolted.
Immediately the bridegroom puts aside the donkey garb;
 when his old hide has been laid away, **he becomes a new man**.
The maiden, seeing the **noble body of a handsome man**
 whose **appearance previously had been repulsive**,
having *marveled* before long at the **unbelievable charm of her spouse**,
 rushed headlong into the bond of lovemaking.
Then at once the two embrace their necks with their arms
 and join their mouths to mouths.
Immediately he leaps into bed and the girl follows.

---

[32] *Cf.* Apul. *Met.* 10.20 (Corinthian *matrona*): 'Nec dominae voluptates diutina sua praesentia morati, **clausis cubiculi foribus** facessunt'; and *Met.* 3.15 (Lucius and Photis): '**pessulis iniectis et uncino firmiter immisso**'.

[33] *Cf.* Apul. *Met.* 10.21 (Corinthian *matrona*): 'Tunc ipsa cuncto prorsus spoliata tegmine […]'.

[34] *Cf.* Apul. *Met.* 5.22 (Psyche): 'videt omnium ferarum mitissimam dulcissimamque bestiam'.

[35] *Cf.* Apul. *Met.* 2.17 (Lucius and Photis): '**simul ambo** corruimus inter mutuos amplexus animas anhelantes'.

[36] *Cf.* Apul. *Met.* 3.15 (Lucius and Photis): 'sic ad me reversa **colloque meo manibus ambabus implexa** […]'.

[37] *Cf.* Apul. *Met.* 6.24: Cupid clasping Psyche in his lap ('maritus, Psychen gremio suo complexus'); 5.28: seagull diving 'ad Oceani profundum gremium'; 5.14: Psyche's sisters recklessly 'leap' ('prosiliunt') from the crag; 4.3: woman 'ad eum statim prosilit'.

What follows they know—and the bed itself knows.
(Nor do I think that the man hiding could have failed to notice
  which games and what sorts of games were conducted there by night!)
For a time he tempers the heat of amorous desire,
  and she fulfills the offices of a wife for her husband.
And as soon as rosy dawn returns once darkness has been dispelled,
  he leaps up from the lap of his bride.
Then he is again clothed in the donkey garb
  and becomes a little donkey just as he had been before.
(301–26)

The detail of the mysterious husband leaving at dawn is common to Fulgentius *and* Apuleius:

Iamque aderat ignobilis maritus, et **torum inscenderat**, et uxorem sibi Psychen fecerat, **et ante lucis exortum propere discesserat**.

Now her unknown husband had arrived, had mounted the bed, had made Psyche his wife, and had quickly departed before the rising of daylight.
(Apul. *Met.* 5.4)

Nocte enim adueniens maritus ueneris præliis obscure peractis: ut inuise uespertinus aduenerat: ita crepusculo incognitus etiam discedebat.

For her husband, in the same way that he came to her unseen in the evening and waged the warfare of Venus in the dark, so too, at dawn, he went away, unknown.
(Fulgentius, *Mitologiae* 3)

But in the next two passages we see the king taking the taboo-violating part of Psyche,[38] by spying upon his son-in-law and daughter while they lie in bed, deep in post-coital sleep.[39]

Rex ergo **thalamum** sub opace tempore noctis
  Intrat et ecce thorum nata generque premunt. [370]
Et quia **post Venerem** mos est obrepere **somnum,**
  Oppressi fuerant **ambo sopore gravi.**
Leniter accedens rex appropriansque cubile,
  Formosum cernit **accubitare virum.**
Qui mox exuvias asinini veleris aufert [375]
  Et genero **minime comperiente** fugit
Fornacem iubet **accendi** fomite multo
  In qua **fit pellis** rege iubente **cinis.**

Accordingly the **king enters the bridal chamber** at the time of **dark night**
  and look! His **daughter and son-in-law** lie **abed.**
And because it is usual for **sleep** to creep up **after love-making,**

---

[38] *Cf.* Apul. *Met.* 5.22 (Psyche): '**sexum** audacia **mutatur**' ('in her boldness, she changes her sex').

[39] *Cf.* Ov. *Met.* 8.82–86 (Scylla and the rape of Nisus' lock): 'with the shadows, her boldness grew. [...] the daughter steals silently into her father's room, and (alas, the evil!) robs him of the fateful lock of hair' ('tenebrisque audacia crevit. [...] thalamos taciturna paternos / intrat et (heu facinus!) fatali nata parentem / crine suum spoliat').

they both are **held fast by deep sleep**.[40]
Gently approaching and drawing near the marriage-**bed**, the king
   perceives **a handsome man reclining**.
A little later he **removes the skin of the donkey's hide**
   and escapes with his son-in-law **hardly noticing**,[41]
and he orders a **furnace** to be set **ablaze** with much kindling
   In which at the king's bidding the **skin becomes ashes**.[42]
(369–74)

The king 'perceives a handsome man reclining' ('Formosum [...] accubitare', picking up Psyche's first view of the recumbent Cupid at Apul. *Met.* 5.22: 'formosum deum formose cubantem').[43] Like Psyche, the king burns the young man's skin, although, in his case, the act of burning is intentional and complete. Both young men respond to the violation with immediate flight ('fuga' is the common term), and, in each case, the violator does his or her best to block that departure, although only the king succeeds:

Ergo gener mane surgit sompno satiatus
   Pelle volens asini sicut et ante tegi.
Quam non inveniens **multo stimulante dolore**
   De **sola** cepit **anxius** esse **fuga**   [384]
Egrediturque foras, sed **rex** foris **obstat** aitque;
   'Quo properas, fili? Quid pateris? Quid habes?
Omnino certe cassabitur ista voluntas
   Atque **tuum** penitus **impedietur iter** [...]'

Therefore the son-in-law arises in the morning satisfied with sleep,
   Wishing to be covered with the donkey skin just as before.
Not finding it and goaded by a **great grief**,[44]
   he begins to be **anxious only about flight**,[45]
and he **goes outside**, but outside the **king blocks his way**[46] and says:
   'Where are you rushing, son? What are you suffering? What's wrong?
Certainly this intention will be altogether in vain
   and your **route will be completely hindered**. [...]'
(381–88)

---

[40] *Cf.* Apul. *Met.* 5.21: 'Nox aderat et maritus aderat priusque **Veneris** proeliis velitatus **altum in soporem** descenderat'.

[41] *Cf.* Apul. *Met.* 5.23: 'de somni mensura metuebat'.

[42] *Cf.* Apul. *Met.* 5.23: 'lucerna [...] evomuit de summa luminis sui **stillam ferventis olei super umerum** dei dexterum. Hem audax et temeraria lucerna [...] ipsum **ignis** totius deum **aduris**, [...] Sic **inustus exsiluit deus** visaque detectae fidei colluvie protinus ex osculis et manibus infelicissimae coniugis **tacitus avolavit**'.

[43] *Cf.* Apul. *Met.* 5.22: '**videt** omnium ferarum mitissimam dulcissimamque bestiam, ipsum illum Cupidinem **formosum** deum **formose cubantem**'.

[44] *Cf.* Apul. *Met.* 5.26: 'lucerna fervens oleum rebullivit in eius umerum. Quo **dolore** statim somno recussus [...]'.

[45] *Cf.* Apul. *Met.* 5.24: 'te vero **tantum fuga** mea punivero'.

[46] *Cf.* Apul. *Met.* 5.24: 'At Psyche, statim resurgentis eius **crure dextero** manibus ambabus **arrepto** [...]'.

Metamorphic modes

One obvious difference between the two works is the mode (and mechanism) of asinine–human transformation. The *Asinarius* poet sidesteps all of the standard medieval objections to actual human–animal metamorphosis[47] by having the queen simply give birth to a donkey:

> Continuis igitur **precibus pia numina pulsans**,
>   Ut mater fiat, nocte dieque rogat.
> Quod petit, assequitur et fit mater—sed aselli,
>   Eius enim partus pulcher asellus erat.

> Therefore, entreating the faithful gods with uninterrupted prayers,
>   She asks by night and day that she be made a mother.
> What she seeks, she obtains and she becomes a mother—but of a little donkey,
>   For her offspring was a beautiful little donkey!
> (21–24)

In his ability to doff and don his asinine hide, the 'little donkey' serves as an inverted image of Avianus' fifth fable. Lucius, in contrast, undergoes a full-body metamorphosis (inside and out)—at the beginning and at the end of the novel (Apul. *Met.* 11.13).[48] Apuleius gives the asinine metamorphosis the full Ovidian treatment, showing us the stages of elongation, contraction, hardening, softening, and so on. There is no question of an outer skin merely being shed. Yet, at certain points in the novel, at least at the level of metaphor, the asinine identity *is* seen as a garment that can be taken off. Isis enjoins Lucius at Apul. *Met.* 11.6: 'pessimae mihique iam dudum detestabilis beluae istius corio te protinus exue' ('cast off at once the hide of that wretched beast which I have long detested'). And Lucius himself recounts at Apul. *Met.* 11.14: 'Nam me cum primum nefasto tegmine despoliaverat asinus […]' ('For as soon as the ass had stripped me of his abominable coat […]').[49]

Putting poem and novel together, we could say that, instead of confirming the conventional wisdom of the Aesopic / Avianan apologue, the medieval poem realizes the potential of the Apuleian auctioneer's mocking (indeed, multiply ironic) sales-pitch at *Met.* 8.25: 'sed prorsus ut in asini **corio** modestum hominem inhabitare credas' ('You would really think that inside this ass's hide dwelt a mild-mannered human being'). The poem mimics (and perhaps even mocks) standard medieval hermeneutics, particularly as applied to the apologue or fable—the notion that the fiction is merely a *cortex*, the bark, the shell, the outer casing that can be taken off and discarded, leaving behind the thing that actually matters, the *nucleus* or kernel of meaning.[50]

The poet focuses, instead, on the normal (yet still 'wonder-filled') metamorphoses that can occur within (and between) human beings: physiological and pedagogical; textual as well as sexual (*cf.* Psyche's change of sex at Apul. *Met.* 5.22: 'sexum audacia mutatur'). Consider

---

[47]   R. H. F. Carver, 'Of donkeys and d(a)emons: metamorphosis and the literary imagination from Apuleius to Augustine', and 'Defacing god's work: metamorphosis and the "Mimicall Asse" in the age of Shakespeare', chapters 5 and 7 of *Transformative Change in Western Thought: A History of Metamorphosis from Homer to Hollywood*, eds I. Gildenhard and A. Zissos (London 2013) 237–46 and 284–300.

[48]   If the second person of the Christian Trinity is theandric (fully God and fully Man), the *Esel-Mensch* may be said to be onandric: fully asinine and fully human.

[49]   *Cf.* Thrasyleon's fateful donning of the bearskin in Apul. *Met.* 4.14–21.

[50]   *Cf. cortex* / *nucleus* reading / jewel in the dung-heap analogy endorsed by the *Speculum stultorum*.

the young donkey's encounter with a master harp-player whom he asks to teach him to play (57–66). In Apuleian terms, Music takes the place of Magic as the forbidden 'art' in which he wishes to meddle.[51] The *mimus* or *citharista* attempts to dissuade him,[52] invoking the conventional wisdom (*mos*) embodied in the fable of the *Asinus ad Lyram* ('The Ass with the Lyre') that donkeys can neither sing nor play:

[Asinus ad Lyram]

Quomodo ingenia saepe calamitate intercidant

Asinus iacentem vidit in prato lyram;
accessit et temptavit chordas ungula.
sonuere tactae. 'Bella res mehercules
male cessit' inquit 'artis quia sum nescius.
si reperisset aliquis hanc prudentior,
divinis aures oblectasset cantibus.'
    Sic saepe ingenia calamitate intercidunt.

The Ass and the Lyre

How genius is often lost through the accidents of fortune

An ass saw a lyre lying in a meadow.
He went up to it and tried the strings with his hoof;
they sounded at his touch. 'A pretty thing, on my faith,'
said he, 'but it has ended in failure, because I am ignorant of the art.
If only someone of greater skill had found this,
he might have charmed all ears with **notes divine**.'

Thus men of genius are often lost to fame through the accidents of fortune.[53]

The donkey, however, insists, and he quickly surpasses his teacher in the musical arts. Yet this successful musical metamorphosis leads immediately to a painful *anagnorisis*: while playing his harp and singing, the donkey sees his own reflection for the first time and is appalled. Having escaped the shackles of one verbal and mental construct, he is immediately caught by a second: convinced that the 'golden' baubles of monarchical office will never sit comfortably on a 'little donkey' ('asellus'), he embarks on a ship which takes him to the western limits of the world, and an encounter with the king's daughter:

Virgo puellares tunc iam compleverat annos,
    Iam dederant teneros membra pudenda pilos. [130]
Ubera mammarum dederant iam signa, quod ipsa
    Vix queat absque viro sola cubare thoro.

---

[51]   Plato makes Music (more precisely, harmonics) the final subject in the advanced curriculum that he outlines in Book 7 of the *Republic*.

[52]   *Cf.* Photis (and Byrrhena) attempting to warn Lucius against meddling in the magic arts.

[53]   Phaedrus, Appendix Perottina 14, in *Babrius and Phaedrus: Fables*, ed. and trans. B. E. Perry (London 1965) 390-91. *Cf.* Boethius, *De consolatione philosophiae*, I. Prosa iv, s. 1; W. S. Gibson, '*Asinus ad Lyram*: from Boethius to Bruegel and beyond', *Simiolus: Netherlands Quarterly for the History of Art* 33.1 (2007/2008) 33–42.

At that time the maid had already completed her years of girlhood:
  her private parts had already given forth fine hairs,
the nipples of her breasts had already given signs that she
  can hardly sleep alone on her bed without a man.
(129–32)

We observe that the girl has recently undergone the natural transformations associated with puberty, but we might contrast her 'fine' pubic hairs ('teneros [...] pilos') with Lucius' body-hair 'thickening into bristles' ('plane pili mei crassantur in setas') as the first stage of his metamorphosis into a donkey at *Met.* 3.24.[54]

Another gap in the poem's narrative is the fact that the donkey only seems to gain (or discover) the ability to doff and don his asinine hide on the night of his wedding. This sexual initiation of an adolescent ass (*asellus*) will, in all senses of the word, 'make a man' of him. We might compare Photis' initiation of Lucius into the erotic and necromantic mysteries (beginning with 'heus tu, scolastice' at Apul. *Met.* 2.10). There is a kind of chiasmus at work: in *The Golden Ass* (at least according to traditional moralizing readings), sex and then magic turn a man into an ass. In the *Asinarius*, music and then sex turn an ass into a man.

Laughter

The donkey is initially denied admission at the king's gate (*cf.* Photis' initial reluctance to admit Lucius to Milo's house at Apul. *Met.* 1.22),[55] but he wins over the gatekeeper with his music:

Hic rarus mimus, o rex, est foedus asellus,
  Qui psallit cithara psallit et ore simul.

This unusual mime player, O king, is a foul little donkey
  who makes music with the harp and makes music with his mouth at the same time.
(155–56)

Immediately before the unknown husband makes Psyche his wife in bed, she is entertained by a banquet and by invisible performers, a singer and a lyre-player (Apul. *Met.* 5.3: 'Post opimas dapes quidam introcessit et **cantavit invisus**, et **alius citharam pulsavit, quae videbatur nec ipsa**'). We note that the *asellus* singing and playing so harmoniously outside the king's gate is heard before he is seen by the guests at table.

No one in the poem seems to be shocked that a donkey can speak (talking animals fit easily within the conventions of medieval Beast Fable). What does amaze onlookers is the donkey's ability to sing and to play the harp:

---

[54] *Cf.* 'squalens pilus' ('coarse bristles') at Apul. *Met.* 11.13; 'pilum liberali nitore nutriveram' (the nourishing effect of the bakers' dishes on his hide) at 10.15; the boar that attacks Tleopolemus ('pilis inhorrentibus corio squalidus') at 8.4. *Cf.* Photis' 'glabellum feminal' ('smooth-shaven pubes') at 2.17, and Cupid's hairless body ('corpus glabellum') at 5.22.

[55] Having heard the racket of the little donkey knocking, the doorkeeper asks, 'Why are you shouting? You, who are you? From where do you come? Why do you beat so importunately at the king's front door? [140] Why do you strike the door panels with such presumptuousness?'. *Cf.* Apul. *Met.* 1.22: 'ianuam firmiter oppessulatam pulsare vocaliter incipio. Tandem adulescentia quaedam procedens, "Heus tu," inquit "qui tam fortiter fores verberasti [...]".' On the soteriological implications of importunate door-knocking, see Luke 13:22–27.

Tunc **mimus cordas asinino pollice tangens**
    Ingreditur modulos articulando novos.⁵⁶ [160]
Quem rex intuitus **in risum laxat habenas**
    Et tanti **risus** fit modus **absque modo**.
At regina suo ridens ridente marito
    Nil poterat risu prepediente loqui.
Omnis condicio iuvenumque senumque **cachinnat**
    Perstrepit et **risu curia tota** pari.   [165]

Then the mime-player, striking the strings with the thumb of a donkey,
    steps inside, fingering new melodies.
Having gazed at him, the king relaxes his restraints upon laughter,
    and the measure of such great laughter becomes measureless.
For her part the queen, laughing as her husband laughs,
    could not say anything because laughter prevents.
Every class of young people and old guffaws,
    and the **entire court responds with equal laughter**.
(161–66)

In terms of its position in the narrative sequence, and the intensity and extent of the laughter, this scene may put us in mind of the conclusion of the *Risus* Festival in Book Three, when Lucius pulls back the sheet that covers the bodies of the men he has 'murdered' only to see that they are merely inflated goat-skins:

conspicio prorsus **totum populum**—**risu** cachinnabili diffluebant—nec secus illum bonum hospitem parentemque meum Milonem risu maximo dissolutum [...] 'insuper exitium meum **cachinnat**.'

I [...] caught sight of the audience: absolutely the entire populace was dissolved in raucous laughter, and even my kind host and uncle, Milo, was broken up by a huge fit of laughing [...] '[...] [He] is even laughing at my downfall.'
(Apul. *Met.* 3.7)

Tunc ille quorundam **astu** paulisper **cohibitus risus libere iam exarsit in plebem**. Hi gaudii nimietate gratulari, illi dolorem ventris **manuum compressione** sedare. Et certe laetitia delibuti meque respectantes cuncti theatro facessunt. At ego, ut primum illam laciniam prenderam, fixus in lapidem steti gelidus nihil secus quam una de ceteris theatri statuis uel columnis.

Then the **laughter**, which some people had **guilefully repressed** for a time, now **broke out unrestrainedly** among the **entire mob**. Some were rejoicing with excessive mirth, while others were **pressing their stomachs** with their hands to ease the pain. At any event they were all drenched with happiness, and they kept turning round to look at me as they made their way out of the theatre. As for me, from the moment I had pulled back that cloth I stood stock still, frozen into stone just like one of the other statues or columns in the theatre.
(Apul. *Met.* 3.10)

---

⁵⁶   *Cf.* 'novos [...] tonos' in the *Speculum stultorum* (2900; R 132).

In both cases, we note the tension between containment and release. But the contrast in *function* is quite marked: Apuleius' Festival of Laughter traumatizes the still-human Lucius: it isolates him from the society of Hypata (Apul. *Met.* 3.10–11); makes him suspect the good faith of his host, Milo (3.7), his aunt, Byrrhena (3.12), and even his lover, Photis; and sets in motion the chain of events that will lead, quite quickly, to his metamorphosis into an ass (we notice that, as a consequence of this performance, he has already undergone a figurative— indeed, theatrical—transformation, into one of the stone 'statues or columns' of the theatre).[57]

In the *Asinarius*, the laughter helps, instead, to integrate the donkey into his new society, and, in this respect, it is closer to the episode (or suite of episodes) in Book Ten that serves as an inverted image of the *Risus* Festival: the bakers' astonishment when they spy upon the asinine Lucius as he feasts upon sweet-meats; the delight of their master, Thiasus; the desire kindled in the Corinthian *matrona*; the fate assigned to Lucius of being exhibited (once again!) in a theatre, but this time as a sexually performing *mimus* in a pantomime, the climax of which is to be the eating alive (by a second beast) of a woman condemned for murder. And, finally, Lucius' escape from the theatre, his double vision of the goddess; his return to human form; and his decision to commit himself to the religious life, as a devotee first of Isis and then of Osiris.

The Baker Brothers

Et hora consueta velut balneas petituri, clausis ex more foribus, per quandam modicam cavernam rimantur me passim expositis epulis inhaerentem. [...] mirati monstruosas asini delicias **risu maximo dirumpuntur**, vocatoque uno et altero ac dein pluribus conservis, demonstrant infandam memoratu hebetis iumenti gulam. **Tantus denique ac tam liberalis cachinnus** cunctos invaserat ut ad aures quoque praetereuntis perveniret domini. Sciscitatus denique quid bonum **rideret** familia, cognito quod res erat, ipse quoque **per idem prospiciens foramen** delectatur eximie. Ac dehinc **risu** ipse quoque **latissimo adusque intestinorum dolorem redactus**, iam patefacto cubiculo proxime consistens coram arbitratur. Nam et ego [...] gaudio praesentium fiduciam mihi sumministrante, nec tantillum commotus securus esitabam, quoad novitate spectaculi laetus **dominus aedium** duci me iussit, immo vero suis etiam **ipse manibus ad triclinium perduxit**, mensaque posita omne genus edulium solidorum et illibata fercula iussit apponi.

At their customary hour they locked the door as usual, as if they were going to the baths, and spied on me through a small crack. When they saw me tucking into the banquet which was spread all about [...], in their amazement at this monstrous taste in an ass, they split their sides laughing. They called a couple of fellow-servants, and then several more, to show them the unspeakable gluttony of a lazy ass. They were all attacked by such **loud and unrestrained laughter** that the sound even reached their **master's ears** as he was passing nearby. He inquired what in heaven's name [16] the servants were **laughing** at, and when he discovered what it was, **the master also peeped through the same hole.** He too was exceptionally amused, and **laughed so hard and long that his belly ached.** Then he had them open the door to the room so that he could stand close to me and watch openly. For my part, because

---

[57] Apul. *Met.* 3.10. See Carver, 'Of donkeys and d(a)emons' (n. 48, above) 233.

I [...] was inspired with confidence by the delight of the people in the room, I was not a bit disturbed, but unconcernedly kept right on eating. Soon the **master of the house,** delighted by the novelty of the spectacle, ordered me to be taken—or rather **conducted me himself with his own hands**—to the dining room; there he had a table set and all sorts of whole dishes and untasted plates put before me.
(Apul. *Met.* 10.15–16)

In the case of the bakers and Thiasus, we might note the double act of looking—first by the servants, then by the master. We will find the same pattern in *Asinarius*, where the servant (and then the king) spy on the donkey making love to the king's daughter.

The close personal attention paid by Thiasus ('the master of the house') to Lucius' dining arrangements is mirrored in the *Asinarius*, where the king goes to inordinate lengths to accommodate his asinine guest at table, even making him his daughter's dining-companion or 'messmate' (the same word, 'conviva', is also used by Thiasus).[58] Thiasus' freedman ('libertus') enrols Lucius in an intensive course of instruction:

Et primum me quidem mensam accumbere suffixo cubito, dein alluctari et etiam **saltare sublatis primoribus pedibus** perdocuit, quodque esset apprime mirabile, verbis nutum commodare, ut quod nollem relato, quod vellem deiecto capite monstrarem, sitiensque pocillatore respecto, ciliis alterna conivens, bibere flagitarem. [...] Iamque rumor publice crebuerat, quo conspectum atque famigerabilem meis miris artibus effeceram dominum: 'Hic est qui sodalem **convivam**que possidet asinum luctantem, **asinum saltantem**, asinum **voces humanas intellegentem,** sensum nutibus exprimentem.'

First he **taught me** to **recline at table** leaning on my elbow; then he taught me to wrestle, and even to **dance with my forefeet in the air**. Most amazing of all, he taught me to respond to words with a gesture: I would show what I did not want by raising my chin and what I wanted by dropping it; and when I was thirsty I would look round at the cupbearer and wink my eyelids alternately to ask for a drink. [...] Soon word of me had spread among the public, and I had made my owner illustrious and famous with my remarkable talents. 'This is the man,' they said, 'who owns as **companion and dinner-guest** an ass who wrestles, **an ass who dances**, an ass who understands men's language and can say what he wants by nods.'
(Apul. *Met.* 10.17)

The *Asinarius* poet goes one stage further, by enabling a donkey to serve food and wine to a human. And for his account of the wedding festivities, the poet turns, I suggest, not so much to the conclusion of 'Cupid and Psyche', as to the pantomime at the end of Book Ten, where Lucius the donkey is billed to star as a sexually performing *mimus* in a mock marriage. Not only is the whole city ('polis', 291) decked out for the *Asinarius*' royal wedding so that it shines like heaven ('polus', 292), a huge swarm of *mimus*-performers ('mimorum magna caterva', 293) is called in, including a female mime-player who (perhaps in inverted mimicry of Lucius' unnatural bipedalism as an ass dancing with 'forefeet in the air', '**sublatis primoribus pedibus**', *Met.* 10.17), moves about on her hands.[59]

---

[58]   *Cf.* Apul. *Met.* 10.18 (Thiasus' view of Lucius' double function): 'summe se delectari profitebatur quod haberet in me simul et **convivam** et vectorem'.

[59]   *Asinarius* 295–96: 'Crura levans sursum suspensa caputque deorsum / Ambulat, atque manus dat pedis officium'

Almost as soon as he enters the dining hall, the King asks the Little Donkey if he likes his daughter:

'Pape, quid inquiris? O rex, quid nosse laboras?
  Cur non deberet ista placere michi?
Immo placet, placet illa michi, multum placet,' inquit   [195]
  '**Ferreus** est certe cui placet illa nichil.
Candida delectat facies permixta **rubore**,
  Ac si contemplor lilia mixta **rosis**
Caesariesque placet, delectat **eburnea cervix**
  Et **corpus** fateor **omne** placere michi.' [200]

'Amazing! Why do you ask? O king, why do you labour to know?
  Why ought I not like her?
On the contrary, I like her, I like her very much.' He said,
  'Certainly the man who does not like her at all is **made of iron**.
Her fair face, suffused with **rosiness**, brings delight,
  as if I should contemplate lilies mixed with **roses**.
And I like her **hair**; her **ivory-white neck** brings delight;
  and I confess that I like her **whole body**.'
(193–200)

Once again, we may detect echoes of Psyche's vision of Cupid at Apul. *Met.* 5.22:

ferrum quaerit abscondere, sed in suo pectore. [...] Videt capitis aurei genialem **caesariem** ambrosia temulentam, **cervices lacteas genasque purpureas** pererrantes crinium globos decoriter impeditos [...] **Ceterum corpus** glabellum atque **luculentum** [...]

She tried to hide the weapon [lit. '**iron**']—in her own heart. [...] On his golden head she saw the glorious **hair** drenched with ambrosia: wandering over his **milky neck** and **rosy cheeks** were the neatly shackled ringlets of his locks [...] The **rest of his body** was hairless and resplendent [...]

We should not make extravagant claims for these correspondences: white necks and rosy cheeks are standard catalogue items in a *blason*, or exercise in *effictio*, and the parallels are suggestive rather than decisive. But the use of 'caesaries' ('hair') in both passages is note-worthy, especially in a sequence which includes notions of 'iron-heartedness' ('ferreus') and 'iron' being 'hidden in the heart' ('ferrum quaerit abscondere, sed in suo pectore').[60] So too is 'contemplor'.[61] We might note, etymologically, the connection with 'templum' (and hence with augury or divination); and the fact that the donkey's erotic devotion to a beautiful young woman whose face seems to be made up, in part, of roses ('lilia mixta rosis'), will lead, in due course, to his being able to shed his asinine hide.[62]

('A female mime-player, balanced with her feet upward and her head downward, walks and accords to her hands the function of her feet').

[60] *Teste* Lewis & Short, *A Latin Dictionary*, 265, 'caesaries' is used most frequently of men. But *TLL* shows plenty of use for females in the Vulgate Bible, as well as in Catullus, Virgil, Claudian, and others.

[61] *Cf.* 'mihi renidentis fortune contemplatus faciem' at Apul. *Met.* 10.16.

[62] *Cf.* Apul. *Met.* 11.6 and 11.13.

These acts of domestic service function as a kind of sexual—and textual—foreplay: Ovid is the obvious source for 'Singula quid memorem?' ('Why should I recall the individual details?'),[63] and this passage becomes the conduit linking (mutually pleasing) service at table ('discumbendo') to (mutually pleasing) service in bed ('concumbendo', 221).

> Ascendensque gradum sedem sortitur in alto
> Convivamque locat hunc domicella sibi.
> Inter cenandum bene servit asellus eidem
> Comminuens panes colliridasque secans.
> Ipse ciphos paterasque levans offert bibiture
> Et mensale tenet, dum domicella bibit.[64]
> Singula quid memorem? Breviter simul omnia tangam:
> Omnia composite doctus asellus agit.
> Nonnihil ergo suus placuit conviva puellae
> Sed, ni fallor, adhuc plus placiturus erit. [220]
> Discumbendo placet, plus concumbendo placebit,
> Huic dum dilecto nupserit illa viro.

> And mounting a step, he takes possession of a seat up high,
>   and the little lady seats him as her tablemate.
> While dining the little donkey serves her well,
>   breaking the bread into pieces and cutting the cakes.
> Raising goblets and drinking bowls, he himself offers to her when she wishes to drink,
>   and he holds up the tablecloth as the little lady drinks.
> Why should I recall every single fact? I should touch upon all of them succinctly in one statement:
>   insofar as he is an ass, he does everything competently.
> Therefore her tablemate pleased the girl to no little extent
>   but unless I am mistaken, he is going to please her even more.
> In sitting together he pleases; in lying together he will please more,
>   when she has wedded him as her beloved husband.
> (211–22)

The last two lines form an astonishing prolepsis. 'Nupserit' may be the key term—all of the actual sexual activity in the poem takes place within the legitimizing confines of wedlock—but the leaps are still shocking, especially given the fact that bestiality is involved.

When the Little Donkey (in spite of the limitless wealth offered to him) becomes homesick (just like Psyche at *Met.* 5.6–7), the king plays his final card:

> 'Una tibi' rex inquit 'adhuc datur opcio, fili,
>   Quam si respueris, semper asellus eris.
> Vis, ut nostra tuas tibi filia detur in ulnas,
>   Tecum nocturnis ut vacet ipsa iocis?'

---

[63]   *Cf.* Ov. *Am.* 1.5.23–26: 'singula quid referam? nil non laudabile vidi, / et nudam pressi corpus ad usque meum. / cetera quis nescit? lassi requievimus ambo. / proveniant medii sic mihi saepe dies'.

[64]   Note the significance of the wine cup going back and forth before Lucius and Photis make love for the first time (Apul. *Met.* 2.16).

'One option is still to be given to you, son,' said the king.
  'If you reject it, you will **always be a little donkey**.
Do you wish that **our daughter** should be **given between your arms**,
  so that **she can occupy herself with you in night-time games**?'
(253–56)

What kind of father invites a donkey to have sex with his daughter? What kind of king asks the heir to his kingdom to marry an ass? The king's generosity—his willingness to give his only child to a 'foedus asellus' ('a foul little ass')—only makes sense if he knows something that other people in the poem do not. He certainly seems to understand (in positive terms) the metamorphic power that sexual love can have, when he says that 'If you reject this option, you will **always be a little donkey**'.

The donkey's response hints at a soteriological dimension to the king's offer: 'as if awakening from a sleep', the donkey recognizes the proposed union as a 'porta salutis', not merely a 'door to well-being' (as Ziolkowski puts it),[65] but a 'gateway to salvation':

Tunc velud evigilans a sompno[66] clamat asellus:
  Hec place, hoc fateor, pactio sola michi.
Ista michi finis meroris et anxietatis,
  Ianua leticie, **porta salutis** erit. [260]

Then, as if awakening from a sleep, the little donkey shouts out:
  'This arrangement alone pleases me, I admit this.
For me she will be the end of sorrow and anxiety,
  the gateway to happiness, the door to well-being [...]'
(257–60)

The *Asinarius* poet is here transforming or repurposing the apologue. Nigel's *Speculum* is consistently anti-metamorphic. It reinforces the message of Avianus' fifth fable, 'De asino pelle leonis induto': if you start life as a donkey, whatever you do (whether you put on a lion's skin, as in Avianus; or do your best to lengthen your tail, or to acquire learning or high position, as with Burnellus), 'you will always' (as the final line of Avianus' fable puts it) 'be a little ass' ('semper asellus eris').

The daughter's response to her father's offer (287: '**Non mea**, sed **patris fiat** liberta **voluntas**') may sound shockingly blasphemous in its echo of Christ's Agony in the Garden of Gethsemane (Luke 22:42: 'dicens **Pater** si vis transfer calicem istum a me verumtamen **non mea voluntas sed tua fiat**'). Yet it also configures the king's daughter as a sacrificial victim who, like Psyche (Apul. *Met.* 4.33–35), is willing to make a 'monstrous' marriage for the greater good.

We are dealing here with very complex webs of inter-textual play. But the king's motivation is still one of the many gaping holes in the plot that I would see as being intentional *lacunae*—

---

[65] On the therapeutic potential of sexual intercourse, see Plin. *Nat.* 28.10 and 28.16. According to William of Newburgh (*Historia rerum anglicarum* 1.3.4), Thomas the Younger, Archbishop of York (d. 1114), preferred his chastity to his life when he disobeyed his doctors' orders to engage in sexual intercourse as the sole remedy for his disease. *Cf.* Mozley and Raymo eds, *Speculum* (n. 10, above) 159, commenting on *Speculum stultorum* 1529–30; and the *De coitu* of Constantinus Africanus (monk of Monte Cassino in the late eleventh century).

[66] *Cf.* Lucius falling asleep (Apul. *Met.* 10.35) and waking to a theophany which seems to offer him 'the hope of salvation' ('spem salutis', 11.1).

gaps that should, or *can*, be filled by readers, depending on the extent of their learning. The poet will expect most, if not all, of his audience to pick up the allusions to the Aesopic fables and admire his bold inversions of them. A far smaller percentage of readers will have heard, thanks to Saint Augustine (*C. D.*, 18.18), of Apuleius the Platonic Philosopher's account of being turned into a donkey. Such readers may even have encountered a version of 'Cupid and Psyche' in Fulgentius or the first of the so-called 'Vatican Mythographers',[67] and, thus, albeit at second or third hand, they may have been able to spot some of the Apuleian links made in the poem.

However, it is also possible (this is our boldest claim) that the poet is working within an elite circle, a network (perhaps tiny) of people who have (or, at some point, have *had*) direct access to *The Golden Ass*. The evidence does not create a clear picture of the poet composing his poem with a manuscript of Apuleius lying open on his desk (in such a scenario, even after taking metrical issues into account, one might expect more mosaic or *cento*-like effects, with specifically Apuleian diction as in Guaiferius). But it does, I think, suggest that the poet has absorbed and digested Apuleius' work, and that he is redeploying its constituent parts, for his own pleasure, and for that of an esoteric readership.

'*Spurcum additamentum*'

If our hypothesis is correct, the *Asinarius* may provide a context for the composition and circulation of the so-called *Spurcum additamentum*, the obscene interpolation (literally, 'dirty addition') found in some manuscripts alongside Apuleius' account of the asinine Lucius' love-making with the *matrona* of Corinth (Apul. *Met.* 10.21). The author is anonymous (Eduard Fraenkel playfully dubbed him 'Spurcus') and the passage has been added to the margin, not of F but of φ, in a hand identified by Billanovich as that of the fourteenth-century humanist Zanobi da Strada. The text below is reproduced from Boccaccio's manuscript (L4) in order to indicate the level of corruption that seems to have already accumulated by the 1350s:

> et hercle orcium pigam [H: bigam] perteretum hyaci fragrantis et chie rosacee lotionibus expurgauit [M: expiauit]. At dein **digitis**, ypate, lichanos, meso, paramese et nete hastam inguinis niuei mei spurciciei pluscule excorias [φ and M: **excorians**] emundauit. Et cum ad inguinis cephalum formosa mulier concitim [H: confestim] ueniebat ab orcibus ganniens ego et dentes ad Iouem eleuans priapo [H: Priapum; M: Priapon] frequenti frictura porrixabam ipsoque pando et repando uentrem sepiuscule tractabam [φ: tactabam]. Ipsa quoque inspiciens quod genius [H: genitus] inter anthteneras [H: anteas teneras; M: antheras] excreuerat modicum illud morule qua lustrum sterni mandauerat anni sibi reuolutionem autumabat.[68]

> And, by Hercules, she cleansed my round scrotum, my balls, with perfumed wine and **rosewater of Chios**. And then with her fingers, thumb, forefinger, middle finger, ring finger and little finger, she withdrew the foreskin, and cleared the shaft of my penis of the plentiful whitish dirt. And when the beautiful woman arrived very soon at the

[67] Carver, *Protean Ass* (n. 1, above) 41–47 (Fulgentius), 97–98 and 103 ('Vatican Mythographers').

[68] Text based on L4 (*Laur.* 54.24), as presented in *Lucii Apulei Metamorphoseon libri XI*, ed. J. Van der Vliet (Leipzig 1897) 238–39, with emendations ('H' and 'M') in square brackets proposed, respectively, by L. Herrmann, 'Le fragment obscène de l'Âne d'or (x, 21)', *Latomus* 10 (1951) 329–32, and S. Mariotti, 'Lo *Spurcum Additamentum* ad Apul. *Met.* 10, 21', *SIFC* 27–28 (1956) 229–50. See Carver, *Protean Ass* (n. 1, above) 67–71; Gaisser, *Fortunes of Apuleius* (n. 6, above) 63–66.

top of my penis from my testicles, braying and lifting my teeth toward the sky, I got, through the regular friction, an erection of the penis, and while it moved up and down I often touched her belly with it. She as well, when she saw what came out of my penis among her perfumes, declared that that small delay, during which she had ordered our love-nest to be prepared, had been to her the orbit of a year.[69]

In Apuleius, Lucius is concerned that, with his 'huge legs' and 'hard hooves' (*Met.* 10.22), he might hurt the soft-skinned *matrona*. Those fears turn out to be ill-founded, as she easily accommodates the full endowment of the ass. When the Little Donkey sees his image in the water for the first time, 'he considers his **legs** and **feet**, and his whole body displeases him'.[70] Thinking himself unfit for kingly office, he leaves. But immediately prior to this, the lyre-player has objected to his attempting to learn to play on the basis of his physical attributes:

O rex, quid queris, quod non tibi competit? Eheu!
   Erras, deciperis, irrita vota geris.
Discere nequaquam potes hanc **artem**, quoniam sunt
   Enormes digiti, mi domicelli, tui.
Ac si pace tua liceat michi vera fateri:
   Quod natura negat, hoc, domicelle, petis.
Non potes absque manu **cithare distinguere cordas**,
   Que puto dissilient, si pede tangis eas.
More suo rudit asinus, nunquam bene ludit,   [65]
   Sacciferi vox est feda canentis ya.

O king, why do you seek what does not become you? Alas, alas!
   You are mistaken, you are deceived, you entertain idle hopes:
you cannot **learn this art** at all, since
   your **fingers are enormous**, my little lord.
And if, by your leave, it be permitted me to speak home truths,
   you seek, little lord, what nature denies.
Without a hand **you cannot distinguish the strings of the harp**,
   which (I think) will blow apart if you touch them with a foot.
According to its custom, an ass brays and never plays well;
   the wild sound of a sack-bearing ass is hee haw.
(57–66)

The *asellus* is told that, with his 'enormous fingers' ('Enormes digiti'), he cannot even distinguish the strings of the harp, but he promptly proves his teacher wrong by mastering the instrument.[71] In the *Spurcum additamentum*, the asinine narrator (let us call him 'Pseudo-Lucius') displays the knowledge befitting a *mimus* or *citharista*: in the midst of a sexual blending (or dissolution) of identities, the ass is (quite literally) able to 'distinguish the strings of the harp' by spelling out their names ('At dein digitis, ypate, lichanos, meso, paramese et

---

[69] Translation from M. Zimmerman, *Apuleius Madaurensis Metamorphoses: Book X: Text, Introduction and Commentary* (Groningen 2000) X 434 (based on Mariotti's Latin text).

[70] 91–92: 'Luminibusque suis percurrens **crura pedesque** / Respicit, et corpus displicet omne sibi' ('Surveying with his eyes, he considers his **legs** and **feet**, and his whole body displeases him').

[71] *Cf.* Lucius' lament at Apul. *Met.* 10.29 that he cannot unsheathe a sword (to kill himself, thus avoiding a public mating with a condemned women) because of his 'round and misshapen hoof' ('ungula rotunda atque mutila').

nete [...]'), but, in an erotic hypallage, he transfers that knowledge to his human lover's fingers as she plays upon *his* instrument. The word 'Excorians' is noteworthy, as it helps to tie together both ass fables: as she pulls back his foreskin, the pseudo-*matrona* is both playing the lyre and 'skinning the hide' off the beast; while the donkey, in turn, is 'singing' ('ganniens', 'growling') to the tune of that lyre ('asinus ad lyram').[72] Spurcus, it seems to me, is taking in hand a somewhat tired, indeed, flaccid common-place and perking it up—teasing it, and squeezing it to an unexpected climax.[73]

More than a decade ago, I tentatively suggested as a plausible candidate for the authorship of the *Spurcum additamentum* the twelfth-century scholar Peter the Deacon (Petrus Diaconus; b. *c.* 1107; d. after 1153), Monte Cassino's most accomplished forger.[74] Peter remains a suspect, but the circle should surely now be widened to include the German-Italian Hohenstaufen networks in southern Italy (*e.g.* Salerno, Naples, with links to Monte Cassino) and perhaps even Sicily.

Conclusion

Ziolkowski points, helpfully, to the pedagogic milieu of the *Asinarius* and its concern with liminal states, with puberty or adolescence.[75] The work may be aimed at (or speak to) those young men who do not feel called to the *vita contemplativa* of monastic life. It is not simply secular, but displays a complex blend of the subversive and the conservative. It manages to be both titillating *and* homiletic, anticipating that modern beatitude, 'The Geek shall inherit the earth'. Even an ass can 'get the girl' (*and* the gold) if he is sufficiently learned.

But the *Asinarius* is also engaging, it would appear, with the complexities of the *translatio studii et imperii*, reflecting the political and cultural resonances (and anxieties) of German power operating within the heartland of the original Roman empire. The 'little ass' ('asellus') is not merely the son of a 'king' ('rex'); he is a 'pignus imperiale' (an 'imperial child' or heir, but also, more literally, a 'pledge' or 'proof' or 'assurance' of the imperial line) and he wonders how well the purple will look upon an ass. In fact, he ends up inheriting both kingdoms (his father's and that of his father-in-law).

As Apuleianists, seeing the ass finally identified at the end of the poem as Neoptolemus,[76] we may be reminded of Tlepolemus, the husband of Charite (the immediate recipient of the tale of 'Cupid and Psyche') and someone who claims (Apul. *Met.* 7.8) to have disguised himself as a 'donkey woman' ('mulier asinaria').[77] But a medieval audience, recalling Virgil's image of Achilles' son (Neoptolemus or Pyrrhus), 'new and glittering' ('nouus [...] nitidusque', Verg. *A.* 2.473), like a snake which has finally cast off its old skin, might be more responsive to the 'Neo-' part of the name (literally, 'new warrior'), particularly in the context of Naples,

---

[72] Gaisser, *Fortunes of Apuleius* (n. 6, above) 65, notes (following Mariotti), the *matrona*'s 'sweet moans' ('dulces gannitus') at Apul. *Met.* 10.22. We might also compare 'sic nobis gannientibus' (an alternative reading for 'garrientibus') at Apul. *Met.* 3.20, where 'libido mutua' ('mutual desire') simultaneously 'excites the minds and bodies' of Lucius and Photis ('et animos simul et membra suscitat').

[73] *Cf.* the hint of the metamorphic in the 'rosewater of Chios'. See Gaisser, *Fortunes of Apuleius* (n. 6, above) 65.

[74] Carver, *Protean Ass* (n. 1, above) 70–71.

[75] Ziolkowski, 'The Beast and the Beauty' (n. 26, above) 58–60.

[76] See Apul. *Apol.* 13.

[77] The suggestive banter between the two in the cave offends the on-looking Lucius, but the situation is redeemed by the revelation that they are espoused (Apul. *Met.* 7.9–12).

the 'new city' ('Neapolis') which retained long memories of its Greek past.[78] The *Asinarius* can be read as a locus of hybridity and of cultural and imperial intersection: the Hohenstaufen dynasty is a relatively new entity but with an ancient lineage (possibly 'degener', as Priam describes Neoptolemus at *Aeneid* 2.549, although still *entitled* in all senses of the word). What we might be seeing is an early (if anxious) flexing of German intellectual muscle, something which the poet's countryman, Konrad Muth (Conradus Mutianus Rufus, 1471–1526), would articulate in explicitly Apuleian terms three hundred years later:

> Postquam vero renatus es et pro Iheger Crotus, pro Dornheim Rubianus salutatus, ceciderunt et aures prelonge et cauda pensilis et **pilus impexus**, quod sibi accidisse dicit Apuleius, cum adhuc asinus esset [...] restitueretur sibi, hoc est humanitati [...] facile cogniscis, quam **miseri sint**, qui nondum barbariam **exuerunt** [...]

> But after you were reborn and greeted as Crotus instead of 'Jaeger', Rubianus instead of 'Dornheim', your enormously long ears fell off along with your drooping tail and uncombed hide, which is what Apuleius said happened to him when, having hitherto been an ass, [...] he was restored to his real self, that is, to humanity [...] You easily recognize the wretchedness of those who have not yet shed their barbarousness.[79]

Reception and transmission are symbiotic: it is not simply a case of 'reception' being the cart pulled behind the horse (or donkey) of 'transmission': the copying and diffusion of texts may also depend on 'receptivity'—on appetites, desires, expectations, and the perception of textual gaps by individuals and/or networks at particular times and in particular places. As academics, we have a duty to be sceptical, to wield Psyche's *novacula* (as Bernardus Silvestris advises us) with the zeal of an Ockhamite in the service of Reason—in this case, cutting off the heads (or skins) of Apuleian imposters.[80] But after examining the *Asinarius* with a loving, yet scholarly gaze, one is tempted to say: if it looks like a Golden Ass, sounds like a Golden Ass, even *smells* like a Golden Ass, perhaps that is because, at the end of a long night of inter-textual games ('ioci'), it actually *is* a *Golden Ass*.

If the foregoing hypothesis is accepted, and if the traditional dating of the *Asinarius* to *c.* 1200 is correct, then we have narrowed the gap between Guaiferius and the next demonstrable imitator of Apuleius' novel (hitherto Mussato) by nearly 120 years. It is difficult to say, at this stage, whether the *Asinarius* poet had access to the Apuleian manuscripts most famously associated with Monte Cassino (F or φ), or whether his knowledge of the *Metamorphoses* depended on a lost ancestor (perhaps even the archetype) of Class-1 manuscripts which was already circulating beyond the immediate confines of the abbey (but probably still within southern Italy). From this new vantage point, however, we are now able to look more positively and receptively at other potential instances of Apuleian influence, such as the apparent echoes of Isiac theophany and pageantry (*Met.* 11) in a clear piece of Hohenstaufen propaganda, Pietro da Eboli's account (completed, probably at Palermo, *c.* 1196–1197) of the triumphal entry of Empress Constance (mother of Frederick II) into Salerno, the capital of Apulia, after her husband, Henry VI's conquest of the kingdom of Sicily. Constance is depicted as Salerno's very own goddess Juno (l. 430). Her appearance at dawn seems to

---

[78]   We might also note the bust of Pyrrhus (the Hellenistic general) at the National Archaeological Museum of Naples.

[79]   See Carver, *Protean Ass* (n. 1, above) 247–49, quoting *Der Briefwechsel des Conradus Mutianus*, ed. K. Gillert (Halle 1890), no. 260, 344.

[80]   On Bernard and Psyche, see Carver, *Protean Ass* (n. 1, above) 102–03.

trigger an immediate rush of devotees, reminiscent of the *praeludia* to the Festival of Isis.[81] In each text, birds and people unite in voicing praise at the sudden end of winter and the arrival both of spring and its divine embodiment.[82] The description of the 'sandy shore' ('arenosum litus', l. 424) where exotic fragrances 'excite the nostrils' ('Cinnama, thus, aloe, nardus, rosa, lilia, mirtus / Inflamant nares', ll. 426–27) as 'each person brings new balsams to be poured out' ('Quod nova perfundi balsama quisque ferat', l. 429) is fraught, I would suggest, with Apuleian resonances.[83]

What remains to be established, however, is the precise point at which *The Golden Ass* moved north and crossed into France.[84] The testimony of the *Asinarius* and Pietro da Eboli potentially strengthens the case for thirteenth-century works such as the *Roman de la Rose* (written in two parts, *c.* 1230 and *c.* 1275) being beneficiaries of Apuleian influence. We are probably still not in a position to claim direct Apuleian input into the great French writers of the twelfth century—Chrétien de Troyes, Marie de France, Alanus de Insulis—but this new evidence suggesting that *The Golden Ass* was being read and imitated outside Monte Cassino in the late 1190s may add fuel to our suspicions and serve as a goad to further research.

University of Durham

---

[81]   Pietro da Eboli, *Book in Honor of Augustus (Liber ad honorem Augusti)*, trans. G. Hood (Tempe, AZ 2012) ll. 418–19: 'Sol ubi sydereas ammovit crastinus umbras, / Urbs ruit et domine plaudit osanna sue'. *Cf.* Apul. *Met.* 11.7: 'Nec mora cum noctis atrae fugato nubilo Sol exsurgit aureus, et ecce discursu religioso ac prorsus triumphali, turbulae complent totas plateas'. *Cf.* 'influunt turbae' (Apul. *Met.* 11.10) and 'Occurrit [...] turba' (l. 423).

[82]   ll. 432–34: 'Ut modulantur aves foliis in vere renatis / Post noctes yemis, post grave tempus aque, / Non aliter verno venienti plauditur ore' ('As the birds sing in the spring when the leaves are reborn, /After the winter nights, after the season of heavy rain, / Not otherwise is her coming applauded by the voice of spring'). *Cf.* Apul. *Met.* 11.7: 'Nam et pruinam pridianam dies apricus ac placidus repente fuerat insecutus, ut canorae etiam aviculae prolectatae verno vapore concentus suaves assonarent, matrem siderum, parentem temporum orbisque totius dominam blando mulcentes affamine' ('For a sunny and calm day had come close on the heels of yesterday's frost, so that even the songbirds were enticed by the spring warmth to sing lovely harmonies, soothing with their charming greetings the mother of the stars, parents of the seasons, and mistress of the whole world').

[83]   *Cf.* Apul. *Met.* 11.9: 'illae quae ceteris unguentis et geniali balsamo guttatim excusso conspargebant plateas' ('Still others shook out drops of delightful balsam and other ointments to sprinkle the streets'). But note also (especially in the light of our discussion of the *Spurcum additamentum*) the possible echoes of Lucius' congress with the Corinthian *matrona* at Apul. *Met.* 10.21: 'multo sese perungit oleo balsamino [F: balsamo] meque indidem largissime perfricat, sed multo tanta impensius; tura [F: cura] etiam nares perfundit meas' ('she anointed herself all over with oil of balsam [...] and lavishly rubbed me down with the same, but with much greater eagerness. She even moistened my nostrils with frankincense [F: 'with care']').

[84]   For potential pathways from Monte Cassino into France, see Carver, *Protean Ass* (n. 1, above) 73–76.

THE WHITE GODDESS IN MEXICO:
APULEIUS, ISIS, AND THE VIRGIN OF GUADALUPE
IN LATIN, SPANISH, AND NAHUATL SOURCES[1]

ANDREW LAIRD

In *The White Goddess* (1948) Robert Graves linked the origins of poetry to the veneration of a lunar Muse. According to Graves,

> the most comprehensive and inspired account of the Goddess in all ancient literature is contained in *The Golden Ass*, where Lucius invokes her from the depth of misery and spiritual degradation and she appears in answer to his plea; incidentally it suggests that the Goddess was once worshipped [...] in her triple capacity of white raiser, red reaper and dark winnower of grain.[2]

Although there was no mention of Mexico in his book, the attributes of the goddess whom Graves described (named by Apuleius as Isis) have a remarkable affinity with those of the white-clad Aztec divinity Cihuacoatl.[3] In turn, Cihuacoatl has long been associated with the Catholic Virgin of Guadalupe: in the decades that followed the Spanish conquest of Mexico, a cult of the Virgin, supplanting that of the Aztec goddess at Tepeyac, came to be promoted by creoles or American-born Spaniards from the mid-1600s.

The present chapter will contend that Isis, Cihuacoatl, and the Virgin of Guadalupe were connected by the rich and complex afterlife of Apuleius' *Metamorphoses* or *Golden Ass* in New Spain (as colonial Mexico was known). The discussion to follow will survey the first glancing allusions to Apuleius in Nahuatl texts and Latin manuscripts from the 1500s (I), before examining some more sustained evocations of the *Metamorphoses* in seventeenth-century narratives of the apparitions of the Virgin of Guadalupe and in Sor Juana Inés de la Cruz' *Neptuno alegórico* (II). It will be argued in the final section (III) that apparent analogues between different religious traditions highlighted by the reading of Apuleius' *Metamorphoses*

---

[1] The discussion that follows, versions of which were presented at the Warburg Institute in May 2016 and at the UNAM Instituto de Investigaciones Filológicas in September 2017, is a more systematic extension of an earlier paper 'Les *Métamorphoses* et le métissage religieux au Mexique colonial', in *La Réception de l'ancien roman du Moyen Âge au début de l'époque classique*, eds C. Bost-Pouderon and B. Pouderon (Lyon 2015) 163–79. I am grateful to the editors and anonymous readers of the present volume, and especially to Claudio García Ehrenfeld, for comments on what follows.

[2] R. Graves, *The White Goddess* (London 1997) 91 (orig. 1949). Graves' own translation of *The Golden Ass* was first published as *The Transformations of Lucius* (Harmondsworth 1951).

[3] Graves visited Mexico in 1965, but his interest in the teonancatl mushroom, which led to an indirect association with María Sabina, the celebrated Mazatec *curandera*, had begun in 1949: M. Pharand, 'The mythophile and the mycophile: Robert Graves and R. Gordon Wasson', *Gravesiana: The Journal of the Robert Graves Society* 1.2 (December 1996) 204–15. Fray Bernardino de Sahagún's influential description of Cihuacoatl in book 1, chapter 6 of his *Historia general de las cosas de la Nueva España*, compiled in the later 1500s, is translated in Sahagún, *Florentine Codex, Book 1: The Gods*, eds A. J. O. Anderson and C. E. Dibble (Santa Fe 1970) 11.

may have originally served as a caution against connecting or comparing the Christian Virgin to any pagan divinity.

I. Apuleius in early Mexican literature

Following the Spanish conquest of 1521, Mexico-Tenochtitlan, the former seat of the Aztec empire, was soon transformed into a colonial metropolis.[4] Mexico City functioned as an imperial and educational centre in the New World even before Madrid became the capital of Spain in 1561. The Royal University of Mexico, inaugurated in 1554 with the same ordinances as Salamanca, was a match for any in Europe.[5] But the religious orders had already instituted several convents and colleges in Mexico City, including the Imperial College of Santa Cruz in Tlatelolco which the Franciscans established in 1536 to provide youths from native elites with a Latin humanist education.[6] A large number of manuscript and printed works were produced and there was a flourishing book trade: among many classical works, *El asno de oro*, the Spanish translation of Apuleius' *Metamorphoses* first published in 1513, was imported to New Spain.[7] The translator, Diego López de Cortegana, had a longstanding association with the volume's Sevillian printers, the Crombergers, who helped to establish the first press in Mexico City, at the prompting of Bishop Juan de Zumárraga in 1539.[8]

There is an early trace of the story of Apuleius' *Metamorphoses* in the indigenous Mexican language of Nahuatl. The Basque missionary Fray Andrés de Olmos' *Tratado de hechicerias y sortilegios*, 'Treatise on sorcery and spells' (*c.* 1553), makes reference to a description in Augustine's *City of God* of how the Devil could cause people to confuse dreams with reality:

> Çan no yui, yehuatl yn Diablo uel quitepololtiz yn tenematiliz ynitoca sentidos, yn iuhqui uey cochizpan, poliui ynic momatiz yehuatl yn tleyn ypan mochioa yn çan uel ompa cah yn campa, in Diablo ynic quitlapololtia, quilnamictia. Yn momat yn uel yc yxpan mochioa, in tleyn cochizpan quitta. Aug. 18 deciui. c. 18.[9]

[4]   B. E. Mundy, *The Death of Aztec Tenochtitlan, The Life of Mexico City* (Austin 2015) is an authoritative account of the transition.

[5]   A. María Rodríguez Cruz, *Salmantica docet: la proyección de la Universidad de Salamanca*, 2 vols (Salamanca 1977) I 53–82.

[6]   R. Ricard, *The Spiritual Conquest of Mexico: An Essay on the Apostolate and the Evangelizing Methods of the Mendicant Orders in New Spain, 1523–1572* (Berkeley 1974) 217–37; M. Mathes, *Santa Cruz de Tlatelolco: la primera biblioteca académica de las Américas* (Mexico City 1982); A. Laird, 'The teaching of Latin to the native nobility in Mexico in the mid-1500s: contexts, methods and results', in *Learning Latin and Greek from Antiquity to the Present*, eds E. Archibald, W. Brockliss, and J. Gnoza (Cambridge 2015) 118–35.

[7]   Diego López de Cortegana, *Apuleyo, 'El asno de oro'* (Seville 1513), ed. C. García Gual (Madrid 1988). López de Cortegana is discussed in J. H. Gaisser, *The Fortunes of Apuleius and the 'Golden Ass': A Study in Transmission and Reception* (Princeton-Oxford 2008) 269–78. N. Maillard Álvarez, 'The early circulation of classical books in New Spain and Peru', in *Antiquities and Classical Traditions in Latin America*, eds A. Laird and N. Miller (Chichester 2018) 26–40 describes the sixteenth-century book trade. A discussion of the Inquisition's suppression of *El asno de oro* in New Spain is cited at n. 38 below.

[8]   J. García Icazbalceta, *Bibliografía mexicana del siglo XVI: catálogo razonado de libros impresos en México de 1539 a 1600* (Mexico City 1954); C. Griffin, *The Crombergers of Seville: The History of a Printing and Merchant Dynasty* (Oxford 1988) 82–9.

[9]   Fray Andrés de Olmos, *Tratado de hechicerias y sortilegios*, ed. G. Baudot (Mexico City 1990). Olmos' manuscript work was a translation of Fray Martín de Castañega, *Tratado muy sotil y bien fundado de las supersticiones y hechicerias* (Logroño 1529): V. Ríos Castaño, 'El *Tratado de hechicerias y sortilegios* que "avisa y no emponzoña" de Fray Andrés de Olmos', *1611: Revista de historia de la traducción* 8 (2014), unpaginated [http://www.traduccionliteraria.org/1611/art/rios.htm (accessed 12 November 2019)].

The Devil can disrupt someone's consciousness—the consciousness we know under the name of 'sensations'—of one who disappears into a deep sleep; he may think the Devil is presenting to him things that are far off and this bothers him and makes him think. He thinks that what he saw in a dream appeared to him. Augustine, *De civitate Dei* book 18, chapter 18.

The passage of Augustine cited by Olmos contains a reflection on the possibility of Apuleius' transformation into an ass:

Sicut Apuleius, in libris, quos asini aurei titulo inscripsit, sibi ipsi accidisse, ut accepto ueneno humano animo permanente asinus fieret, aut indicauit aut finxit.[10]

So Apuleius said, in the books which he entitled *The Golden Ass*, that after taking poison he had turned into an ass but with his human mind intact, whether he revealed or made up what had happened to him.

Olmos deemed it appropriate to discuss such questions with native converts because the belief that sorcerers or 'naguales' had the capacity to transform themselves into jaguars, wolves, and other animals was widely held at the time. Indeed, it continues to this day throughout Mesoamerica.[11]

Indigenous fascination with 'nagualism' could explain why elements from Apuleius' *Cupid and Psyche* becoming incorporated into two fables ('zazanilli') in Nahuatl, which were transcribed at the beginning of the twentieth century by the folklorist and linguist Pablo González Casanova.[12] There are parallels for the rendition of classical texts into the Mexican language in the 1500s, and interactions between missionary friars and their native students may have led to the first Nahuatl version or versions of *Cupid and Psyche*.[13] Such a percolation into Mexican oral narrative is of interest because the Madauran Apuleius' story may itself have originated in oral narratives—those of the ancient Berbers which were precursors of North African folktales recorded in the twentieth century.[14] But such a percolation is also

[10]   August. *C. D.* 18.18.12–15.

[11]   D. G. Brinton, *Nagualism: A Study in Native American Folk-Lore and History* (Philadelphia 1894) was a pioneering account. A. López Austin, *Cuerpo humano e ideología. Las concepciones de los antiguos nahuas* (Mexico City 2012) 1, 420–30, and R. Martínez González, 'Sobre el origen y significado del término nahualli', *Estudios de cultura náhuatl* 37 (2006) 95–105 are among more recent studies.

[12]   'The Virgin and the Beast', recounted by Juan Hidalgo, a native of Tepotzlan, south of Mexico City; and 'A sickness afflicting three girls', related by Ignacia Maldonado from the neighbouring town of Milpa Alta: P. González Casanova, 'Un cuento griego en el folklore azteca', *Ethnos* 3 (1925) 16–24, reprinted in P. González Casanova, *Estudios de lingüística y filología nahuas* (Mexico City 1977) 199–208. The linguist assumed that the story's features were common to many peoples of the world but G. Baudot, 'La belle et la bête dans le folklore náhuatl du Mexique central', *Cahiers du monde hispanique et luso-brésilien* 27 (1976) 53–61 introduced his French translation of 'The Virgin and the Beast' ('Cizuanton huan yolcatl') with the suggestion that the Mexican story may have resulted from 'transfert littéraire et métissage culturel'.

[13]   Fray Juan de Torquemada, *Monarchia indiana* (Seville 1615), book 15, chapter 43 attests a sixteenth-century translation of Cato's *Distichs* into Nahuatl, and there are manuscripts of a version of forty-seven of Aesop's fables from the same period: A. Laird, 'A Mirror for Mexican princes: Reconsidering the context and Latin source for the Nahuatl translation of Aesop's *Fables*', in *Brief Forms in Medieval and Renaissance Hispanic Literature*, eds B. Taylor and A. Coroleu (Newcastle 2017) 132–67.

[14]   O. Weinreich, 'Eros und Psyche bei den Kabylen', *Archiv für Religionswissenschaft* 28 (1930) 1–2, 88–94; É. Dermenghem, *Contes kabyles* (Algiers 1945) and 'Les mythes de Psyché dans le folklore nord-africain', *Revue africaine* 89 (1945) 41–81; and J. Öjvind Swahn, *The Tale of Cupid and Psyche: Aarne-Thompson 425 & 428* (Lund 1955) compared Apuleius' story to the north African traditional accounts; E. Plantade and N. Plantade, '*Libyca*

important because it might help to account for connections between European texts and Mesoamerican traditions which are otherwise difficult to explain: on this basis, a parallel between the manifestations of Cihuacoatl and Apuleius' Isis discussed below (III) may not be coincidental.

Two sixteenth-century Latin letters in Mexico City recall Apuleius' language, rather than the content of his work. A letter to Philip II of Spain by an indigenous noble, Pablo Nazareo of Xaltocan, contains the following *captatio benevolentiae*:

> Itaque cum ergo regia corona Sacrae Catholicae Majestatis sit admodum quercus aut abies, quae in montibus altis aeditur, tam in adversis quam in prosperis maxima commoditas, merito sub umbra foliorum regiae pietatis refocillare protendimus [...] quod artem gubernandi rem publicam mare tranquillum non ostendit, cum impulsu venti contrariorum aliquod adversum occurrat in hoc salo mentis.[15]

> And so since the royal crown of your holy Catholic Majesty may be a kind of oak or pine, which grows on high mountains, the greatest comfort in favourable and adverse conditions alike, only rightly do we stretch forth to revive ourselves under the shade of its leaves of royal piety [...] because it is not a quiet sea which shows the skill needed to govern a state, when by the impulse of the wind of contrary forces, adversity looms in this sea of the mind.

The final two words of the Latin sentence, 'salo mentis' ('sea of the mind'), were used in Apuleius' *De deo Socratis*; there are similar formulations—'isto cogitationis salo' and 'mentis salo'—in the *Metamorphoses*.[16] Although Saint Augustine could also have transmitted 'salo mentis' to Nazareo, the evocations above of Virgil and of Quintilian's remark on Horace's ship of state ode (as well as a quotation from Ovid's *Ars amatoria* in his previous sentence) demonstrate the writer's acquaintance with classical sources.[17]

The second Latin author, Fray Cristóbal Cabrera, a Franciscan humanist in New Spain, wrote an epistolary preface to a Latin translation of some Greek commentaries on Paul's *Epistles* in 1540:

> Nam, vt ad doctos me convertam, quis adeo tetricus est, aut livore corruptus, aut lippis oculis caecutiens, vt non videat haec quantulacumque sunt, non parum lucis allatura studiosis lectoribus, sacrarumque litterarum candidatis, illisque potissimum Graecanicae linguae ignaris, in quorum gratiam haec Latinis auribus reddita sunt?[18]

Psyche: Apuleius' narrative and Berber folktales', in *Apuleius and Africa*, eds B. Todd Lee, E. Finkelpearl, and L. Graverini (New York-Abingdon 2014) 174–202 make a strong case for Libyan oral sources informing the literary narrative of Apuleius' *Metamorphoses*. Such investigations, though, are problematic: K. Dowden, 'Ass-men and witches', *Classical Review* 35.1 (1985) 41–3, a short review of A. Scobie, *Apuleius and Folklore: Toward a History of ML 3045, AaTh 567, 449A* (London 1983).

[15]   Pablo Nazareo de Xaltocan, *Sacrae Catholicae Magestati Hispaniarum Indiarumque*, 17 March 1566 [ms. Archivo General de Indias, F 1229/ P37], fol. 2. The letter is edited in Ignacio Osorio Romero, *La enseñanza de latín a los indios* (Mexico City 1990) 11–34.

[16]   Apul. *Soc.* 12; *Met.* 4.2 and 9.19: S. J. Harrison, 'Waves of emotion: an epic metaphor in Apuleius' *Metamorphoses*', in *Metaphor and the Ancient Novel, Ancient Narrative Supplementum 4*, eds S. J. Harrison, M. Paschalis, and S. A. Frangoulidis (Groningen 2005) 163–76.

[17]   August. *C. D.* 9.3 and 9.6–7; Verg. *Aen.* 4.441–6; Hor. *Odes* 1.14; Quint. *Inst.* 8.6.44: 'navem pro re publica, fluctus et tempestates pro bellis civilibus'.

[18]   Fray Cristóbal Cabrera, *Argumenta in omnes Beati Pauli Epistolas* (Biblioteca Apostolica Vaticana, ms. Vat.

Now to turn to those who are educated: who is so odious, or corrupted by malice, or squints so dimly with swollen eyes as not to see that, whatever these efforts amount to, they do bring some light for studious readers and trainees in sacred letters, and especially for those who do not know the Greekish tongue, for whose sake all this has been rendered for Latin ears?

Cabrera's words play on the first sentence of Apuleius' prologue to the *Metamorphoses*:

At ego tibi sermone isto Milesio uarias fabulas conseram auresque tuas benivolas lepido susurro permulceam – modo si papyrum Aegyptiam argutia Nilotici calami inscriptam non spreueris inspicere [...] Fabulam Graecanicam incipimus. Lector intende: laetaberis.[19]

But for you I will sew various stories in this Milesian speech, and soothe your benevolent ears with a pleasant whisper, if you don't despise looking at Egyptian papyrus inscribed with a sharp reed from the Nile [...] we begin a Greekish tale. Pay heed reader: you'll be glad.

Apuleius' conceit of a text that could either be heard or scrutinised by sight was thus redeployed and embellished—with the mention of Latin listeners and an adversarial reader modelled on Horace's critic with 'swollen eyes full of ointment' ('oculis [...] lippus inunctis').[20] The friar also appropriated the term 'Graecanicam' ('Greekish') to signal his recognition of the distinction, made long ago by Isidore of Seville, between the *koinē* of the New Testament and classical Greek.[21] Like Apuleius, Cabrera was translating Greek into Latin—which was not his first language either. These allusions show that the Latin text of the *Metamorphoses*, or at least of its opening, was known in New Spain by the mid-1500s, as well as López de Cortegana's popular translation in *El asno de oro*.

II. Accounts of the Virgin of Guadalupe and Apuleius' Metamorphoses

Apuleius' Prologue was also echoed more than a century later in another Mexican Latin preface: Bernardo Ceinos de Riofrío's introduction to his *Centonicum Virgilianum Monimentum* of 1680.[22] This Virgilian cento narrated what is still the most famous miracle on the American continent: the apparition, which supposedly occurred in 1531, of the Virgin of Guadalupe to an indigenous Mexican—a foundation myth which continues to be of potent religious and political significance in Mexico today, as well as for people in many other Spanish-speaking countries and regions of the Americas (fig. 1).[23]

Lat. 1164, 1540), ed. Fr. Leopoldo Campos, 'Métodos misionales y rasgos biográficos de Don Vasco de Quiroga según Cristóbal Cabrera', in *Don Vasco de Quiroga y el arzobispado de Morélia*, ed. M. Ponce (Mexico City 1965).

[19] Apul. *Met.* 1.1.

[20] Hor. *Sat.* 1.3.25.

[21] Isid. *Etym.* 10.4–5.

[22] Riofrío, *Centonicum Virgilianum Monimentum mirabilis apparitionis purissimae Virginis Mariae de Guadalupe* (Mexico City 1680); A. Laird, 'The Virgin of Guadalupe and the birth of Latin epic in Mexico: Bernardo Ceinos de Riofrío's *Centonicum Virgilianum Monimentum*', in *Mexico 1680: Cultural and Intellectual Life in the 'Barroco de Indias'*, eds. J. Andrews and A. Coroleu (Bristol 2007) 199–220.

[23] J. Lafaye, *Quetzalcoatl and Guadalupe: the Formation of Mexican National Consciousness, 1531–1813* (Chicago 1987) 276–302; D. A. Brading, *Mexican Phoenix: Our Lady of Guadalupe: Image and Tradition across Five Centuries* (Cambridge 2001); J. Rodríguez, *Our Lady of Guadalupe: Faith and Empowerment among Mexican-American Women* (Austin 1994).

Figure 1. Original image of the Virgin of Guadalupe in the New Basilica of Tepeyac, Mexico. Public domain.

One of the first published accounts of the miracle, Luis Becerra Tanco's *Origen milagrosa del santuario de Nuestra Señora de Guadalupe* (Mexico City 1666), was summarized by Riofrío in the Latin preface to his cento.[24] On the ninth of December 1531, a poor and humble Indian called Juan Diego was walking at dawn past the hill now known as Guadalupe to hear mass. He caught sight of a colourful rainbow and heard the sound of beautiful singing. As he turned towards the sound, the Virgin Mary appeared and spoke to him, declaring that she was the mother of God and that a temple should be established on the hill from where she might stretch out her hand to help him and all those devoted to her. She enjoined him to give a faithful account of this to the bishop, who at first did not believe him and sought a sign. The Indian returned and unfastened his cloak, in which the Virgin had instructed him to gather roses from the hill. The bishop then saw the image of the Virgin on the cloak and ordered a church to be built in the place she appeared: the very site where, Riofrío remarks, 'the ancient inhabitants had once in their foolish and empty superstition worshipped an expiatory goddess whom they had persistently called the mother of gods' ('ubi antea inepta, vanaque veterum superstitio, expiatricem Deam colebat, quam deorum matrem appellitabat').[25]

The very first sentence of Riofrío's preface, however, took the form of a *captatio benevolentiae* to the reader:

---

[24] L. Becerra Tanco, *Origen milagrosa de santuario de Nuestra Señora de Guadalupe* (Mexico City 1666) in *Testimonios históricos guadalupanos*, eds E. de la Torre Villar and R. Navarra de Anda (Mexico City 2005) 309–33.

[25] Riofrío, *Centonicum Virgilianum Monimentum* (n. 22, above) 'Ad lectorem', fol. 13 (unnumbered).

En, candide lector, unum indicum opusculum, tibi obvium procedens centonibus peraratum, non tibi sordeat, nec inusitatum putes.[26]

Behold fair reader, may this one little work of Indian colour not seem grubby to you as it advances to meet you down a route ploughed by centos, and may you not think it out of the ordinary.

This resembles Apuleius' address to his reader in the opening sentence of the prologue to the *Metamorphoses* quoted above, and Riofrío's playful apology for the 'Indian colour' of the work corresponds to the ironic bashfulness about using 'Egyptian paper' and a 'Nile reed pen' on the part of the African Apuleius' narrator. Riofrío characterized his cento as an 'indicum opusculum' because of the supposed indigenous origin of that story: the native Mexicans had indeed venerated their deity Tonantzin, 'Our Mother', in Tepeyac at the site where the Virgin supposedly appeared.[27] It was, however, creole Spaniards, not Indians, who were responsible for generating and promoting the Guadalupan myth from the mid-1600s onwards.[28]

Riofrío's prominent and pronounced allusion to Apuleius' Prologue may have a further significance. The first apparition of the Virgin of Guadalupe in Becerra Tanco's narrative has some elements in common with the epiphany of Isis to Lucius in book 11 of the *Metamorphoses*. Although not in the desperate situation of Lucius, the Indian Juan Diego was still an abject figure, 'plebeian and poor, lowly and simple'. The clothing of the 'beautiful lady' ('hermosíssima señora') he saw was described as follows:

[...] brillaba tanto, que hiriendo sus esplendores en los peñascos brutos que se levantan sobre la cumbre del cerillo, le parecieron piedras preciosas labradas y transparentes, y las hojas de las espinos y nopales, que allí de finas esmeraldas, y sus brazos, tronco y espinas de oro bruñido y reluciente; y hasta el suelo de un corto llano que hay en aquella cumbre, le pareció de jaspe matizado de colores diferentes.[29]

[...] her garments shone so brightly that, as their splendour struck the rough crags that rise above the top of the hill, they looked like carved and transparent precious stones, and the leaves of thorns and nopal were like fine emeralds, and their branches, trunk, and thorns of burnished and glistening gold; and even the ground of the short plateau on that summit looked to him like jasper tinted in different colours.

This part of Becerra Tanco's description is a Spanish translation of a passage from the *Huey Tlamahuiçoltica* (fig. 2), a version of the story that had been printed in Nahuatl in 1649:

In itlaquentzin iuhquin tonatiuh ic motonameyotoia inic pepetlaca; auh in tetl, in texcalli inic itech moquetza, inic quimina in itlanexyotzin yuhqui in tlaçòchalchihuitl, maquiztli; inic neci yuhquin ayauhcoçamalocuecueyoca in tlalli; auh in mizquitl, yn nòpalli, ihuan oc cequi nepapan xiuhtotontin oncan mochìchihuani yuhquin

---

[26]   Riofrío, *Centonicum Virgilianum Monimentum* (n. 22, above) 'Ad lectorem', fol. 12 (unnumbered).

[27]   Sahagún, *Florentine Codex, Introductory Volume*, eds A. J. O. Anderson and C. E. Dibble (Santa Fe 1982) 90; A. Laird, 'Aztec and Roman gods in sixteenth-century Mexico: classical learning in Sahagún's missionary ethnography', in *Altera Roma: Art and Empire from Mérida to Mexico*, eds J. Pohl and C. Lyons (Los Angeles 2016) 147–67 (161).

[28]   This consideration is central to Brading, *Mexican Phoenix* (n. 23, above).

[29]   Becerra Tanco, *Origen milagrosa de santuario de Nuestra Señora de Guadalupe* (Mexico City 1666), in *Testimonios históricos guadalupanos*, (n. 24, above) 313.

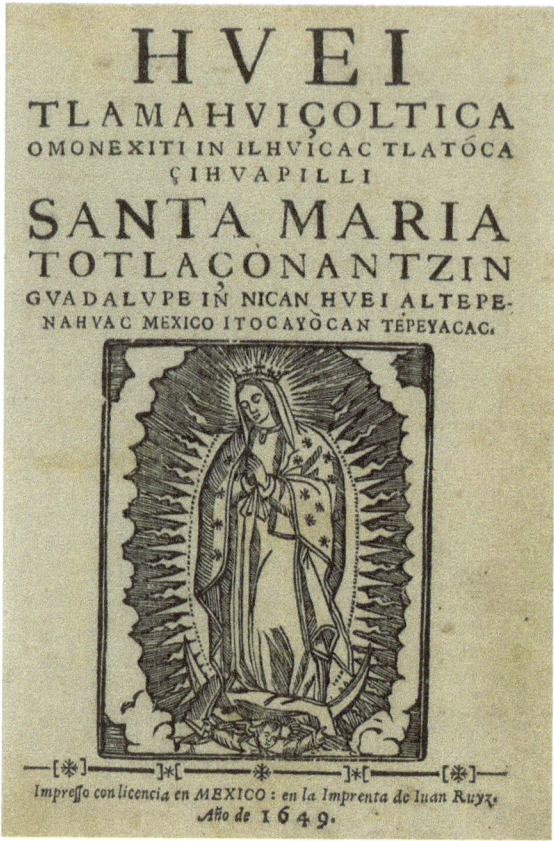

Figure 2. *Huei tlamahuiçoltica*, 'By a Great Miracle' (Mexico 1649), title page. Courtesy of the John Carter Brown Library at Brown University.

quetzaliztli, yuhqui in teoxihuitl in iatlapallo ic neci; auh in iquauhyo, in ihuitzyo, in iàhuayo yuhqui in coztic teocuitlatl ic pepetlaca.[30]

Her clothes were like the sun in the way they gleamed and shone. Her resplendence struck the stones and boulders by which she stood, so that they seemed like precious emeralds and jewelled bracelets. The ground sparkled like a rainbow and the mesquite, the prickly pear cactus, and other various kinds of weed that grow there seemed like green obsidian, and their foliage like fine turquoise. Their stalks, their thorns, and spines gleamed like gold.

That Nahuatl version of the passage more directly recalls the iridescent raiment of the image of the goddess that was treated in equivalent detail in chapter 3 of book 11 of the *Metamorphoses*:

Tunica multicolor, bysso tenui pertexta, nunc albo candore lucida, nunc croceo flore lutea, nunc roseo rubore flammida et, quae longe longeque etiam meum confutabat optutum, palla nigerrima splendescens atro nitore.[31]

[30] Luis Laso de la Vega, *Huei tlamahuiçoltica* (Mexico City 1649), edited and translated as *The Story of Guadalupe*, eds L. Sousa, S. Poole, and J. Lockhart (Stanford 1988) 62–5.

[31] Apul. *Met.* 11.3, ed. D. S. Robertson (Paris 1945) II 140; other texts have 'vestis' for 'tunica'. Compare *El asno de oro*, trans. López de Cortegana (Madrid 1988) 308 (book 11, chapter 1 of this translation): 'traía un vestido de

Her multicoloured garment woven of fine linen, now gleaming in clear white, now yellow as a saffron flower, now flaming in a rosy red, and, what was confounding my gaze even as I was far away, the blackest cloak shining with a dark splendour.

In Becerra Tanco's narrative, the Virgin then makes a speech to Juan Diego, which parallels the speech Isis made to Lucius. Both of the speeches, reproduced below, exhibit the same thematic correspondences in the same order, here enumerated [1]–[4] and highlighted in bold type. The Virgin and Isis present themselves respectively as the mother of God and the mother of gods; both pledge their compassion and protection to their addressee, whom they charge with a mission; and both engineer a miracle in which roses are involved. The relevant parts of Becerra Tanco's narrative are as follows:

Sábete, hijo mío, muy querido, que soy la siempre Virgen María, [1] **Madre del verdadero Dios**, autor de la vida, creador de todo, Señor del Cielo y de la tierra que está en todas partes y es mi deseo que se me alce un templo en este lugar donde, como Madre piadosa tuya y de sus semejantes, [2] **mostraré mi clemencia amorosa y la compasión** que tengo de los naturales, de aquellos que me buscan y aman y de todos los que soliciten mi protección o me invoquen en sus trabajos o aflicciones. Y donde enjugaré las lágrimas y oiré sus ruegos para darles **consuelo y alivio.** y [3] **para que tenga efecto mi voluntad has de ir** a la ciudad de México y al palacio del obispo que ahí reside a quien dirás que yo te envío, y como es gusto mío que me edifique un templo en este lugar; les referirás cuanto has visto y oído, y ten por cierto tú, que te agradeceré lo que por mí hicieres en esto que te encargo y te afamaré y te sublimaré por ello; ya has oído, hijo mío, mi deseo; vete en paz y advierte que te pagaré el trabajo y diligencia que pusiereis; y así harás en esto todo esfuerzo que pudiereis [...]³²

Dixole Maria Santísima: 'Sube, hijo mio muy querido y tierno, á la cumbre del cero en que me has visto y hablado, y [4] **corta las rosas** que hallares alli, y recogelas en el regazo de tu capa, y traelas á mi presencia y te diré lo que has de hacer y decir.'³³

My son, very dear to me, you should know that I am the ever Virgin Mary, [1] **Mother of the true God** who is author of life, creator of all, Lord of Heaven and of the earth, who is present everywhere. And it is my wish that a temple should be founded for me in this place where, as dutiful Mother to you and others like you, [2] **I will show the loving mercy and compassion** I have towards the native people, for those who look for me, love me, and all who seek my protection or invoke me in their labours and afflictions. And there I shall wipe away their tears and hear their prayers to grant them counsel and relief; and [3] **for my will to be accomplished you have to go** to the city of Mexico and to the palace where the bishop lives, and tell him I am sending you, and that it is my pleasure that he should build a temple in this place; you should relate to them all you have seen and heard, and be sure that I will thank you for doing what I ask by promoting and exalting you. Now my son you have heard what is my wish. Go in peace and bear in mind that I will repay your work and diligence, so that you do the very best you can [...]

---

lino tejido de muchos colores: ahora era blanca y muy luciente, ahora amarilla como flor de azafrán, ahora inflamada con un color rosado, que aunque estaba yo lejos, me quitaba la vista de los ojos, traía encima otra ropa negra, que resplandecía la obscuridad de ella'.

³² Becerra Tanco, *Origen milagrosa* (n. 29, above), 'Primera aparición' 313.

³³ Becerra Tanco, *Origen milagrosa*, 'Cuarta aparición' 318.

Most Holy Mary said to him 'Go, my dear and beloved son, to the top of the hill on which you saw and spoke with me, and **[4] cut the roses** that you will find there, and put them in the fold of your cape, bring them to me and I will tell what you have to do and say.'[34]

Isis speaks these words to Lucius thus in Apuleius' *Metamorphoses*:

Inde primigenii Phryges Pessinuntiam **[1] deum matrem**, hinc autochthones Attici Cecropeiam Mineruam, illinc fluctuantes Cyprii Paphiam Venerem, Cretes sagittiferi Dictynnam Dianam, Siculi trilingues Stygiam Proserpinam, Eleusinii uetusti Actaeam Cererem [...] priscaque doctrina pollentes Aegyptii caerimoniis me propriis percolentes appellant **uero nomine reginam Isidem. [2] Adsum tuos miserata casus, adsum fauens et propitia.** Mitte iam fletus et lamentationes omitte, depelle maerorem; iam tibi prouidentia mea inlucescit dies salutaris. **[3] Ergo igitur imperiis istis meis animum intende sollicitum.**

Diem, qui dies ex ista nocte nascetur, aeterna mihi nuncupauit religio, quo sedatis hibernis tempestatibus et lenitis maris procellosis fluctibus nauigabili iam pelago rudem dedicantes carinam primitias commeatus libant mei sacerdotes. Id sacrum nec sollicita nec profana mente debebis opperiri. Nam meo monitu sacerdos in ipso procinctu pompae **roseam** manu dextera sistro cohaerentem gestabit **coronam**. Incunctanter ergo dimotis turbulis alacer continuare pompam mea uolentia fretus et de proximo clementer uelut manum sacerdotis osculabundus **[4] rosis decerptis** pessimae mihique iam dudum detestabilis beluae istius corio te protinus exue.[35]

The first-born Phrygians thus call me the Pessinuntine **[1] Mother of the Gods**, the Athenians sprung from their own earth call me Cecropean Minerva, the Cypriots surrounded by sea call me Paphian Venus, the Cretans with their arrows call me Dictynna and Diana, those from Sicily with its three tongues call me Stygian Proserpina, those of Eleusis call me Ceres [...], and the Egyptians, revered for their ancient wisdom, worship me with their rites and call me by my true name of queen Isis. **[2] I am here, taking pity on your misfortunes, I am here to favour and help you.** Now cease weeping and forget your lamentation, drive away your sorrow; now through my providence a day of salvation is dawning for you. **[3] So now turn your mind to my commands.**

My eternal rites have dedicated the day born of this night to my rites: on this day the winter storms are stilled, the ocean's stormy waves are becalmed, and my priests commit a new ship to the sea now that it can be sailed, and dedicate it to me as the first offering of the trading season. You must await this ceremony with a mind neither distracted nor irreverent. Then on my instructions the high priest will carry in the procession a **[4] garland of roses** attached to the sistrum in his right hand. Then, without hesitation, part the crowd and promptly join the procession, and relying on my protection, push your way towards the priest, then, as if you wished to kiss his hand, **pluck at the roses**, and so at once throw off the skin of the worst and most detestable beast.

---

[34] An initiate seeking or being bidden to make an ascent is a *topos* of Christian protreptic and humanist writing (Petrarch, *Epistolae familiares* 4.1) with precedents in classical literature (Lucian, *Hermot.* 59; *Cebetis Tabula* 15).

[35] Apul. *Met.* 11.5–6, ed. Robertson, II 143 (n. 31, above).

The Virgin of Guadalupe identifies herself as a divine mother, assuring Juan Diego of her pity and compassion. Like Isis, she also issues a command and promises benefits to her mortal addressee if it is fulfilled: Juan Diego should inform the bishop of her wish for a temple to be built in Tepeyac where she has appeared. Most strikingly, roses and a high-ranking priest have a role in the resolutions of both the pagan and the Christian stories: Isis instructs Lucius to approach the high priest and snatch at the garland of roses to recover his human form; the Virgin locates some 'fresh roses of Castile' which Juan Diego is to wrap in his cloak to present to the bishop—an action which led to the manifestation of the Virgin's sacred image.

Passages from Scripture and accounts of Marian apparitions in Europe were the principal sources and inspiration for the Guadalupan testimonies by Becerra Tanco and others. Even so, Venus' appearance to her son in *Aeneid* book 1 offers a classical model for Riofrío's verse narrative of the epiphany in his Virgilian cento.[36] What is more, his Latin prose summary of the Virgin's speech to Juan Diego has a pronounced resemblance to Isis' speech in Apuleius:

> Filiole mi, scias [1] me veram altissimi Dei Matrem esse, meque incenso exoptare molimine, ut iuxta montem hunc, templum in mei honorem constituatur, vbi tibi, cunctisque me diligentibus [2] auxiliatricem porrigam manum: sicque libet, vt [3] Episcopum adeas, cuncta haec ei expromas, et fideliter pandas.[37]

> My dear little son, you should know that [1] I am the true mother of God on high, and that my great wish is to spark the endeavour for a temple to be built in my honour on the side of this hill—from where I can stretch out a helping hand to you and to all those who love me [2]—and I would like [3] you to go to the bishop and convey and explain to him all this in faithful detail.

The convergence may not be coincidental. López de Cortegana's translation of the *Metamorphoses* had circulated widely in the colony of New Spain long before it was prohibited by Gaspar de Quiroga in his inquisitorial Index of 1583.[38] A century later, in 1680, the same year as Riofrío's *Centonicum Virgilianum Monimentum* appeared, the Jeronymite nun Sor Juana Inés de la Cruz published her *Neptuno alegórico*, a prose text replete with displays of learning characteristic of much baroque literature. The *Neptuno alegórico* celebrated the entry of the new viceroy into Mexico City—Sor Juana playfully associated him with Neptune on account of his name, *Laguna*. Citing the unreliable Italian humanist Natale Conti, the poetess affirmed that Neptune's mother 'was the goddess Isis [...] whom they called *Magna mater*, mother of the gods':

> Fue madre suya [Neptuno] la diosa Opis o Cibeles, lo cual es lo mismo que Isis, por representar estos dos nombres la Tierra, a la cual llamaron Magna Mater, y creyeron ser madre de todos los dioses, y aun de las fieras, como la llamaron Laercio: Quare Magna Deum Mater, Materque ferarum y Sílio Itálico en el libro 6: At grandaeva Deum praenoscens omnia Mater. Lo mismo signfica Isis en sentir de Nadal [...]. Digo que esta Isis tan celebrada fue aquella reina de Egipto, a quien Diódoro Sículo con

---

[36] Verg. *Aeneid* 1.327–34, recalled in Riofrío, *Centonicum Virgilianum Monimentum* (n. 22, above) v. 201–8. Laird, 'The Virgin of Guadalupe and the birth of Latin epic' (n. 22, above) 208.

[37] Riofrío, *Centonicum Virgilianum Monimentum* (n. 22, above), 'Ad lectorem'.

[38] I. A. Leonard, *Books of the Brave: Being an Account of Books and of Men in the Spanish Conquest* (Cambridge, MA 1967) 248.

tanta razón elogia desde los primeros renglones de su Historia: la cual fue la norma de
la sabiduría gitana. Un libro entero escribió Plutarco de este asunto: Pierio Valeriano
muchos capítulos; Platón muchos elogios, el cual en el lib. 2 de Legib., tratando de la
música de los egipcios, dijo: Ferunt, antiquissimos illos apud eos concentus Isidis esse
poemata. [...] Cartario, in Minerv. Pág. 259, equivocando con Minerva a Isis, a quien
los autores antiguos han nombrado con grandísima diversidad: Apuleyo la llama Rea,
Venus, Diana, Belona, Ceres, Juno, Proserpina, Hécate y Ramnusia. Dióduro Sículo
dice que Isis es la que llamaron Luna, Juno y Ceres; Macrobio afirma no ser sino la
Tierra, o la naturaleza de las cosas.[39]

Neptune's mother was the goddess Opis or Cybele, who, since both these names
represent the Earth, is identical to Isis, who was called *Magna Mater* and thought to
be the mother of all the gods, as well as of wild beasts—as Diogenes Laertius referred
to her: 'The Mother of the Gods and the Mother of Wild Beasts'; and as Silius Italicus
referred to her in his sixth book: 'The longstanding Mother of the Gods foreknowing
all things'. Isis stands for the same in Natale Conti's opinion [...]. I declare that this
Isis was that renowned queen of Egypt whom Diodorus Siculus praises with good
reason from the first lines of his *History*: this was the conventional wisdom of Egypt.
Plutarch wrote a whole book on the subject; Pierio Valeriano devoted several chapters
to it; and Plato provided eulogies such as the one in book 2 of the *Laws*, where, treating
the music of the Egyptians, he said: 'They note that the oldest compositions in their
possession are poems to Isis'. [...] Cartario, *On Minerva*, p. 259 identifies Minerva
with Isis; to the latter ancient authors ascribe very different names: Apuleius calls
her Rhea, Venus, Diana, Bellona, Ceres, Juno, Proserpina, Hecate, and Rhamnusia.
Diodorus Siculus says that, to speak of Isis, they used names such as Moon, Juno, and
Ceres; Macrobius affirms she is nothing other than the Earth, or the nature of things.

Sor Juana adduced other sources for Isis, including all the names given to her by Apuleius,
which she had absorbed from Athanasius Kircher's *Oedipus Aegyptiacus* (fig. 3).[40] All in all,
Apuleius' Isis and the Virgin of Guadalupe were oddly similar figures, but it remains to be
shown that a direct association had already been made between them earlier in New Spain's
history.

III. Serpent women: Cihuacoatl, Isis, and Eve

The evidence is in the *Monarchia indiana*, an ambitious history of New Spain—reminiscent
of Livy's *Ab urbe condita*—from Mexico's beginnings in pre-Hispanic myth to the time the
work was brought to completion in the 1590s. Its Franciscan author, Fray Juan de Torquemada,
taught in the Indian college of Tlatelolco in Mexico City and had a good command of the
Mexican language of Nahuatl. In book 2 of his history, Torquemada recounted how the Aztecs
left Aztlan, their mythical place of origin, often supposed to be in North America, and came
to be called the *Mexica*. In the course of their long migration, when they reached Apanco, a
strange event occurred. A witch named Quilaztli appeared before two of their commanders

---

[39]   Sor Juana Inés de la Cruz, *Neptuno alegórico* (Mexico City 1680) in *Obras completas*, ed. A. G. Salceda,
(Mexico City 1957) IV 355–410 (360–2).

[40]   Athanasius Kircher, *Œdipus ægyptiacus hoc est vniuersalis hieroglyphicæ veterum doctrinae* [...] *instauratio*,
vol. 1 (Rome 1652) 189.

Figure 3. The *Magna Deorum Mater*, based on Apuleius' Isis, in Athanasius Kircher, *Oedipus Aegyptiacus* (Rome 1652). Public domain.

as a great and beautiful eagle perched on a nopal cactus. The men aimed their arrows at her, but she made fun of them, telling them not to shoot, for she was their sister, of their people, and they would pay the price if they killed her. On a second occasion, Quilaztli assumed the guise of a warrior in order to terrify the same two men. She spoke to them, listing her various names:

> Porque si vosotros me conocéis por Quilaztli (que es el nombre común con que me nombráis) yo tengo otros cuatro nombres conque me conozco; el uno de los cuales es Cohuacihuatl. que quiere decir. mujer culebra; el otro Quauhcihuatl. mujer águila; el otro Yaocihuatl. mujer guerrera; el cuarto Tzitzimicihuatl que quiere decir mujer infernal; y según las propiedades que se incluyen en estos cuatro nombres veréis quién soy y el poder que tengo y el mal que puedo haceros [...][41]

> For, if you know me as Quilaztli (the common name you give me), I have another four names by which I know myself. One is Cohuacihuatl which means Serpent Woman; another Quauhcihuatl which means Eagle Woman; another Yaocihuatl which means Warrior Woman; the fourth Tzitzimicihuatl means Devil Woman. And by the qualities contained in these four names you will see who I am, the power I have and the harm I can do you [...]

---

[41]   Fray Juan de Torquemada, *Monarchia indiana* (Seville 1615) book 2, chapter 2.

Figure 4. Pre-Hispanic sculpture of Cihuacoatl, Cuernavaca *c.* 1325–1521 AD.
Museo Nacional de Antropología, Mexico City, inv. no. 11-3298.

Quilaztli was an unpleasant avatar of the Aztec goddess Cihuacoatl, the Serpent Woman, who was often represented visually as framed by the mouth of a serpent, holding an ear of maize in one hand and a snake in the other (fig. 4). As Torquemada describes her, Cihuacoatl-Quilaztli has a lot in common with a female divinity described in Virgil's *Aeneid*: the loathsome Allecto, an infernal agent of Discord. Allecto too is a snake-wielding goddess with many names who can take any form she likes, including the appearance of people known to those whom she aims to terrorize. Allecto also makes her entrance at the very point that the Trojans are reaching their own promised land of Italy. There is another glancing convergence: Allecto induces Aeneas' son to kill with his arrow a pet stag cherished by the Latins, directly causing the war between them and the Trojans:

> Luctificam Allecto dirarum ab sede dearum
> infernisque ciet tenebris, cui tristia bella
> iraeque insidiaeque et crimina noxia cordi [...]
>
> odit et ipse pater Pluton, odere sorores
> Tartareae monstrum: tot sese uertit in ora,
> tam saeuae facies, tot pullulat atra colubris.[42]

---

[42] Verg. *Aen.* 7.324–6, 7.328–9.

Grievous Allecto from the seat of grim goddesses and infernal darkness, whose heart is set on grim war, rage, trickery, and noxious crimes [...]

Her father Pluto himself loathes her, her Tartarean sisters loathe her as a monster, so many forms she assumes, so fierce their visage, so many her black sprouting snakes.

But the speech of Quilaztli also pointedly recalls that of Isis at the end of the *Metamorphoses*. What is more, Isis wears a crown adorned with coiled serpents, a mirror, and ears of wheat. After she too has listed her numerous names and her true identity as Isis, she says to Lucius: 'Adsum tuos miserata casus, adsum favens et propitia' ('I am here to take pity on your misfortune, to favour and help you').[43]

Torquemada's Quilaztli, who threatens hindrance and harm rather than providing help to the Mexicans, is a pointed inversion of Apuleius' goddess, and indeed of the Virgin of Guadalupe. Narratives and demonologies transmitted in works of *speculum* literature (such as Gervase of Tilbury's *Otia imperialia* considered below) could have possibly inspired Torquemada's portrayal of Quilaztli, but Isis' speech to Lucius has the most obvious bearing on the construction of the Mexican goddess' speech to the Aztec leaders.

That is not accidental. The reason for this evocation emerges in the prior account of the Mexican goddess Cihuacoatl by Torquemada's predecessor as a missionary ethnographer of pre-Hispanic Mexico, Fray Bernardino de Sahagún. In his Spanish chapter on Cihuacoatl, Sahagún states that this goddess was also called Tonantzin, which means 'Our Mother'. The friar took her two names, 'Snake Woman' and 'Mother', to mean that 'this goddess is our Mother Eve, who was tricked by a serpent'.[44] Sahagún was drawing from a tradition of Eve herself as a serpent woman (fig. 5a). In the second century, Clement of Alexandria claimed that the aspirated Hebrew name of Eve, 'Hevva', translated into Greek as 'female serpent'— both Clement and Eusebius linked this to the use of serpents and the ritual invocation of Eve ('Euhoe') in Greek Bacchic orgies.[45]

The association of women with snakes became a more general convention, and depictions of Eve directly associating her with a serpent were widespread in medieval Europe: the restored bas-relief on the Portail de la Vierge of the Cathedral of Notre Dame in Paris shows Eve almost as a reflection of Lilith, who is rendered as a serpent with a woman's head (fig. 5b).[46] A passage in Gervase of Tilbury's *Otia imperialia*, an influential work composed in the thirteenth century for the Holy Roman Emperor Otto, helps throw light on this convention and also has a tangential relation to the story of Apuleius' *Metamorphoses*:

[43] Apul. *Met.* 11.5. Isis' crown is described in *Met.* 11.3.

[44] Fray Bernardino de Sahagún, *Historia general de las cosas de la Nueva España*, book 1, chapter 6, ed. J. C. Temprano (Madrid 2009).

[45] Clement of Alexandria, *Protrepticus* 2.12.2: 'The exact pronunciation of the aspirated Hebrew name of "Eve" translates into Greek as "female serpent"'. Eusebius, *Praeparatio evangelica* 2.3.3: 'The bacchants celebrate with their orgies the madness of Dionysus, and organize a festival day each month on which they eat raw flesh and when they distribute the flesh of slaughtered victims; they are crowned with garlands of serpents, and they invoke Eve, that Eve through whom every treachery was admitted and who was closely followed by death'.

[46] A. Giallongo, *The Historical Enigma of the Snake Woman from Antiquity to the 21ˢᵗ Century*, trans. A. C. Foster (Newcastle upon Tyne 2017). A. Rojas Silva, 'Gardens of origin and the Golden Age in the Mexican *Libellus de medicinalibus indorum herbis* (1552)', in *Antiquities and Classical Traditions* (n. 7, above) 51, suggests that an image of two snakes in a native Mexican herbal could allude to Eve and Lilith, noting that 'coatl', serpent in Nahuatl, also means 'twin'.

Figure 5a. Drawing of Snake Woman, *Florentine Codex c.* 1577, book 8, fol. 12 r, detail. World Digital Library.

Nec erit omittendum quid ait Beda, loquens de serpente qui Euam seduxit. Elegit enim diabolus quoddam genus serpentis femineum uultum habentis, quia similia similibus applaudunt, et mouit ad loquendum linguam eius. De serpentis tradunt uulgares quod sunt quedam feminae que mutantur in serpentes, que ita dinoscuntur: habent enim ligaturam albam quasi uittam in capite.

Sane quod in serpentes mutari dicunt feminas mirandum quidem est, sed non detestandum. Vidimus enim frequenter in Anglia per lunationes homines in lupos mutari, quod hominum genus 'gerulfos' Galli nominant, Angli vero were wolf dicunt; were enim Anglice uirum sonat, wolf lupum. Creberrimum quoque apud mulieres Grecas et Ierosolimitanas extitit, ut aiunt, quod contemptores sue libidinis in asinos transformant miro incantationis genere, ita quod facie asini laborem et onus sustinent, quousque ipsarum auctricum miseratio penam releuet.[47]

We should not pass over what Bede says about the serpent which seduced Eve: that the devil chose a particular kind of serpent with a woman's face, because like approves of like, and he prompted its tongue to speak. Popular tradition on serpents has it that there are some women who turn into serpents and that they can be recognized by this means: they wear on their head a white band like a fillet.

---

[47]   Gervase of Tilbury, *Otia Imperialia: Recreation for an Emperor*, eds and trans S. E. Banks and J. W. Binns (Oxford 2002) 87 [1.15] (my translation). Book 1 relates the creation and early history of the world as a kind of commentary on Genesis. Banks and Binns note *ad loc.* that (i) Petrus Comestor's twelfth-century work on Genesis was the proper source for the remark Gervase misattributed to Bede; and (ii) that Augustine (*C. D.* 18.18) had heard of Italian landladies who turned their guests into beasts of burden. Augustine (cited in n. 10, above) next mentions Apuleius' transformation, having considered werewolves in his preceding chapter (18.17), but makes no mention of women who changed into snakes.

Figure 5b. Relief showing Adam,
Eve, and Lilith, Portail de la Vierge,
Notre Dame, Paris. Photograph by
author.

Of course, it is certainly astonishing that they say women change into serpents, but this should not be dismissed, as in England we have often seen that men change into wolves according to phases of the moon. The Gauls call men of this kind '*gerulfi*', but the English say *werewolf,* because in English '*vir*' [man] is pronounced *were,* and '*lupus*' becomes 'wolf'. It has also been very common, so they say, for women of Greece and Jerusalem to transform men who scorn their desire into asses by means of an extraordinary enchantment, so that they have to endure burdens and toil in the form of an ass, until pity from the women responsible relieves them of their punishment.

The rest of Gervase's chapter is taken up with a purportedly veridical account he heard in Aix of a local knight whose wife changed into a serpent. Such a discussion of women who turn into snakes, which incorporates legends about men being transformed into asses, would naturally bring Apuleius' *Metamorphoses* to mind—the protagonist and principal narrator became an ass and was relieved from his predicament by a goddess adorned with snakes, while a monstrous serpent intruded into the embedded narrative of *Cupid and Psyche*.[48]

---

[48]   D. Felton, 'Apuleius' Cupid considered as a Lamia (*Metamorphoses* 5.17–18)', *Illinois Classical Studies* 38 (2013) 229–44.

Gervase of Tilbury's discussion, however, has a further resonance with native Mexican testimony about Cihuacoatl—at least as it was given in Sahagún's Nahuatl text: the goddess imposed heavy burdens and toil on menfolk and was clad all in white with a womanly hairdress (fig. 6).[49] The Aztec goddess could thus be seen to conjoin the European snake women in their white headbands with the Mediterranean enchantresses who imposed heavy loads and labour on the men they had turned into asses. In the end, Sahagún's alignment of Cihuacoatl with Eve was probably disingenuous. The Franciscan missionary's real concern was with a far more threatening identification fuelled by the secular clergy and prompted by Cihuacoatl's alternative name of Tonantzin: the church of the Lady of Guadalupe in Tepeyac had been built on the site of the Aztec temple of Tonantzin, which means 'Our Mother'. 'Now', Sahagún complained, 'the Indians also call *her* "Tonantzin"'.[50]

Torquemada attributed the association of Cihuacoatl with Eve to Sahagún—perhaps because he did not subscribe to it himself. Instead, Torquemada decided to discredit the woman snake goddess with figures who were not biblical but classical: the nightmarish Allecto and the Mother goddess Isis, as she was characterized in Apuleius' *Metamorphoses*. But all the Franciscans of the sixteenth century objected to the cult of the Virgin of Guadalupe because of its connections with the veneration of Cihuacoatl-Tonantzin. This is why Torquemada *inverted* the portrayal of Isis as a benign mother in Apuleius. The friar wanted to emphasize the danger and the threat posed by these resemblances and he used Isis to highlight the dangerous ambivalence of the Guadalupan Virgin and her confusing identification with an Aztec divinity.[51]

Conclusions

Lexical echoes of Apuleius' *Metamorphoses* indicate that the Latin text was available in New Spain from as early as 1540, even before the first imports of Diego López de Cortegana's Spanish translation were recorded. A citation of the *Florida* by Fray Juan de Torquemada suggests that other works by Apuleius circulated as well.[52] The popularity of the *Metamorphoses*, or at least of *El asno de oro*, in sixteenth-century New Spain may have been due to the influential commendations of Erasmus—Thomas More's *Utopia* and his Latin versions of Lucian were also enthusiastically absorbed by missionary friars and educators.[53]

---

[49]   Sahagún, *Historia natural*, book 1, ch. 6: *Florentine Codex, Book 1: The Gods*, eds A. J. O. Anderson and C. E. Dibble (Santa Fe 1970) 11: 'Ciuacoatl (sic) [...] was an evil omen to men; she brought men misery. For it was said: she gave men the digging-stick, the tump-line; she visited men therewith. And as she appeared before men, she was covered with chalk, like a court lady. She wore ear-plugs, obsidian ear-plugs. She appeared in white, garbed in white, standing white, pure white. Her womanly hair-dress rose up'.

[50]   Sahagún, *Historia natural*, book 11, ch. 12 para. 6: *Florentine Codex*, eds A. J. O. Anderson and C. E. Dibble (Santa Fe 1982) 90.

[51]   S. Gruzinski, *The Mestizo Mind: The Intellectual Dynamics of Colonization and Globalization* (London 2002) 19–21 outlines the evident problems and contradictions inherent in the notion of 'syncretism'; *Theological and Philosophical Responses to Syncretism: Beyond the Mirage of Pure Religion*, eds P. Fridlund and M. Vähäkangas (Leiden 2018) seeks to rehabilitate the term.

[52]   Torquemada, *Monarchia indiana* (n. 41, above), book 15, chapter 30.

[53]   R. Ricard, *The Spiritual Conquest of Mexico* (Berkeley 1974) 299–300; M. Bataillon, *Érasme et l'Espagne: recherches sur l'histoire spirituelle du XVIᵉ siècle* (Genève 1998; orig. Paris 1937) 580–90; G. Bataillon, *Érasme au Mexique* (Algiers 1932); S. Zavala, *Sir Thomas More in New Spain: Utopian Adventure of the Renaissance* (London 1955); A. Laird, 'The classical foundations of Utopia in sixteenth-century Mexico: Lucian, Virgil, More, and Vasco de Quiroga's *Información en derecho* (1535)', *Comparatismes en Sorbonne* 6 (2015), 1–9 [Online: http://www. crlc.paris-sorbonne.fr/pdf_revue/revue6/1-Laird.pdf (accessed 15 January 2020)]. In Lucian's *Dream*, the narrator

Figure 6. Cihuacoatl dressed in white, *Florentine Codex* (*c.* 1577), book 1, preliminary folio, detail. World Digital Library.

Although separated by an interval of 150 years, the Latin prefatory texts of Fray Cristóbal Cabrera's letter and of Bernardo Ceinos de Riofrío's introduction to his cento were both modelled on the opening of the *Metamorphoses*. As well as the stylistic debt to Apuleius in his opening sentence, Riofrío's account of the Virgin of Guadalupe's speech to Juan Diego in the same preface calls attention to the thematic and structural correspondences between narratives of the apparitions of the Virgin of Guadalupe and the description of Isis in *Metamorphoses* book 11. Those formal correspondences bring into greater relief the essential similarities between the two divinities: each was called the 'queen of heaven'; the Virgin Mary was the Mother of God, while Isis, also associated with virginity, was the mother of the gods.[54] Moreover, Sor Juana Inés de la Cruz recognized the multiple divine identities Apuleius had accorded Isis. The Egyptian deity who had been called different names by the different races of the ancient Mediterranean was also comparable in that respect to the Virgin whose cult had originated in Tepeyac, where there had been a pre-Hispanic temple to a goddess whom the Aztecs had called Tonantzin.

Yet Apuleius' Isis had already provided Fray Juan de Torquemada with a formula for countering misleading identifications of the Virgin of Guadalupe with the Aztec mother goddess. In addition, the coherent presentation of paganism in Apuleius' *Metamorphoses*,

---

describes how as a youth he was accosted by female personifications of Sculpture and Eloquence, but the accounts of the Virgin of Guadalupe and Quilaztli have far more salient parallels to Apul. *Met.* 11.5–6.

[54] W. Drexler, 'Isis (mit Jungfrau Maria identifiziert)', *Ausführliches Lexikon der Mythologie*, ed. W. H. Roscher, 2.1 (Leipzig 1890–4) 428–32; R. E. Witt, *Isis in the Ancient World* (Baltimore 1971) 270–8; J. McGuckin. 'The early cult of Mary and inter-religious contexts in the fifth-century church', in *The Origins of the Cult of the Virgin Mary*, ed. C. Maunder (London 2008) 23–40 are among the many treatments.

popularized in Spanish translation, may well have offered other missionary friars a ready and engaging (if unofficial) resource for making sense of the alien polytheism they encountered in New Spain. After all, Sahagún had openly drawn from Virgil's *Aeneid* as well as from Augustine's *City of God* in his analysis of Mexican belief—and accounts of Greco-Roman religion in Renaissance encyclopaedias and *speculum* literature were used in a similar way.[55]

The particular example of Gervase of Tilbury's testimony considered in this chapter also serves as a salutary reminder that boundaries between some classical texts and popular tradition (or 'folklore') in ancient and early modern Europe alike were never as firm as is often supposed. On that basis, the passage of Apuleius' *Cupid and Psyche* into Nahuatl oral narrative in sixteenth-century New Spain should be no more surprising than the transmission of Augustine's insights on metamorphosis to indigenous Mexican audiences by Fray Andrés de Olmos.

Brown University

---

[55] Laird, 'Aztec and Roman gods' (n. 27, above) 152–7.

THE ASS GOES EAST:
APULEIUS AND ORIENTALISM

CAROLE BOIDIN

Artistic and intellectual 'afterlives' often rely on powerful and long-lasting comparisons. Most of the earliest commentaries on *The Golden Ass* that have come down to us (that by Macrobius for example) draw parallels between Apuleius' stories and Plato's fictions, working on the assumption that Apuleius was a Platonist. This comparison played a crucial role in ulterior interpretations and artistic receptions of the text.[1] Readings in terms of other strong paradigms, such as conversion narratives or picaresque novels, have also had long-lasting effects. In this chapter, I will consider a few instances of another comparison that is frequently drawn when framing the reception of *The Golden Ass*. My purpose in doing so is to ask why commentators have so frequently compared this book with famous collections of oriental tales.

The invention of the oriental tale and the genealogy of fiction

Nearly forty years ago, Edward W. Said identified the tendency, common to classical scholarship, to consider Eastern traditions from a Greco-Roman perspective. According to his views on 'Orientalism', the very concept of the Orient was an early modern occidental construction, based on a kind of inverted mirror of occidental values.[2] While Said's model is limited in certain ways, we cannot overlook its validity concerning the way in which this attitude permeated European representations of the collection of beliefs, practices, and artistic works dubbed as oriental. On the other hand, a reverse cultural process also created unexpected associations between many familiar classical texts and the Orient. Through such associations, new aesthetic and intellectual values were defined, and a range of cultural traditions of very different natures (be they ancient or modern, local or extraneous) were consequently labelled as 'oriental' by scientific and artistic discourse, allowing for critical distance and new considerations, as well as for fantastic projections.

The 'oriental tale' was thus invented by European literate circles, as an archetypal literary genre that was believed to have its origins in Antiquity, in an attempt to trace the history of modern fiction and to give it some cultural legitimacy. As the progressive autonomy of literary fiction elicited a collective reflection on the morality of storytelling and the limits of invention, the reconstructed entity that was the 'oriental tale' provided a distant model against which it was possible to delineate what modern fiction should be.

---

[1]   On this subject, see for example S. J. Harrison, 'Constructing Apuleius: the emergence of a literary artist', *Ancient Narrative* 2 (2002) 143–171; R. H. F. Carver, *The Protean Ass: The 'Metamorphoses' of Apuleius from Antiquity to the Renaissance* (Oxford-New York 2007); J. H. Gaisser, *The Fortunes of Apuleius and the 'Golden Ass'. A Study in Transmission and Reception* (Princeton-Oxford 2008).

[2]   E. W. Said, *Orientalism* (New York 1978). Although the terms 'orientalism' and 'orientalist' only appear towards the end of the eighteenth century, Said invokes pre-modern precedents for European interests directed towards Eastern cultures.

In 1669, Pierre-Daniel Huet thus defined the modern (European) novel or 'romance' by reference to a historical or genealogical narrative. He described modern romances as elaborate and moral versions of 'fables' that had originally come from the Orient, considered as the well-known source of all wisdom and fantasy. He particularly stressed the distance between the modern novel and ancient oriental tales that conveyed the mystical secrets of the Egyptians, the 'unnatural metaphors' of the Arabians, the Persian 'art of falsifying agreeably', and so on regarding Indian, Syrian, or Hebrew forms of fiction.[3] These 'fables' were first transmitted to the Greeks, who invented the very genre of romance, then to the Romans, and then onwards to their medieval successors.

The Golden Ass holds a special position in this historical account. Huet suggests that Apuleius found inspiration in a specific vein of oriental writing known as the *sermo Milesius*. He argues that certain ancient oriental traditions were transformed by writers from Miletus (in Asia Minor—the oriental Greece), giving birth to a lesser form of fiction that remained peripheral to, but a historically constitutive element of, the European canon. The writers from Miletus knew of oriental traditions but they translated them in corrupted, lascivious taste:

> Il y a assez d'apparence que les romans avaient été innocents jusqu'alors, que la galanterie y était traitée modestement et rarement, que les Milésiens les corrompirent les premiers et les remplirent de narrations lascives et déshonnêtes.[4]

It is quite probable that romances had been innocent until then and included only limited and scarce gallantries. But the Milesians were the first to corrupt them and fill them with lascivious and dishonest narrations.

Apuleius' book thus, according to Huet, inherited its dubious morality from this doubly oriental ancestry:

> Il nous a donné une idée des fables milésiennes par cette pièce, qu'il déclare d'abord être de ce genre. Il l'a enrichie de beaux épisodes, et entre autres celui de Psyché, que personne n'ignore, et il n'a point retranché les saletés qui étaient dans les originaux qu'il a suivis.[5]

He has given us an idea of the Milesian fables in this piece of work, which he declares in the very first words to be of this genre. He has enriched it with beautiful episodes, and among others that of Psyche, of which nobody is ignorant; and he hasn't removed the filth that was in the original texts he followed.

In addition to these Milesian roots, Huet also mentions Apuleius' own African origins, which are supposed to confer an oriental sensibility of another kind to his stories: 'Son style est d'un sophiste, plein d'affectation et de figures violentes, dur, barbare, digne d'un Africain' ('His style is that of a sophist, full of affectation and violent figures, hard, barbarous, most befitting an African').[6] *The Golden Ass* was therefore perceived as being an oriental tale *squared*, due to its Asian origins and its African author. The old debate about Apuleius'

---

[3] P.-D. Huet, *Lettre-traité sur l'origine des romans* (first published as a preface to *Zayde, histoire espagnole*, attributed to Segrais, Paris 1670). I quote F. Gégou's edition (Paris 1971). All translations from French or Latin are my own.

[4] Huet, *Lettre-traité* (n. 3, above) 70.

[5] Huet, *Lettre-traité* (n. 3, above) 109.

[6] Huet, *Lettre-traité* (n. 3, above) 109.

African style was not the only issue underlying this assessment:[7] Apuleius' work provided a singular piece of evidence, a surprising oriental milestone, for Huet's historical apology of the novel. *The Golden Ass* belonged to an internal Orient which was imagined to be the birthplace of fiction, constructed within the classical tradition for both strategic and rhetorical reasons. Despite its obscenity and its ambiguity towards magic, *The Golden Ass* thus became part of the common patrimony: it was published in the collection *Ad usum Delphini* in 1688 and was constantly referred to by such authors as Sorel, La Fontaine, and Perrault, albeit at a sufficient distance from its origins to allow for the affirmation of the modern romance and its morality. This 'orientalization' thus became a way of addressing the peculiar status of *The Golden Ass*, a status that was relatively new in the history of its reception.

A fashionable oriental tale

This rhetorical construction gave way to a more complex process in the following decades, in the context of the growing knowledge and popularity in Europe of narratives with a real Eastern origin. The first European translation of the *Arabian Nights* in 1704, by Antoine Galland, a regular correspondent of Huet's, was also introduced as another piece of documentation in this genealogy of fiction.[8] The foreword claimed that European readers could finally have direct access to what Galland presented as a genuinely oriental tradition of fairy-tales and romances.[9] The particular treatment of verisimilitude and morality in these tales had a fascinating effect on literary production, creating a European vogue for 'oriental tales' in the eighteenth century. A whole series of forged 'translations' from Arabic, Turkish, and Persian were published alongside authentic ones, based on the common formal basis of a sensational use of imagination, relaxed morality, and exoticism. This proved to be an excellent pattern for philosophical fictions. Not only were oriental tales postulated as ancient paradigms for the novel but they were now accessible to non-specialists and, at the same time, constituted a living, modern literary genre.[10] This new European genre of the oriental tale can, in retrospect, be seen to have contaminated other narrative genres and, indeed, the whole Western patrimony. For example, the *Heptameron* of Marguerite de Navarre was republished in 1740 under the title of *Les Mille et une faveurs*.

The 'orientalization' of *The Golden Ass* thus acquired a new and enduring dimension. Eastern connotations were eagerly looked for in the text and were sometimes heavily underlined by translators, in both texts and peritexts. For example, in 1707 the Abbot Compain de Saint-Martin deliberately translated the famous mention of 'modo si papyrum Aegyptiam argutia Nilotici calami inscriptam non spreveris inspicere' (*Met.* 1.1) as an allusion to this oriental style of the text, omitting the reference to the material writing *realia*: the Ego promises the reader a delightful experience 'provided you don't despise reading a

---

[7]   On this debate, see, for example, the article by C. Marsico in this volume.

[8]   In 1702 he explicitly compared these tales to the works of Apuleius and Lucian in a letter to G. Cuper: 'Ces contes sont de la nature de l'Âne d'Apulée, et de l'Histoire véritable de Lucien', in *Correspondance d'Antoine Galland*, ed. M. Abdel-Halim (Paris 1964) 436.

[9]   'Si les Contes de cette espèce sont agréables et divertissants par le merveilleux qui y règne d'ordinaire, ceux-ci doivent l'emporter en cela sur tous ceux qui ont paru, puisqu'ils sont remplis d'événements qui surprennent et attachent l'esprit, et qui font voir de combien les Arabes surpassent les autres nations en cette sorte de composition'. *Les Mille et une nuits, Contes arabes*, trans. A. Galland, eds A. Chraïbi and J.-P. Sermain, 3 vols (Paris 2004, based on the *princeps* edn Paris 1704–1717) I 21.

[10]   For further detail concerning this literary vogue, see J.-F. Perrin, *L'Orientale allégorie. Le conte oriental au XVIIIᵉ siècle en France (1704–1774)* (Paris 2015).

book written in the merry and facetious style of Egyptian authors'.[11] Footnotes also draw parallels between a number of details in Apuleius' text and contemporary oriental customs: the religious mortifications performed by the priests of Cybele and Attis in *Met.* 8.27 or the purifying 'lavacrum' of Lucius in *Met.* 11.1 are likened to Islamic rites in Turkey and India.[12]

This form of naturalization of a text allegedly imbued with some sort of oriental sensibility—and not devoid of esoteric connotations—also accounted for its later integration within a collection of 'Imaginary travels, dreams, visions, and cabalistic novels' in 1788.[13] This development accorded with the peculiar status that Egyptian antiquity had progressively acquired in the imagination of eighteenth-century artists and intellectuals. In a quite fascinating way, the oriental flavour of the text could be taken as accounting for both its lack of explicit morality and its spiritual significance, obscure as that may have appeared.

Oriental Psyches

Several literary allusions to the story of Psyche in the eighteenth century also integrate these oriental connotations. In the *Ricciardetto* by Niccoló Forteguerri (1738), an imitation of Ariosto, we meet Psyche as a well-meaning fairy, desperately looking for her husband Cupid, who has fallen in love with a fifteen-year-old Arabic girl in Rome, and whose fatal attraction holds him prisoner. In a closer and more elaborate relationship with the Apuleian Psyche story, the French 'historiette' *La Nouvelle Psyché* (1711) introduces its main character using an oriental set of criteria, in spite of her blond hair:

> Psyché (c'était son nom) avait la taille noble et dégagée, ni petite ni grande, les yeux bleus aussi brillants, aussi pleins de feu que s'ils eussent été petits et noirs ; le regard tendre et modeste tout ensemble, le nez un peu retroussé, une bouche petite et riante, qui en s'ouvrant laissait voir deux rangs de perles orientales [...][14]

> Psyche (such was her name) had a noble and supple waist, was neither short nor tall, with blue eyes as bright, as full of fire, as if they had been small and black; with a gaze both tender and modest, a slightly turned-up nose, a small cheerful mouth, showing two rows of oriental pearls [...]

Psyche passes the time in mundane pleasures and is courted by three princes: the first comes from Happy Arabia, the second from the Distant Islands, and the last from Monomotapa, with an escort of elephants and giants. All three princes die of desperation upon Cupid's arrival.

We can thus see that *The Golden Ass* was read as an analogue of collections of oriental tales, *i.e.* as a free form of fiction, apt to convey different kinds of messages,[15] and as an open and inexhaustible source of narrative motifs from which could be created new fictions. Interestingly, this kind of retroactive contamination of *The Golden Ass* by an Eastern infection reached an unexpected literary climax (albeit confidential and

---

[11] '[P]ourvu que vous ne dédaigniez pas de lire un ouvrage écrit dans le style enjoué des auteurs égyptiens', *Les Métamorphoses, ou l'Âne d'or d'Apulée philosophe platonicien, avec le Démon de Socrate*, 2 vols (Paris 1707) I 1.

[12] *Les Métamorphoses*, trans. Compain de Saint Martin (n. 8, above) II 135, 179. Such comparisons with Eastern customs can still be found in the footnotes to twentieth-century translations.

[13] *Voyages imaginaires, songes, visions et romans cabalistiques*, ed. C. G. T. Garnier, 39 vols (Amsterdam 1787–89). The *Met.* is the 33rd vol.

[14] *La Nouvelle Psyché, par Mme* *** (Paris 1711) 2.

[15] The freemasonic use of this narrative provides an interesting case that I cannot discuss in the present chapter.

unique) in an anonymous 1802 book entitled *L'Âne au bouquet de roses, renouvelé de l'Âne d'Apulée* ('The Ass with a bunch of roses, renewed from Apuleius' *Ass*').[16] In this adaptation of *The Golden Ass*, the story of Psyche undergoes an explicit process of orientalization through specific uses of narrative devices. First of all, the narrative frame of the story is a conversation between Apuleius and his friends about metamorphosis and metempsychosis, which brings him to tell the story of his own adventures. This invention provides a discursive actualization of the dialogical beginning of *The Golden Ass* ('At ego tibi […]') and renews the opinion, common since Augustine's time, that Apuleius describes his personal metamorphosis in this book. Later on, we follow his adventures until the expected point at which he encounters a young maiden and an old woman who tries to comfort her by telling her a fabulous story, with the latter having to try surprisingly hard to find the right tale to tell. First, she starts narrating the mythological challenge of Paris and his attempt to find the most beautiful woman in the world, but the young maiden soon interrupts her, protesting that she has already heard that story. The servant then announces a more astonishing tale, in which she emphasizes the presence of three human sisters instead of three goddesses, thus affording greater pleasure. This proves to be an interesting, although seemingly arbitrary, commentary on the original story of Psyche. Yet again, the maiden starts yawning and interrupts the old woman:

> - Si je ne me trompe, répondit la jeune demoiselle, c'est [l'histoire] de Psyché et de Cupidon. Comment ne la connaîtrais-je pas ? Elle a été écrite de nos jours par un auteur célèbre qui l'a embellie des agréments de son style et des charmes de son heureuse imagination.
>
> - […] Eh bien, voici une histoire que je vous défie bien de savoir, car c'est la mienne, et personne, que je sache, ne l'a encore écrite. […]
>
> Quand on veut peindre une personne accomplie, vous savez que l'on ne manque pas de vanter l'élégance de sa taille, les roses de son teint, l'albâtre de sa gorge, le corail de ses lèvres, l'ivoire de ses dents, les ondulations de ses cheveux flottants. Eh bien, pour tout réunir, en un mot, on m'avait donné le nom d'Azola-Mirza, qui en indien veut dire toutes ces choses-là.[17]

> - If I'm not mistaken, the young maiden answered, it's [the story] of Psyche and Cupid. How could I not know it? It was recently written by a famous author who has embellished it with the ornamentation of his style and of his felicitous imagination.
>
> - […] Well, here's a story that I really defy you to know, since it is my own and no one, to my knowledge, has yet written it. […]
>
> When one wishes to portray an accomplished person, as you know, they certainly will praise her elegant waist, rosy complexion, alabaster breast, coral lips, ivory teeth, and wavy curls. Well, to sum it all up in a word, I was named Azola-Mirza, which in the Indian language means all of those things.

---

[16]   In a footnote to the preface of an 1802 printed and illustrated version of *Fable de Psyché*, we read that 'une sorte de mutilation en deux volumes in-18 sous le titre de *L'Âne au bouquet de roses*' was published, probably drawing from Compain de Saint-Martin's translation in *La Fable de Psyché, figures de Raphaël* (Paris 1802) 16. However, the adaptation I quote below is quite different from Compain's translation.

[17]   Anon., *L'Âne au bouquet de roses, renouvelé de l'Âne d'or d'Apulée*, 2 vols (Paris 1802) I 117–18, 120–21.

The complex transformation of the passage announcing the expected story of Cupid and Psyche arouses multiple effects in the readers. The 'famous author' may refer to Apuleius, who explicitly figures as the main character and narrator in the novel but has not yet written the tale of Psyche at this point in the story. This first reading, paradoxically enough, is certainly influenced by the knowledge of the original framing that is to be found in the Latin text, together with the comic regrets of the ass who is unable to transcribe the *fabella* for lack of a tablet (*Met.* 6.25). For the readers of the time, it may also have alluded to La Fontaine, or to a more recent translator or adaptor. However, the most important point is the way in which these words underline the radical change at stake here: the central story of Psyche is overtaken by a first-person narrative of the old woman's story, and this story happens to be an oriental tale. Furthermore, the need for a more amazing story, and the use of the first-person narrative, might also consciously echo the celebrated narrative patterns of the *Arabian Nights*. The whole design thus belongs to the typical, oriental-like, construction of the modern novel: the oriental tale turns out to be a romanesque and playful one, full of twists and turns, situated in an antique Indian setting and narrated by an antique Roman philosopher, who later confesses that the whole adventure actually occurred in a dream he had one amorous night, lying next to his beloved Photis. Literature here expresses a unified vision of the Orient as the birthplace of all fictions, and such representations framed the reception of Apuleian stories through both texts and illustrations.[18]

The orientalization of *The Golden Ass* was also progressively supported by science. Several folklore specialists devoted the same attention to *The Golden Ass* as they did to oriental narrative traditions, hunting for evidence of circulation and influence, mostly in order to prove the existence of an Indo-European connection. Psyche was thus attributed an Indian origin by such scholars,[19] although this method was satirized from an early stage.[20]

In all these examples, the discussion about the oriental identity of Apuleius and his masterpiece offered a way by which to establish paradigms for modern fictions, as already noted. However, such a conception is also quite reversible: the oriental tale proved to be a generic category functioning, more or less, as a modern way of designating a genre of literary discourse missing in Aristotle's categorization. It had a pragmatically analogous function to that of the 'Milesian tales' in early modern times.[21]

---

[18]   One might easily compare, for instance, the figure of Psyche in illustrations by Edmond Dulac, *e.g.* in *The Marriage of Cupid and Psyche* (New York 1951), with his representation of certain female protagonists from the *Arabian Nights*, inspired by Persian miniatures, *e.g.* in *La Princesse Badourah : Conte des Mille et une nuits* (Paris 1914).

[19]   Emmanuel Cosquin traces the oriental origins of the story in 'Contes populaires lorrains recueillis dans un village du Barrois – suite', *Romania* 10.37 (1881) 117–193. He claims that the monstrous husband is a snake in what he calls the 'forme primitive' of the tale: 'cette forme primitive est tout indienne' ('this primitive form is entirely Indian', 130).

[20]   See, for example, French writer Charles Nodier's claims that 'Les Indiens n'ont pas tout imaginé, quoi qu'en puisse dire l'Académie des Inscriptions et Belles Lettres à qui ces théories crues fourniront longtemps encore de savantes élucubrations, mais qui ne parviendra pas aisément à prouver que l'esprit d'invention ait été réservé, par une faveur exceptionnelle, à une seule branche de la famille humaine' ('the Indians did not imagine everything, despite the opinion of the Academy of Inscriptions and Belles Lettres, whose learned ramblings those raw theories will continue to stoke for a long time, but shall not easily prove that inventiveness would have been granted to one branch of the human family only, because of some exceptional favour'), *Description raisonnée d'une jolie collection de livres* (Paris 1844) 308.

[21]   A catalogue of the oriental manuscripts in the Bodleian Library seems to indicate that a fragment of a story from the *Arabian Nights* is registered under the title *Fragmentum Fabulae Milesiae* (*Bibliothecae Bodleianae codicum manuscriptorum orientalium (...) catalogus*, eds J. Uri and C. Nicoll, 2 parts in 3 vols (Oxford 1787–1835) part 2 II

Orientalism and the ideological exploitation of an 'alien'

This process had gained a new momentum by the middle of the nineteenth century, in the wake of the Romantic quest for exotic literary sensibilities and the Symbolists' fascination with Apuleius. A series of new European translations were published, which both explained and were shaped by this renewed interest of a slightly different kind. The old debate about Apuleius' African style continued, but now with a new phrasing, as we find in the prefaces of two English translations. In 1893, Charles Whibley introduced a new edition of William Adlington's 1566 translation as follows:

> It is among the marvels of history that an alien of twenty-five—and Apuleius was no more when he wrote his Metamorphoses—should have revolutionised a language not his own, and bequeathed us a freedom, which, a thousand times abused, has never since been taken away.[22]

This designation of Apuleius as an 'alien' was not new *per se*. In the same vein as many other commentators, Whibley took the initial portrayal of the ego-narrator in *Met.* 1.1 as a definite truth about Apuleius: 'A barbarian born, a Greek by education, Apuleius only acquired the Latin tongue by painful effort'.[23] But this traditional way of accounting for Apuleius' style is here renewed by the dedication of 'this metamorphosis of an Ancient Decadent' to the French poet Mallarmé. It is the French-speaking 'alien poets' who are in the observer's mind:

> Were he alive today Paris would have been his field, and he the undisputed master of Decadence and Symbolism. The comparison is close at all points. Would he have not delighted in the Black Mass, as celebrated on the heights of Mont Parnasse? Like too many among the makers of modern French literature he was an alien writing an alien tongue.[24]

This declaration received a most virulent reply a few years later, in Francis D. Byrne's introduction to his new translation (1905):

> This seems to me a hastily written sentence; and I am prepared to maintain that it contains four mistakes in as many lines. Apuleius was not an alien: he wrote his Metamorphoses, since called 'The Golden Ass', at an advanced age: he did not revolutionise the Latin language, but exhibited it at the stage in which he found it: lastly, Latin was his native tongue, as much as English is Mr. Rudyard Kipling's.[25]

The allusion here to Kipling is rather interesting, as Apuleius seems to have become at the time a precocious master of the new literary genre of Orientalism, illustrated by Kipling's novels about the Empire. In reply to Whibley's depiction of Apuleius' education, Byrne writes:

> It would be just as accurate to write of Mr Kipling 'A Hindoo by birth, a cosmopolitan by education, Kipling only acquired the English language under the birch'.[26]

---

153. I owe this reference to Ibrahim Akkel; I have not yet been able to consult this manuscript.

[22] *The Golden Ass of Apuleius*, translated out of Latin by W. Adlington, anno 1566, With an Introduction by Ch. Whibley (London 1893) xviii.

[23] *The Golden Ass of Apuleius* (n. 22, above) xvi.

[24] *The Golden Ass of Apuleius* (n. 22, above) xvii.

[25] *The Golden Ass of Apuleius*, Newly translated with Introduction and Notes by F. D. Byrne (London 1905) xiv.

[26] *The Golden Ass of Apuleius* (n. 25, above) xvi.

The orientalization of Apuleius had thus reached, by the end of the nineteenth century, a literary and scientific climax, with the ancient author becoming an involuntary witness to ideological considerations about civilization hierarchies. On the one hand, a colonial propagandist such as Louis Bertrand could later rise against this notion of an oriental Apuleius and claim a reappropriation of *The Golden Ass* as proof of the Latin identity of Northern Africa, discarding its Arabic and Islamic past. Apuleius was, thus, used as a tool to 'de-orientalize' the Orient and to promote the reintegration of North Africa into Western (and Christian) civilization. Louis Bertrand tried to invent a new tradition (to paraphrase Hobsbawm's formula): the 'Afrique latine' novel.[27]

On the other hand, *The Golden Ass* was also to be used as a postcolonial 'counter-text' in answer to colonialist ideology in North Africa, through a process of indigenization, both in French, Arabic, and Amazight texts, creating a new sort of 're-orientalization'.[28] But this is quite another story.

Concluding remarks

This oriental dimension in the European reception of *The Golden Ass* proves interesting with regard to what it tells us about cultural identity and literary characterization within the European canon. Rather unexpectedly, we might even suggest that the enigma of the *Madaurensis* character speaking in *Met.* XI (thus originating from Africa) could be the textual reason why so many readers and artists have felt free to fantasize about the oriental dimensions of the text. Many of the texts I have mentioned here could, thus, be considered as imaginary extensions that take their starting point from this vexed passage. They all testify to an acute consciousness of the seminal value of this text in modern literary tradition, in spite of its moral ambiguities.

I would like to insist on the fact that such 'afterlife' phenomena should ultimately bring us back to the source texts and help us read them in a new, retrospective light. I only wish to suggest that, in considering the ways in which European modernity elected the Orient as a fantastic and constructed origin for the pleasures of pure fiction, we may find a pragmatic equivalent of this imaginary origin in the way Apuleius uses a purely literary and fantastic Greek setting for his delectable story. The statement that the whole story is a *fabula graecanica* should not only be tackled from a *Quellenforschung* perspective that would study how Apuleius re-wrote an originally Greek model.[29] A more anthropological investigation allows us to focus on the cultural and literary connotations of this Greek affiliation, to consider why Apuleius needed to promote his work as a story 'à la grecque'.

Université Paris Nanterre

---

[27] See, for example, his *Nuits d'Alger* (Paris 1929). I suggest an intertextual reading of this novel as a peculiar rewriting of *The Golden Ass* in 'La "voie du retour" ? Le modèle de *l'Âne d'or* dans le parcours du mythe de l'Algérie latine chez Louis Bertrand', *Recherches & Travaux* 81 (2012) 17–40. I freely refer here to Hobsbawm's concept of the invention of traditional cultural practices, defined in *The Invention of Tradition*, eds E. Hobsbawm and T. Ranger (Cambridge 1983).

[28] I can only allude here to a scientific work in progress. Some useful references can be found in V. Gély's 'Latinité, hybridité culturelle et migritude : L'Afrique du Nord et Apulée (Ahmed Hamdi, Assia Djebar et Kebir M. Ammi)', *Silène* (2011) [http://www.revue-silene.com/f/index.php?sp=comm&comm_id=86 (accessed 7 April 2017)].

[29] For this type of investigation, see *e.g.* H. J. Mason, '*Fabula Graecanica*: Apuleius and his Greek sources', in *Aspects of Apuleius' 'Golden Ass'*, eds B. L. Hijmans and R. T. van der Paardt (Groningen 1978) 1–15.

HOW TO TELL THE STORY
OF CUPID AND PSYCHE: FROM FULGENTIUS
TO GALEOTTO DEL CORRETTO

JULIA HAIG GAISSER

A story changes with each retelling. Details of the plot may be altered or added or omitted altogether. The narrator may be an omniscient third person or one of the characters. The story may be free-standing or imbedded in another narrative; it may appear in different genres; and its action may begin or end at different points. It is inevitably coloured by the perspective and purposes of the narrator and audience, whether these are internal to the narrative or external or both. Sometimes, factors like these affect the story only in subtle ways. Sometimes, however, they make it a different story. In what follows I will explore the ways in which this universal truth about storytelling is manifested in the reception of Apuleius' tale of Cupid and Psyche, from its earliest retelling by Fulgentius the Mythographer around 550, through that of Giovanni Boccaccio some 800 years later, to its flowering in the courts of Ferrara and Mantua in the period around 1470–1500. These retellings use and revise not only Apuleius but also each other, for the reception of an ancient author is like a snowball rolling down a hill, constantly picking up (and shedding) elements of earlier readings as it goes.

Fulgentius and Boccaccio are both allegorists.[1] Each follows the same procedure, first telling Psyche's story and then allegorizing it; both allegories are religious and explicitly identify Psyche as Soul.[2] I will touch on their allegories as needed, but my principal interest is in the stories themselves. The stories are essentially different both from each other and from the one told by Apuleius.

Fulgentius tells the story of Cupid and Psyche in *Mitologiae* 3.6 (*Fabula deae Psicae et Cupidinis*).[3] His narrative is characterized by significant omissions. He leaves out every detail connected with Psyche's redemption and final happiness: her pregnancy and the birth of Voluptas, her rescue by Cupid from Stygian sleep, her award of immortality, and her joyous marriage in heaven.[4] He also omits any reference to Fortune, so important in Apuleius,

---

[1] For Fulgentius (*fl.* 550), see B. G. Hays, *Fulgentius the Mythographer* (Ann Arbor, MI: University Microfilms 1996). For Boccaccio (1313–1375), see V. Branca, *Giovanni Boccaccio: Profilo biografico* (Florence 1977).

[2] In Fulgentius, Psyche is Anima (Soul), her sisters Caro (Flesh) and Ultronietas (Free Will). Boccaccio's discussion exists in two versions: the autograph and the vulgate (see below). In the autograph, Psyche is the rational soul, her sisters the vegetative and sensitive souls; in the vulgate, the three sisters are not three souls but three faculties ('potentie') of the soul.

[3] Fulgentius, *Mitologiae* in *Opera*, ed. R. Helm (Leipzig 1898). For Fulgentius' narrative, see J. H. Gaisser, *The Fortunes of Apuleius and the 'Golden Ass': A Study in Transmission and Reception* (Princeton-Oxford 2008) 53–59. For Fulgentius as an allegorist and a text and translation of *Mit.* 3.6, see R. H. F. Carver, *The Protean Ass. The 'Metamorphoses' of Apuleius from Antiquity to the Renaissance* (Oxford 2007) 41–47.

[4] The only reference to Psyche's immortality appears in the title, which is quite possibly a later addition; see Hays, *Fulgentius* (n. 1, above) 173. It is not even hinted at in the narrative or the allegory. Cupid marries Psyche, but not joyously: 'Postea Iove petente in coniugio accepit' (*Mit.* 3.6.116).

and, in a series of editorializing intrusions in the narrative, he makes it clear that the fault is entirely Psyche's. She is thrice guilty. She is guilty of disobedience: 'her affection for her blood kin overshadowed her husband's command'.[5] She is guilty of curiosity and credulity: 'she seized curiosity, stepmother of her safety, and she seized easy credulity, which is always the mother of deception'.[6] Worst of all, she is guilty of carnal lust: raising the fatal lamp, she recognizes *Cupido*—surely both the god and the force of erotic desire—and 'is on fire with the licentious passion of love'.[7] Cupid deserts her, and she is an exile, driven from her home.[8] All this, it should be noted, is in the narrative—not in the allegory. In the allegory, Fulgentius likens her to Adam, who, 'although he sees, does not see that he is naked until he eats of the tree of concupiscence'.[9] He evokes Adam again at the end of the allegory, saying that Psyche—'as if made naked by desire'—loses everything and is driven from her palace.[10]

Boccaccio knew Fulgentius but revised his account, perhaps polemically.[11] He tells the story in *Genealogia Deorum Gentilium* 5.22, in a chapter entitled *De Psyce XV^a Apollinis filia*.[12] This is his first change in the story. In Apuleius, Psyche's parents are the unnamed king and queen of fairytale, allegorized by Fulgentius as god and matter. But Boccaccio follows Martianus Capella, who made them Apollo and Endelichia.[13] This detail is important, for in the allegory Boccaccio explains that Psyche's father Apollo, the sun, is God, 'the true light of the world'; her husband is 'divine stock, that is, honourable love, or God himself'.[14] She is forbidden to see him because he is to be known by faith alone.

Two versions of the *Genealogia* have come down to us: the autograph and the vulgate which supersedes it.[15] They tell subtly but significantly different stories. In the autograph, Boccaccio's narrative follows Apuleius very closely, except for the detail of Psyche's parentage, but there are some important changes in the vulgate. There, like Fulgentius, Boccaccio omits Psyche's pregnancy, her wedding in heaven, and her gift of immortality,

[5]   'consanguineae caritatis invincibilis ardor maritale obumbravit imperium' (*Mit.* 3.6.115). All translations in this chapter are my own.

[6]   'curiositatem, suae salutis novercam, arripuit et facillimam credulitatem, quae semper deceptionum mater est [...] arripit' (*Mit.* 3.6.115).

[7]   'inmodesto amoris torretur affectu' (*Mit.* 3.6.115).

[8]   'Cupido [...] domo extorrem ac profugam derelinquit' (*Mit.* 3.6.115).

[9]   'Adam quamvis videat nudum se non videt, donec de concupiscentiae arbore comedat' (*Mit.* 3.6.118).

[10]   'quasi cupiditate nudata' (*Mit.* 3.6.118).

[11]   Gaisser, *Fortunes of Apuleius* (n. 3, above) 112–13; B. L. Hijmans Jr., 'Boccaccio's *Amor and Psyche*', in *Symposium apuleianum groninganum*, eds B. L. Hijmans and V. Schmidt (Groningen 1981) 30–45.

[12]   For Boccaccio's narrative, see Gaisser, *Fortunes of Apuleius* (n. 3, above) 110–18. Carver, *Protean Ass* (n. 3, above) 133–41, presents a text and translation of the vulgate version and a discussion of Boccaccio on fiction.

[13]   Mart. Cap. 1.7. But Boccaccio read the name as Entelochia, which he glosses in his allegory as 'perfecta aetas'. He would have seen Entelochia in his manuscript, for in texts from the tenth century onwards it wrongly replaced Endelechia. See Gaisser, *Fortunes of Apuleius* (n. 3, above) 53, with earlier bibliography.

[14]   'Hec autem Apollinis, id est solis, filia dicitur, eius scilicet qui mundi vera lux est Deus, cum nullius alterius potentie sit rationalem creare animam, nisi Dei' (*Gen.* 5.22.12); 'divine stirpi [...], id est amori honesto, seu ipsi Deo' (*Gen.* 5.22.13).

[15]   G. Martellotti, 'Le due redazioni delle *Genealogie* del Boccaccio', in *Dante e Boccaccio e altri scrittori dall'umanesimo al romanticismo* (Florence 1983) 137–63; P. G. Ricci, 'Contributi per un'edizione critica della "Genealogia deorum gentilium"', in *Studi sulla vita e le opere del Boccaccio* (Milan 1985) 189–225. The autograph is printed in the edition of Vincenzo Romano, *Genealogie deorum gentilium*, 2 vols (Bari 1951), the vulgate in that of V. Zaccaria, *Genealogie deorum gentilium*, vols 7–8 in *Tutte le opere di Giovanni Boccaccio*, ed. V. Branca, 12 vols (Milan 1998).

but, unlike Fulgentius, he gives her a happy ending. Here it is:

> She performed Venus' tasks with the aid of her husband, and because of his prayers
> to Jupiter she came into favour with Venus, and when she had been taken into heaven
> she enjoyed a perpetual union with Cupid to whom she bore Pleasure ('Voluptas').[16]

This story, unlike that in the autograph (and in Apuleius), is abstract and metaphysical. Psyche
is taken up ('assumpta') into heaven but not brought there by Mercury. There is no wedding
celebration and no gift of immortality. Since the preceding narrative omitted her pregnancy,
it seems that Voluptas, born of her divine union and more abstraction than child, was not only
born in heaven but conceived there. In the vulgate, then, Boccaccio changed his story. But he
did not change his allegory. In both versions it ends in the same way:

> When she is purged through toil and suffering of her haughty presumption and
> disobedience, she regains the good of divine love and contemplation and is joined to
> it forever, until having put away transitory things, she is carried to everlasting glory
> and there gives birth to Pleasure, or eternal joy and delight, the child of Love.[17]

Fulgentius and Boccaccio have both told new stories (Boccaccio has told two). Fulgentius'
is a story of Psyche's Fall, Boccaccio's of her redemption. Each has written a story to fit
his allegory—not the other way around, as we might imagine. But the process is clearer in
Boccaccio, since one can almost watch him changing the end of his narrative to make a closer
fit for the allegory.

The fortunes of Boccaccio's work remind us that words are not the only way to tell a
story. In Florence, his telling (with a significant change) was painted on 'cassoni', or wedding
chests. The earliest example, a pair of 'cassoni' dated c. 1470–75, was painted by the Master
of the Argonauts for a Medici wedding.[18] The story is told in a series of scenes on the frontals
of the chests.[19] The first frontal takes us from Psyche's conception to the catastrophe of
the lamp, the second from Cupid lecturing Psyche from his cypress tree to their glorious
wedding. The first and last scenes identify the story as Boccaccio's. In the scene of Psyche's
conception, the golden ball in the marriage chamber represents her father Apollo, the sun,
'the light of the world'. The last scene shows the action in two registers. In the upper register,
a kneeling Cupid pleads with Jupiter for Psyche's hand as Venus looks on. There is no sign
of the messenger Mercury or Psyche or the cup of immortality. Here, as in the opening scene,
we are seeing Boccaccio's story. But in the lower register the artist writes a different ending,
with a fine picture of the wedding omitted by Boccaccio. Naturally: he is painting a wedding
chest. And like all good storytellers, he suits his telling to the occasion and the audience.
But he has not forgotten Boccaccio's allegory. Boccaccio had allegorized Psyche's marriage

---

[16]   'Opera viri adiuta perfecit iniuncta; cuius postremo ad Iovem precibus actum est ut in Veneris deveniret gratiam
et in celis assumpta, Cupidinis perpetuo frueretur coniugio, cui peperit Voluptatem' (*Gen.* 5.22.10, ed. Zaccaria).

[17]   'Et erumnis et miseriis purgata presumptuosa superbia atque inobedientia, bonum divine dilectionis atque
contemplationis iterum reassumit, eique se iungit perpetuo, dum perituris dimissis rebus in eternam defertur gloriam,
et ibi ex amore parturit Voluptatem, id est delectationem et letitiam sempiternam' (*Gen.* 5.22.17, ed. Romano and
ed. Zaccaria.)

[18]   The 'cassoni' are dated around 1470 by H. Nützmann, 'Verschlüsselt in Details: Hochzeitbilder für Lorenzo
de'Medici', *Jahrbuch Preussischer Kulturbesitz* 34 (1997) 223–35. They are dated around 1475 by S. Cavicchioli,
The Tale of Cupid and Psyche: An Illustrated History (New York 2002) 66.

[19]   The frontals are illustrated in Cavicchioli, *The Tale of Cupid and Psyche* (n. 18, above) plates 35–36; Gaisser,
Fortunes of Apuleius (n. 3, above) plates 15–16.

as the union of the soul with God. The painter treats the human marriage of his Medici patrons as a mortal reflection of that everlasting union: the members of the wedding party are standing on the ground, but with clouds under their feet so that the wedding seems to take place in heaven and earth at the same time.

Psyche had an excellent reception in Florence from Boccaccio and the 'cassoni' painters, but her story received even more attention in the courts of Ferrara and Mantua, where it was told and retold in various genres by a series of writers and artists. The process began in the 1470s—at about the same time as the 'cassoni'—and it continued for a generation or so. The courtly storytellers undoubtedly knew and used the Florentine versions, especially that of Boccaccio, but they relied on a different source for Apuleius himself. Boccaccio had read the story in a manuscript. (There were several in Florence, including the one he transcribed himself.) [20] The 'cassoni' painters took Boccaccio as their starting point, as we have seen. But the first person to tell the story in Ferrara, Matteo Maria Boiardo, used the first edition, printed in 1469.[21] His successors built on his telling and—as the process continued—on those of each other.

Boiardo, count of Scandiano (1440/41–94), was a noble by birth and a courtier by profession.[22] But he was also a famous poet and translator. He plied his trades at the glittering court of Ercole d'Este, Duke of Ferrara, who had a deep interest in Apuleius. Boiardo's first treatment of Psyche seems to have been in the verse captions he wrote for a set of tarot cards created for someone at the court.[23] Most of the deck is lost, including the Psyche card, but we have a detailed account of the whole set by a contemporary, Pier Antonio Viti (*fl.* 1470–1500), who described it for a noble lady of Urbino who wanted to have a deck made for herself.[24] Psyche, Viti tells us, appeared as the eighth card in the suit of Triumphs, representing the quality of Patience. Boiardo told her story in this tercet:

> Psyche had Patience in her misfortunes
> And for that reason was aided in her distress,
> And in the end was made a goddess who is an example to us.[25]

This is a very short story, but Boiardo's tercet is only part of the text presented on the card: the card's verse and its picture were to be read together. From Viti's ecphrasis for the lady in Urbino we can almost see the image. He says:

> The picture is of a beautiful young woman clad in a violet mantle with a white dress underneath, and she holds part of her mantle with both hands, and she has at her feet

[20] Gaisser, *Fortunes of Apuleius* (n. 3, above) 108–10; J. Gaisser, 'Apuleius in Florence: from Boccaccio to Lorenzo de'Medici', in *Classica et Beneventana: Essays Presented to Virginia Brown on the Occasion of her 65th Birthday*, eds F. T. Coulson and A. A. Grotans (Turnhout 2007) 43–70.

[21] E. Fumagalli, *Matteo Maria Boiardo volgarizzatore dell''Asino d'Oro': contributo allo studio della fortuna dell'Apuleio nell'Umanesimo* (Padua 1988) 1–28, 31–91.

[22] See F. Forti, 'Matteo Maria Boiardo', *Dizionario biografico degli Italiani* 11 (1969) 211–23.

[23] Boiardo, *Tarocchi*, ed. Simona Foà (Rome 1993), see 9–10 for 1469–78 as the date of the work. See also R. Renier, 'I Tarocchi', in *Studi su Matteo Maria Boiardo* (Bologna 1894) 229–59; C. Baldi, 'I tarocchi di Boiardo nella cultura rinascimentale', *Acme* 61.3 (2009) 77–108.

[24] Viti also presented an allegory; Gaisser, *Fortunes of Apuleius* (n. 3, above) 183–84. Foà, *Tarocchi* (n. 23, above) edits and discusses his description.

[25] 'Patientia hebbe Psiche ai casi soi, / E perhò fu soccorsa nelli affanni, / E fatta Dea nel fin che è exemplo a noi'. Boiardo, *Tarocchi* (n. 23, above) 25–7.

on one side a broken bow with a reversed inscription below it, and on the other side two wings stripped of their feathers and a dapple-grey horse with a violet bridle, which, being patiently valiant, would endure every labour. And above the head of the aforesaid Psyche are three verses that tell about her.[26]

Psyche is young and beautiful. The colour of her cloak presents her as a lover, for purple is the colour of the suit of Love.[27] The broken bow and unfeathered wings at her feet take us further into her story, alluding to a particular moment: the scene in which Venus lists the punishments she would like to inflict on the errant Cupid. These include unstringing his bow and shearing his wings.[28] The image on the card shows these penalties fulfilled and tells us how to read the scene: with Cupid powerless, the painted Psyche is alone and without resource—that is, in precisely the situation in which she is to show the quality of Patience that she represents. The horse beside her also embodies Patience, for Psyche, like all the characters in the suit of Triumphs, is accompanied by an animal signifying her quality.[29] If we read back from the picture to the tercet, however, we see that, despite appearances, Psyche is not alone after all: even at the moment shown on the card she is 'aided in her distress' and she will achieve her reward of immortality.

But the story on the tarot card is not only short—Psyche's adventures boiled down to an irreducible minimum. It is also radically different from those we have seen before—Psyche's story without the lamp, one might say. By beginning with Psyche's misfortunes and making her an example of Patience, Boiardo and the artist have written a new story, not of curiosity punished and finally redeemed, but of endurance rewarded by immortality. Their story is what we might call a mixed-media production, told with word and image at the same time and with both being necessary to the understanding of its plot.

Boiardo's principal engagement with Psyche, however, appears in *Apulegio volgare*, his translation of Apuleius' novel into Italian for Ercole d'Este.[30] Boiardo had finished his translation by 1479 but it did not appear in print until 1518.[31] Since the work is a translation, Boiardo for the most part follows the story in Apuleius very closely. But he is not a slavish translator, and the changes he makes to Apuleius' novel in order to please himself and his courtly audience produce a subtly different story.

Two of his changes are major. First, he omits Apuleius' book 11 (the Isis book), and substitutes the farcical conclusion of Pseudo-Lucian's *Onos* ('The Ass'), in which Lucius,

---

[26]   'La pictura de Psiche è in forma di Nynfa, di morello manto vestita, con il bianco camiso di sotto, e tiene cum ambedue le mane parte del suo manto; et ha a suoi piedi, da l'un de canti, uno arco ropto, con uno scrito riverso a lui di sotto; e da l'altro canto due ali spenachiate et uno cavallo leardo, col freno morello, che pazientemente essendo generoso, patisse ogni fatica. E sopra el capo di dicta Psiche sono tre versi che di lei ragionano'. Viti, *Illustrazione*, in Foà, *Tarocchi* (n. 23, above) 52.

[27]   'El campo de le qual carte è colore morello nel gioco de Amore, che significa Amore, cioè colore violaceo'. Viti, *Illustrazione*, in Foà, *Tarocchi* (n. 23, above) 31.

[28]   In Apul. *Met.* 5.30.5–6 Venus suggests destruction of two sorts: of Cupid's equipment (undoing his quiver, blunting his arrows, unstringing his bow, and putting out his torch) and of his person (shaving his hair and clipping his wings). The artist has selected an easily depicted item from each list, showing the bow broken rather than unstrung for the sake of clarity.

[29]   'Et a piede di tucti li Trionfi sono animali di quella medesima natura che è il trionfo'. Viti, *Illustrazione*, in Foà, *Tarocchi* (n. 22, above) 47. Toil ('Fatiga'), for example, is accompanied by ants (Viti, 48).

[30]   There is no modern edition of the translation as a whole, but the story of Psyche has been edited by Fumagalli, *Boiardo* (n. 21, above) 217–335.

[31]   Ercole's jealously limited its circulation. For its publication history, see Fumagalli, *Boiardo* (n. 21, above) 163–84.

now restored to human shape, is unkindly rejected by the amorous matron because she liked him better as an ass.[32] The substitution deprives the novel of any hint of religious seriousness, but it also has implications for Psyche. In Apuleius, her story is imbedded in the larger story of Lucius, and we can read it as essentially the same story: both come to grief through curiosity, both suffer many afflictions, and both are finally redeemed by divine favour despite being essentially undeserving. Boiardo's racy conclusion, which would have been more entertaining for his audience than the Isis book, takes away Psyche's connection with Lucius.[33] She is still in the centre of the novel, but her story is now free-standing—as independent as it was in Fulgentius or Boccaccio, or on the tarot card discussed above.

Boiardo's second major change is in the sex of Psyche's child. In Apuleius, of course, she has a daughter, Voluptas (*Met.* 6.24.4). But Boiardo makes the child a boy instead, Dilecto.[34] In Apuleius, Voluptas comes as a surprise; all along we have been led to expect a boy.[35] And as readers we have to wonder what that surprise means. Is Voluptas a 'divine child', as some would have it, or is she the mortal child Cupid predicts if Psyche reveals his secrets?[36] Since Apuleius does not say, Voluptas can bear more than one interpretation, including the abstract reading ('eternal joy and delight') in Boccaccio's religious allegory. Boiardo has Cupid make the same prediction to Psyche that he did in Apuleius, but for him the child is all boy from the beginning: a 'fanciullino', 'fanciullo', or 'figliolo'.[37] We can still speculate about whether he is mortal or divine, but there is no surprise at the end to set us wondering.

Boiardo also makes dozens of small changes in his translation. He was a nobleman writing for Ercole's sophisticated court, and many of his changes give the story a luxurious and sensual tone. One, in particular, would be picked up by his successors: his embellishment of Psyche's reception in Cupid's palace. Apuleius' Psyche has a nap and a bath: 'Et prius somno et mox lavacro fatigationem diluit' (*Met.* 5.3.1). Boiardo's enjoys a *fragrant* bath and rests on a *snow-white bed*: 'ne lo odorifero bagno ralegrata e ristaurata nel candido lecto' (*Apulegio Volgare* 5.3).[38] She sits at a table of citrus wood adorned with gold and precious gems and eats from bejewelled golden dishes, all absent in Apuleius. After dinner, both Psyches are entertained by invisible musicians. Apuleius' Psyche hears a singer, someone playing the cithara, and a many-voiced choir (*Met.* 5.3.5). Boiardo's hears *two* choirs:

> A harmony of various voices, brought together with great art, could be heard singing. These were two large choirs [...] and now separately, now together they brightened the empty loggia and the whole enclosed garden with many songs.[39]

---

[32] For Lucian Boiardo's reliance on the translation of Niccolò Leoniceno (1428–1524), who was also active in the Este court in the 1470s, see M. Acocella, '*L'Asino d'oro' nel rinascimento: Dai volgarizzamenti alle raffigurazioni pittoriche* (Ravenna 2001) 17–75.

[33] See M. Trecca, *La magia rinnovata* (Florence 1995) 71–72.

[34] 'Cosí pervene Psiche in mano de Cupido, e di lor nacque quello figliolo che Dilecto è chiamato'. Boiardo, *Apulegio volgare* 6.24, ed. Fumagalli, *Boiardo* (n. 21, above) 345.

[35] See Apuleius, *Cupid and Psyche*, trans. with intro. and comm. by E. J. Kenney (Cambridge 1990) 224.

[36] For 'divine child', see Kenney, *Cupid and Psyche* (n. 35, above) 224.

[37] For Cupid's prediction, see Apul. *Met.* 5.11.6 and Boiardo, *Apulegio volgare* 5.11, ed. Fumagalli, *Boiardo* (n. 21, above) 257: 'Già cresceremo la famiglia nostra, perché nel ventre tuo mi porti un fanciullino, il quale, scoprendo tu li secreti nostri, nascerà omo mortale, e guardandoli fidelmente, serà divino'.

[38] Fumagalli, *Boiardo* (n. 21, above) 241.

[39] 'Una concordantia de voce varie e diverse, unita con mirabile arte, se fece udire cantando. Erano questi dui cori de molta gente [...] et ora separatamente et ora insieme con molte cancione la solitaria logia alegrarno e tutto el chiuso giardino'. Boiardo, *Apulegio volgare* 5.3, ed. Fumagalli, *Boiardo* (n. 21, above) 241.

It has been suggested that Boiardo's two choirs singing back and forth would have reminded his readers, including Ercole, of musical performances at the court.[40] But perhaps one should put it the other way and consider that his antiphonal choirs were inspired by the court performances.

Boiardo's translation was soon followed by three new retellings associated with the Este, each in a different genre: a verse narration by Niccolò da Correggio, a fresco cycle by Ercole de' Roberti and its ecphrasis, and a play by Galeotto del Carretto.[41] Niccolò da Correggio (1450–1508) was a cousin of Boiardo's and, like him, was both a courtier and an accomplished poet.[42] Around 1491, he dedicated his long Italian poem, *Fabula Psiches et Cupidinis*, to Ercole's daughter Isabella d'Este, who had married Francesco Gonzaga, Marquis of Mantua, in 1490. The first edition was printed in 1507.

Correggio's work is the first literary telling of the story we have seen, and it is very literary indeed.[43] As in Apuleius, Psyche's story is an inset in the narrative. The frame story is told in the first person by a poet struck by love's arrow with unrequited love for a nymph. Pursuing her in vain, he finally falls asleep in a beautiful garden and, in a dream, sees Amor (whom Correggio never calls Cupido). In the imbedded story, Amor, himself a victim of love, tells the poet of his adventures with Psyche. In the concluding panel, the poet awakes and encounters Pan, another victim of unhappy love, who vouches for the truth of Amor's story. In the end, the poet, considering his own misfortunes and those of Amor himself, renounces love altogether and advises the reader to do the same: 'Flee fast and far because love's arrow kills and not just stings you'.[44]

The story that Amor tells has essentially the same plot as that of Cupid and Psyche in Boiardo—including the baby Dilecto (although the birth announcement does not use the word 'son').[45] It also includes (and further enhances) Boiardo's enhancements of Psyche's entertainment, emphasizing the loggia and the enclosed garden—which Amor takes nine stanzas to describe (*Fabula*, stanzas 65–73). Nonetheless, it is not the same story, and it is unlike any of its predecessors. It does not tell of punishment for curiosity, or of the soul's union with God or Love, or of patience rewarded. Instead, it is a cautionary tale of the vulnerability of gods and men alike to the vicissitudes of love. More to the point, however, it is not the story of Cupid and Psyche at all, but rather of Cupid (or Amor), the first-person narrator. The point of view, the emotions, the misfortunes all belong to him, and we see everything through his eyes, including himself. When Apuleius' Psyche lights her lamp and sees her beautiful husband, we register every detail through her eyes: from his golden hair to his gorgeous wings, to the bow and arrows at his feet (*Met.* 5.22.5–7). Correggio's Amor, by contrast, filters Psyche's reaction through his own vision of himself: 'I don't think I ever looked better', he says, and then proceeds with his description.[46] The story of Amor, with

---

[40]   Fumagalli, *Boiardo* (n. 21, above) 241 n.

[41]   See Gaisser, *Fortunes of Apuleius* (n. 3, above) 184–95, with earlier bibliography.

[42]   P. Farenga, 'Niccolò da Correggio', *Dizionario biografico degli Italiani* 29 (1983) 466–74.

[43]   Trecca, *La magia rinnovata* (n. 33, above). See also R. Stillers, 'Erträumte Kunstwelt. Niccolò Correggios *Fabula Psiches et Cupidinis* (1491)', in *Der Mythos von Amor und Psyche in der europäischen Renaissance*, eds J. Jankovics and S. Katalin Németh (Budapest 2002) 131–50.

[44]   'Fuggiti presto, di buon passo e longie, / Ché'l stral d'amor ucide e non pur pongie'. Niccolò da Correggio, *Fabula Psiches et Cupidinis* 179.7–8, in *Opere*, Scrittori d'Italia 244, ed. A. Tissoni Benvenuti (Bari 1969).

[45]   'Psiche divenne mia, como io t'ho decto, / e gravida, di nui nacque il Dilecto'. Correggio, *Fabula* (n. 44, above) 169.7–8.

[46]   'Io ero credo alor di più bellezza / che mai nel mio trïonfo io mi mostrassi'. Correggio, *Fabula* (n. 44, above) 107.1–2.

Psyche no longer the focus of interest, is not edifying and is not intended to be. Rather, it is a piquant entertainment for courtly readers who knew other tellings and would appreciate something new.

Even more, it is also the centrepiece of a highly self-conscious poem about stories, storytellers, and their audiences.[47] The external audience is specifically the new bride, Isabella d'Este. The external narrator is Correggio, who perhaps resembles the primary internal narrator, the suffering poet, who is of course the audience of the second internal narrator, Amor. In the concluding frame, the poet, our primary internal narrator, again speaks in his own voice and tells us that he told his dream (and Amor's story), as well as his own story, to Pan, and that Pan related it back to him. But no more. The poem is a literary Rubik's cube of intersecting and imbedded stories, narrators, and audiences, too complicated to disentangle in the present discussion.

Not long after Correggio's poem, Ercole d'Este began to work with his court painter, Ercole de' Roberti, on the programme for a frescoed hall in his country palace, Belriguardo.[48] The Duke had a long-standing interest in Apuleius, but it has been suggested that his acquisition of Boccaccio's *Genealogies* in 1489 inspired him to think seriously about Psyche.[49] I will come back to this point. Belriguardo is largely destroyed and the Psyche room with it, but we have a contemporary description dedicated to the Duke by Sabadino degli Arienti in 1497.[50]

Both Sabadino's description and the painted story are indebted to Correggio.[51] It seems clear, however, that the tone of the cycle did not come from Correggio. The Duke is known to have been a deeply religious man with a particular interest in the soul, and Sabadino describes the work as a moral allegory. At the beginning, he says, 'On the walls one sees depicted with rare piety, under a poetic veil of allegory, with most felicitous painting, the celestial nymph Psyche'.[52] And at the end: 'These events and acts of pious love, full of rare wisdom, were represented [...] by the hands of the excellent painter who painted such a great pious subject following your ducal instruction'.[53] Sabadino does not identify the pious message, but since most of the frescoes seem to have shown Psyche's labours, one might infer that it had to do with the earthly trials of the soul. But there are two tantalizing details at the end. First: Psyche is not offered a cup of immortality, although Mercury escorts her to heaven for her marriage

[47]   See especially Trecca, *La magia rinnovata* (n. 33, above) 72–75, 133.

[48]   W. L. Gundersheimer, *Art and Life at the Court of Ercole I d'Este: The 'De triumphis religionis' of Giovanni Sabadino degli Arienti* (Geneva 1972) 64 n. 55. See also S. Cavicchioli, 'Amore e Psiche nella delizia estense di Belriguardo', *La Diana* 1 (1995) 125–45.

[49]   Cavicchioli, 'Amore e Psiche' (n. 48, above) 128.

[50]   G. Ghinassi, 'Giovanni Sabadino degli Arienti', *Dizionario biografico degli Italiani* 4 (1962) 154–56. The description is edited in Gundersheimer, *Art and Life* (n. 48, above).

[51]   The story in the cycle began at the same place as in Correggio: with Venus' envy and her instructions to Cupid. Sabadino takes many phrases from Correggio, and he mentions his telling of the story: 'Di che anchora tanta beata cosa in legiadro e dolce verso materno Nicolao da Coregio, signore claro e facundo e d'arme valido huo[mo] ha depincto, secondo Apoleio autore prestate scrive'. Sabadino, *De triumphis religionis*, ed. Gundersheimer, *Art and Life* (n. 48, above) 64–5. But Sabadino does not follow Correggio and Boiardo in changing the sex of Psyche's child (see below).

[52]   'In le pariete si vede con moralità singulare, sotto poetico velamento hystoriata con felicissima pictura, Psyche celeste nympha'. Sabadino, *De triumphis religionis*, ed. Gundersheimer, *Art and Life* (n. 48, above) 62.

[53]   'Questi accidenti et acti de morale amore, pieni de singulari sentimenti sono effigiati [...] de mane de optimo pictore ferrariense che tanta morale cosa pinse secondo la tua ducal instructione'. Sabadino, *De triumphis religionis*, ed. Gundersheimer, *Art and Life* (n. 48, above) 64.

and she joins the gods at the celestial feast.[54] I think that the omission is deliberate and that the Duke took his cue from Boccaccio, who also omitted this detail. Why? I would say that it is because, for both Boccaccio and Ercole, Psyche is Soul and the soul is immortal by definition. The second detail is Psyche's child: 'a charming daughter named Voluptas, fruit of the wretched world'.[55] What are we to make of her? Is she divine since she is born in heaven, or mortal as a product of the wretched world?

The room housing the frescoes was large, Sabadino says, with six glass windows overlooking the secluded garden—a clear echo of the loggia and enclosed garden described by Boiardo and, more lavishly, by Correggio.[56] The room, then, was intended to recall a distinguishing feature of Cupid's palace. But there is more: the frescoes show Zephyr bringing Psyche down to a grassy wooded spot, 'where there is a palace of marvellous beauty—like this one'.[57] That is, like the Duke's palace, Belriguardo, itself. Scholars have suggested that the fresco actually depicted Belriguardo.[58] If they are right, one could say that the Duke was bringing his world into that of the story—or perhaps the other way around. In either case, the telling of the tale has been adjusted in order to create a resemblance between two fairy-tale realms, the one of Apuleius' Cupid, the other of the Duke of Ferrara.[59]

Soon after Ercole's frescoes, yet another courtier and poet, Galeotto Del Corretto (c. 1455–1530), completed a play called *Noze de Psiche e Cupidine*, which is probably to be identified with the 'new comedy' he sent Isabella d'Este around 1500.[60] Del Carretto used language from Boiardo and perhaps also from Correggio.[61] His story is the familiar one until it takes a surprising turn at the end. The gods agree to Psyche's becoming immortal and marrying Cupid, but at Venus' request something else must happen first: Psyche's sisters must be brought back to life. Accordingly, Mercury stages a grand reunion, bringing Psyche together with her sisters, parents, and brothers-in-law at her father's house. All this, so that

---

[54]   Sabadino, *De triumphis religionis*, ed. Gundersheimer, *Art and Life* (n. 48, above) 64. Cf. Cavicchioli, 'Amore e Psiche' (n. 48, above) 133: 'si ha l'impressione che fosse omessa anche l'offerta a Psyiche dell'ambrosia, cioè del segno tangibile dell'immortalità'.

[55]   'una vaga figlia nominata Voluptate, fructo del misero mondo'. Sabadino, *De triumphis religionis*, ed. Gundersheimer, *Art and Life* (n. 48, above) 64.

[56]   Sabadino, *De triumphis religionis*, ed. Gundersheimer, *Art and Life* (n. 48, above) 62.

[57]   'dove è uno palazo come questo de maravigliosa belleza'. Sabadino, *De triumphis religionis*, ed. Gundersheimer, *Art and Life* (n. 48, above) 62.

[58]   'The phrase "come questo" raises the possibility that this was a depiction of Belriguardo itself'. Gundersheimer, *Art and Life* (n. 48, above) 62 n. 54. Cavicchioli, 'Amore e Psiche' (n. 48, above) 131–2, suggests that Correggio's detailed description of Amor's gardens might have been inspired by those of the Duke.

[59]   The idea of likening a grand contemporary villa to Cupid's palace had an interesting *fortuna* that would be worth investigating. For example, in 1500, Filippo Beroaldo, commenting on *Met.* 5.1, whether independently or influenced by the treatment of Ercole's palace by Boiardo, Correggio, and Ercole himself in the Sala di Psiche, described the villa of his friend Mino de' Rossi as like 'Cupid's country house ('diversorium')'. See Gaisser, *Fortunes of Apuleius* (n. 3, above) 233–37. It has also been suggested that contemporary descriptions of the garden of Agostino Chigi's Farnesina (whose loggia is decorated with Raphael's Psyche fresco cycle) closely match that of Cupid's garden in Correggio. J. Shearman, 'Die Loggia der Psyche in der Villa Farnesina und der Probleme der letzten Phase von Raffaels graphischem Stil', *Jahrbuch der Kunsthistorischen Sammlungen in Wien* 60 (1964) 59–100 (73).

[60]   See R. Riccardi, 'Galeotto Del Carretto', *Dizionario biographico degli Italiani* 36 (1988) 415–19. For the text, see Galeotto Del Carretto, *Noze de Psiche e Cupidine*, in *Teatro del Quattrocento: Le corti padane*, eds A. Tissoni Benvenuti and M. P. Mussini Sacchi (Torino 1983) 611–725. The history of the comedy is discussed by Tissoni Benvenuti in the same volume, 559–67. For a detailed modern discussion, see M. Minutelli, 'Poesia e teatro di Galeotto dal Carretto. Riflessioni in margine al carteggio con Isabella d'Este', *Nuova Rivista di Letteratura Italiana* 7.1–2 (2004) 123–78.

[61]   See Fumagalli, *Boiardo* (n. 21, above) 145–50.

the penitent sisters can receive Psyche's forgiveness. Their resurrection, it seems, has been for her spiritual benefit, and the scene ends with Psyche's farewell as she departs for the 'triumphant chorus of the glorious court in heaven'.[62] Mercury then duly escorts her to heaven, where she drinks the cup of immortality and is married to Cupid. Del Carretto has told yet a different story—as religious as any we have seen before, but one whose happy ending requires not just patience from Psyche, but reconciliation and forgiveness, and this by the design of the formerly vengeful Venus.

Psyche—not Cupid as in Correggio—is Del Carretto's principal subject. And since the story is a drama, for once it is Psyche's own voice we hear—not the narrator's or Cupid's—exclaiming over Cupid's beauty: 'Oh, what wings he has! Oh what beautiful / golden hair! Ah, what a beautiful face!'[63] In fact, the story is told in many voices. Everyone has something to say: the familiar principals, of course, but also Psyche's parents, the sisters' husbands, and even the ants and other helpers. But it is more complicated than that, for there are also voices outside the action: the voice of Del Carretto himself in the long *argumentum* that tells the whole story before the play begins, and of the otherworldly chorus of Psyche's invisible servants, whose songs comment on and interpret the events. Their songs, written for performance and perhaps scored by the famous court musician Tromboncino, appear throughout, and also end each act, except for the last, which ends in epithalamia sung by Apollo and the Graces.[64]

Writers and artists from late antiquity to the end of the fifteenth century retold Apuleius' 'Cupid and Psyche' many times, constantly changing it to produce new stories suited to their own times and interests. Fulgentius and Boccaccio rewrote it to fit their Christian allegories of the soul's fall or redemption. 'Cassoni' painters changed the ending of Boccaccio's story to put it on a marriage chest. Boiardo told a short tale without curiosity and the lamp that made Psyche an exemplum of patience rewarded. He also wrote a translation whose luxurious embellishments and change of the sex of Psyche's child, were used in later retellings. Correggio fashioned an elaborate literary *tour de force* of interlocking stories and storytellers, with the first-person narrator Amor at the centre. Ercole d'Este, using Correggio and probably Boccaccio together with his own religious vision, created a fresco programme that apparently both emphasized the earthly trials of the soul and presented his villa as the house of Cupid. Del Carretto wrote a play with musical interludes in which Psyche had to forgive her enemies in order to earn her place in heaven. We can imagine that Apuleius would have shaken his head in amazement at these retellings, so different from his own 'Cupid and Psyche', but since he was a consummate borrower of other people's stories, he surely would have understood.

Bryn Mawr College

---

[62]　'Vale, mio padre, e tu mia matre posa, / che me ne vado al trïunfante coro / de la corte superna e glorïosa'. Del Carretto, *Noze* (n. 60, above) *Act* 5, 323–25.

[63]　'Ohimè ch'egli ha le piume! Ohimè che belli / et aurati capelli! ahi che bel viso!' Del Carretto, *Noze* (n. 60, above) *Act* 3, 12–13.

[64]　For the music, see C. Cavicchi, 'D'alcune musiche sul tema d'Amore e Psiche nel Cinquecento,' in *Psyché à la Renaissance: Actes du LIIe Colloque international d'études humanistes (29 juin – 2 juillet 2009)*, eds M. Bélime-Droguet, V. Gély, L. Mailho, and P. Vendrix (Turnhout 2013) 159–77.

PSYCHE'S TEXTUAL JOURNEY FROM APULEIUS TO BOCCACCIO AND PETRARCH

IGOR CANDIDO

In the envoy of the *Filocolo*, Giovanni Boccaccio draws a key distinction between the epic tradition of the *magni auctores*—Virgil, Lucan, Statius, and Ovid, all models of high rhetorical style—and his new prose writing, labelled as the 'middle way' ('mezzana via'), with no authoritative father. Some years later, the literary canon of the *Amorosa visione* would finally include, among other authors, Apuleius of Madauros (canto 5, ll. 37–38). Platonic philosopher, rhetorician, and narrator, Apuleius was one of Boccaccio's dearest authors and the most congenial narrative model he had encountered since his early education.[1] In the history of the transmission of classical literature, the significance of Boccaccio's encounter with Apuleius cannot be underestimated: Boccaccio had in his library the most important extant manuscripts of the *Metamorphoses* and, like Petrarch, he was able to rejoin the two Apuleian traditions, the philosophical and the rhetorical, in the autograph manuscript *Laurentianus* 54.32. His interest in and imitation of Apuleius laid the foundation for the linguistic tradition of Renaissance Apuleianism as well as for the modern fortune of the Madaurensis at large.[2]

During the last years of his stay in Naples, if not earlier, Boccaccio read Apuleius' *Metamorphoses* (or *The Golden Ass*) and his rhetorical works in the manuscript *Laurentianus* 29.20, which Zanobi da Strada had most likely sneaked out of the Monte Cassino library.[3] A palaeographic examination of *Laurentius* 29.2 shows that books 4–6 of the *Metamorphoses*, in which the fable of Cupid and Psyche is contained, are the most glossed section of the entire manuscript, heavily by the hand of Zanobi and sporadically by that of Boccaccio.[4] This, along with other evidence, complements and confirms the results of intertextual analysis, which indicate that the fable of Cupid and Psyche was a myth that was unique in the way it stimulated Boccaccio's narrative imagination. Yet the Apuleian *fabula*, notwithstanding its immense influence on late ancient, medieval, and Renaissance literature and art, has so far received only scant attention from Boccaccio scholars, with the sole exception of the exposition of the Platonic myth in the *Genealogia*. Here the narration is a synthesis of Apuleius' text and Fulgentius' own exposition of the myth, followed by an allegorical reading that depends on

---

[1] Apuleius' works are cited with no further reference from Apulée, *Les métamorphoses*, ed. D. S. Robertson, 3 vols (Paris 1940–45) and *Opuscules philosophiques et fragments*, ed. J. Beaujeu (Paris 1973). Boccaccio's works are cited from *Tutte le opere di Giovanni Boccaccio*, ed. V. Branca, 10 vols (Milan 1964–98).

[2] See, in particular, G. F. Gianotti, 'Da Montecassino a Firenze: la riscoperta di Apuleio', in *Il 'Decameron' nella letteratura europea*, ed. C. Allasia (Rome 2006) 11.

[3] See G. Billanovich, *I primi umanisti e le tradizioni dei classici latini* (Fribourg 1953) 16–19.

[4] See M. Cursi, M. Fiorilla, 'Boccaccio', in *Autografi dei letterati italiani: le origini e il Trecento*, tome 1, eds G. Brunetti, M. Fiorilla, and M. Petoletti (Rome 2013) 53. Emanuele Casamassima has instead attributed most of the glosses to Boccaccio's hand. See his 'Dentro lo scrittoio del Boccaccio: i codici della tradizione', in *Il 'Decameron': pratiche testuali e interpretative*, ed. A. Rossi (Bologna 1982) 253–260 (254).

ancient and medieval sources (mainly Aristotle, Calcidius, Martianus Capella, and Dante) and aims to shed light on the agreement between Aristotelian psychology and the Christian view of the soul.[5]

In Boccaccio's *Decameron*, three tales owe their *inventio* to Apuleius' *fabula* (*Dec.* 2.7 and 9; 10.10). These are audacious narrative experiments aimed at translating and rethinking the ancient model for the new bourgeois readership, mature examples of a totally new and surprisingly modern mythopoesis. Within their narratives, they show common elements drawn from Apuleius, allowing us to presume that Boccaccio composed the three tales at the same time. The most important themes are those of marriage between unequals, the power of fortune influencing human life, male 'mad bestiality' as opposed to the Aristotelian virtue of 'mesòtes', and the unfortunate consequences of female beauty. In *Dec.* 2.7, Alatiel, like Psyche, becomes a slave of Venus. Boccaccio's invention of her countless sexual adventures must depend, in fact, not only on the parody of the trials of faith that the main characters must undergo in the ancient novel, but, more properly, on the metaphorization of Psyche's enslavement. In the ancient novel, moreover, the trials of faith are essentially tests of virginity. Likewise, at the end of both the tale of Psyche and that of Alatiel, as well as in the Griselda story, the happy ending is made possible only through the offer of a symbolic compensation for the stolen virginity and is sanctioned by an actual marriage. If Alatiel is the antitype of Psyche, Zinevra, the wise wife of Bernabò in *Dec.* 2.9, owes most of her virtues and dispositions to Psyche, and her character helps the reader cover the Apuleian inventive space between Alatiel and Griselda.

Far from being isolated within Boccaccio's *œuvre*, the case of Apuleianism in *Dec.* 10.10 is unique and striking, as the Griselda tale can be considered a careful rewriting of the fable of Cupid and Psyche.[6] In my comparative reading of the two texts, I would like to focus on the narrative nucleus of the marriage between unequals (Apuleius' 'impares nuptiae'), around which the novella's plot entirely revolves. The difference in the social conditions of Gualtieri and Griselda is, indeed, the only reason Boccaccio introduces to justify the intolerable trials Griselda must undergo to show her unconditional faith in her husband's will (the fictitious killing of the children, her husband's choice of a new spouse). According to Boccaccio, Gualtieri's 'vassals were most sorely dissatisfied with her by reason of her base condition, and all the more so since they saw that she was a mother'.[7] This motive strictly depends on Apuleius: in the fable, Venus likewise does not accept her son's union with a mortal woman and devises all sorts of trials for Psyche in order to impede it:

> 'Look at her!' she said. 'She is moving us to pity with that alluring swollen belly of hers. With that illustrious progeny she no doubt means to make me a happy

---

[5]   On the influence of the Apuleian fable upon Boccaccio, see my *Boccaccio umanista: studi su Boccaccio e Apuleio* (Ravenna 2014).

[6]   I proposed that the Cupid and Psyche fable should be identified as the source of the Griselda tale in 'Apuleio alla fine del 'Decameron': la novella di Griselda come riscrittura della *lepida fabula* di Amore e Psiche', *Filologia e critica* 32.1 (2007) 3–17. Prior to my article, Luca Carlo Rossi, examining the Apuleian elements in Petrarch's Griselda, had also considered plausible an influence on Boccaccio. See 'In margine alla Griselda latina di Petrarca', *Acme* 63 (2000) 139–160 (152). Later, Jessica Lara Lawrence Harkins devoted a chapter of her dissertation ('Translations of Griselda', unpublished doctoral thesis (Washington University 2008)) to the comparison between the Apuleian fable and *Dec.* 10.10.

[7]   §27, trans. J. M. Rigg: 'i suoi uomini pessimamente si contentavano di lei per la sua bassa condizione e spezialmente poi che vedevano che ella portava figliuoli, e della figliuola che nata era tristissimi altro che mormorar non faceano'. All passages quoted from Boccaccio's *Decameron* follow Rigg's translation unless otherwise noted.

grandmother. Lucky me! In the very flower of my youth I shall be called grandmother; and the son of a cheap slave-girl will be known as Venus' grandson. But how foolish I am to misuse the word *son*, since the marriage was between unequals ('impares nuptiae'); besides, it took place in a country house without witnesses and without the father's consent ('in villa sine testibus et patre non consentiente'). Hence it cannot be regarded as legal and therefore your child will be born illegitimate—if indeed we allow you to go through with the birth at all.'[8]

In both the novella and the fable, therefore, the problem of marriage between unequals only reveals itself before the fruit of the marriage itself, the birth of a child.

The discourse of Venus has more to tell us. Her use of the formula 'in villa sine testibus et patre non consentiente' to designate the illegal conditions under which the marriage was celebrated is singled out in the manuscript *Laur.* 29.2 by a *manicula* drawn by Boccaccio (see figs 1 and 2 on the next pages).

The legal question of a marriage celebrated in a country house is also one of the problems at stake in the *Apologia*. In chapter 67 Apuleius refers to the fourth accusation levelled against him, that his marriage with the widow Pudentilla would be invalid 'because the marriage contract was sealed not in the town but at a country house'.[9] But the law, as he later objects in chapter 88, does not prohibit the celebration of a marriage in a country house: 'The Julian marriage-law nowhere contains a clause to the effect that no man shall wed in a country house'.[10] In this case, anyhow, there existed the legal evidence of the marriage contract ('tabulae nuptiales') as guarantee of the mutual agreement between the partners ('consensus'), while the union of Cupid and Psyche must certainly be defined as a 'coniunctio occulta' and therefore be invalid. Psyche, in fact, is overtly aware that her marriage is invalid, as she lets both of her sisters believe that Cupid, having divorced her, will this time marry each of them according to the sacred rites the law strictly requires:

> 'On account of your dreadful crime,' Cupid declared, 'you are forthwith to depart from my couch and take what is yours with you ('res tuas habeto'). I shall now wed your sister in holy matrimony ('ego vero sororem tuam [...] iam mihi confarreatis nuptis coniugabo')'—and he spoke your full name. Then at once he commanded Zephyr to waft me beyond the boundaries of his house.[11]

The marriage between Cupid and Psyche is thus invalid because it is not configured as 'nuptiae confarreatae', the most ancient and solemn form of marriage among the Roman patricians.[12]

---

[8]   *Met.* 6.9, trans. J. A. Hanson: 'Et ecce' inquit 'nobis turgidi ventris sui lenocinio commovet miserationem, unde me praeclara subole aviam beatam scilicet faciat. Felix vero ego quae in ipso aetatis meae flore vocabor avia et vilis ancillae filius nepos Veneris audiet. Quamquam inepta ego quae frustra filium dicam; impares enim nuptiae et praeterea in villa sine testibus et patre non consentiente factae legitimae non possunt videri ac per hoc spurius iste nascetur, si tamen partum omnino perferre te patiemur'. All passages quoted from Apuleius' *Metamorphoses* follow Hanson's translation unless otherwise noted.

[9]   §3, trans. H. E. Butler: 'quod in villa ac non in oppido tabulae nuptiales sint consignatae'. All passages quoted from Apuleius' *De magia* follow Butler's translation unless otherwise noted.

[10]   §3: 'Lex quidem Iulia de maritandis ordinibus nusquam sui ad hunc modum interdicit: uxorem in uilla ne ducito'.

[11]   *Met.* 5.26: '"Tu quidem" inquit "ob istud tam dirum facinus confestim toro meo divorte tibique res tuas habeto, ego vero sororem tuam"—et nomen quo tu censeris aiebat—"iam mihi confarreatis nuptis coniugabo" et statim Zephyro praecipit ultra terminos me domus eius efflaret'.

[12]   On the terms of Latin matrimonial law used by Apuleius ('dos', 'iustum matrimonium', 'concubinatus',

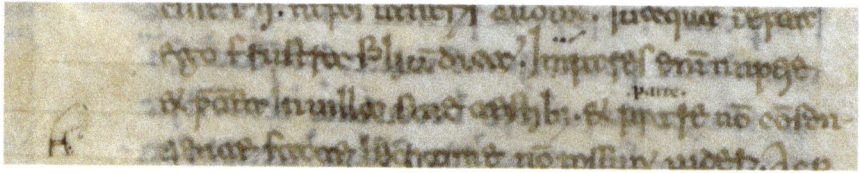

Figure 1. Florence, Biblioteca Medicea Laurenziana, *Laur.* 29.2, f. 45v.

Now, it is certainly no coincidence that the Apuleian formula uttered by Venus, 'in villa sine testibus et patre non consentiente', lists the same three negative conditions under which the marriage between Gualtieri and Griselda was also celebrated. In Boccaccio's text, in fact, at her first appearance on the narrative scene, Griselda is described as 'a poor girl that dwelt on a farm hard by his [Gualtieri's] house'.[13] Likewise, on the wedding day Gualtieri is said to have arrived with his company at a village. Moreover, while the reader is generally told that he 'married her before them all',[14] no mention is made of any specific witnesses. Last but not least, textual evidence allows us to infer that the marriage was celebrated without the consent of Griselda's father, Giannucole. During the first dialogue between Gualtieri and Giannucole, the latter, being a very poor man, has no voice in the question and can only accept the former's request to marry his daughter. So, on the wedding day Gualtieri simply informs Giannucole of his resolution: 'I am come to wed Griselda'.[15] Finally, only when Griselda is sent back home to her father do we learn that 'Giannucolo, who had ever deemed it a thing incredible that Gualtieri should keep his daughter to wife, [...] had looked for this to happen every day, and had kept the clothes that she had put off on the morning that Gualtieri had wedded her'.[16]

We should note at this point that in both Apuleius and Boccaccio two weddings are celebrated and these events perform the same narrative function in each of the texts. The first union, between Cupid and Psyche, is, as we have seen, illegal, and the second therefore requires its final legitimate consecration by Jove himself before the council of the gods. In particular, Jove's intervention aims to remove the last two obstacles to a legitimate union: the condition of a marriage between unequals and the fact that Cupid has stolen Psyche's virginity.

> 'I have decided that the hot-blooded impulses of his early youth must be restrained by some bridle. There has been enough scandal from the daily tales of his adulteries and all sorts of immoralities. We must remove every opportunity, and chain his boyish self-indulgence with the shackles of matrimony. He has selected a girl and robbed her of her maidenhood: let him keep her to have and to hold, and in Psyche's arms let him indulge his passion forever.' Then he added, turning to Venus, 'Now, my

---

'confarreatio', 'divortium', 'repudium', 'tempus lugendi', 'novus contractus'), and known to Boccaccio from his studies of canon law at the University of Naples, see F. Norden, *Apulejus von Madaura und das römische Privatrecht* (Leipzig-Berlin 1912, reprinted 1974) 90–125. See also C. Fayer, *La 'familia' romana: aspetti giuridici e antiquari. Sponsalia. Matrimonio. Dote*, 2 vols (Rome 2005) II 223–26.

[13]   § 9: 'una povera giovinetta che d'una villa vicina a casa sua era'.

[14]   § 22 : 'in presenza di tutti la sposò'.

[15]   § 17 : 'Io son venuto a sposar la Griselda'.

[16]   § 48 : 'Giannucolo, che creder non avea mai potuto questo esser ver che Gualtieri la figliuola dovesse tener moglie, e ogni dí questo caso aspettando, guardati l'aveva i panni che spogliati s'avea quella mattina che Gualtier la sposò'.

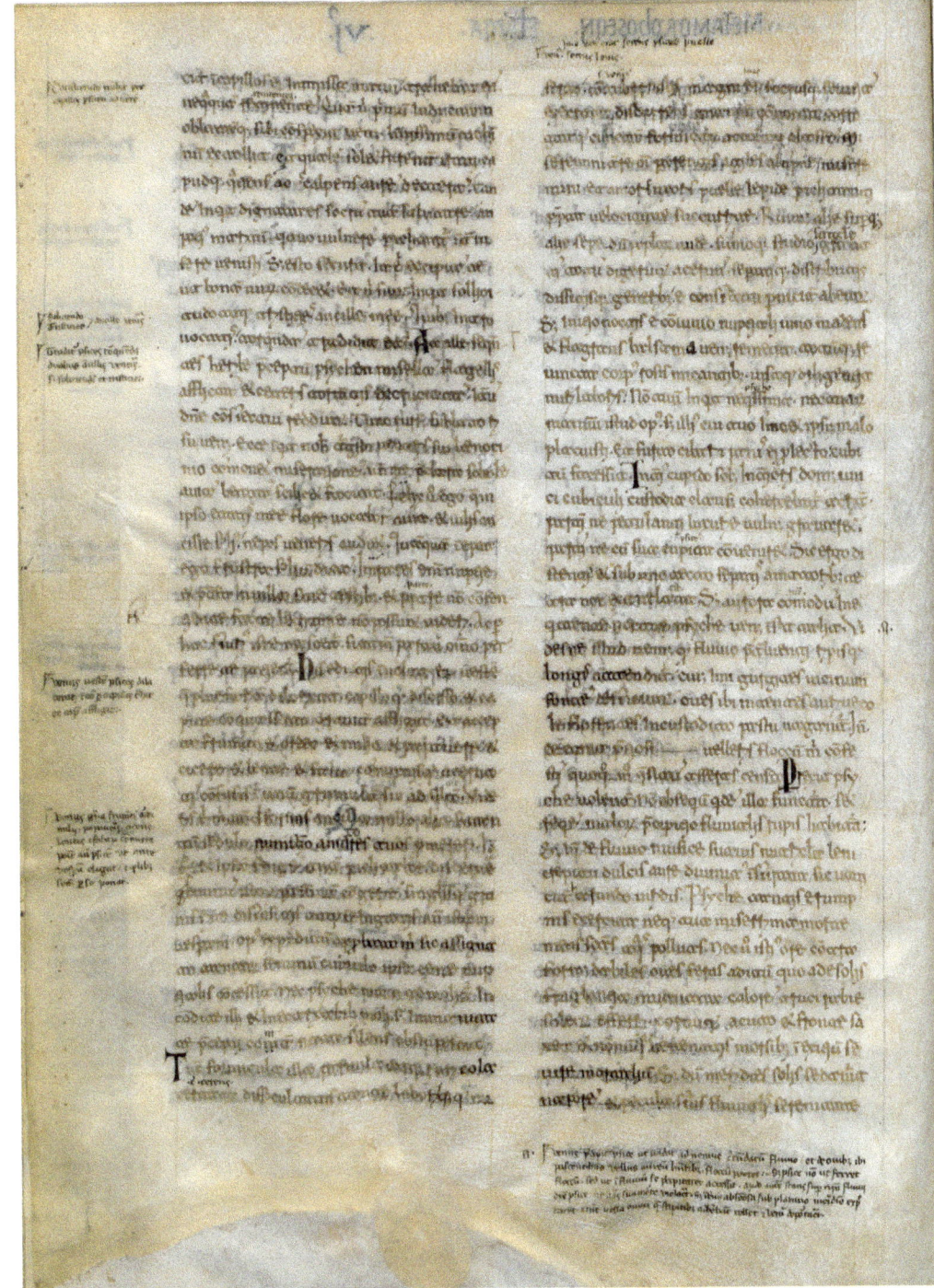

Figure 2. Florence, Biblioteca Medicea Laurenziana, *Laur.* 29.2, f. 45v.

daughter, do not be so gloomy and do not be afraid for your excellent pedigree and your status because of a mortal marriage. I will make the wedding no longer uneven, but legitimate and in accordance with civil law.' He immediately ordered Mercury to take hold of Psyche and bring her to heaven. Then he handed her a cup of ambrosia, saying, 'Drink this, Psyche, and you will be immortal. Cupid will never leave your embrace, and your marriage will last for ever.'[17]

The conditions under which this second marriage is celebrated are completely different: the council of gods in heaven is the noblest place; the gods are the witnesses; Jove himself is the father of the newly deified Psyche. This narrative plot is closely imitated by Boccaccio. The fictitious wedding between Gualtieri and the twelve-year-old girl, who is actually his own daughter, finally turns into the second wedding between Griselda and himself, which, just as in the Apuleian model, serves the purpose of reaffirming the first unfortunate union on new and more stable foundations. This is, in the end, the true meaning of Gualtieri's final words:

> 'I now [...] am minded to restore to thee at once all that, step by step, I took from thee, and by extremity of joy to compensate the tribulations that I inflicted on thee. Receive, then, this girl, whom thou supposest to be my bride, and her brother, with glad heart, as thy children and mine, [...] and I am thy husband.'[18]

The conditions of this second marriage also positively overturn those implied in the Apuleian formula 'in villa sine testibus et patre non consentiente'. Gualtieri's noble house is the new location, his newly recovered sons and the count of Panago are the witnesses, and Giannucole is the finally recognized and consenting father: 'Gualtieri took Giannucolo from his husbandry, and established him in honour as his father-in-law, wherein to his great solace he lived for the rest of his days'.[19]

Last but not least, as in the fable, the second marriage finally removes the same two obstacles to the legitimate union of Gualtieri and Griselda: the condition of a marriage between unequals and the fact that Gualtieri has stolen Griselda's virginity. In fact, the sole reason for Gualtieri's rejection of Griselda is, as she herself admits, her poor social status, which is unworthy of her husband's noble status. In addition, the last part of Griselda's speech brings up the problem of stolen virginity as a good that is impossible to give back.

> 'Twas not without travail most grievous that the lady, as she heard this announcement, got the better of her woman's nature, and suppressing her tears, made answer: 'My lord, I ever knew that my low degree was on no wise congruous with your nobility, and acknowledged that the rank I had with you was of your and God's bestowal, nor did I

---

[17] *Met.* 6.23: '"Cuius primae iuventutis caloratos impetus freno quodam coercendos existimavi; sat est cotidianis eum fabulis ob adulteria cunctasque corruptelas infamatum. Tollenda est omnis occasio et luxuria puerilis nuptialibus pedicis alliganda. Puellam elegit et virginitate privavit: teneat, possideat, amplexus Psychen semper suis amoribus perfruatur." Et ad Venerem conlata facie: "Nec tu" inquit "filia, quicquam contristere nec prosapiae tantae tuae statuque de matrimonio mortali metuas. Iam faxo nuptias non impares sed legitimas et iure civili congruas", et ilico per Mercurium arripi Psychen et in caelum perduci iubet. Porrecto ambrosiae poculo: "Sume" inquit "Psyche, et immortalis esto, nec umquam digredietur a tuo nexu Cupido sed istae vobis erunt perpetuae nuptiae"'.

[18] § 62–63: 'intendo di rendere a te a un'ora ciò che io tra molte ti tolsi e con somma dolcezza le punture ristorare che io ti diedi. E per ciò con lieto animo prendi questa che tu mia sposa credi, e il suo fratello, per tuoi e miei figliuoli: [...] e io sono il tuo marito'.

[19] § 67: 'Gualtieri, tolto Giannucolo dal suo lavorio, come suocero il pose in istato, che egli onoratamente e con gran consolazione visse e finí la sua vecchiezza'.

ever make as if it were mine by gift, or so esteem it, but still accounted it as a loan. 'Tis your pleasure to recall it, and therefore it should be, and is, my pleasure to render it up to you. So, here is your ring, with which you espoused me; take it back. You bid me take with me the dowry that I brought you; which to do will require neither paymaster on your part nor purse nor packhorse on mine; for I am not unmindful that naked was I when you first had me. And if you deem it seemly that that body in which I have borne children, by you begotten, be beheld of all, naked will I depart; but yet, I pray you, be pleased, in guerdon of the virginity that I brought you and take not away, to suffer me to bear hence upon my back a single shift—I crave no more—besides my dowry.'[20]

Here Boccaccio is most likely relying on *Apol.* 92, where Apuleius makes a legal distinction between the dowry brought by the maiden and that brought by the widow:

A beautiful maiden, even though she be poor, is amply dowered. For she brings to her husband a fresh untainted spirit, the charm of her beauty, the unblemished glory of her prime. The very fact that she is a maiden is rightly and deservedly regarded by all husbands as the strongest recommendation. For whatever else you receive as your wife's dowry you can, when it pleases you and if you desire to feel yourself under no further obligation, repay in full just as you receive it; you can count back money, restore the slaves, leave the house, abandon the estates. Virginity only, once it has been given, can never be repaid; it is the one portion of the dowry that remains irrevocably with the husband. The widow on the other hand, if divorced, leaves you as she came.[21]

One last consideration concerns Boccaccio's decision to imitate Apuleius' fable of Cupid and Psyche in the three novellas we have examined, and particularly in the Griselda tale that seals his narrative masterpiece. This choice is fully explained by Boccaccio himself in his *Genealogia deorum*, book 14, chapter 9:

Fiction has, in some cases, sufficed to lift the oppressive weight of adversity and furnish consolation, as appears in Lucius Apuleius; he tells how the highborn maiden Charis, while bewailing her unhappy condition as captive among thieves, was in some degree restored through hearing from an old woman the charming story of Psyche.[22]

---

[20] § 44–45: 'La donna, udendo queste parole, non senza grandissima fatica, oltre alla natura delle femine, ritenne le lagrime e rispose: "Signor mio, io conobbi sempre la mia bassa condizione alla vostra nobiltà in alcun modo non convenirsi, e quello che io stata son con voi da Dio e da voi il riconoscea, né mai, come donatolmi, mio il feci o tenni ma sempre l'ebbi come prestatomi; piacevi di rivolerlo, e a me dee piacere e piace di renderlovi: ecco il vostro anello col quale voi mi sposaste, prendetelo. Comandatemi che io quella dota me ne porti che io ci recai: alla qual cosa fare né a voi pagatore né a me borsa bisognerà né somiere, per ciò che di mente uscito non m'è che ignuda m'aveste; e se voi giudicate onesto che quel corpo nel quale io ho portati i figliuoli da voi generati sia da tutti veduto, io me n'andrò ignuda; ma io vi priego, in premio della mia virginità che io ci recai e non ne la porto, che almeno una sola camiscia sopra la dota mia vi piaccia che io portar ne possa"'.

[21] § 6–8: 'Virgo formosa etsi sit oppido pauper, tamen abunde dotata est; affert quippe ad maritum novum animi indolem, pulchritudinis gratiam, floris rudimentum. Ipsa virginitatis commendatio iure meritoque omnibus maritis acceptissima est; nam quodcumque aliud in dotem acceperis, potes, cum libuit, ne sis beneficio obstrictus, omne ut acceperas retribuere, pecuniam remunerare, mancipia restituere, domo demigrare, praediis cedere: sola virginitas cum semel accepta est, reddi nequitur, sola apud maritum ex rebus dotalibus remanet. Vidua autem qualis nuptiis uenit, talis diuortio digreditur'.

[22] Trans. C. G. Osgood: 'Fabulis laborantibus sub pondere adversantis fortune non nunquam solamen inpensum est, quod apud Lucium Apuleium cernitur. Quem penes Carithes, generosa virgo infortunio suo apud predones captiva, captivitatem suam depolorans, ab anicula fabule Psycis lepiditate paululum refocillata est'. All passages

The fable can give relief to those who are troubled by misfortune, as teaches Apuleius, who offers the story to Charis, a maiden taken prisoner by bandits. Throughout the fable, Boccaccio therefore aims to console all women 'restrained by the will, the caprice, the commandment of fathers, mothers, brothers, and husbands'.[23] So Charis' request to her warder to show some 'human kindness' ('pietas humana') and help her a little in her harsh misfortune (*Met.* 4.26) might have contributed to inspire Boccaccio's memorable beginning: ''Tis humane to have compassion on the afflicted'.[24]

In early 1373, Petrarch received in Padua a copy of Boccaccio's *Decameron* and would later admit to having devoted only cursory attention to his younger friend's work. Petrarch nonetheless did dwell at length on the *Decameron*'s last tale, the story of Griselda, which he first learned by heart and then translated into Latin. The poetic and intellectual reasons underlying this unprecedented work of his are committed to two of his *Seniles*, book 17, epistles 3 and 4, both sent to Boccaccio. Together with the attached Latin translation of the Griselda tale, these form a pre-humanist treatise entitled *De insigni obedientia et fide uxoria*. Ascribed to Petrarch's programme of reviving classical antiquity in the Christian era, the Latin Griselda is a meditated and learned literary enterprise that far surpasses the boundaries of free *imitatio*. In many respects, it is in fact a rewriting of the source tale rather than a faithful translation. By following the precepts on the falsehood of the *fabula* in the *Rhetorica ad Herennium* (1.8.12) and Cicero's *De inventione* (1.19.27), Petrarch chose to substitute the free inventiveness of the *fabula* with the pattern of historical *exemplum*, to turn an absolute model of patient conjugal love into an example of moral virtue for Christian imitation.[25] In the second part of this chapter, I would like to focus on Petrarch's understanding of the Griselda tale while also trying to provide answers to important questions that are at stake when we study the complex intellectual process of his translation. What idea did he entertain of the 'Griselda fable', the very apex of Boccaccio's masterpiece? Did his predilection for historical verisimilitude lead him to misunderstand Boccaccio's idea of *fabula*? Last but not least, was he aware of the Apuleian source of Boccaccio's tale?

Petrarch's ideal programme for restoring classical antiquity in the Christian era, as far as it concerns his Latin Griselda, was not limited to the twofold task of dignifying the original vernacular text and imposing a Christian allegory upon it. It also aimed to raise questions concerning the principles and effects of narrative invention. As a matter of fact, Petrarch's resort to the concept of historical verisimilitude was meant to call into question Boccaccio's use of the *fabula* as a privileged narrative genre. In the proem to the *Decameron*, Boccaccio—with an evident *sprezzatura*—had defined his hundred tales as 'stories or fables or parables or histories or whatever you like to style them',[26] and in a letter to Francescuolo da Brossano lamenting the death of Petrarch, he would refer to the Griselda tale as 'the last of my fables' ('ultima fabularum mearum', ep. 24, § 41). If we now turn our attention to epistle 3 of Petrarch's *Seniles*, we will discover that the source of the Griselda tale is instead termed 'ystoria':

quoted from Boccaccio's *Genealogia* follow Osgood's translation unless otherwise indicated.

[23]   *Proem* § 10: 'ristrette da' voleri, da' piaceri, da' comandamenti de' padri, delle madri, de' fratelli e de' mariti'.

[24]   *Proem* § 1: 'Umana cosa è aver compassione degli afflitti'.

[25]   For an introduction to the most important questions at stake in Petrarch's Griselda, see G. Boccaccio and F. Petrarca, *Griselda*, ed. L. C. Rossi (Palermo 1991) 9–21.

[26]   *Proem* § 13: 'novelle, o favole o parabole o istorie che dire le vogliamo'.

I was struck by the idea that maybe such a sweet story ('dulcis ystoria') would appeal also to those who do not know our language, since it had always pleased me after hearing it many years earlier, and I gathered it had pleased you to the point that you considered it not unworthy of your vernacular style, and of the end of your work, where the art of rhetoric tells us to put whatever is more powerful.[27]

Rather than emphasizing Petrarch's use of the term 'ystoria', scholars have focused instead on the Latin expression 'cum et michi semper ante multos annos audita placuisset', suggesting that Petrarch has here in mind a popular story heard many years earlier and widely circulating in Florence. Indeed, a few have examined both the popular narrative tradition and, in particular, the folklore cycle of Cupid and Psyche.[28] However, it is very unlikely that Petrarch is here referring to a popular antecedent of the novella, as Vittore Branca has rightly pointed out.[29]

Another possible reading of the 'dulcis ystoria' is suggested by the conclusion of epistle 3, where Petrarch introduces the key question of the novella's authorship: 'Whoever asks me whether it is true; that is, whether I have written a history or just a tale, I shall reply with the words of Crispus, *Let the responsibility fall on the author*, namely my Giovanni'.[30] For the first time in the letter, the opposition between *fabula* and *historia* finally comes to the fore. By stressing this difference in favour of *historia*, Petrarch attempts to restore verisimilitude to a story that would otherwise be unbelievable. He then touches upon the question again at the beginning of epistle 4:

Whether the contents are true or fictitious I know not, since they are no longer histories but just tales; but I have done it for one reason: that they belong to you and were written by you, although, foreseeing this challenge, I prefaced that the guarantee would rest with the author, that is, with you. And I shall tell you what happened to me in connection with this story ('historia'), which I would rather call a tale ('fabula').[31]

The most relevant question for us is whether Petrarch's distinction between *fabula* and *historia* was simply rhetorical, or whether he attributed a connotative meaning to the former term. If applied to the Griselda tale, in fact, the notion of *fabula* could not only refer to the classical genre of fictive narrative, to which the tale properly belongs, but also to the most

[27] 'subito talis interloquendum cogitatio supervenit, fieri posse ut nostri etiam sermonis ignaros tam dulcis ystoria delectaret, cum et michi semper ante multos annos audita placuisset, et tibi usque adeo placuisse perpenderem ut vulgari eam stilo tuo censueris non indignam et fine operis, ubi rhetorum disciplina validiora quelibet collocari iubet'. All passages quoted from the two letters follow Pétrarque, *Lettres de la vieillesse (Rerum senilium)*, ed. E. Nota, 5 vols (Paris 2002–13) V (2013) 161–99 (citation, 163, § 4). For the English translation, Petrarch, *Letters of Old Age*, trans. A. Bernardo, S. Levin, and R. A. Bernardo, 2 vols (New York 2005) II 655–71.

[28] For the definition of the Griselda story as 'a development of some rationalized form of the Cupid and Psyche folktales', G. L. Kittredge, 'Arthur and Gorlagon', *Studies and Notes in Philology and Literature* 4 (1903) 149–275 (241, n. 4). Discussion in A. de Gubernatis, *De Sacountala à Griselda: le plus ancien des contes aryens* (Rome 1905); D. D. Griffith, *The Origin of the Griselda story* (Chicago 1931); W. Armistrad Cate, 'The problem of the origin of the Griselda story', *Studies in Philology* 29 (1932) 389–405; W. E. Bettridge and F. Lee Utley, 'New light on the origin of the Griselda story', *Texas Studies in Language and Literature* 13 (1971) 153–208.

[29] See G. Boccaccio, *Decameron*, ed. V. Branca, 2 vols (Turin 1992) II 1232, n. 6.

[30] § 1: 'Quisquis ex me queret, an hec vera sint, hoc est an historiam scripserim an fabulam, respondebo illud Crispi: Fides penes auctorem, meum scilicet Iohannem, sit'.

[31] § 1: 'nescio an res veras an fictas que iam non historie sed fabelle sunt ab hoc unum: quod res tue et a te scripte erant, quanvis hoc previdens fidem rerum penes auctorem, hoc est penes te, fore sim prefatus; et dicam tibi quid de hac historia, quam fabulam dixisse malim, mihi contingerit'.

important source of the tale itself, the Apuleian *fabula* of Cupid and Psyche, just as both meanings are implied in Boccaccio's defining of Griselda as 'ultima fabularum mearum'. In this latter case, Petrarch's use of *fabula* in epistles 3 and 4 would aim to establish a sort of pre-humanist dialogue with his friend and disciple Boccaccio on the Christian interpretation of the Cupid and Psyche myth. Petrarch had indeed a good knowledge of Apuleius' works, although he maintained in *Fam.* 22.2 (dated 1359) that he had read them with no attention:

> I read once amongst the works of Ennius, of Felix Capella, of Apuleius, and I read snatchingly, hastily, making no delay except, as it were, for other ends. As I passed over them in this way, it happened that I saw many things: I gathered a few; an even smaller number, I placed in the open and in the very forecourt—as I called it—of the memory.[32]

As both Robert Carver and Julia Gaisser have pointed out, Petrarch's *Legi semel* is contradicted by the evidence of his own manuscript copy.[33] Here the text of *The Golden Ass* has notes in Petrarch's hand written in two periods, *c.* 1340–43 and *c.* 1347–50, which suggests prolonged and repeated exposure to Apuleius' work. Textual echoes from Apuleius can be found in Petrarch's *Rerum memorandarum libri* and *Africa*. Moreover, he frequently introduces Apuleius into his letters, for example in the first epistle of the *Familiares* to Ludwig van Kempen, as well as in the penultimate epistle of the *Liber sine nomine*, in which the allusion is precisely to the fable of Cupid and Psyche.[34]

The evidence of Petrarch's sensitivity to Boccaccio's borrowings from Apuleius is not to be found in plain sight. Nor could it be, given the profound transformation of Boccaccio's original text—aptly defined as a *retexere*—and, more generally, Petrarch's humanistic attitude to dissimulating too close an imitation.[35] The most important thematic evidence that can confirm Petrarch's attention to the Apuleian model as a source of the Griselda tale is certainly his understanding of the common plot, which, as we have seen in both Apuleius and Boccaccio, revolves dialectically around two marriages. Upon this complex narrative dynamic of the Cupid and Psyche story, as well as on its later interpretations, Petrarch was able to build the allegory of his text.

The discovery of the Apuleian source in the *Decameron* must have suggested to Petrarch the invention of Griselda as a figure of the soul, according to Fulgentius' allegorical interpretation of the Cupid and Psyche story in *Myth.* 3.6. In Fulgentius, Psyche's betrayal of Cupid's faith allegorizes the soul's fall into sin due to an excessive desire for knowledge, a fall which requires a second covenant to restore the original faith. In Fulgentius' interpretation, Psyche's journey corresponds to the journey of the soul that tries to rejoin God, or in other words the history of Adam and, ultimately, the story of Griselda. And if this is true, a new

---

[32] 'Legi semel apud Ennium, apud Plautum, apud Felicem Capellam, apud Apuleium, et legi raptim, propere, nullam nisi ut alienis in finibus moram trahens. Sic praetereunti multa contigit ut viderem, pauca decerperem, pauciora reponerem eaque ut communia in aperto et in ipso, ut ita dixerim, memorie vestibulo'. See F. Petrarca, *Le familiari*, ed. V. Rossi, 4 vols (Florence 1933–42) IV (1942) 105–06, ll. 64–69.

[33] Vatican City, Biblioteca Apostolica Vaticana, *Vat. Lat.* 2193.

[34] See R. H. F. Carver, *The Protean Ass: The 'Metamorphoses' of Apuleius from Antiquity to the Renaissance* (Oxford 2007) 124–27; J. H. Gaisser, *The Fortunes of Apuleius and 'The Golden Ass': A Study in Transmission and Reception* (Princeton-Oxford 2008) 77–82. For Petrarch's glosses, see C. Tristano, 'Le postille del Petrarca nel ms. Vat. Lat. 2193 (Apuleio, Frontino, Vegezio, Palladio)', *Italia medioevale e umanistica* 17 (1974) 365–468.

[35] See, for example, his letter *Fam.* 22.2 to Boccaccio, which includes alternative readings for his *Bucolicum carmen* in order to avoid too close an imitation of Virgil and Ovid.

question arises: if Griselda always keeps her faith, why is she abandoned? That is, what is the actual reason for her fall? To answer this question, we need to reread Petrarch's envoy of the novella, which provides the necessary starting point for interpretation. The story of Griselda does not offer a model of patience that women should imitate but, rather, a model of firmness of faith in God that all Christians should follow. And if God puts us to the test— Petrarch adds—it is because He wants us to become aware of our own weakness. The text's final message is therefore entrusted to the praise of three virtues: patience in misfortunes, obedience to the divine law, and firmness of the faith. A more careful analysis can show that Griselda's virtues exactly correspond to the three Christian theological virtues, through which Griselda-Psyche, or the soul, can aspire to rejoin God. Gualtieri chooses Griselda, in fact, because she possesses Charity; she then keeps the Faith notwithstanding the terrible trials she has to undergo; and, finally, she does not abandon Hope even when Gualtieri sends her back to her father's house. Faith, as the most important of the three virtues, is mentioned again at the very end when Gualtieri reveals to his wife that he has intentionally put her to the test: 'Dear Griselda, I know your faithfulness well enough, I have observed it; and I do not believe there is anyone under the heavens who has reaped such great proofs of conjugal love'.[36] But Griselda's journey to salvation, like Psyche's, has been a hard path studded with trials. If she, unlike Psyche, accepts everything obediently, the divine secrets remain hidden from her and it is precisely this that represents her inner weakness. Griselda, like Psyche, is finally safe because she is disposed to lose everything, even her own life, for an infinite love, supported by the faith that is the authentic way to trust in God.

I believe it is clear at this point that the 'alius stilus' Petrarch adopted to translate the Griselda tale does not allude only to the choice of Latin as a linguistic medium, but also, and more properly, to the new allegorical interpretation hidden under the veil of the *fabula*. However, it has so far passed unnoticed that some allegorical elements were already present in Boccaccio's Griselda, elements which must have directed Petrarch's attention to the moral meaning of the novella. As Luca Carlo Rossi has pointed out, when Gualtieri sends Griselda away, Petrarch's formula 'Et camisiam tibi unicam habeto' (§ 31) depends not only on Boccaccio ('E tu una camiscia ne porta', § 46), but ultimately on Apuleius' 'tibique res tuas habeto' (*Met.* 5.26.6), which Petrarch glossed as 'formula divortii' in his MS.[37]

This provides clear evidence that Petrarch also drew on the source of the Griselda tale, the fable of Cupid and Psyche. But already in Boccaccio, Griselda's garment is an element that bears the allegorical meaning of wisdom. It is Martianus Capella, one of Boccaccio's sources for his exposition of the Cupid and Psyche myth in the *Genealogia*, who clarifies this meaning: among Minerva's gifts to Psyche, he says in *De nuptiis* 1.7, there is also the 'interula', which Remigius of Auxerre in his commentary on Capella's locus interprets as an allegory of the virtue of wisdom.[38] This allegory is clear to Petrarch, who uses not only the term 'camisia', like Boccaccio, but also 'tunica', like Remigio.[39] Wisdom is, in fact, the greatest of Griselda's virtues, and it is through wisdom that she can conquer Gualtieri's

---

[36] § 35: '"Satis" inquit "mea Griseldis, cognita et spectata michi fides est tua, nec sub cielo aliquem esse puto qui tanta coniugalis amoris experimenta perceperit"'.

[37] See Rossi, 'In margine alla Griselda' (n. 4, above) 154. For the meaning of the legal formula, Norden, *Apulejus von Madaura und das römische Privatrecht* (n. 10, above) 120.

[38] 'interiore tunica, hoc est supparo quod vulgo dicitur camisia. Per interulam designatur interior quaedam virtus, qua ipsam solam diligimus sapientiam quaque spretis omnibus aliis ipsi soli cupimus inhaerere'. See *Tutti i commenti a Marziano Capella*, ed. I. Ramelli (Milan 2006) 886. For the word 'interula', see *Florida* 9.18.

[39] § 31: 'Senex [...] tunicam eius hispidam et attritam senio, abdita parve domus in parte servaverat'.

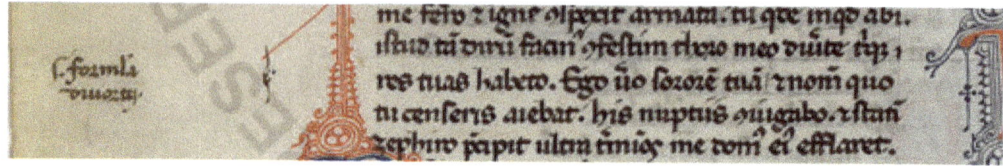

Figure 3. Vatican City, Biblioteca Apostolica Vaticana, *Vat. Lat.* 2193, f. 58v.

love. If Griselda's request to take only a garment with her already in Boccaccio allegorizes Salomon's request for wisdom, Petrarch makes this parallel explicit by representing Griselda as a public judge.

In *Seniles* 3 and 4, Petrarch argues that the inspiration for and content of Boccaccio's Griselda was fictive rather than historical. Such a criticism was probably aimed at his friend's declared unwillingness to clarify the genre to which his own tales properly belonged. We saw, in fact, that in the proem to the *Decameron*, one of the few sections that attracted Petrarch's attention ('libri principium finemque perspexi', ep. 3, § 3), Boccaccio vaguely termed his tales 'stories or fables or parables or histories', somewhat as Apuleius does in Lucius' metanarrative account of the Chaldaean oracle foretelling his future adventures: 'I will become a long story, an unbelievable tale, a book in several volumes'.[40] If this really were the content of Petrarch's criticism, a new reading of the *Decameron*, and this time a careful and thorough one, would have persuaded him that Boccaccio did not mean to seek refuge in the abstract fancies of *fabula*. Rather, Petrarch would have seen that Boccaccio sought to provide through it a different conception of history, one that would turn everyday life into a source of narrative realism of the type revealed in Fiammetta's principle of verisimilitude, described in her prologue to the last tale of the Calandrino cycle: 'in the telling of a story, to depart from the truth of things betided detracteth greatly from the listener's pleasure'.[41]

According to Vittore Branca, in the three Latin treatises *De mulieribus*, *De casibus*, and *Genealogia*, Boccaccio would go on to investigate the relationship between reality (or history) and imagination, and in *Genealogia* 14.9 he seems to answer Petrarch's persistent questions on this very relationship. Here, Boccaccio provides a general definition of *fabula* and particular definitions of its four kinds. The general definition reads: 'fiction is a form of discourse, which, under the guise of invention, illustrates or proves an idea; and, as its superficial aspect is removed, the meaning of the author is clear'.[42] But Boccaccio's focus is on the second kind of *fabula*, which at times superficially mingles fiction with truth. In this very blending, Boccaccio equates the writings of the Old Testament with those of the ancient poets: 'where history is lacking, neither one concerns itself with the superficial possibility, but what the poet calls fable or fiction our theologians have named figure'.[43]

In 'A philologist's remarks on memoria', Friedrich Ohly has emphasized the chronological continuity between ancient and medieval worlds, as well as the continuity between myth and history:

---

[40] *Met.* 2.12: 'nunc historiam magnam et incredundam fabulam et libros me futurum'.

[41] *Dec.* 9.5.5: 'il partirsi dalla verità delle cose state nel novellare è gran diminuire di diletto negl'intendenti'.

[42] 'Fabula est exemplaris seu demonstrativa sub figmento locutio, cuius amoto cortice, patet intentio fabulantis'.

[43] 'Nam, ubi absit hystoria, neuter de possibilitate superficiali curat, et quod poeta fabulam aut fictionem nuncupat, figuram nostri theologi vocavere'.

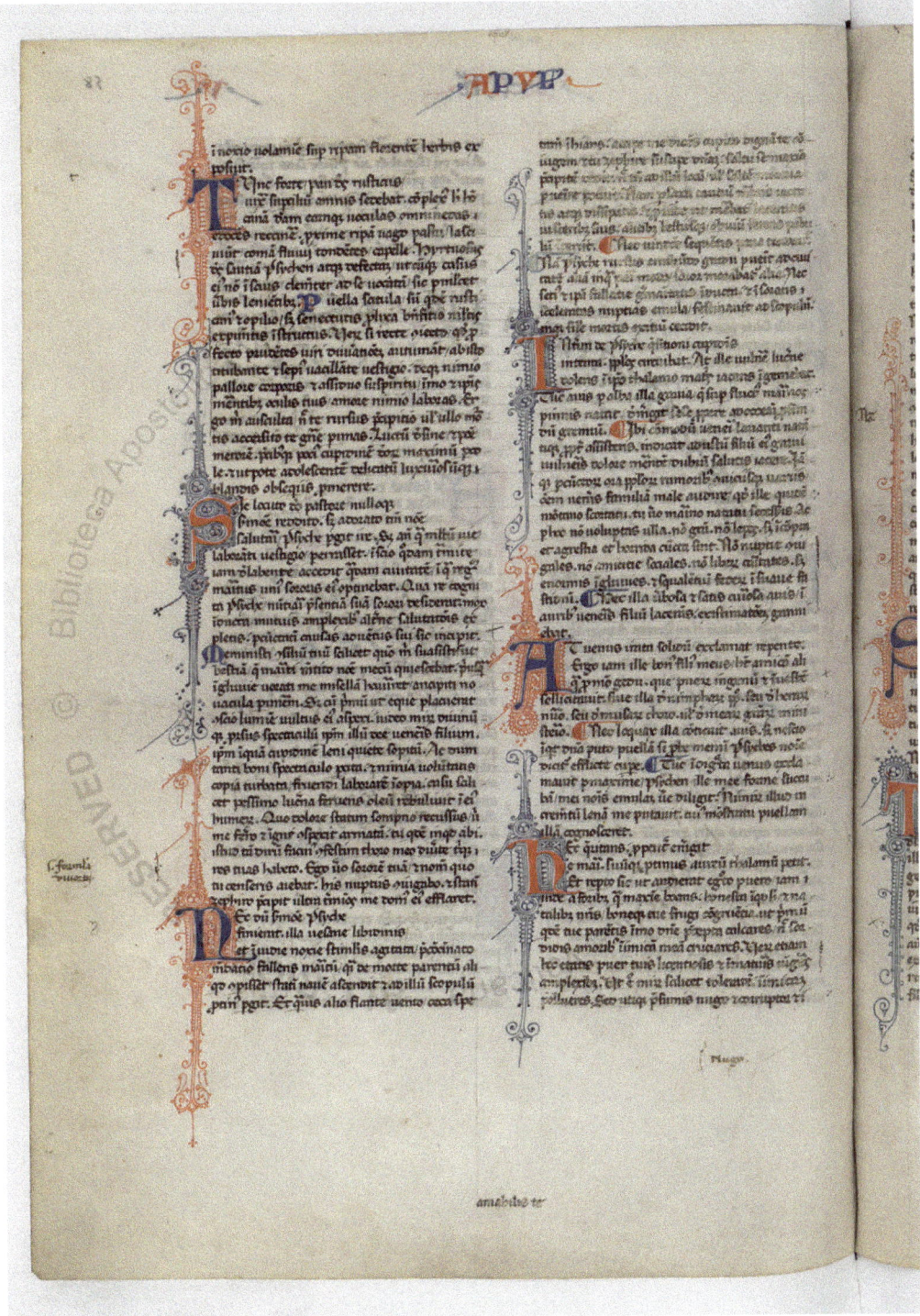

Figure 4. Vatican City, Biblioteca Apostolica Vaticana, *Vat. Lat.* 2193, f. 58v.

The clear distinction that was made, in antiquity and the Middle Ages, between the memory of the sufferings of the great, in the Middle Ages in history, and in antiquity in myth, in the Middle Ages in the *historia*, and in antiquity in the *fabula* or *fictio*, never excluded the possibility of a convergence and transmission of patterns between the two, or of a convergence between the mythical heroic legends of antiquity and a hagiography that claims to be historical.[44]

This continuity is palpable in narrators such as Apuleius and Boccaccio, who have so much in common, but also in Petrarch, whose Griselda tale, his unique narrative experiment, aims at historicizing fiction without losing the allegorical potential of the Apuleian fable. In *The Golden Ass*, the character of Lucius observes and registers reality from a new point of view, leading Gianfranco Gianotti to aptly speak of a peculiar and humorous application of the 'autopsìa' and the 'akoé', or the fundamental criterion of truthfulness that the ancient historiographical legacy has established for a reliable reconstruction of events. This is the only way that '*fabula* sanctions the historical importance of everyday life, putting it on the same level of important public events, while erudite historiography provides the *fabula* with the narrative tools it needs'.[45] Seen in this light, Apuleius' method shows a striking affinity with that of Boccaccio, as both aim at 'docere' and 'delectare', or in other words to provide 'diletto' and 'utile consiglio', upon which Boccaccio's own narrative art is entirely based. Likewise, Apuleius, through Boccaccio, lends Petrarch a unique narrative material upon which to build his own story of Griselda, destined to enjoy great appreciation from later writers precisely because it was meant to be history and hagiography at the same time.

Trinity College Dublin

---

[44]   F. Ohly, *Sensus Spiritualis: Studies in Medieval Significs and the Philology of Culture*, trans. K. J. Northcott, ed. S. P. Jaffe (Chicago 2004).

[45]   G. F. Gianotti, *Romanzo e ideologia: Studi sulle 'Metamorfosi' di Apuleio* (Naples 1986) 102–03 and 111.

AN APULEIAN MASQUE?
THOMAS HEYWOOD'S *LOVE'S MISTRESS* (1634)

STEPHEN HARRISON

I. Introduction

Thomas Heywood (*c.* 1570–1641) was a contemporary of Shakespeare and Jonson, and a vastly prolific author of dramas for the English stage as well as of many other literary works.[1] In 1633, towards the end of his career, he describes himself as having had 'an entire hand or at least a maine finger in two hundred and twenty plays'.[2] Twenty-three plays and eight masques survive which are wholly or partly by him, the best known of which is his tragedy *A Woman Killed with Kindness* (1603).[3] The classical education Heywood pursued at Cambridge is clear from the time of his early work in the 1590s: the poem *Oenone and Paris* (1594) makes use of Ovid's *Heroides* 5 as well as Shakespeare's *Venus and Adonis* (1593). Later, he published prose translations of Sallust's *Catiline* and *Jugurtha* (1608; from the French) and the first complete English verse translation of Ovid's *Ars Amatoria*, *Love's School* (*c.* 1610, popular and much reprinted).[4] His narrative poem *Troia Britannica* (1609) in seventeen *ottava rima* cantos, dedicated to James I, begins with the Creation and moves through classical mythology and the fall of Troy, before ending with a whirlwind history of Britain, from Brute's founding of London (or 'New Troy') to the accession of James (a structure which recalls that of Ovid's *Metamorphoses*). His spectacular, pageant-like plays known as *The Ages* followed, using many of the same classical myths. *The Golden Age* (printed 1611) tells the story of Saturn, Titan, and Jupiter; *The Silver Age* (printed 1612) concerns the further adventures of Jupiter and the early labours of Hercules; *The Brazen Age* (printed 1613) concerns the later labours of Hercules, and Jason and the Golden Fleece; and the two-part *The Iron Age* (printed 1632) tells the story of the Trojan War, strongly influenced by Shakespeare's *Troilus and Cressida*. In 1624, Heywood adapted Plautus' comedy *Rudens* for the London stage under another Plautine title, *The Captives*.[5]

Heywood's *Love's Mistress, or the Queen's Masque*, the object of this study, was a successful commercial play in 1634–5, which was then given court performances at Queen Henrietta Maria's personal theatre at Denmark House, including one on the king's birthday, 19 November 1635, as a present from the queen.[6] In its royal productions it was given new

---

[1]   For a convenient summary of his life and works, see D. Kathman, 'Heywood, Thomas (*c.* 1573–1641)', *ODNB* [http://www.oxforddnb.com/view/article/13190 (accessed 20 June 2016)].

[2]   T. Heywood, 'To the Reader', in *The English Traveller* (London 1633) A3.

[3]   For his dramatic career, see R. Rowland, *Thomas Heywood's Theatre, 1599–1639: Locations, Translations, and Conflict* (Farnham 2010).

[4]   For a study, see M. L. Stapleton, *Thomas Heywood's 'Art of Love'* (Ann Arbor 2000).

[5]   See Rowland, *Thomas Heywood's Theatre* (n. 3, above) 173–201.

[6]   The text used here is R. C. Shady, *Thomas Heywood, Love's Mistress, or The Queen's Masque* (Salzburg 1977); for the play's performance history, see R. C. Shady, 'The stage history of Thomas Heywood's *Love's Mistress*',

scenery by Inigo Jones and probably acquired its sub-title;[7] the text may well have been revised to give it more features of the contemporary court masque,[8] although it remains fundamentally a play-text (one much longer than those of masques, which are rarely more than a few hundred lines). Masques were spectacular big-budget entertainments for royal pleasure and participation with music, dance, and splendid scenery. In these productions, elevated characters were sometimes contrasted with low-life characters in an 'anti-masque' episode (*cf.* the clown and swains in *Love's Mistress*, discussed below).[9]

In *Love's Mistress* we see not only an interesting adaptation of the Apuleian story of Cupid and Psyche that has features of the Caroline court masque, but also a commentary by the author Apuleius, appearing as a character, which uses the kind of allegorical interpretation of the narrative favoured in Renaissance editions of the *Metamorphoses*. This allegorical element is another link with masques, in which characters were often allegorical abstracts and quasi-mythological plots had contemporary symbolism. We also see an eclectic use of other classical authors to generate a text which classically educated elite contemporaries would have appreciated, as well as clear uses of Shakespeare. The play was a success and was re-produced a number of times after the 1660 Restoration (Samuel Pepys records seeing it five times in the years 1661–68).[10] The present chapter adds to recent work on this drama, focusing particularly on the issue of its adaptation of classical sources.[11]

II. Cupid and Psyche: the Apuleian material

For the reader's convenience, I here set out a brief summary of the story of Cupid and Psyche as it is narrated in Apuleius' *Metamorphoses* (4.28–6.24), followed by a rough division of Apuleius' material into possible dramatic scenes. It is worth noting that dramatic adaptations of the Cupid and Psyche story were common from its first appearance in print in 1469.[12]

II.1. Summary of Apuleius 'Metamorphoses' 4.28–6.24

Psyche, a princess feted for her great beauty, thereby incurs the wrath of Venus and is told by an oracle that she will marry a terrifying winged monster and should be exposed on a rock. On the rock, and expecting death, she is taken away to the luxurious but mysterious palace of Cupid, who has fallen in love with her. Cupid visits her bed nightly but forbids her to see him face-to-face or to ask his identity. Psyche asks for her sisters to visit. They, jealous, make her curious and trick her into finding out who her husband is, suggesting that he is a monster and that she should kill him. On discovering what Psyche has done, Cupid leaves

Theatre Survey 18 (1967) 86–95; Rowland, *Thomas Heywood's Theatre* (n. 3, above) 234–35.

[7]   So Rowland, *Thomas Heywood's Theatre* (n. 3, above) 236.

[8]   So Rowland, *Thomas Heywood's Theatre* (n. 3, above) 286–87. For some of these, see below.

[9]   For the court masque genre, see *The Court Masque*, ed. D. Lindley (Manchester 1984) and, for some sample texts, D. Lindley, *Court Masques: Jacobean and Caroline Entertainments, 1605–1640* (Oxford 1995).

[10]   See Shady, *Thomas Heywood, Love's Mistress* (n. 6, above) xxxiv–xl.

[11]   For other work on the play's classical sources, see Shady, *Thomas Heywood, Love's Mistress* (n. 6, above) xli–lxiv, and, for its Apuleian adaptation, see briefly R. H. F. Carver, *The Protean Ass: The 'Metamorphoses' of Apuleius from Antiquity to the Renaissance* (Oxford 2007) 349–54. Rowland, *Thomas Heywood's Theatre* (n. 3, above) 233–97, the most recent and fullest study, concentrates on the play's cultural and political context, although it includes interesting observations on the figure and contemporary value of Apuleius.

[12]   *Cf. e.g.* C. Moreschini, *Il mito di Amore e Psiche in Apuleio* (Naples 1994) 12–26; J. H. Gaisser, *The Fortunes of Apuleius and the 'Golden Ass'* (Princeton-Oxford 2008) 193–95.

her. Psyche, now pregnant, tries and fails to commit suicide and searches for Cupid in various wanderings, while Venus, still hostile, harasses her. Psyche surrenders to Venus and is set a number of arduous tasks. Psyche completes these with indirect help from Cupid, but on her return from the final task, involving a descent to the Underworld, Psyche is again overcome by her curiosity and almost perishes on her return journey. She is rescued by Cupid and admitted to the company of the gods, where the pair, reconciled with Venus, live happily ever after, and have a daughter, Pleasure.

II.2. Division of original narrative into possible dramatic scenes[13]

AP1. *Met.* 4.28–35: The beginning of Psyche's story up to her arrival at Cupid's palace. [5 pages]

AP2. *Met.* 5.1–4: Psyche comes to the palace and is united with Cupid. [2 pages]

AP3. *Met.* 5.5–8: Psyche's sisters arrive at the palace and see its wonders. [2.5 pages]

AP4. *Met.* 5.9–20: Psyche's sisters incite her to kill Cupid as a monster. [7.5 pages]

AP5. *Met.* 5.21–4: Psyche's attempt to kill Cupid and the revelation of his true identity. [2.5 pages]

AP6. *Met.* 5.25–27: Psyche attempts suicide in the river, which rescues her, is comforted by Pan, and takes vengeance on her sisters. [2 pages]

AP7. *Met.* 5.28–31: Venus discovers Psyche's identity, rebukes Cupid, and furiously pursues Psyche, heedless of the attempts of Ceres and Juno to soften her. [3 pages]

AP8. *Met.* 6.1–5: Psyche asks Ceres and Juno for help in vain. [3 pages]

AP9. *Met.* 6.6–10: Psyche is sought by Venus via Mercury's proclamation and surrenders to her on Olympus. She is harshly treated and beaten. [3 pages]

AP10. *Met.* 6.11–16: First part of Psyche's enforced labours for Venus: (i) sorting out a heap of mixed grains, aided by ants; (ii) getting wool from golden-fleeced sheep, aided by the reed; (ii) fetching water from the cliff-top spring, aided by the eagle. [3 pages]

AP11. *Met.* 6.16–22: Psyche's last labour: descent to the Underworld to fill a box with Proserpina's face-powder. Psyche is advised in detail by a magic tower as to how to succeed and does so. On her return, Psyche opens the box and falls into a deep and deadly sleep, from which she is rescued by Cupid. [3 pages]

AP12. *Met.* 6.22–4: Jupiter makes Psyche a goddess after some negotiation. Cupid and Psyche are married and have a daughter, Pleasure. [1.5 pages]

---

[13] The page totals for particular scenes here should be set against the total of 38 pages for the whole tale in the English translation of P. G. Walsh, *Apuleius: The Golden Ass* (Oxford 1994).

III. Heywood's 'Love's Mistress'

Here, again for the reader's orientation, I give a summary of Heywood's play, which is approximately the same length as Apuleius' original. The metre is largely iambic pentameter, with occasional heroic couplets, some prose scenes, and lyric songs, very much in the Shakespearian manner. It is a free adaptation which retains the main narrative arc of Apuleius' plot. I have tried to indicate Heywood's main imitations and innovations, marking with an asterisk new scenes added by him.

Act 1 [Act 1 Scenes 2–4 = scene **AP1** from original; Scene 5 = scene **AP2** from original]

   Scene 1 Dialogue between Apuleius (holding a pair of ass' ears, alluding to his supposed identity with the asinine protagonist of his novel) and Midas, who tells the Ovidian story of his golden touch. Apuleius claims that his story of Cupid and Psyche will show (like Apollo's song in Ovid) that he is a true artist.
   Scene 2 Admetus the Arcadian king comes with his three daughters (Astioche, Petraea, and Psyche) to the Delphic oracle to ask about the future husband of the youngest (Psyche). Apollo replies with the response that Psyche should be exposed on a rock (as in Apuleius) and will marry a monster, but also reveals more of the future than the original (Psyche must not look at her husband but will eventually become immortal).
   Scene 3 Venus calls for her son Cupid, who comes and reports that Juno and Ceres were summoned but say they will come 'anon—forsooth'. Enter Pan and Apollo. Venus reports to them that men honour Psyche and not herself and appeals to them for help in revenge (if they encounter Psyche, they should get Mercury to bring her to Venus or imprison her themselves; Venus promises them a 'sweet kiss'). Cupid is asked to make Psyche fall in love with 'some ill-shapen drudge', but after all the others leave he says he has fallen in love with Psyche himself and calls on Zephyrus to carry Psyche to his palace.
   Scene 4 Psyche and her family are at the foot of the rock of exposure; Psyche's two noble brothers-in-law, Menetius and Zelotis, try to save her, but she insists on facing apparent death all alone. All lament, and Psyche's sisters promise to visit her the next day if she is still alive.
   Scene 5 Zephyrus rescues Psyche and takes her to a banquet in Cupid's palace. Her hesitant monologue is met by echoes (in the manner of Echo's speech in Ovid's *Metamorphoses* 3.359–401), and then by disembodied laughter. Zephyrus serves her with drink, and Cupid enters invisible to Psyche. The two lovers converse, and Cupid warns Psyche about her sisters.
   Scene 6 Re-enter Apuleius and Midas (*cf.* Scene 1). Apuleius refers to his time as an ass (*i.e.* the rest of the *Metamorphoses*), and introduces a sequence of dancing asses of various kinds and also some human types deemed to be asinine. Midas attacks poets and the story of Cupid and Psyche. Apuleius justifies his tale by a symbolic and allegorical moral interpretation of the story.

Act 2 [Act 2 Scene 1 = scene **AP3** from original; Scene 4 = scene **AP4** from original]

   Scene 1 Psyche welcomes her sisters to Cupid's palace [Echo again]—Astioche is envious of her sister's husband, Petraea glad for Psyche's good fortune.
   Scene 2 Admetus, Menetius, and Zelotis await the sisters' return; the sisters report Psyche's good fortune and return to her with Admetus' blessing.

Scene 3 Prose scene. A clown appears with several swains. They discuss Cupid and his powers, as celebrated by poets. On poetry, the clown gives a parodic summary of the *Iliad* as a pastoral comedy and of pastoral love, and gives cod translations of Latin phrases, defying Cupid. Cupid enters and punishes the clown with his arrow, which inspires love.

Scene 4. Psyche enters in doubt about her sisters. Cupid warns her. Her sisters return and Astioche urges Psyche to reveal and kill her monstrous husband.

Scene 5 Midas and Apuleius re-enter (*cf.* end of Act 1). Midas criticizes Apuleius' story and offers an Arcadian rustic dance in response. Apuleius then gives an allegorical moralizing account of his story (*cf.* end of Act 1 again).

Act 3 [Act 3 Scene 1 = scene **AP5** from original; Act 3 Scene 2 includes parts of **AP 9** and **AP 10**]

Scene 1 Psyche seeks to kill Cupid but is discovered and sent away [with dialogue] back to her father.

Scene 2 Clown, Amaryllis, and swains: in prose, the Clown reports a poetic contest between Pan and Apollo which is then staged in verse with Midas as judge; Apollo is represented by a choir of voices, Pan by the Clown (each sings a praise of their own god, short and elevated for Apollo, longer and more comic for Pan). Midas rules in favour of Pan and is cursed with ass's ears by Apollo. Psyche, transformed and ugly, returns to her father but is rejected by him and her sisters as an impostor. Her sisters recognize her eventually, her father still hesitates; Cupid intervenes but reluctantly rejects her for her disobedience. Her father now knows her but disowns her, banishing her from his court. Enter Mercury, who arrests Psyche to take her to Venus (she goes willingly). Venus, angry at Adonis' death, beats Psyche and imposes the first test of grain-sorting. Mercury helps Psyche and liberates Cupid to aid her in this task.

Scene 3 Dialogue of Midas and Apuleius commenting on the action of the story, punctuated by a dance; more allegorical moralizing interpretation of the narrative.

Act 4 [Act 4 Scene 1 has elements from **AP10** and **AP11** in the original]

Scene 1 Vulcan in his workshop with the Cyclopes complains of his workload and is visited by his son Cupid, who charms him into striking off his shackles despite Venus's ban. Psyche enters, having completed her first task, and seeks help from Cupid directly with her second, the filling of a vessel with infernal water. He cannot intervene personally but advises her what to do and she leaves. Enter Pan and Venus, Pan revealing to Venus that Cupid has fled to Vulcan for help. Venus rebukes both Cupid and Vulcan, who appeals to Pan, who asks for more work from Vulcan and makes fun of him as a cuckold. Psyche enters with the water and is given a third task, despite the pleas of Vulcan, Cupid, and Pan, to fetch a 'box of beauty' from Proserpina. Enter Mercury, who summons all the gods to appear 'at Ceres' plain / To entertain the fair Proserpina'. They all leave except Cupid. Psyche re-enters and Cupid gives her detailed advice on how to navigate the Underworld. Psyche's continuing ugliness is stressed (*cf.* Act 3 Scene 3).

Scene 2 Enter clown and swains, who comment on the actions of Cupid (prose scene). The clown again holds forth about poets (*cf.* Act 2 Scene 2): 'Homer was honourable, Hesiod Heroical, Virgil a Vicegerent, Naso Notorious, Martial a Provost, Juvenal a Jovial lad, and

Persius a Paramount'. Amaryllis is comically compared in beauty to Mopsa, with allusions to contemporary court fashions. The clown sings a comic song in praise of Amaryllis. The scene ends with a plan to steal for Amaryllis the box of beauty carried by Psyche.

Scene 3 As is now regular at the end of an act, Midas and Apuleius enter, Midas commending the last scene. Apuleius, to please the low taste of his companion, asks the Cyclopes to perform: ''Tis musick fitting thee, for who but knows / The vulgar are best pleased with noise and shows?'. They dance with Vulcan. The scene finishes with another allegorical commentary, this time on the meaning of Psyche's labours, and with a promise of successful passage through the Underworld and a happy ending.

Act 5 [Act 5 Scenes 1–2 expand scene **AP11** from original; Act 5 Scene 3 expands **AP 12**]

Scene 1 Mercury speaks to the assembled gods of the Underworld. It is a festival of Ceres to which Proserpina is invited, but first Psyche must carry out her errand. Proserpina and Pluto seem to support Venus in opposing Psyche and wishing to retain her in the Underworld. Comic Underworld apparatus (Charon, Aeacus, Minos [who sees fair play], Rhadamanthus, Cerberus); Mercury says Psyche has been forewarned of how to succeed, and the scene recalls the tests she passes in her journey in the original. Psyche abases herself and refuses infernal hospitality, vexing Pluto but allowing return to the world above with the box. Pluto admits she is worthy of being Cupid's wife and asks Proserpina to intervene with Venus in her favour. Proserpina is taken off to the festival by Mercury.

Scene 2 Back on earth, Cupid sees Psyche on her way back from the Underworld and witnesses her encounter with the Clown, who seeks to steal her box (see Act 4 Scene 2); he hopes to be a new Phaon (*cf.* Ovid, *Heroides* 15) or Corydon (Virgil, *Eclogue* 2). Psyche opens the box and falls asleep; Cupid substitutes another box for that of Proserpina, and this box is appropriated by the Clown, whom Cupid charms asleep. Cupid inveighs against women's vanity. Psyche awakes and is told by Cupid that she will be a goddess and to use the beauty. The Clown awakes after the magic and opens the box, which is full of ugly cosmetics. He now hopes to exceed Ganymede, Phaon, Cupid, and Corydon. Enter swains, Colin, Dickon, Hobinall, summoning the Clown for his wedding to Amaryllis. They laugh at his new appearance, but the Clown believes he looks good, and offers others the beauty from his box.

Scene 3 Venus comes to Arcadia to seek Psyche. Admetus says he would surrender her but she is not there. Apollo, Vulcan, and Pan plead for Psyche. Mercury enters with Proserpina and summons all those present to Ceres' annual festival. The queen is elaborately welcomed by all present. Cupid enters with a retransformed Psyche, who presents the box. Cupid reports their marriage and her apotheosis. Venus yields. Mercury asks Admetus to judge the two wicked sisters. Psyche asks for pity rather than revenge and the pair volunteer to be her handmaids. All are to attend Ceres' festival paired for dancing. A dance. Enter Midas and Apuleius. The former criticizes the latter's work, but Apuleius suggests that more intelligent spectators will understand its depth. Cupid intervenes and judges Midas a dull ass, Apuleius a poet, and suggests that the story of Psyche can be seen as 'doubly crown'd', concluding with an exhortation to faithful love.

IV. Heywood's modifications of the Apuleian original

Structurally, some of the most significant modifications in Heywood's version are the framing scenes between Apuleius and Midas, which commence each act and begin and end the play as a whole. In these scenes, the pair contest whether the play has a serious moral or not, a contest which, in some ways, symbolizes the dual nature of the piece as both comic entertainment and intellectually serious classical adaptation. The presentation of the tale's author as a character is unusual in versions of Cupid and Psyche, and here seems to encourage the spectator/reader to think about the Latin original and its author. The play's comic plot gains dignity from its explicit association with a Latin writer and text popular with Heywood's generation, especially since Adlington's English translation of 1566 and Lyly's adoption of Apuleius' elaborate prose style in English in *Euphues* (1578).[14] It also gathers intellectual weight from the allegorical commentary on the Psyche story repeatedly offered by Apuleius as character. This reflects the tradition of interpreting the love story of Cupid and Psyche as a moral and philosophical allegory, a tradition which goes back at least to Fulgentius in the sixth century CE and was popularized in the Renaissance by Beroaldo's commentary of 1500.[15] In the scenes in which this commentary is offered, it is commonly presented as a correction by Apuleius of the vulgar and foolish views of Midas, as, for example, in Act 1 Scene 6:

> *Apuleius*
> Misunderstanding fool, this much conceive,
> Psyche is *Anima*, Psyche is the Soul,
> The Soul, a virgin, longs to be a bride,
> The Soul's immortal, whom then can she woo
> But heaven? Whom wed but immortality?
> O blame not Psyche, then, if mad with rage
> She long for this so divine marriage.

Cupid's judgement as the divine arbiter in the final scene is that the story appeals to 'both the apt and dull', to both the intellectual and non-intellectual, but once again Apuleius the author is given what looks like an authoritative statement approving the more sophisticated approach (Act 5 Scene 3):

> *Apuleius*
> But there's an understanding that hath depth
> Beyond thy shallow nonsense; there's a wit,
> A brain which thou want'st, I to that submit.

The other key structural modification is the addition of the scenes with the clown and swains and their comic plot, which, as we shall see below, owes something to both the masque form and to Shakespearian comedy.

Another feature is the introduction of material from the other books of Apuleius' novel outside the Cupid and Psyche story (4.28–6.24) in Act 1 Scene 6. There Apuleius as character refers to his time in the shape of an ass in the *Metamorphoses* (3.25–11.13, two-thirds of the novel), incorporating the belief, common since Augustine's time (*De Civitate Dei* 18.18) and found in the preface to Adlington's 1566 translation, that Apuleius was narrating the story

---

14   See Carver, *Protean Ass* (n. 11, above) 327–64; Rowland, *Thomas Heywood's Theatre* (n. 3, above) 287–88.

15   See Carver, *Protean Ass* (n. 11, above) 174–82; Gaisser, *Fortunes of Apuleius* (n. 12, above) 197–242.

of his own metamorphosis in the person of his protagonist Lucius. To illustrate this episode, Heywood's Apuleius introduces a dumb-show sequence of dancing asses of various kinds[16] and also some human types deemed to be asinine:

> *Apuleius*
> If this displease thee, Midas, then I'll show thee
> Ere I proceed with Cupid and his love,
> What kind of people I commerced withal
> In my transhape.
> *Midas*
> That's when thou wert an ass?
> *Apuleius*
> The very same.
> *Midas*
> Yes, that I fain would see.

The list of asinine human types which then appear (the proud, the prodigal, the drunken, the usurer, a foolish young girl, the ignorant young man) looks like the *anteludia* or pre-festival parade of *Met.* 11.8, where a similar passing series of figures (including an ass) seems to represent some of the (often dubious) characters Lucius the protagonist has encountered in his time as an ass, shortly to come to an end.[17]

More generally, Heywood's version contains much more interaction between the two lovers than the original, where, after their initial marriage and separation, Cupid and Psyche really only meet up again when he saves her towards the end. This greater air-time for the couple together is shared with many Renaissance and early modern adaptations, putting romantic love at the centre of the story in a way that appealed to the period (we may compare La Fontaine's 1669 *Les Amours de Psyché et de Cupidon* for this same feature). In particular, Heywood makes Cupid help Psyche in her tasks for Venus directly rather than indirectly via the agency of others. There is also a larger role for Psyche's royal father and sisters, who acquire names (they are anonymous in the original). We shall see below that her father's name of Admetus recalls another specific classical source, as is also the case for her sisters' husbands (again named in Heywood but not in Apuleius), whose virtuous conduct, contrasted with the bad behaviour of their wives, perhaps has a Shakespearian source (see further below). In Heywood's version, the bad sisters are not killed but pardoned, reflecting a more Christian and decorous approach; he also allocates a more pronounced role to the pagan gods. The latter might reflect not only a feature of the masque genre (see further below) but also the context of the court of Charles I and Henrietta Maria, for which (as we have seen above) at least the revised extant version of the play was framed.

In the final act, the assembled gods are greeted by Mercury on behalf of Ceres and Jupiter (neither of whom appears) and invited to Ceres' festival (Act 5 Scene 3):

> To all these gods, to Venus and this train
> Health from the son of Saturn and queen Ceres.

---

[16]   On this scene, see Rowland, *Thomas Heywood's Theatre* (n. 3, above) 236.

[17]   See S. J. Harrison, 'Interpreting the *anteludia* (Apuleius, *Metamorphoses* 11.8)', *Trends in Classics* 4 (2012) 377–87.

The pairing of these two gods here (and the immediately following mention of their daughter Proserpina) suggests that they are a divine couple parallel to the royal couple. In this regard, it is notable that Juno, Jupiter's usual divine consort, is only mentioned once, early on in a passing allusion to the Latin original (in Act 1 Scene 3), and does not appear as a character, even though (as already noted) Heywood's version allots more space to the pagan gods, with Pan, Apollo, Mercury, Vulcan, Pluto, and Proserpina all making personal appearances. In the last act, Ceres' role as an honoured but non-speaking hostess and 'queen of fertility' (Act 5 Scene 3) might in fact reflect the role of Henrietta Maria, who would have been heavily pregnant at the performance of the play on the king's birthday in November 1635, since she was to give birth to Princess Elizabeth on December 28th. There are further possible hints towards the royal pair at the end of Heywood's play, where Cupid refers to Psyche as 'doubly crown'd' and exhorts the audience to fidelity in love, highly appropriate for a queen's birthday present to a king (Act 5 Scene 3):

And then this legacy I leave behind,
Where'er you love, prove of one faith, one mind.

Another clear feature of Heywood's adaptation of the original is the insertion of a range of non-Apuleian classical material. Amongst the more evident instances, in Act 1 Scene 1 we have a summary of the story of Midas' acquisition of his golden touch (from Ov. *Met.* 11.85–145), while Midas receives his own ass' ears as a mark of his ignorance as a poetic judge in Act 3 Scene 2, reworking another story about him from the same sources (Ov. *Met.* 11. 172–193). Ovid's *Metamorphoses*, perhaps the most read classical text of Heywood's period,[18] is again drawn upon for a contribution in Act 1 Scene 5 and Act 2 Scene 1, where Psyche's speeches in Cupid's palace are answered by exact echoes of her closing words in the manner of Echo's speeches in Ov. *Met.* 3.359–401. No doubt Heywood was aware of Apuleius' own great debt to Ovid's poem, prominently advertised in the title of his work, *Metamorphoses*, and clear enough to intelligent readers of both texts.[19] Epic allusion is not limited to Ovid: in Act 4 Scene 1, where Vulcan, in his workshop with the Cyclopes, complains of his workload, we clearly have an entertaining version of the episode in which Vulcan urges on his workers to complete the shield of Aeneas in Virgil's *Aeneid* (*Aen.* 8.423–53). Vergilian poetry is alluded to again in Act 4 Scene 2, where Amaryllis is comically compared in beauty with Mopsa. Amaryllis is a common name of a beloved in the *Eclogues* (*Ecl.* 1, 2, 3, and 8), in which Mopsus (the masculine version of Mopsa, not a classical name itself) is also used as a shepherd's name (*Ecl.* 5 and 8). Similarly, in Act 5 Scene 2 the clown hopes to be a new Corydon (the male lover of *Ecl.* 2) once equipped with Proserpina's beauty. Pastoral allusions are not restricted to Latin pastoral: the names of Heywood's swains (Act 2 Scene 3)—Colin, Dickon, and Hobinall—are drawn from Spenser's *The Shepheardes Calender* of 1579. As we shall see, pastoral colour was a common feature of the masque genre.

Another classical text deployed in the play is the *Homeric Hymn to Demeter*, which emerges in Act 5 Scene 1. There, in an elaborate simile spoken by Mercury, we find the

---

[18] See *e.g.* S. Keilen, 'Shakespeare and Ovid', H. James, 'Ben Jonson's Light Reading', P. Hardie, 'Spenser and Ovid', and D. Hooley, 'Ovid translated: early modern versions of the *Metamorphoses*', all in *A Handbook to the Reception of Ovid*, eds J. F. Miller and C. E. Newlands (Chichester 2014) 232–45, 246-61, 291–305, and 339–354.

[19] For this debt, see S. J. Harrison, 'Ovid in Apuleius' *Metamorphoses*', in *A Handbook to the Reception of Ovid*, eds J. F. Miller and C. E. Newlands (Chichester 2014) 86–99.

curious story of Iambe (*h. Dem.* 202–5), the old woman who made Demeter laugh despite her mourning for her kidnapped daughter, and who thus became the origin of iambic poetry:

> singing mirthful lays,
> Such as Iambe, Metaneira's maid,
> Sung, when she mourned her daughter's ravishment.

Later in the same scene we find Mercury commanded by Pluto to take Proserpina off to the festival of Ceres for six months, using Ovid's doubling in the *Metamorphoses* (5.564–7) of the three-month stay that we find in the *Homeric Hymn* (460–69):

> Here, Hermes, take my queen Proserpina;
> Return her when the sister of the sun
> Hath six times compassèd her silver sphere.

It may be that these allusions were prompted by George Chapman's relatively recent first translation of the *Homeric Hymns* into English (1624).[20]

A further classical genre found in Heywood's play is that of Greek tragedy. The naming of Psyche's royal father, anonymous in the original, as Admetus inevitably points the classically educated reader to the plot of Euripides' *Alcestis*. There, the noble queen Alcestis is willing to suffer death to save her husband Admetus, and it is in the spirit of Alcestis that, in Act 1 Scene 4, Heywood has Psyche insist on facing apparent death all alone. This context of a daughter nobly insisting on self-sacrifice as the consequence of a prophecy also looks to the story of Euripides' *Iphigenia at Aulis*, in which Psyche plays the part of the dutiful Iphigenia and Admetus that of the agonized royal father Agamemnon, torn between sparing his daughter and insisting on the fulfilment of the prophecy.

This deployment of material from various classical genres in his version of the Cupid and Psyche story might reflect an intelligent reading of Apuleius' narrative by Heywood. Modern scholars agree that Apuleius' *Metamorphoses*, and especially its Cupid and Psyche section, draws on a broad range of classical poetic genres, primarily epic but also pastoral, elegy, tragedy, comedy, and satire, to create a rich and entertaining literary texture.[21]

Given the work's subtitle and the likelihood that it was made more masque-like for its later court performances (see section 1 above), it is also worth considering what features of the masque tradition it displays in its adaptation of the original.[22] The overall argument between Apuleius and Midas as to whether the story has a substantive content and moral significance perhaps points towards the general anxiety of the masque genre about its intellectual seriousness, given that it was essentially aimed at dazzling the audience with spectacular effects. This is famously expressed in Jonson's introduction to *Hymenaei*, a masque written for the marriage of the third Earl of Essex in 1606, in which the poet presents two levels of appreciation of his work:

---

[20] In G. Chapman, *The Crowne of All Homers Works* (London 1624).

[21] See *e.g. Cupid and Psyche: Aspects of Apuleius' 'Golden Ass' II*, eds M. Zimmerman, T. D. McCreight, D. van Mal-Maeder, S. Panayotakis, V. Schmidt, and B. Wesseling (Groningen 1998), and S. J. Harrison, *Framing the Ass: Literary Texture in Apuleius' 'Metamorphoses'* (Oxford 2013). Literary allusions in 'Cupid and Psyche' may be fully traced via M. Zimmerman, S. Panayotakis, V. Hunink, W. H. Keulen, S. J. Harrison, T. D. McCreight, B. Wesseling, and D. van Mal-Maeder, *A Commentary on Apuleius 'Metamorphoses' IV.28–VI.24* (Groningen 2004).

[22] More particular suggestions on masque-style staging in *Love's Mistress* are made by K. Britland, *Drama at the Court of Queen Henrietta Maria* (Cambridge 2006) 140–41.

This it is hath made the most royal princes, and greatest persons (who are commonly the personaters of these actions) not only studious of riches, and magnificence in the outward celebration or shew, which rightly becomes them ; but curious after the most high and hearty inventions, to furnish the inward parts ; and those grounded upon antiquity, and solid learning : which though their voice be taught to sound to present occasions, their sense or doth or should always lay hold on more removed mysteries. And howsoever some may squeamishly cry out, that all endeavor of learning and sharpness in these transitory devices, especially where it steps beyond their little, or (let me not wrong them,) no brain at all, is superfluous: I am contented, these fastidious stomachs should leave my full tables, and enjoy at home their clean empty trenchers, fittest for such airy tastes.[23]

This nicely parallels the Apuleius/Midas contest in Heywood, and we may also note the reference to 'inventions [...] grounded upon antiquity, and solid learning'. Classical learning is a regular feature of Jacobean and Caroline masques, and pagan deities are regular figures in them; Jonson's own *The Hue and Cry after Cupid* (1606) is a dramatized version of Moschus' Hellenistic poem on Eros the runaway (Moschus 1). Allegorization of classical figures is also common, not just in the representation of monarchs, princes, and royal favourites as gods or heroes like Hercules (as in Jonson's *Pleasure Reconciled to Virtue*, 1618), but also in more explicitly allegorical functions, as in the presentation of Circe as Desire in Aurelian Townshend's *Tempe Restored* (1632). As already noted, the comic elements of the pastoral clown and swains parallel similar characters found in the anti-masque sections of masques which presented low-status characters for humorous effect, for example the Country Clown in Francis Beaumont's *The Masque of the Inner Temple and Gray's Inn* (1613). Indeed, even the comic Vulcan and his hammering Cyclopes recall the Cyclopes hammering on stage in Jonson's *The Hue and Cry after Cupid*.

A final element of adaptation would seem to be the likely use of two Shakespearian plays, readily available after the Second Folio of 1632; as we saw earlier, Heywood had imitated Shakespeare from the earliest days of his literary career. The first of these is *A Midsummer Night's Dream*. In Act 1 Scene 3, Cupid is ordered by Venus to make Psyche fall in love with 'some ill-shapen drudge', following the Apuleian original (*Met.* 4.31.3, 'See that the girl is seized with consuming passion for the lowest possible specimen of humanity').[24] In Apuleius, this is ironically reversed as it is Cupid himself who falls in love with the girl, as also happens in Heywood. But in *Love's Mistress*, the idea of Cupid making a figure fall catastrophically in love is also repeated, in Act 2 Scene 3 where Cupid enters and punishes the clown with his arrow for defiance of his power, which inspires love (eventually) for the old and ill-favoured Amaryllis. The mild resemblance of this scene to the Oberon-inspired infatuation of Titania for the lowly weaver Bottom in *A Midsummer Night's Dream* is clear (both are punishments from a male power figure), but it is in Act 5 Scene 2 that the parallel with Shakespeare's play seems most likely. There the clown awakes after being charmed to sleep by Cupid and uses the ointments from the box Cupid has left him, which he thinks make him handsome but in fact make him ugly, as his lowly companions confirm. Here, it is hard not to see an allusion to *A Midsummer Night's Dream* Act 3 Scene 1, where Bottom's transformation into an ass feels good to him but terrifies his companions.

[23]   B. Jonson, *Hymenaei or The Solemnities of Masque, and Barriers* (London 1606) A3–4.

[24]   Trans. Walsh, *The Golden Ass* (n. 13, above).

The second Shakespearian play relevant to Heywood's Apuleian adaptation is *King Lear*. Apuleius' scenario of one virtuous sister and two less virtuous ones would naturally recall Shakespeare's plot of the sisters Cordelia, Goneril, and Regan. Heywood's extension of the roles of the two evil sisters' husbands (already noted above), making them virtuous characters who contrast with their wives (*cf.* Act 1 Scene 4, where they try to save Psyche), might recall the ultimate attempts of Goneril's husband Albany to restrain his wife and her sister in their villainy. The link with *King Lear* seems irresistible in Act 3 Scene 2, where Psyche, disfigured by Cupid's intervention and unrecognizable, is banished from her father's court with her sisters approval, a comic and softer version of Lear's effective exiling of Cordelia in the opening scene of Shakespeare's tragedy. When Admetus says, not recognizing Psyche, 'Thou art no child of mine', it is hard not to see a reference to Lear's fully conscious denial of his daughter, 'we / Have no such daughter'.[25]

A fascinating question arises in connection with both of these Shakespearian plays. Modern scholarship on the reception of Apuleius is clear that Lucius' metamorphosis into an ass in Apuleius' *Metamorphoses* is a very likely source for the asinine transformation of *A Midsummer Night's Dream*, and that Psyche and her two sister princesses are probable models for the three royal daughters of *King Lear*.[26] Could Heywood have realized that the Shakespearian episodes he imitates were, themselves, probably Apuleian in origin? Given his considerable classical learning, it is not impossible.

V. Conclusion

This analysis hopes to have shown that *Love's Mistress* is a literary work of considerable interest which deploys a number of sophisticated strategies in its adaptation of Apuleius' Latin prose fiction tale of Cupid and Psyche into a verse play for the English Caroline stage and court. It reshapes the original in the light of the Renaissance tradition of allegorical Apuleian commentary, uses elements from a range of classical literary genres other than that of the novel, shows evidence of crossing the traditional stage play with the courtly masque, and likely echoes some famous Shakespearian scenarios. Above all, the classically educated Heywood seems to have realized the literary complexity and allusivity of his Apuleian original, and to have sought to reflect this in the complex texture of his own work.

Corpus Christi College, University of Oxford

---

[25]   On this link, see further Carver, *Protean Ass* (n. 11, above) 352.

[26]   See Carver, *Protean Ass* (n. 11, above) 429–445.

ECHOES OF APULEIUS' NOVEL IN MARY TIGHE'S *PSYCHE*: ROMANTIC IMAGINATION AND SELF-FASHIONING

REGINE MAY

Mary Tighe (1772–1810) wrote a Spenserian adaptation (first published in 1805) of 'Cupid and Psyche' in six cantos: *Psyche or The Legend of Love*.[1] This paper argues that despite Tighe's claims to know little of the rest of the *Metamorphoses*, there is ample evidence from her poem that she read Apuleius' novel beyond 'Cupid and Psyche', especially in cantos III–VI, which are less close to the story as set out in Apuleius. This explicit denial of much knowledge of Apuleius beyond 'Cupid and Psyche' appears in a letter to a close friend and mentor: 'I know little of it I assure you but my own story'.[2] However, her claim here is both part and consequence of Tighe's self-fashioning as a poet. In the preface to *Psyche* (xiii–xiv), she goes to great lengths to reassert her own originality, denying knowledge of other imitations of Apuleius, who alone is her model, and only in the first two cantos:[3]

> The loves of *Cupid and Psyche* have long been a favourite subject for poetical allusion, and are well known as related by Apuleius: to him I am indebted for the outline of my tale in the two first cantos; / [xiv] but even there the model is not closely copied, and I have taken nothing from Moliere, La Fontaine, Du Moustier, or Marino. I have seen no imitations of Apuleius except by those authors; nor do I know that the story of Psyche has any other original. I should willingly acknowledge with gratitude those authors who have, perhaps, supplied me with many expressions and ideas; but if I have subjected myself to the charge of plagiarism, it has been by adopting the words or images which floated upon my mind, without accurately examining, or being indeed able to distinguish, whether I owed them to my memory or my imagination.

Taking this claim to originality literally may be one of the reasons why English scholars tend not to study Tighe's reception of ancient texts, especially not beyond the narrower focus of 'Cupid and Psyche' rather than the *Met.* as a whole,[4] have not so far critically tested Tighe's claims of independence from Apuleius, and have not analysed the similarities and differences to Apuleius in all six cantos. But Tighe was an excellent Latinist, capable of reading and

---

[1] M. Tighe, *Psyche; or The Legend of Love* (London 1805).

[2] Mary Tighe to Joseph Cooper Walker (co-founder of the Royal Irish Academy), 6 September 1803, cited in A. Buchanan, *Mary Blachford Tighe: The Irish Psyche* (Newcastle upon Tyne 2011) 175 n. 41.

[3] Unless otherwise stated, quotations from Tighe follow M. Tighe, *Psyche. With Other Poems. By the Late Mrs. Henry Tighe* (London 1811, 3rd edn).

[4] For an overview of authors and topics, see H. Linkin Kramer, 'Mary Tighe and literary history: the making of a critical reputation', *Literature Compass* 7 (2010) 564–76. Even A. Hoffmann, *Das Psyche-Märchen des Apuleius in der englischen Literatur* (Strasbourg 1908) 61–81 does not notice allusions to the rest of the *Metamorphoses*, stating that 'die Abhängigkeit von Apuleius ist auf das Mindestmass reduziert' (69).

using the whole novel.[5] My intention is to show that this is precisely what she did.

Educated by her formidable Methodist mother, and encouraged by her husband, who loved the Classics[6] and taught her to read Latin, Tighe was a voracious reader; her reading journal, kept from 1806 to 1809, lists over 200 items.[7] She was well versed in Latin, French, Italian, and other languages, and liberally cited poems in these languages in her work. She was familiar with Catullus, Horace, Tibullus, and Aulus Gellius, and in the footnotes to her own works she cites authors from Valerius Flaccus to Achilles Tatius.[8]

Her motto for *Psyche* sets the scene for her Latinate readership. It is a quotation of Martial 10.35.8, a poem about the poetess Sulpicia: 'Sed castos docet et pios amores'.[9] She thus claims the ability of female authors not only to write about chaste love affairs, but also to be able to make them acceptable to a contemporary mindset influenced by sensibility and Christianity.

Her preface to the 1805 edition furthermore cites La Rochefoucauld in French and Ben Jonson's *The Alchemist*, and ends with Terence's *Eunuchus* quoted in Latin, while Ariosto is quoted in Italian between her dedicatory sonnet to her mother and the actual text of *Psyche*. Even the adaptations of Apuleius she admits to having read[10] are already classics in their own right, and Tighe's status is enhanced by her ability to appreciate French and Italian poems while maintaining her independence from them at the same time. The Spenserian form of the poem nods to Psyche's brief presence in *The Faerie Queene*.[11] There is no doubt that Tighe wants to present herself as a learned yet original poetess.

Studies of Tighe in recent years have focused on her self-fashioning as a female poet. Linkin Kramer, for example, highlights the obvious parallels between Psyche and Tighe's own life as a society beauty, which Tighe stresses repeatedly,

> but with an important difference: she contrasts Psyche as the archetypal romanticized object of desire who transgresses when she looks at Cupid with herself as the narrating woman poet who insists on her capacity to compose visionary poetry when Romantic-era culture teaches her to be the muse.[12]

---

[5]   See Hoffmann, *Psyche-Märchen* (n. 4, above) 69–70 for evidence that Tighe studied the text in Latin.

[6]   Buchanan, *Mary Blachford Tighe* (n. 2, above) 34, 77, and 81. It was also Henry Tighe who encouraged her to publish *Psyche*: H. Linkin Kramer, 'Skirting around the sex in Mary Tighe's 'Psyche'', *Studies in English Literature, 1500–1900* 42 (2002) 731–52 (733).

[7]   Buchanan, *Mary Blachford Tighe* (n. 2, above) 8.

[8]   In footnotes to her 1803 manuscript, V. Fl. 5.109–11. On Sinope, on the Greek novels on Pan and Syringa, see M. Tighe, *The Collected Poems and Journals*, ed. H. Linkin Kramer (Lexington, KY 2005) 301–302, and xv for an astonishing list of influences.

[9]   In Tighe, *The Collected Poems* (n. 8, above) 295, Linkin Kramer notes that Tighe changed the Latin from 'probos' to 'pios', but both readings are transmitted in respective archetypes, see M. Valerii Martialis, *Epigrammata*, ed. D. R. Shackleton Bailey (Stuttgart 1990) *ad loc.*

[10]   Molière's *Psyché* (1671); Jean de La Fontaine's *Les Amours de Psyché et Cupidon* (1669); Charles Albert Demoustier's *Lettres à Emilie sur la mythologie* (1792–98); Giovan Battista Marino's *L'Adone* (1623).

[11]   In Spenser, Psyche appears briefly for nine lines (book 3, canto 6), as the teacher in true femininity of Amoret (3.6.51), together with her daughter Pleasure. For a detailed discussion of Tighe's reception of this passage, see E. M. Goss, 'A training in "feminitee": Edmund Spenser, Mary Tighe, and reading as a lover', *Texas Studies in Literature and Language* 56 (2014) 259–91, who argues that Tighe's poem offers the prequel and background story to Spenser's instructress of love; Tighe sets out how Psyche was able to become the kind of teacher needed for Amoret as a model of achievable earthly love. For Spenser's wider use of Apuleius, see R. H. F. Carver, *The Protean Ass: The 'Metamorphoses' of Apuleius from Antiquity to the Renaissance* (Oxford 2007) 384–428.

[12]   Tighe, *The Collected Poems* (n. 8, above) xxiii. See also: A. Henderson, 'Keats, Tighe, and the chastity of

Psyche's transgression is to look at something forbidden, while Tighe's visionary inspiration continues until the very last stanza of the poem, when the inspiration ceases. Tighe knows that any unpleasant associations between herself and Psyche would damage her own reputation as a poet.

I will put Tighe's claims of relative ignorance of the rest of the *Metamorphoses* to the test by looking at echoes of and references to the rest of the novel in her *Psyche* poem. This is important because if Tighe claims little knowledge of the bawdy story of Lucius while still making considerable use of it, this has implications for our understanding of her self-fashioning as a poet and her reluctance to be associated with anything Apuleian other than the more romantic story of 'Cupid and Psyche'. We therefore need to analyse any evidence for the use of the whole of the *Metamorphoses*, both in the first two cantos, which are more directly inspired by 'Cupid and Psyche', as well as in the more allegorical, quest-like Spenserian cantos III–VI. Linkin Kramer calls the latter four cantos a 'sharp revision of the myth', which has 'nothing to do with the completion of punitive domestic tasks for Venus', and stresses their difference from Apuleius.[13] At first glance, Tighe seems to be correct to claim some distance from Apuleius' story.

In the first two cantos, Tighe starts *medias in res*[14] with Psyche, exhausted, resting on a flowery bank after having discovered Cupid's true identity and having lost both Cupid and his palace. In a flashback, her story up to this point is told, partly echoing Apuleius' version, partly deviating from it. At the end of canto II, the ring closes and we see Psyche again on that flowery bank. In cantos III–VI, Tighe takes Psyche on a Spenserian allegorical *psychomachia*,[15] visually echoing Redcrosse, Una, and her lion: accompanied by a knight in armour (Cupid in disguise) who places her on his white steed, his attendant Constance, and a lion symbolizing passion, Psyche goes on a quest to find the urn of Beauty for Venus. Once this urn is placed on Venus' altar, Cupid and Psyche can be reunited. On this quest, they encounter several allegorical figures, including Innocence, Vanity, Ambition, Chastity, and Jealousy. Although personifications of emotions, virtues, and sins are already present in Apuleius, where Sobriety is Venus' servant and Sadness her enemy,[16] it is clear that the last four cantos are indeed different from Apuleius' story. Therefore, let us first look at some similarities and differences between 'Cupid and Psyche' and Tighe's first two cantos, in which Tighe claims at least some inspiration from Apuleius.

Differences between Tighe and Apuleius in cantos I and II

In terms of plot, Tighe does not follow Apuleius slavishly. For example, like a contemporary society belle, and like Tighe herself, Psyche had many suitors (12):

> [...] By many a royal youth had oft been wooed;
> Low at her feet full many a prince had sued,

---

allegory', *European Romantic Review* 10 (1999) 279-306; G. Kucich, 'Gender crossings: Keats and Tighe', *Keats-Shelley Journal* 44 (1995) 29–39.

[13]   Tighe, *The Collected Poems* (n. 8, above) xxii–iii.

[14]   One of the many epic features; others include epic similes or appeals to the Muse. Buchanan, *Mary Blachford Tighe* (n. 2, above) 68 argues that Tighe can rely on the familiarity of her readers with the story.

[15]   Tighe herself calls it 'the beautiful ancient allegory of Love and the Soul' (preface to 1811 edition, x).

[16]   Apul. *Met.* 5.30; 6.8–9. Carver, *Protean Ass* (n. 11, above) 398–405 points out that Una's character in Spenser is already inspired by Apuleius' Psyche. Tighe's Psyche thus comes full circle.

And homage paid unto her beauty rare;
But all their blandishments her heart withstood [...]

In Apul. *Met.* 4.32,[17] Psyche is devastated because no suitor is interested in her at all:

Meanwhile, Psyche, for all her striking beauty gained no reward for her ravishing
looks. She was the object of all eyes, and her praise was on everyone's lips, but no
king or prince or even commoner courted her to seek her hand.

Psyche's family, too, is sketched in a more realistic way in Tighe; her sisters are jealous
of her already before her marriage to Cupid,[18] because Psyche was worshipped and courted
far and wide (13):

But envy of her beauty's growing fame
Poisoned her sisters' hearts with secret gall,
And oft with seeming piety they blame
The worship which they justly impious call;
And oft, lest evil should their sire befall,
Besought him to forbid the erring crowd
Which hourly throng'd around the regal hall,
With incense, gifts, and invocations loud,
To her whose guiltless breast, ne'er felt elation proud.

There is no mention of their jealousy in Apuleius until they visit her several times after her
marriage (*Met.* 5.4).

Tighe's Psyche never feels a desire to avenge her fate on her sisters, whereas Apuleius'
Psyche lures both of them to their deaths. Psyche wishes to visit her parents, especially her
mother, in Tighe, who herself had a very close relationship with her own mother (canto I,
38),[19] and even leaves Cupid's palace to visit her family (canto II, 47), thus turning into a
more actively engaged young lady than Apuleius' Psyche, who can merely beg Cupid to
allow her sisters to visit. Whereas Apuleius' parents never see their daughter again, Tighe's
royal parents are relieved to see their daughter happily married to a figure whom they guess
rightly to be a god (48).

Apuleius' Psyche attempts suicide several times, but Tighe's sensible Psyche both never
contemplates it and more actively seeks help in her quest (67):

Hoping to find some skilled in secret fate,
Some learned sage who haply might disclose
Where lay that blissful bower the end of all her woes.

In Apuleius we hear about Cupid's love at first sight for Psyche only after her betrayal and
from his own mouth (*Met.* 5.24):

'Poor, ingenuous Psyche, [...] I preferred to swoop down to become your lover. I
admit that my behaviour was not judicious; I, the famed archer, wounded myself with
my own weapon, and made you my wife.'

---

[17]   All Apuleius translations are taken from: Apuleius, *The Golden Ass*, trans. P. G. Walsh (Oxford 1994).

[18]   Also noticed in Hoffmann, *Psyche-Märchen* (n. 4, above) 69–70.

[19]   The introductory sonnet to Psyche is addressed to her mother, making the poem a present of daughterly duty to
Theodosia Blachford.

Tighe's report of the events is both chronological and sensual, in a celebrated scene of mutual gazing (21):

> He sought the chamber of the royal maid;
> There, lulled by careless soft security,
> Of the impending mischief nought afraid,
> Upon her purple couch was Psyche laid,
> Her radiant eyes a downy slumber sealed.

Tighe's scene is generally very different from Apuleius' depiction: Cupid gives the sleeping Psyche the cup of anguish first (22), but also wounds and wakes her with his own arrow, and then, possibly accidentally, uses the same arrow on himself (23), whereupon he adds drops of joy for Psyche. The moment of falling in love is mutual, and Psyche has a vision of Cupid, although she is not sure whether it is real or a dream.[20] In Apuleius, Psyche only falls in love with Cupid much later, in the moment she holds the lamp over him and accidentally handles his arrows. Tighe's romantic couple falls in unceasing mutual love with each other at the same time.

Whereas there is doubt about the legality of the marriage of Cupid and Psyche in Apuleius,[21] Tighe's poem of sensibility ensures that there is no doubt that the marriage is valid. Hymen is invoked during the coyly described wedding night (34) and becomes an allegorical helper figure for the couple in the later cantos. Despite Psyche's betrayal of trust, Cupid never falls out of love with her. Crucially, there is no conversation between Cupid and Psyche after she wounds him with her lamp, and Tighe's Psyche does not try to cling on to Cupid flying away: Cupid's palace simply disappears around her (58). Then she hears the unseen Cupid's voice, who prophesies a future union between them if she only manages to appease Venus (62). His continued invisibility here, whereas Apuleius' Cupid no longer attempts to hide his shape, facilitates his role in cantos III–VI as her knight errant in disguise.

Apuleius' Cupid, wounded by the oil, takes flight of his own accord, hurt by Psyche's betrayal. Tighe's Cupid never leaves her in doubt that he loves her, and that a union between the two is achievable. His undying love for her continues despite her betrayal (63):

> Yet still attentively she stands unmoved,
> To catch those accents which her soul could cheer,
> That soothing voice which had so sweetly proved
> That still his tender heart offending Psyche loved!

Similarities between Tighe and Apuleius

Despite these important differences, there are some close echoes of 'Cupid and Psyche' in Tighe, especially in her ecphrastic set pieces. For example, Cytherean Venus' shrines are left unattended and neglected by humans who worship Psyche instead (12):

---

[20]   Tighe's imagined 'graceful champion' (22) of course already anticipates Cupid's function in cantos III–VI; on the importance of themes of the female gaze, see H. Linkin Kramer, 'Romanticism and Mary Tighe's 'Psyche': peering at the hem of her blue stockings', *Studies in Romanticism* 35 (1996) 55–72 (64); on viewing and blindness in Tighe as a new feminine aesthetics, see A. P. Hobgood, 'The bold trespassing of a "proper romantic lady": Mary Tighe and a female, romantic aesthetic', *European Romantic Review* 18 (2007) 503–19.

[21]   See R. May, *Apuleius and Drama: The Ass on Stage* (Oxford 2006) 225–28.

Lo! all forsaking Cytherea's shrine,
Her sacred altars now no more embrace,
But to fair Psyche pay those rites divine,
Which, Goddess! are thy due, and should be only thine.

This corresponds closely with the equivalent passage in *Met.* 4.29:

No one took ship for Paphos, Cnidos, or even Cythera to catch sight of the goddess
Venus. Sacrifices in those places were postponed, shrines grew unsightly […] It was
the girl who was entreated in prayer.

Venus' outburst on discovering a mere mortal has usurped her place is given quite some
space in Tighe (14–16), and shows echoes of Apuleian phrasing: both Venuses refer bitterly
to their victory in the judgment of Paris, perform a suppliant prayer to their sons, ask for the
lowest possible husband for Psyche and finally seal the deal with a rather passionate kiss.

Indignant quitting her deserted fanes,
Now Cytherea sought her favourite isle,
And there from every eye her secret pains
Mid her thick myrtle bowers conceal'd awhile;
[…]
And bade her favourite boy her vengeful will obey.
Bathed in those tears which vanquish human hearts,
'Oh, son beloved!' (the suppliant goddess cried,)
'If e'er thy too indulgent mother's arts
'Subdued for thee the potent deities
'Who rule my native deep, or haunt the skies;
'Or if to me the grateful praise be due,
'That to thy sceptre bow the great and wise,
'Now let thy fierce revenge my foe pursue,
'And let my rival scorned her vain presumption rue.
'For what to me avails my former boast
'That, fairer than the wife of Jove confest,
'I gained the prize thus basely to be lost?
'With me the world's devotion to contest
'Behold a mortal dares; though on my breast
'Still vainly brilliant shines the magic zone.
'Yet, yet I reign: by you my wrongs redrest,
'The world with humbled Psyche soon shall own
'That Venus, beauty's queen, shall be adored alone.
'Deep let her drink of that dark, bitter spring,
'Which flows so near thy bright and crystal tide;
'Deep let her heart thy sharpest arrow sting,
'Its tempered barb in that black poison dyed.
'Let her, for whom contending princes sighed,
'Feel all the fury of thy fiercest flame
'For some base wretch to foul disgrace allied,
'Forgetful of her birth and her fair fame,
'Her honours all defiled, and sacrificed to shame.'

Then, with sweet pressure of her rosy lip,
A kiss she gave bathed in ambrosial dew;
The thrilling joy he would for ever sip,
And his moist eyes in ecstasy imbrue.

Compare *Met.* 4.30–31:

'Here am I, the ancient mother of the universe, the founding creator of the elements, the Venus that tends the entire world [...]. What a waste of effort it was for the shepherd [*i.e.* Paris] whose justice and honesty won the approval of great Jupiter to reckon my matchless beauty superior to that of those great goddesses! But this girl, whoever she is, is not going to enjoy appropriating the honours that are mine; I shall soon ensure that she rues the beauty which is not hers by rights!'

She at once summoned her son [Eros], that winged, most indiscreet youth, whose own bad habits show his disregard for public morality [...], and showed him Psyche in the flesh (that was the girl's name). She told him the whole story of their rivalry in beauty, and grumbling and growling with displeasure added: [31] 'I beg you by the bond of a mother's affection, by the sweet wounds which your darts inflict and the honeyed blisters left by this torch of yours: ensure that your mother gets her full revenge, and punish harshly this girl's arrogant beauty. Be willing to perform this single service which will compensate for all that has gone before. See that the girl is seized with consuming passion for the lowest possible specimen of humanity, for one who as the victim of Fortune has lost status, inheritance and security, a man so disreputable that nowhere in the world can he find an equal in wretchedness.'—With these words she kissed her son long and hungrily with parted lips.

Apollo's oracle also closely mirrors Apuleius' version (26, *cf.* Apul. *Met.* 4.33):

'On nuptial couch, in nuptial vest arrayed,
'On a tall rock's high summit Psyche place:
'Let all depart, and leave the fated maid
'Who never must a mortal Hymen grace:
'A winged monster of no earthly race
'Thence soon shall bear his trembling bride away;
'His power extends o'er all the bounds of space,
'And Jove himself has owned his dreaded sway,
'Whose flaming breath sheds fire, whom earth and heaven obey.'

Even Psyche's Apuleian characterization as 'simple'[22] finds its echo in Tighe's 'her simple heart' (49).

Echoes of Apuleius' 'Metamorphoses' outside 'Cupid and Psyche'

Importantly, other books of the *Metamorphoses* are echoed in the first two cantos as well, directly contradicting Tighe's own claim of ignorance. After Venus' outburst, she retires to the Island of Pleasure (17):

---

[22] Her simplicity is alluded to four times in *Met.* 5 alone: 5.11, 15, 19, and 24.

[…] Pleasure had called the fertile lawns her own,
And thickly strewed them with her choicest flowers;
Amid the quiet glade her golden throne
Bright shone with lustre through o'erarching bowers:
There her fair train, the ever downy Hours,
Sport on light wing with the young Joys entwin'd:
While Hope delighted from her full lap showers
Blossoms, whose fragrance can the ravished mind
Inebriate with dreams of rapture unconfined.

This recalls in some ways the depiction of the pantomime of Venus, the 'mistress of pleasure', in *Met.* 10.31 with its train of Hours and beautiful flowers. Interestingly, this is also the place to which Tighe's Zephyrus brings Psyche after her marriage (28):[23]

But now Venus becomingly took the centre of the stage […] She was surrounded by a throng of the happiest children; […] Next floated in charming children, unmarried girls, representing on one side the Graces at their most graceful, and on the other Hours in all their beauty. They were appeasing their goddess by strewing wreaths and single blossoms before her, and they formed a most elegant chorus-line as they sought to please the mistress of pleasures with the foliage of spring.

Throughout Tighe's text, there are several references to change and metamorphosis, a central theme in Apuleius. For example, at the beginning of canto II (45), we read:

Change is the lot of all. Ourselves with scorn
Perhaps shall view what now so fair appears;
And wonder whence the fancied charm was born
Which now with vain despair from our fond grasp is torn!

This theme is also touched upon in the advice to Psyche on how to gain Venus' forgiveness and be reunited with her husband (66):

[…] from immortal Beauty's sacred spring,
'Which foul deformity to grace can turn,
'And back to fond affection's eyes can bring
'The charms which fleeting fled on transient wing […]'

The most tell-tale scene in canto II, which belies Tighe's claim to know little of Lucius' story, follows on immediately from Cupid's telling Psyche that she needs to appease Venus. Psyche reaches a temple adorned with 'immortal roses' (64), which is then revealed to be the temple of Ammon, a Libyan-Egyptian god. Here she encounters a kind old priest who will look familiar to readers of *Met.* 11:

Round the soft scene immortal roses bloom,
While lucid myrtles in the breezes play;
No savage beast did ever yet presume
With foot impure within the grove to stray,
And far from hence flies every bird of prey;
Thus, mid the sandy Garamantian wild,

---

23 'To Pleasure's blooming isle their lovely charge they bear'.

When Macedonia's lord pursued his way,
The sacred temple of great Ammon smiled,
And green encircling shades the long fatigue beguiled:
With awe that fearfully her doom awaits
Still at the portal Psyche timid lies,
When lo! advancing from the hallowed gates
Trembling she views with reverential eyes
An aged priest. A myrtle bough supplies
A wand, and roses bind his snowy brows:
'Bear hence thy feet profane (he sternly cries)
'Thy longer stay the goddess disallows,
'Fly, nor her fiercer wrath too daringly arouse!'
(65) His pure white robe imploringly she held,
And, bathed in tears, embraced his sacred knees;
Her mournful charms relenting he beheld,
And melting pity in his eye she sees [...]

This echoes Isis' instructions to Lucius in *Met.* 11.6:

As the procession forms up, a priest at my prompting will be carrying a garland of roses tied to the rattle in his right hand. So without hesitation part the crowd and join the procession, relying on my kindly care.

And the appearance of the priest in *Met.* 11.12:

A priest approached bearing with him my future fortune and my very salvation. Exactly in keeping with the divine promise, his right hand held an adorned rattle for the goddess and a crown of flowers for me.

It is Tighe's old priest who advises Psyche how to gain Venus' forgiveness and instructs her what to do. The roses, the white garments, and the helpful old priest of an Egyptian deity find close parallels in Lucius' encounter with the priests of Isis in *Met.* 11. It would be odd to assume that Tighe had reached her decision to include him here and fashion him in in this way without detailed knowledge of the rest of the *Metamorphoses*.

Spenser's 'Temple of Isis' (*Faerie Queene* book V canto vii) also features priests of Isis, but their description, with their linen shirts and moon-shaped mitres, although possibly inspired by Apuleius,[24] is not as close to the *Metamorphoses* as is that of Tighe:

All clad in linen robes with silver hemd;
And on their heads with long locks comely kemd,
They wore rich Mitres shaped like the Moone,
To shew that Isis doth the Moone portend [...].

Apuleius, more so than Spenser, is the inspiration for Tighe's old priest. In Psyche's reaction, and during other important passages from this scene onwards, Tighe stresses the observance of mystic silence (67):

---

[24]   Discussed in Carver, *Protean Ass* (n. 11, above) 393–95. The statue of Isis in this canto is clad in linen and silver, with a golden crown. Lusinga's description, too (as 'a gentle nymph of lovely form [...] In robe of fairest white, with scarf of pleasant green' (97)), is closer to Isis' depiction in Apuleius than in Spenser.

With meek submissive woe she heard her doom,
Nor to the holy minister replied;
But in the myrtle grove's mysterious gloom
She silently retired her grief to hide.

Although Spenser's Britomart prays silently, mysteries are absent from his Isiac temple. Tighe even imposes mystic silence on herself when she begins to describe Chastity's palace in canto V (149):

Celestial temple! 'tis not lips like mine
Thy glories can reveal to mortal ear,
Or paint the unsullied beams which blaze for ever here.

The language of mystery cult, prominent in the *Metamorphoses*, is evident in Apuleius' depictions of both Psyche and Lucius, and is also found in Tighe's 'Apuleian' and 'Spenserian' cantos. In fact, Tighe here proves herself a perceptive reader of Apuleius by aligning these two characters with each other long before 'Cupid and Psyche' was identified as a 'mise en abyme' of Apuleius' novel.[25] Consequently Tighe's reception of the *Metamorphoses* offers a subtle and intelligent, and surprisingly modern, interpretation of Apuleius' story.

Another important plot element in Tighe is the presence of the helper figures with which she surrounds her Psyche: a dove, symbolising innocence (68), joins her immediately; it is clearly identified as 'The messenger of Cupid'. In the following cantos the dove is joined by a lion ('passion'), and of course Cupid himself in disguise as a knight with his white horse, and with him his attendant Constance. In Apuleius, Psyche does have helpers, too, often animals like ants or an eagle, or talking objects like reeds or towers, and it is subtly suggested that it is Cupid himself who has sent her these aides.[26] Tighe makes Cupid's continued involvement as a helper in Psyche's tasks much more explicit, again offering a perceptive and inspired interpretation of Apuleius' original tale. Psyche and Cupid in Tighe become equals in their quest for reunion. Cupid wears a disguise to avoid being recognized by her, but confides in her that he too, like Psyche, needs to placate Venus to find his lover again (82):

As he revealed how he himself was bound
By solemn vow, that neither force nor art
His helmet should unloose, till he had found
The bower of happiness, that long sought fairy ground.
'I too (he said) divided from my love,
'The offended power of Venus deprecate,
'Like thee, through paths untrodden, sadly rove
'In search of that fair spot prescribed by fate,
'The blessed term of my afflicted state,
'Where I the mistress of my soul shall find [...]

---

[25]   On 'mise en abyme' (embedded narratological miniaturization), see L. Dällenbach, *The Mirror in the Text* (Oxford 1989).

[26]   Cupid may help Psyche behind the scenes: P. James, *Unity in Diversity: A Study of Apuleius' 'Metamorphoses'* (Hildesheim 1987) 183–85; M. Zimmerman, S. Panayotakis, V. Hunink, W.H. Keulen, S.J. Harrison, T. D. McCreight, B. Wesseling, and D. van Mal-Maeder, *Apuleius Madaurensis, 'Metamorphoses', book IV 28–35, V and VI 1–24. The Tale of Cupid and Psyche: Text, Introduction and Commentary.* Groningen Commentaries on Apuleius (Groningen 2004) 446 are more sceptical.

Tighe's innovation neither discredits nor undermines Apuleius' work, but puts some of its important key themes centre stage, showing her to be an excellent classicist and an attentive reader of the *Metamorphoses*.

Apuleius' 'Metamorphoses' in cantos III–VI

Expanding our analysis to the allegorical cantos III–VI, I would argue that here, too, we find echoes of Lucius' adventures. Like Psyche, Lucius also wanders from place to place, and encounters many different characters on his way. Just as Charite attempts to escape on the donkey Lucius (*Met.* 6.27–29), so Psyche mounts Cupid's horse (81):

> The timid Psyche mounts his docile steed,
> Much prayed, she tells to his attentive ear
> (As on her purposed journey they proceed).

This action is repeated now and again, as, for example, when they flee the bower of loose Delight (91):

> While trembling Psyche on the steed they place,
> Which swift as lightning flies far from the dreadful chase.

But it is in the description of her allegorical personifications, I argue, that Tighe relies most prominently on Apuleius' characters. As we will see, Tighe uses these personifications to create negative images of the emotions and temptations that Psyche needs to overcome on her quest.

There may be an echo of the Isis procession of *Met.* 11 when, in canto III, Psyche and her companions meet the group of young men and women who will take them to the bower of loose Delight (85):

> A joyous goodly train appear around,
> Of many a gallant youth and white robed maid,

Compare *Met.* 11.10:

> Next, crowds of those initiated into the divine rites came surging along, men and women of every rank and age, gleaming with linen garments spotlessly white.

In Apuleius, various articles associated with the worship of Isis are carried along in the procession (*Met.* 11.9f.), including garlands, mirrors, combs, perfumes, lamps that copy divine light, and musical instruments:

> A numerous crowd of both sexes who sought the favour of the creator of the celestial stars by carrying lamps, torches, tapers and other kinds of artificial light. Behind them came musical instruments, pipes and flutes which sounded forth the sweetest melodies. There followed a delightful choir of specifically chosen youths clad in expensive white tunics, who kept hymning a charming song […]. Their leader held out a lamp gleaming with brilliant light […]

The depiction of the bower of loose Delight, a place of temptation, focuses on the sensual nature of the Isis procession. The attendants wear similar clothes and carry comparable items of worship, such as lamps, and they also worship a divine queen (87):

White bosomed nymphs around with loosened zones
All on the guests obsequiously tend,
Some sing of love with soft expiring tones,
While Psyche's melting eyes the strain commend;
Some o'er their heads the canopy suspend,
Some hold the sparkling bowl, while some with skill
Ambrosial showers and balmy juices blend,
Or the gay lamps with liquid odours fill
Whose many coloured fires divinest sweets distil.
And now a softer light they seemed to shed,
And sweetest music ushered in their queen [...]

This charming scene is, however, a delusion, and on the discovery of its fallacious nature the whole edifice collapses (89):

And foul deformity, and filth obscene,
With monstrous shapes appear on every side;
But vanished is their fair and treacherous queen,
And with her every charm that decked the enchanted scene.

We are even introduced to a version of Isis herself in canto III, where Psyche encounters Vanity and Lusinga (Flattery) together on a chariot. Vanity's eyes are fixed on the mirror that this allegory usually carries as her symbol (98):

Her eyes she fixes on a mirror clear
Where still by fancy's spell unrivalled charms appear.

This image allows Tighe to explore Vanity's similarities with Isis, whose acolytes take great pains to let Isis see her own face in the mirrors they hold for her. Apuleius writes at *Met.* 11.9:

Others [*i.e.* women] had gleaming mirrors attached to their backs to render homage to the goddess as she drew near them [...]

Vanity's multi-coloured garments with images of the universe, her exotic perfume, and her elaborate curly hairstyle also recall Isis as she appeared to Lucius in his dream:

And, as she looked with aspect ever new,
She seemed on change and novel grace intent,
Her robe was formed of ever varying hue,
And whimsically placed each ornament;
On her attire, with rich luxuriance spent,
The treasures of the earth, the sea, the air,
Are vainly heaped her wishes to content;
Yet were her arms and snowy bosom bare,
And both in painted pride shone exquisitely fair.
(99) Her braided tresses in profusion drest,
Circled with diadem, and nodding plumes,
Sported their artful ringlets o'er her breast,
And to the breezes gave their rich perfumes;
Her cheek with tint of borrowed roses blooms:

Used to receive from all rich offerings,
She quaffs with conscious right the fragrant fumes
Which her attendant from a censer flings,
Who graceful feeds the flame with incense while she sings.

Compare Isis in *Met.* 11.3:

To begin with, she had a full head of hair which hung down, gradually curling as it
spread loosely and flowed gently over her divine neck. Her lofty head was encircled
by a garland interwoven with diverse blossoms, at the centre of which above her
brow was a flat disk resembling a mirror, or rather the orb of the moon, which emitted
a glittering light [...] She wore a multi-coloured dress woven from fine linen, one
part of which shone radiantly white, a second glowed yellow with saffron blossom,
and a third blazed rosy red. But what riveted my eyes above all else was her jet-
black cloak [...] Stars glittered here and there along its woven border and on its flat
surface, and in their midst a full moon exhaled fiery flames. Wherever the hem of that
magnificent cloak billowed out, a garland composed of every flower and every fruit
was inseparably attached to it [...] She breathed forth the fertile fragrance of Arabia
as she deigned to address me in words divine: [...]

Isis transforms from Lucius' benevolent saviour goddess into the treacherous allegory of
flattery, thus allowing for a more problematic reflection on the nature of Isis' involvement
in the novel. Again, this displays a sceptical view of the goddess more familiar to modern
scholars than to Tighe's contemporaries. It is only much more recently that scholars have
pointed to Isis' role as a somewhat flawed saviour, whose priests display a degree of self-
serving and greedy behaviour, and whose involvement in Lucius' re-transformation is not as
crucial as Lucius portrays it to be, since he could have found the Isis procession and eaten the
saving roses without Isis' epiphany to him on Cenchreae's beach.[27]

Lusinga then tricks Psyche into stepping into the chariot, where she is kidnapped and
from which she cannot escape. She is finally brought to Vanity's brother Ambition, whose lair
lies in a true *locus horridus*, with a castle situated amidst craggy cliffs and dark woods (103):

High o'er the spacious plain a mountain rose,
A stately castle on its summit stood:
Huge craggy cliffs behind their strength oppose
To the rough surges of the dashing flood;
The rocky shores a boldly rising wood
On either side conceals; bright shine the towers
And seem to smile upon the billows rude.
In front the eye, with comprehensive powers,
Sees wide extended plains enriched with splendid bowers.
Hither they bore the sad reluctant fair [...]

Compare the cave of the robbers who hold Charite in *Met.* 4.6:

---

[27] See n. 24, above, on the lack of similarities between Lusinga and Spenser's Isis. For a sceptical view of Isis'
involvement, see S. J. Harrison, *Apuleius: A Latin Sophist* (Oxford 2000), following through suggestions in the
seminal J. J. Winkler, *Auctor & Actor: A Narratological Reading of Apuleius' 'Golden Ass'* (Berkeley 1985).
For more conciliatory readings, see May, *Apuleius and Drama* (n. 21, above), and especially S. Tilg, *Apuleius'
'Metamorphoses': A Study in Roman Fiction* (Oxford 2014).

A bristling mountain rose up, shadowy with its woodland foliage, to a towering height. Its slanting and precipitous slopes, girt with rocks which were razor-sharp and therefore insurmountable [...]. A high tower rose over the cavern where the mountain's edges ended.

In canto IV, we briefly meet Credulity, an old woman riding on a donkey. In her *argumentum*, Tighe misleadingly cites a painting by Apelles[28] as her source (112) for her unsympathetic portrait of Credulity as (117) 'blind', 'misshaped and timorous', with a 'voracious appetite [...] Though all-devouring, yet unsatisfied'. Credulity tells Psyche many tales, just as the old servant of the robbers tells Charite a story, 'Cupid and Psyche' itself, to calm her down (119):

> And, as they onward went, in Psyche's ear
> Her tongue with many a horrid tale o'erflowed,
> Which warned her to forsake that venturous road,
> And seek protection in the neighbouring grove;
> Where dwelt a prudent dame [...]

When Tighe's Psyche listens to the 'hag loquacious' (120), she consequently shares several features of her early quest with Apuleius' description of the desperate yet brave Charite, whose bridegroom comes in disguise to rescue her from the robbers, just as Cupid aids Psyche in Tighe.

Canto IV's Disfida (Suspicion), in turn, bears echoes of Apuleius' dangerous witch Pamphile, since Disfida's castle is surrounded by allusions to Pamphile's metamorphosis into an owl (Apul. *Met.* 3.21) and her alleged power over the elements, Tartarus, and several cosmic phenomena (*Met.* 2.5; *cf.* 121):

> While to affright her soul at once combine
> A thousand shapeless forms of terror dire,
> Here shrieks the ill-omened bird, there glares the meteor's fire.

The owl reappears on page 123—'Alas! the screaming night-bird only cries;'—and on 132, where Disfida's machinations hand Psyche over to Jealousy:

> Where screaming owls their daily dwelling crave.
> One sickly lamp the wretched master shewed [...]

Disfida lives in a way that is similar to Milo and Pamphile (Apul. *Met.* 1.21) in their voluntary separation from society, as described by another garrulous old woman in Apuleius (121):

> In the deep centre of the mazy wood,
> With matted ivy and wild vine o'ergrown,
> A Gothic castle solitary stood,
> With massive walls built firm of murky stone;
> Long had Credulity its mistress known,
> Meagre her form and tawny was her hue,
> Unsociably she lived, unloved, alone,
> No cheerful prospects gladdened e'er her view,
> And her pale hollow eyes oblique their glances threw.

---

[28]   See Hoffmann, *Psyche-Märchen* (n. 4, above) 79–80 on the disingenuous nature of this claim.

Like Pamphile (*Met.* 1.22), who sits at a 'table before them with nothing on it', inhospitable Disfida offers no food on her table nor lit fires in her hearth (122):

> And at the well known call reluctantly appears.
> In hall half lighted with uncertain rays,
> Such as expiring tapers transient shed,
> The gloomy princess sat, no social blaze
> The unkindled hearth supplied, no table spread […]

And, like Pamphile, she employs magic and binding spells (124):

> Of foul magicians and of wizard spell,
> The poisoned lance and net invisible;
> While Psyche shuddering sees her knight betrayed
> Into the snares of some enchanter fell […]

Geloso (Jealousy) shares Disfida's connections with magic (131, 133, 137), entraps Psyche in the shape of a snake and echoes the shapeshifting old man in *Met.* 8.21, who is apparently able to turn into a snake in order to devour his victims:

> The messenger […] had an extraordinary tale to tell about his fellow-slave: he had seen him lying prostrate, with a monstrous snake perched on top of him gnawing his flesh, so that the youth was now almost entirely gobbled up. There was no sign anywhere of that unhappy old man.

It is Cupid who bravely saves Tighe's Psyche at the last moment from being devoured by jealousy (136):

> The vile magician all his art exerts,
> And triumphs to behold his proud control:
> Changed to a serpent's hideous form, he stole
> O'er her fair breast to suck her vital blood;
> His poisonous involutions round her roll:
> Already is his forked tongue imbrued
> Warm in the stream of life, her heart's pure purple flood.
> Thus wretchedly she falls Geloso's prey!

In canto V, these assimilations of characters from Apuleius' story to Tighe's tale are much less frequent, because Psyche spends more or less the whole canto in the Palace of Castabella (Chastity). Much of the book is an extended epic catalogue of her personified handmaidens, and distinguished chaste men and women from mythology. Canto VI, by contrast, begins with repeated references to roses, spring, and a sea voyage for Psyche and her knight (180f.), a setting similar to the last book of the *Metamorphoses*, with its themes of renewal and Isis' Ploiaphesia festival. After the journey over the sea and a short sojourn at Glacella's (Indifference) icy palace, the group finally arrives on a beach, where Psyche's journeys come to an end as she will now be able to collect the urn of Beauty and place it on Venus' altar (202):

> But safely anchored in the happy port,
> Led by her knight the golden sands she prest […]

Similarly, Lucius' prayer to Isis on the beach of Cenchreae and the announcement of her priest that he has finally reached a safe harbour mark the end of his troubles (*Met.* 11.15): 'You have been driven before the heavy storms and the heaviest gales of Fortune, but now you have finally reached the harbour of peace and the altar of mercy'.

By this stage, Psyche has discovered the real identity of her knight as Cupid, and it is the god's intervention which helps Psyche for a final time here. But it is not Psyche who completes her task. Unexpectedly for Tighe's more proactive heroine, and just like Apuleius' Psyche, who has considerable help from others during her four tasks set by Venus, Tighe's Psyche yields the actual fetching of the urn with the water of Beauty to their attendant, Constance, on Cupid's command (202, 204).[29] The only thing left for her to do is to pray fervently to Venus to restore Cupid to herself, while placing the urn on her altar (204):

> 'Venus, fulfilled is thine adored command,
> Thy voice divine the suppliant's claim allows,
> The smile of favour grant, *restore her heavenly spouse.*'

Lucius, too, begs the Moon Goddess in *Met.* 11.2 to be restored to him and does not really have to do much to help himself apart from prayer—the Isis priest will bring the roses to him, and Lucius merely has to take them. Much friendlier than Apuleius' Venus, Cupid's mother agrees to the marriage and to Psyche's apotheosis. The poem ends with Tighe's farewell to her story and her own divine inspiration.

Tighe is therefore somewhat disingenuous when she claims to know little of the rest of the *Metamorphoses*. This is a clear strategy, a strategy which has worked with many of her modern readers, and it is obvious why she pursues it—her changes to 'Cupid and Psyche' made the story more palatable to the readers of her own time, and turned Psyche into a denizen of the age of sensitivity who struggles against inimical emotions to achieve her happiness in blissful marriage.[30] This is a far cry from Lucius' sexual adventures and serial mishaps. After reshaping Psyche's character based on the behaviour of contemporary society belles, a pattern she herself emulated, Tighe was forced by necessity to cut any connections with the bawdy parts of the novel. By tracing back some of her allegorical characters to Apuleius' Pamphile, old women, or Isis, we can, however, rediscover added depths in her creative imagination and astute interpretations of Apuleius' text.

English scholars have demonstrated how dangerous for the reputation of women in Tighe's lifetime it was to be an authoress.[31] An association with the rest of the *Metamorphoses* would have damaged Tighe, already vulnerable as a female poet, severely indeed. Even basing the portrait of the negative emotions Psyche needs to overcome on characters drawn from the rest of the *Metamorphoses*, and therefore indirectly admitting that she had read these bawdy stories, might have finished both her career and her social status. Her denial of any real

---

[29]   Buchanan, *Mary Blachford Tighe* (n. 2, above) 70: 'it is difficult to see how she has learnt anything at all, or earned the prize of reconciliation with Cupid, since it is Constance, not Psyche herself, who eventually fulfils the quest by fetching the water from the sacred spring'.

[30]   Buchanan, *Mary Blachford Tighe* (n. 2, above) 72 agrees with Tighe's intentions, but does not realise her white lies: 'For this audience, Mary was certainly keen to distance herself from the original story, the opening stanzas preparing the reader for a tale of chivalry and courtly love, and although she acknowledged her debt to Apuleius, she downplayed his influence—he supplied only an outline to her poem, and only in the first two cantos'.

[31]   Linkin Kramer, 'Skirting around the sex' (n. 6, above) 731: 'when in 1801 Mary Tighe began composing Psyche [...], an epic romance that offers a sensual, often erotic reworking of the myth of *Cupid and Psyche*, she knew how dangerous articulating sexual passion could be for a woman's literary reputation'.

knowledge of the rest of Apuleius' novel, and her repeated stressing of her own originality, also preclude any identification of Tighe's inspired female narrator or her muse with the old woman who tells the tale of Cupid and Psyche to Charite;[32] personifications in *Psyche* which echo the old crone are negative, and the old woman is an unsympathetic character in Apuleius as well, with whom identification would have been equally injudicious for Tighe.

It is more widely recognized that she tells a similar white lie when she claims to be innocent of writing erotic tales. Tighe repeatedly addresses a set of idealized readers,[33] in the same way that Apuleius and Lucius do. She, however, does this strategically whenever her story might become too eroticized, as, for example, in the scene in which Cupid falls in love with Psyche. Consequently, she can claim to write an innocent allegorical tale of Love and Soul, just when she is, in fact, depicting some very sensuous scenes. Similarly, when she displays her credentials as a classicist from the beginning, and clothes her erotic tale in ancient dress, she distances herself from the dangerous eroticism her story evokes.

Despite her caution, Tighe, herself a society beauty,[34] was, from an early point, identified with her subject, with her friends giving her the nickname 'Psyche'. The effigy on her tomb by John Flaxman (*c.* 1807) shows a sleeping Mary Tighe with a small weeping Psyche next to her head, extending the identification beyond the grave. The author, her femininity, and her morals became linked in the minds of her readers, proving again that Tighe was right to try to distance herself from Apuleius, for reasons of self-preservation as well as of self-fashioning, despite being one of Apuleius' most innovative, interesting, and perceptive readers of the period. And she almost got away with claiming for herself both ignorance of Lucius' sexual exploits and the status of a learned poetess able to teach chaste and pious love.

University of Leeds

---

[32] E. M. Goss, *Revealing Bodies: Anatomy, Allegory, and the Grounds of Knowledge in the Long Eighteenth Century* (Lewisburg 2013) 126 at least acknowledges the old woman as the teller of the story in Apuleius.

[33] Linkin Kramer, 'Skirting around the sex' (n. 6 above) 733.

[34] See Linkin Kramer, 'Mary Tighe and literary history' (n. 4, above) 564–76.

APULEIUS AND MARTIANUS CAPELLA: RECEPTION, PEDAGOGY, AND THE DIALECTICS OF CANON

AHUVIA KAHANE

I. Is Apuleius a canonical author?

'Is Apuleius a canonical author?' asks Joseph Farrell in a recent essay. In essence, and despite Apuleius' recent acceptance into the late-modern canon, Farrell answers in the negative. Apuleius 'is, literally, marginal'. Yet, as Farrell notes,

> [i]t is odd […] that […] Apuleius seems to have had at least some status in later antiquity—a higher status, in fact, than such pillars of the modern classical canon as Pliny and Tacitus.[1]

In what follows, I want to suggest that, in fact, Apuleius' canonical status in late antiquity, and indeed in general, is not entirely 'odd', or perhaps that it is so by necessity. We should view Apuleius not as being closer to the centre of the canon or further away at its margins but instead as subject to a special canonical dialectic of appeal and exclusion. On the one hand, his work, especially the salacious surplus of *The Golden Ass*, and the exuberance of his language and thought—loud, free, witty, titillating, and learned—give him an alluring voice. He is a useful literary *actor*. Yet, on the other hand, this very same excess is more difficult to socialize within structured cultural contexts that rely on the pedagogical regulatory device of canon to enforce and replicate their values and *praxis*. In this sense, Apuleius is often a liminal *auctor* excluded from speech. The double-sided character of his work makes it inherently more difficult for tradition to position him within its literary hierarchies. It cannot erase him from literary history, but it likewise cannot fully acknowledge his presence.[2] This kind of double status, we should add, is different from the more uniform canonicity of, for example, Homer or Virgil. Yet it is not 'odd', first, because it is essential to Apuleius'

---

[1] J. Farrell, 'Apuleius and the classical canon', in *Apuleius and Africa*, eds B. T. Lee, E. Finkelpearl, and L. Graverini (London 2014) 66–84 (70).

[2] I do not discuss matters of theory at length in this paper. However, loosely adapted, the Apuleian dichotomy *auctor/actor* and the distinction between animal 'voice' ('phonê') and human 'speech' ('logos') provide a useful critical framework for my argument. For *auctor/actor* (*cf. Met.* 3.11 and the scribal correction 'auctorem' - superscr. 'actorem'), see J. J. Winkler, 'Auctor & actor: Apuleius and his metamorphosis', *Pacific Coast Philology* 14 (1979) 84–91 (84); J. J. Winkler, *Auctor and Actor: A Narratological Reading of Apuleius's 'The Golden Ass'* (Berkeley 1985) 171 on 3.11; 249 n. 16. For voice and speech, see Arist. *Hist. An.* 488a32–36, 535a28–535b3, 535b3–13, 535b25–32; *de Anim.* 420b6–17, 420b23–421a2, *etc.*; A. Haltenhoff, 'ΑΛΟΓΑ ΖΩΙΑ: Antike Diskussionen über Tierrechte', in *Translatio humanitatis: Festschrift zum 60. Geburtstag von Peter Riemer*, ed. C. Kugelmeier (St Ingbert 2015) 369–80; J. L. Labarrière, 'Imagination humaine et imagination animale chez Aristote', *Phronesis* 29 (1984) 17–49; W. Ax, 'Ψόφος, φωνή und διάλεκτος als Grundbegriffe aristotelischer Sprachreflexion', *Glotta* 56 (1978) 245–71, *etc.* The Aristotelian distinction has attracted important comments in contemporary philosophy (Arendt, Foucault, Agamben, Braidotti, *etc.*).

reception and, second, because it is also a necessary mechanism working within broader traditions of canon and pedagogy.

II. Apuleius, reception, Martianus Capella

The tradition of Apuleius' reception is long and detailed.[3] However, to argue my point here, I want to look at the work of just one of his closest, most influential, and most instructive imitators, Martianus Min(n)e(i)us Felix Capella. In doing so, I consider the relationship between pedagogy, desire, and pleasure, and their implications for questions of canon and canonicity, with special emphasis, as we shall see, on the interaction of eros and formal learning.

Martianus Capella (fourth century CE) was, like Apuleius, a native of the city of Madauros in North Africa. He is best known for the *De nuptiis Philologiae et Mercurii* (*On the Marriage of Philology and Mercury*), an encyclopaedic didactic work in nine books that outlines the structure and boundaries of the learned disciplines within an allegorical mythological framing narrative. In this narrative, the god Mercury, having come of age, seeks a bride. Turned down by Wisdom, Divination, and the Soul, he marries Philology, who brings with her as gifts her seven maidens: Grammar, Dialectic, Rhetoric, Geometry, Arithmetic, Astronomy, and Harmony.[4] The *De nuptiis Philologiae et Mercurii* was also known by the title *De septem disciplinis* (*On the Seven Disciplines*, *i.e.* the 'Liberal Arts') or, alternatively, as *Satura*. All three appellations seem to be late attributions rather than the original given by Martianus himself.[5] But precisely for this reason these titles provide evidence about Capella's reception and character, and, as we shall see, through this reception also important perspectives on Capella's relation to Apuleius and the position of the work of both authors within the literary canon.

---

[3]   Extended surveys in R. H. F. Carver, *The Protean Ass: The 'Metamorphoses' of Apuleius from Antiquity to the Renaissance* (Oxford 2007); J. H. Gaisser, *The Fortunes of Apuleius and 'The Golden Ass': A Study in Transmission and Reception* (Princeton-Oxford 2008).

[4]   Overview of Capella in A. Hicks, 'Martianus Capella and the liberal arts', in *The Oxford Handbook of Medieval Latin Literature*, eds R. Hexter and R. Townsend (Oxford 2012) 307–34. Capella's name and biography: S. Grebe, *'De nuptiis Philologiae et Mercurii' Darstellung der sieben freien Künste und ihrer Beziehungen zueinander* (Stuttgart 1999) 22; W. H. Stahl and R. Johnson, *Martianus Capella and the Seven Liberal Arts*, 2 vols (New York 1971–77) I (1971) 21–22. Capella's *floruit*: 420–30 CE (A. Cameron, 'Martianus and his first editor', *Classical Philology* 81 (1986) 320–8; R. Martin, 'Petronius Arbiter et le 'Satyricon': quelques pistes de réflexion', *Bulletin de l'Association Guillaume Budé* (2009) 143–68), or the third quarter of the century (D. Shanzer, *A Philosophical and Literary Commentary on Martianus Capella's 'De nuptiis Philologiae et Mercurii' Book 1* (Berkeley, CA 1986); S. I. B. Barnish, 'Martianus Capella and Rome in the late fifth century', *Hermes* 114 (1986) 98–111), or even later in the sixth century (S. Grebe, 'Gedanken zur Datierung von 'De nuptiis Philologiae et Mercurii' des Martianus Capella', *Hermes* 128 (2000) 353–68). Text: J. Willis, *Martianus Capella* (Stuttgart 1983). The Budé edition now has text and commentaries of most of the *De nuptiis*. For books I and IV (the focus of this essay), see esp. D. Shanzer above; J. F. Chevalier, *Martianus Capella, 'Les noces de Philologie et de Mercure'. Tome I, Livre I* (Paris 2014), with bibliography, xic–cxi; M. Ferré, *Martianus Capella, 'Les noces de Philologie et de Mercure', Livre IV, La Dialectique* (Paris 2007); L. Cristante, L. Lenaz, and P. Ferrarino, *Martiani Capellae 'De nuptiis Philologiae et Mercurii'. 1, Libri I–II* (Hildesheim 2011). See also the Medieval commentaries, *e.g.* in C. Lutz, *Remigii Autissiodorensis Commentum in Martianum Capella, Libri I–II* (Leiden 1962–65); H. J. Westra and C. Vester, *The Berlin Commentary on Martianus Capella's 'De nuptiis Philologiae et Mercurii' Book 1* (Leiden 1994) (full list in Chevalier, *Martianus Capella* (this note, above) xci–xcii).

[5]   See Shanzer, *A Philosophical and Literary Commentary* (n. 4, above) 45.

II.1. Capella's 'De nuptiis', 'Protean style'

The most common title of Capella's work, *De nuptiis* (see, for example, Fulgentius, *Expositio sermonum antiquorum* 45), clearly foregrounds the work's allegorical narrative and the erotic, exotic frame of its often technical, dry content. Such allegorical framing directly alludes to Apuleius' 'Cupid and Psyche' episode, the most prominent narrative component of *Metamorphoses*, and suggests a double-sided approach to knowledge and education which, in a different form, is also characteristic of Apuleius' seriocomic, erotico-philosophical tale about Lucius' curiosity.[6] As Stahl, Shanzer, Westra, Carver, Gaisser, and many others point out, Capella is a close imitator of Apuleius' 'Protean' style, and indeed develops it to excess.[7] He has sometimes been described as the *singe d'Apulée*.[8] E. R. Curtius has suggested that 'Modern readers find him insipid'.[9] C. S. Lewis went a step further: 'this universe, which has produced the bee orchid and the giraffe, has produced nothing stranger than Martianus Capella'.[10] F. J. LeMoine says: 'If Horace had read the work, he probably would have compared it to the picture of [a] "human head to [a] horse's neck conjoined"'.[11]

Like Apuleius, Capella was, as we have already noted, an African, a man born far from the centre of the Empire. We must, however, consider such provenance and its implications for canonicity with caution. Our perspectives on canon and canonical diversity have changed considerably in recent decades,[12] as has our understanding of such terms as 'African style' in Latin and Latinity.[13] Yet it is clear that, as an independent author, Capella has an even more complex relationship with the 'golden' centre of the canon of Latin literature than does Apuleius' *The Golden Ass*. We shall have to consider carefully this aspect of his work and its implications for the idea of canon below.

II.2. Capella and the cultural dialectics of canon

The second title of Martianus' book, *De septem disciplinis* (Cassiodorus, *Institutiones* 2.2.17) characterizes the work in exactly the opposite way—a pointed reminder of Capella's double-

---

[6] For a comparison, see, *e.g.*, H. J. Westra, 'The juxtaposition of the ridiculous and the sublime in Martianus Capella', *Florilegium* 3 (1981) 198–214.

[7] Carver, *Protean Ass* (n. 3, above) 36–9; Gaisser, *Fortunes of Apuleius* (n. 3, above) 52–3; Shanzer, *A Philosophical and Literary Commentary* (n. 4, above) *passim*; Stahl and Johnson, *Martianus Capella and the Seven Liberal Arts* (n. 4, above) *passim*; *etc.*

[8] Criticized by Shanzer, *A Philosophical and Literary Commentary* (n. 4, above) 44, also citing L. Lenaz, *Martiani Capellae 'De nuptiis Philologiae et Mercurii liber secundus'* (Padua 1975) 96 n. 398. See below, n. 11.

[9] E. R. Curtius, *European Literature and the Latin Middle Ages* (London 1953) 38.

[10] C. S. Lewis, *The Allegory of Love* (New York 1963) 78.

[11] F. J. LeMoine, 'Judging the beauty of diversity: a critical approach to Martianus Capella', *Classical Journal* 67 (1972) 209–15 (209).

[12] We can no longer speak of 'canon' as an unchanging literary standard. Major discussions in *Critical Inquiry* 10 (1983)—a special issue on canon; *Canons*, ed. R. von Hallberg (Chicago 1984); P. Bourdieu and J.-C. Passeron, *Reproduction in Education, Society and Culture* (New York 1990); J. Gorak, *The Making of the Modern Canon: Genesis and Crisis of a Modern Idea* (London 1993); J. Guillory, *Cultural Capital: The Problem of Literary Canon Formation* (Chicago 1993); F. Kermode, *Pleasure and Change: The Aesthetics of Canon* (Oxford 2004); J. D. Wyrick, *The Ascension of Authorship: Attribution and Canon Formation in Jewish, Hellenistic, and Christian Traditions* (Cambridge, MA 2004); *Canon and Canonicity: The Formation and Use of Scripture*, ed. E. Thomassen (Copenhagen 2010).

[13] See the essays in *Apuleius and Africa*, eds B. T. Lee, E. Finkelpearl, L. Graverini, and A. Barchiesi (London 2014).

sided reception. In contrast to the mythological narrative frame and the allegorical title *De nuptiis*, the 'technical' appellation *De septem disciplinis* marks Capella's work as a learned, non-narrative, and non-allegorical presentation of ordered knowledge ('disciplinae'). The book is one of the prime exponents in the transmission and consolidation of the traditional Western 'enkyklios paideia' and the idea of the 'Seven Liberal Arts'.[14] The Seven Arts define a *prescriptive* rule of pedagogic content as well as the administrative structure of higher education and, thus, the training of elites and the practice of knowledge in the West. This 'rule' was in effect from the fifth century, and perhaps earlier, right up until the Enlightenment, and can still be traced in the intellectual content and administrative departmental structure of present-day higher education. Canon, is, of course, the sublimated instrument of education. Lists of 'the best', socially sanctioned, literary works are at the core of pedagogic ideology and the transfer of values and social practices.[15] Capella is not independently admired as a 'primary' *auctor*. He is not a household name or a literary celebrity. Yet the *De nuptiis*, despite its obscure language and its mix of wild allegory and dull learning, was 'perhaps the most widely used schoolbook of the Middle ages'.[16] *De facto*, it was at the heart of pedagogy and the canon. Consider, for example, that today we possess over 240 extant manuscripts of the *De nuptiis*. Capella's text is problematic, its language and style are exotic and difficult. The work thus presents an enormous challenge to editors. Yet the main witnesses for the text constitute a remarkably coherent stemma, probably going back to a single Carolingian (or Merovingian) archetype.[17] In other words, against the odds of language, style, and content, Capella's manuscript tradition has managed to thrive and exclude 'rogue' independent witnesses. The tradition is authoritative, and in this sense canonical. From this perspective, then, Capella can be regarded as a distinct example of the 'cultural dialectics' of canon which also characterize Apuleius.

II.3. Satura and farrago

Finally, Capella's work is also known as *Satura*. Again, this is probably not an original appellation, but one derived from internal references in the work itself (1.2; 385.4–6; 9.997). It points to the 'Varronian' generic characterization of the *De nuptiis* as a varied, prosimetric 'Menippean' work, a literary and philosophical delicacy, just like the work of Apuleius.[18] *Satura* can also be used to represent Capella's *farrago* of low-brow entertainment

---

[14]   Curtius, *European Literature* (n. 9, above) 37–42; B. Englisch, *Die Artes liberales im frühen Mittelalter* (Stuttgart 1994); Stahl and Johnson, *Martianus Capella and the Seven Liberal Arts* (n. 4, above) I 90–7; S. Grebe, *'De Nuptiis Philologiae et Mercurii'* (n. 4, above) 37–50; P. Olmos, 'Two literary encyclopaedias from late antiquity', *Studies in History and Philosophy of Science* 43.2 (2012): 284–92; *etc*. The date and early formation of the 'seven arts' is a matter of some disagreement; Ferré, *Martianus Capella* (n. 4, above) xiv–xv, citing H. I. Marrou, 'Les arts libéraux dans l'Antiquité classique', in *Actes du quatrième congrès International de philosophie médiévale* (Paris-Montréal 1969) 5–33 and I. Hadot, *Arts libéraux et philosophie dans la pensée antique* (Paris 1984, 1st edn).

[15]   See above, n. 11.

[16]   H. O. Taylor, *The Classical Heritage of the Middle Ages* (New York 1901) 49; *cf.* Stahl and Johnson, *Martianus Capella and the Seven Liberal Arts* (n. 4, above) I 22.

[17]   The main manuscripts are the *Reichenauensis* 73 (R = *Carolsruhensis* 73, ninth century CE), *Bambergensis* Ms class 39 (B, also ninth century CE), *Parisinus* 8670 (D, ninth century CE), *Harleianus* 2685 (A, ninth century CE), and the more-recently collated and partial *Vaticanus Reginensis* 1987; see *Martianus Capella*, ed. Willis (n. 4, above) iv–xvi; more recently, *Martianus Capella*, ed. Chevalier (n. 4, above) lviii–iv. Catalogue of the manuscripts of the *De nuptiis*: C. Leonardi, 'I codici di Marziano Capella', *Aevum* 33 (1959) 443–489 and *Aevum* 34 (1960) 411–524.

[18]   See Westra, 'The juxtaposition of the ridiculous' (n. 6, above); Shanzer, *A Philosophical and Literary*

and high-brow formal pedagogy, of a wild and often erotically charged 'nuptial' narrative and a prescriptive 'disciplinary' programme. In the appellation *Satura*, we might also see an emblem of Capella's strange 'Apuleian' position: on the one hand, a useful source and influential literary *actor*, but, on the other hand, an author not fully admitted into the canon. Martianus, as we have already suggested, enhances this double 'advantage/disadvantage'.

III. Martianus' proem: actor and auctor

In the discussion that follows, I begin with some brief and relatively conventional examples illustrating the general character of the *De nuptiis* and its relation to Apuleius. Later examples will reveal more complicated aspects of intertextuality. These involve not merely acts of reference but also possible acts of occlusion as well, which raise important questions of tradition, pedagogy, and ethics.

The *De nuptiis* opens with a verse invocation to Hymenaeus as the principle of unity among cosmic elements brought together by mutual attraction (1.1):

> You who play the strings in marriage chambers [...] sacred coupler of the gods, who draw together the warring elements with secret embrace [...] you impregnate the universe, and associate the breath of the mind with bodies in that pleasing bond by which Nature is yoked [...] O fair Hymenaeus [...] most beloved of Cypris [...] from her burning desire flickers in your face [...][19]

This proem offers a conventional coupling of allegorical sensuality and philosophical content. It also comprises an unbroken, sixteen-verse sentence,[20] the absurd, circuitous poetics, convoluted syntax, and bombastic poetry of which are immediately derided in the next section, a first-person prose proem that provides a characteristically Apuleian second introduction to the narrative (1.2):[21]

> Dum crebrius isto Hymenaei versiculos nescioquid inopinum intactumque moliens cano, respersum capillis albicantibus verticem incrementisque lustralibus decuriatum nugulas ineptias[22] aggarrire non preferens Martianus intervenit dicens, 'quid istude,

---

Commentary (n. 4, above) 29–44 (esp. 29 n. 2); Grebe, *'De nuptiis Philologiae et Mercurii' Darstellung* (n. 4, above) 24–6.

[19]   'Tu quem psallentem thalamis, quem matre Camena / progenitum perhibent, copula sacra deum, / semina qui arcanis stringens pugnantia vinclis / complexuque sacro dissona nexa foves, / nam elementa ligas vicibus mundumque maritas / atque auram mentis corporibus socias, / foedere complacito sub quo natura iugatur, / sexus concilians et sub amore fidem; / o Hymenaee decens, Cypridis quae maxima curas es / (hinc tibi nam flagrans ore Cupido micat), / seu tibi quod Bacchus pater est placuisse choreas, / cantare ad thalamos seu genetricis habes / comere vernificis florentia limina sertis / seu consanguineo Gratia trina dedid: / conubium divum componens Calliopea / carmina auspicio te probat annuere'. The translation draws heavily on Shanzer, *A Philosophical and Literary Commentary* (n. 4, above) and Stahl and Johnson, *Martianus Capella and the Seven Liberal Arts* (n. 4, above). Further translations, below, unless otherwise stated, are taken from Shanzer. Main discussions of the verse proem in Stahl and Johnson, *Martianus Capella and the Seven Liberal Arts* (n. 4, above); Shanzer, *A Philosophical and Literary Commentary* (n. 4, above); Cristante, Lenaz, and Ferrarino, *Martiani Capellae* (n. 4, above); *Martianus Capella*, ed. Chevalier (n. 4, above).

[20]   See Shanzer, *A Philosophical and Literary Commentary* (n. 4, above) 45.

[21]   For the Apuleian use of the first person, see S. Frangoulidis, *Witches, Isis and Narrative: Approaches to Magic in Apuleius' 'Metamorphoses'* (Berlin 2008) 83–4. For a bibliography of studies discussing Capella's double prologue, see *Martianus Capella*, ed. Chevalier (n. 4, above) 43–4.

[22]   MSS—'nugulas ineptias'; Willis—'nugulas ineptas'. Discussion in Shanzer, *A Philosophical and Literary*

mi pater, quod nondum vulgata materie cantare deproperas et ritu dictantis antistitis, priusquam fores aditumque reseraris, ὑμνολογεῖς?'

While I was repeatedly singing these trifling Hymeneal verses ('Hymenaei versiculos'), [my son, also called] Martianus, not tolerant of that a head sprinkled with whitening hairs through the accumulation of ten lustra[23] should chatter fatuous nothings ('nugulas ineptias aggarrire'), interrupted [me],[24] saying 'What has happened to you, my father ('quid istud, mi pater')? Why are you hurrying to sing of things whose subject has not yet been revealed, and in the fashion of a bleary priest sing hymns (ὑμνολογεῖς) before you have unbolted the door at the entrance?'

Martianus the son rudely interrupts Martianus the father and, using characteristically obscure 'Capellan' vocabulary, speaks both for himself and as an intradiegetic surrogate for the readers, asking 'quid istud, mi pater?', in effect, 'what is going on?'

Martianus the *auctor* of De nuptiis, with the aid of both of his *actors*, Martianus Sr. and Martianus Jr., is speaking in jest, partly at *our* expense although also for *our* benefit. And, as readers of the De nuptiis often point out, Martianus borrows his son's question, *our* question, from Apuleius' *Metamorphoses*.[25] In the first book of the novel, at the beginning of the story of the witches (1.6.2), the speaker, Aristomenes, meets his old friend Socrates, who is 'half covered by a tattered old cloak, almost unrecognizable in his sallowness ('paene alius lurore'), pitiably deformed and shrunken ('ad miseram maciem deformatus'). Socrates has been assumed to be dead by all and his appearance is unexpected. Bewildered by this apparition, Aristomenes says, 'mi Socrates, quid istud?'[26]

Aristomenes and readers of the *Metamorphoses* will yet learn an important lesson ('don't mess with magic') from the ghostly tale's hilarity.[27] This is entertainment in the service of instruction that sets the tone for Capella's readers too. The *Metamorphoses*' question 'quid istud', we might add, replicates (with a change of grammatical gender) the novel's most famous interrogative and the 'anticipatory' bewilderment of its prologue: 'Quis ille?' This uncanny question at the beginning of the book, voicing both the reader's anxiety, not knowing who is speaking, and the unsettling reassurance of precisely that speaker, whoever he is, establishes an essential Apuleian tone of ambiguity.[28] The imperious promise, 'lector, intende, laetaberis', that follows shortly afterward, at the end of the *Metamorphoses*' prologue, only increases our perplexity.[29] The identity and authority of the implied narrator of Apuleius'

Commentary (n. 4, above) 53 *ad loc. Martianus Capella*, ed. Chevalier (n. 4, above): 'nugulas in Nuptiis' is ingenious but too straightforward, given Capella's usual diction.

[23] 'An *incrementum lustrale* was a period of five years': Shanzer, *A Philosophical and Literary Commentary* (n. 4, above) 52.

[24] Shanzer, *A Philosophical and Literary Commentary* (n. 4, above) 52: 'the deprecating tone and diminutive ['nugulas', 'versiculos'] reinforce the modesty topos'. However, as Grebe and others rightly note, this is not modesty but self-deprecation in the interests of comedy: Grebe, *'De nuptiis Philologiae et Mercurii'* (n. 4, above) 22–23 n. 55.

[25] See, *e.g.*, *Martianus Capella*, ed. Willis (n. 4, above) 2 *ad* 2.8.

[26] *Cf.* W. H. Keulen, *Apuleius Madaurensis 'Metamorphoses' book I* (Groningen 2007), 166 *ad Met.* 1.6.2.

[27] M. C. O'Brien, '"Larvale simulacrum": Platonic Socrates and the persona of Socrates in Apuleius, 'Metamorphoses' 1, 1–19', *Echoing Narratives* (2011) 123–37.

[28] See A. Kahane and A. Laird, *A Companion to the Prologue of Apuleius' 'Metamorphoses'* (Oxford-New York 2001) 300–01 for references to a range of views. For the idea that the speaker is the talking book, see S. J. Harrison, 'The speaking book: the prologue to Apuleius' 'Metamorphoses'', *Classical Quarterly* 40 (1990) 507–13.

[29] See Kahane and Laird, *A Companion to the Prologue* (n. 28, above) 303.

novel, like the identity of his secondary narrator Aristomenes, who tells preposterous lies ('tam absurda tamque immania', 1.2), and his tertiary narrator Socrates, who is a walking corpse, are moot. Likewise, the identity of 'Martianus', the implied narrator of the *De nuptiis*' prologic frame is obscured by his formal namelessness and his discourse seems to turn into a game by the confusing presence of an otherwise unknown son and addressee also named Martianus. Adding to this playful atmosphere, it is not immediately clear to us from the prologue of the *De nuptiis*, nor from its allegorical frame narrative and the story of Mercury and Philology, what Martianus Capella's 'chatter of fatuous nothings' has to do with the serious curricular content which his book must deliver. The *De nuptiis*—it may be better to speak of the *De septem disciplinis* here—was a canonical *handbook* for the education of boys who would one day assume real positions of power in their worlds.[30] In its socially-productive capacity, Capella's book is not a piece of light erotic entertainment. The real-life students who will have been tasked to read it by their *magistri* will have been both puzzled and amused by the prologue, and would have wanted to know 'quid istud?', which is, indeed, an essential 'prologic' question.

Martianus Sr.'s immediate response to his son (1.2) is:

'Ne tu' inquam 'desipis admodumque perspicui operis ἐγέρσιμον[31] noscens creperum sapis nec liquet Hymanaeo praelibante disposita nuptiae resultare.'

'Surely you are joking. Do you not recognize like the dawn the opening passage ('perspicui operis ἐγέρσιμον noscens creperum sapis') of the work you see me reciting? Since the poem is addressing Hymen, is it not clear that my theme is a marriage?'

This retort too is, as scholars widely recognize, a direct echo from precisely the same Apuleian story and from Socrates' response to Aristomenes (1.6.16–18):[32]

[...] ne tu fortunarum lubricas ambages et instabiles incursiones et reciprocas uicissitudines ignoras?

[...] do you not know the slippery windings and shifting attacks and alternating reversals of Fortune?

Capella, whose 'real' theme is not 'nuptiae' but the 'disciplinae', knows Apuleius' 'slippery windings'. Like the Apuleian voice in the prologue of the *Metamorphoses* that says 'pay attention: you *will* be entertained', Capella too is bent on entertainment. Yet like Apuleius, he has a more serious, practical mission. At the end of the prologue of the *De*

---

[30]   See, *e.g.*, Curtius, *European Literature* (n. 9, above) 38 n. 5: 'Pierre Daniel Huet (1630–1721), later bishop of Avranches, was in 1670 appointed assistant to Bossuet, who was then tutor to the Dauphin. One of his duties was supervising the edition of the Latin classics for the Dauphin's use. [...] He entrusted the edition of Martianus Capella to Leibniz, who wanted to "restore him honor" (G. Hess, *Leibniz korrespondiert mit Paris [1940]* 22)'.

[31]   Obscure and much discussed. See R. Schievenin, *Nugis ignosce lectitans: studi su Marziano Capella* (Triest 2009) 25: 'Per Marziano dunque ἐγέρσιμον indica anzitutto l'inno che segna l'inizio mattutino del culto. Il termine, sostantivato, sarebbe dunque entrato nel lessico del rito egizio a indicare l'inno della cerimonia di risveglio della divinità. Questo significato spiega anche la valenza della occorrenza del libro nono: da 'inno iniziale dell rito mattutino' a semplice 'inno iniziale in onore della divinità' (musicale nel caso del libro nono, una ouverture potremmo dire con una certa approssimazione)'.

[32]   *Martianus Capella*, ed. Willis (n. 4, above) 2 *ad loc.*; Stahl and Johnson, *Martianus Capella and the Seven Liberal Arts* (n. 4, above) II 4 n. 8; *etc.*

nuptiis, he promises his son Martianus (and the readers) that 'if you are serious, I will unfold before you a tale which Satire taught me' ('si properus scrutator inquiris, fabellam tibi, quam Satura [...] edocuit [...] explicabo').

Nevertheless, if, amidst such games, Capella, his book, and the social order that sanctioned his book are to retain strategic control of pedagogy, they must first maintain control over their means and over the exuberance of the *De nuptiis*' Apuleian source. Capella uses borrowed 'Apuleian windings' but he cannot give them official sanction. This, let me suggest, is why, as Robert Carver, Julia Gaisser, and others note, despite being ever-present in Capella's *De nuptiis*, Apuleius is never named anywhere in the work. *Recognizing* him as a source, giving him the status of canon, would conflate Capella's incongruous, if necessary, means and ends, and could jeopardize the authority of Capella's pedagogic edifice.

IV. The slippage between usage and canonical recognition

Following the verse proem and the prose prologue, Capella begins in the next section (1.3) the frame story of the marriage itself. We are in a world of playful literary allusion, which nevertheless, as we shall see, moves progressively towards a more complex practice of reception and pedagogy.

'There was a time when on all sides among the gods the sacred weddings of a numerous generation were being celebrated', Capella begins. A little later in the narrative (1.5), hearing of such nuptials, Mercury decides that he should also take a wife. His mother Maia recommends it too:

> In quam sententiam [*sc.* uxorem ducere] mater illum anxia, cum annua peragratione zodiaca eam in Pliadum numero salutaret, impulerat, praesertimque quod palaestra crebrisque discursibus exercitum corpus lacertosis in iuvenalis roboris excellentiam toris virilis quadam amplitudine renidebat, ac iam pubentes genae seminudum eum incedere chlamydaque indutum parva, invelatum cetera, umerorum cacumen obnubere sine magno risu Cypridis non sinebat.

> His nervous mother, when he greeted her from among the Pleiades in his annual journey through the Zodiac, had pushed him to this decision [to take a wife], especially because his body, exercised in the palaestra and through constant activity ('creberisque discursibus'), glistened forth in masculine development with muscles bulging in the protuberance of youthful vigour ('in iuvenalis roboris excellentiam toris virilis quadam amplitudine renidebat'). Already his bedowned cheeks did not allow him to walk around half-naked ('seminudum'), draped in a small chlamys, and, with everything else exposed ('invelatum cetera'), to cover only the tops of his shoulders, without great amusement on the part of Cypris.

Capella's narrative, like that of Apuleius, is replete with sexual nudges and winks. In *De nuptiis*, Mercury had been practicing in the palaestra and through 'constant to and fro activity' ('creberisque discursibus'). These are Apuleian words,[33] yet 'discursus' 'is not the

---

[33] See, *e.g.*, *Martianus Capella*, ed. Willis (n. 4, above) 3 *ad loc.* and *Met.* 6.1, 'interea Psyche variis iactabatur discursibus' ('meanwhile Psyche wandered this way and that'). 'Iactabatur', like 'discursus', involves a to-and-fro movement (M. Zimmerman, S. Panayotakis, V. C. Hunink, W. H. Keulen, S. J. Harrison, T. D. McCreight, B. Wesseling, and D. van Mal-Maeder, *Apuleius Madaurensis 'Metamorphoses' Books IV 28–35, V and VI 1–24 The Tale of Cupid and Psyche* (Groningen 2004) 363–4).

normal word to use of running in the track or *palaestra*'.[34] Lexical opaqueness is a Capellan characteristic, but here it is also part of an erotic trope. We and young student readers can only guess at the precise nature of Mercury's 'bustling activity' in the wrestling schools,[35] guided, perhaps, by the description of Mercury's ephebic physique in the next sentence: Mercury's body 'glistens forth in masculine development', his muscles 'bulging in the protuberance of his youthful vigour' ('corpus lacertosis in iuvenalis roboris excellentiam toris virilis quadam amplitudine renidebat'). A moment later, Martianus offers a yet more open hint, pointing out that Mercury was in the habit of walking about 'half-naked ('seminudum'), draped in a small chlamys, with everything else exposed ('invelatum cetera'), so as to cover only the tops of his shoulders, to 'great amusement on the part of Cypris'. Interpreting such hints, it is important to bear in mind the *De nuptiis*' performative context and its perlocutionary effects. As a textbook, Capella's work will have been read in the classroom by adolescent youths who were probably themselves going through the same bodily changes and will have had similar opportunities for exercise. Capella's innuendo seems well aimed at adolescent humour and may have helped in keeping fidgety pupils at their desks.

It is hard to say exactly how much of Martianus' intertext his youthful readers were meant to have known. But, as Chevalier says, 'le portrait de Mercure est vraisemblent inspiré de celui que propose Apulée dans *Apol.* 63'.[36] In the *Apology*, we find an ecphrastic description of a ritual statue of Mercury:

Em uide, quam facies eius decora et suci palaestrici plena sit, quam hilaris dei uultus, ut decenter utrimque lanugo malis deserpat, ut in capite crispatus capillus sub imo pillei umbraculo appareat, quam lepide super tempora pares pinnulae emineant, quam autem festiue circa humeros uestis substricta sit.

Look how charmingly the down creeps over both cheeks, and how his curls show from under the edge of his felt cap. Look how elegantly those little wings stand out just above his temples, how gracefully his cloak is tied up around his shoulders.

A similar description, with its emphasis on Mercury's beauty and nakedness, along with his short chlamys, is also attested in the *Metamorphoses* (10.30.3):[37]

Adest luculentus puer nudus, nisi quod ephebica chlamida sinistrum tegebat umerum, flauis crinibus usquequaque conspicuus, et inter comas eius aureae pinnulae colligatione simili sociatae prominebant; quem [caducaeum] et uirgula Mercurium indicabat.

---

[34]   Shanzer, *A Philosophical and Literary Commentary* (n. 4, above) 64 *ad loc. Cf.* H. Schalk, 'Diskurs: zwischen Allerweltswort und philosophischem Begriff', *Archiv für Begriffsgeschichte* 40 (1997) 56–104; *TLL* 5.1.1369.82; Plin. *Hist. Nat.* 1.2.36 'de discursu stellarum'; *etc.*

[35]   *Cf. OLD s.v.* 'discursus' 3 and, *e.g.*, Sen. *Dial.* 12.6.5, 'discursus et sudor'; Plin. *Ep.* 1.9.7, 'inanum discursum relinque'.

[36]   *Martianus Capella*, ed. Chevalier (n. 4, above) 63. Text: R. Helm, *Apulei Platonici Opera Quae Supersunt Vol. II Fasc. 1: Pro Se De Magia Liber (Apologia)* (Leipzig 1959); trans. S. J. Harrison, J. Hilton, and V. C. Hunink, *Apuleius, Rhetorical Works* (Oxford 2001) 85–6. For a discussion of Mercury's portrait here, see J.-F. Chevalier, 'Le corps du Cyllénien dans le livre I du 'De nuptiis Philologiae et Mercurii' de Martianus Capella: Le portrait d'un éphèbe virgilien?', in *Mélanges en l'honneur de Philippe Heuzé*, eds Y. Hersant and J. Pigeaud (Québec, forthcoming).

[37]   In contrast to Mercury's short chlamys, when, in the modest initiation ceremony at the end of the *Metamorphoses*, Lucius dons a similar garb (11.24.2), it hangs 'all the way to his heels'.

Then a radiantly beautiful boy appeared, naked except for an ephebic cape covering his left shoulder. He attracted all eyes with his blond curls, and from his hair projected little golden wings symmetrically attached, a caduceus and wand identified him as Mercury.

These sources, however, require careful assessment. In Apuleius' *Apology*, otherwise known as the *De magia*, Mercury's description is not mere pleasantry but part of the author's defence against a serious legal charge of sorcery and moral corruption. In our passage, Apuleius is responding to the accusation (*Apol.* 61) that he had commissioned a sinister ritual statuette for secretive magical purposes. Apuleius describes the statue in question, which, he claims, is not a sordid figurine but a graceful image. What Apuleius keeps *sub rosa*, for obvious reasons, is the 'highly dangerous' fact that Mercury is the patron god of magic itself.[38] Using the *De magia* as a source, Capella takes advantage of the alluring eroticism of Apuleius' description, but—almost like Apuleius himself—he seems to elide some of the darker resonance of its context. Capella treads on the cusp of transgression and must maintain a careful balance of exposure and occlusion. To have said, 'as Apuleius says in his *De magia* [...]', may have taken the narrative a step too far.

The dilemmas behind the otherwise playful description of Mercury can be understood even more distinctly when we consider Capella's second Apuleian intertext and the image of Mercury as it appears in Apuleius' best-known work, the *Metamorphoses*. Here, the description of Mercury, although not without charm, is nevertheless part of the ecphrastic *mise-en-scène* of the novel's most grotesque and pornographic scene, one which, happily, even Apuleius forecloses before it reaches its climax. Lucius the narrator, still in the body of an ass, is to play the role of Zeus in disguise and re-enact the myth of Pasiphaea in a bizarre theatrical spectacle: the public execution, by bestial copulation, of a condemned murderess. The *Metamorphoses* describes the slopes of a wooden mock-up of Mont Ida, 'mons ligneous ad instar incluti montis illius quem vates Homeris Idaeum cecinit' (10.30), a rustic vista adorned by a few grazing goats, 'capellae pauculae tondebant herbulas'. Martianus Capella was no doubt smiling to himself (indeed, enjoying a pun?) as he invoked this scene in which Mercury, an actor in costume, makes a brief dancing appearance as he hands a golden apple to the actor playing Paris. Mercury's innocent ephebic nakedness adds perverse detail to this scene.

The relation between eros and pedagogy has many applications. But sexual bestiality takes any such relation beyond what is acceptable or permitted in most cultures.[39] Animal sexuality is a basic appetite that cannot be removed from human experience (as Aristotle and other ancient philosophers knew), but is in many cultures— Greek, Roman, Medieval, Victorian, and no less our own age—often relegated to clearly defined spaces in the silent and occluded peripheries of social order, and especially outside the sphere of public culture and education.[40] Pornography is rarely 'canonical'. Apuleius' *Metamorphoses* takes us to

---

[38]   *Florida*, trans. V. C. Hunink, in S. J. Harrison, J. Hilton, and V. C. Hunink, *Apuleius, Rhetorical Works* (n. 36, above) 84 n. 155.

[39]   With some exceptions, such as representation in Greek vase painting, which lie outside the scope of our discussion and require special consideration. See, *e.g.*, M. F. Kilmer, *Greek Erotica on Attic Red-Figure Vases* (London 1993).

[40]   The relation of pornography to canon in antiquity is an understudied topic (but see, *e.g.*, A. Richlin, *Pornography and Representation in Greece and Rome* (Oxford 1992); L. Kurke, 'Pindar and the prostitutes, or reading ancient "pornography"', *Arion* 4.2 (1996) 49–75. The fate of the *Metamorphoses*' Greek cognate, *Lucius, or The Ass*, which is more pornographic and largely lost, may be indicative. For pornography and canon more generally, see S. Gubar, 'Representing pornography: feminism, criticism, and depictions of female violation', *Critical Inquiry* 13.4 (1987) 712–41.

the brink of bestiality. It does not actually cross the line but, treading so close to the edge, it remains in a 'liminal' position. Martianus Capella's borrowing, the occlusion of the context of the source of his description of Mercury, and exclusion of any open reference to Apuleius are both a confirmation of Apuleius' liminal status and the replication of such a double-sided liminality. Here, I submit, is the operative principle that determines the slippage between usage and canonical recognition.

V. Transgressive vehicles and prescriptive tenors: eros and dialectic

I want to suggest, however, that some of the most interesting and revealing examples of this slippage—an incongruous but productive 'marriage' of transgressive vehicles and prescriptive tenors—occur in the more formal, academically 'hard-core', sections of Capella's didactic treatise. I turn therefore to book IV of the *De nuptiis* and to Capella's discussion of dialectic, the 'science of science' ('disciplina disciplinarum', Aug. *de ord.* 2.1.3.38), of formal inference, syllogisms, and logic.[41] My comments, of course, will focus not on the formal, philosophical, aspects of the *Dialectica* but on its use of the Apuleian source and its pedagogy.

Like the other 'disciplinary' books of the *De nuptiis* (*i.e.* books II–IX), the *Dialectica* is framed by allegory and begins with its own long and convoluted verse proem (327):

> Into the assembly of the gods came Dialectic, a woman whose weapons are complex and knotty utterances. Without her, nothing follows, and likewise nothing stands in opposition [*i.e.* in formal syllogisms] [...] she had ready the school maxim which reminds us that speech consists in words which are ambiguous and judges nothing as having a standard meaning unless it be combined with other words.[42]

By necessity, the topic is more technical and Capella, while preserving the allegorical frame as best he can, must already here mention several of his main sources. These include above all Aristotle, whose *Organon* was the foundation of ancient logic, the Stoics, especially Chrysippus, and the Sceptic Carneades.[43] The more immediate sources of Capella's *Dialectic* were, however, probably Latin works on the subject. Mentioned by name are only the canonical authors, for example Varro (335) and Cicero (350 and *passim*; citations appear especially in the 'hypothetical syllogisms', 414–22). But other, unacknowledged, Latin sources include work by the fourth-century North African rhetorician Marius Victorinus Afer and, most important for us here, the *Peri hermeneias*, which, despite its Greek title, is a Latin work on logic attributed to Apuleius.[44]

---

[41]   For a characterization of the *Dialectica* in relation to knowledge and the sciences, see Ferré, *Martianus Capella* (n. 4, above) viii.

[42]   'Haec quoque contortis stringens effamina nodis / Qua sine nil sequitur nilque repugnant item, / in coetum superum veniens primordia fandi / advehit et scholium praestruit axioma / ambiguis memorans vocem consistere verbis / nil normale putans, ni fuat associum / sed licet ipse modos demum bis quinque profatus / pallens afflictim verset Aristoteles, / Stoica circumeant ludantque sophismata sensus / perdita neque umquam cornua fronte ferant, / Chrysippus cumulet proprium <et> consumat acervum / Carneadesque parem vim great hellebore; / nullus apex tot prole virum par accidit umquam / nec tibi tam felix sortis honos cecidit: / inter temple deum fas est, Dialectica, fari, / et Iove conspecto iure docentis agis'. Trans. Stahl and Johnson, *Martianus Capella and the Seven Liberal Arts* (n. 4, above).

[43]   See Grebe, *'De nuptiis Philologiae et Mercurii'* (n. 4, above) 109–15; Ferré, *Martianus Capella* (n. 4, above) xvi–viii.

[44]   Text of the *Peri hermeneias*: C. Moreschini, *Apulei Platonici Madaurensis Vol. III: De philosophia libri* (Stuttgart-Leipzig 1991). See also D. Londey and C. Johanson, *The Logic of Apuleius* (Leiden 1987); M. W. Sullivan,

The influence of the *Peri hermeneias* is easy to identify in Capella's *Dialectica*, and especially in the section of book IV on 'categorical syllogisms' (406–13). However, to understand his use of Apuleius, we must first say a brief word about this work which Stephen Harrison describes as 'a Latin version of Aristotelian logical doctrine in dry and technical language which offers little of stylistic or literary interest'.[45] Fundamentally, *Peri hermeneias* is indeed a taxonomy of formal propositions. It provides definitions, examples, and explanations of 'predicative' and 'conditional' statements, 'universal' and 'particular' propositions, 'dedicative' and 'abdicative' syllogisms, and so on.[46] Whoever was the author of the *Peri hermeneias*, the work names Apuleius explicitly. Indeed, Apuleius' name is part of the book's formal *exempla*. A proposition, the text explains, has a 'pars subiectiva / subdita' and a 'pars declarativa' (a 'subjective' / 'subordinative' and a 'declarative' element; broadly corresponding to the nominal and verbal parts of the sentence). The text gives an example, 'Apuleius [the nominal element] disserit / non disserit [the verbal element]', then extends the 'subordinative' part 'Apuleius' with the element 'philosophicus Platonicus Madaurensis', which, it explains, is logically interchangeable.[47]

Of course, reference to 'Apuleius, philosophicus Platonicus Madaurensis', like all semantic content, has no impact on the formal logical structure of propositions. Yet in the *Peri hermeneias*, Apuleius' name inevitably frames the readers' horizons of expectation. The formal logical propositions take on the curious flavour of Apuleian narrative—light zest in a bitter scientific draught. In the discussion of the relations between the 'subordinative' and 'declarative' elements, Apuleius' *Peri hermeneias* offers the following proposition: 'qui equus est, hinnibile est', 'he who is a horse is a neigher'.[48] With the author's name and, implicitly, his most famous work, also known as *The Golden Ass*, ringing in our ear, it is hard to miss the deadpan joke ('every horse neighs [[…] and every ass brays]'). A line or two later, 'Apuleius' offers another example of the relations between 'subordinative' and 'declarative': 'omnem hominem animal esse […] omne animal hominem esse', 'every man is an animal […] every animal is a man'.[49] Again, the logical *exempla* trigger Apuleian humour, first, because the author's name is 'Apuleius', second, because they contain the essential narrative and situational theme of Apuleius' *Metamorphoses* ('man turns into animal'), and, finally, because they incorporate a sense of Apuleian innuendo and playful poetics.

Let us now turn again to Martianus Capella's *Dialectica*. Following the verse proem, the book discusses propositions (sections I–IV), the relations between propositions (sections V–VI), 'assertoric' syllogisms (VII–XIV), and, finally, some doxographic comments on the study of logic (XIII). As this text moves forward, Capella's allusive Apuleian hints also develop and take on more substantial moral and pedagogical, but equally more transgressive, resonance.

In one of the most important sections of the *Dialectica* (V), Capella considers the relations between propositions and arranges them within a structured logical diagram otherwise

---

Apuleian Logic: The Nature, Sources, and Influence of Apuleius's 'Peri hermeneias' (Amsterdam 1967). The fact that this work is today excluded from the Apuleian corpus is irrelevant for our purposes here.

[45]   S. J. Harrison, *Apuleius: A Latin Sophist* (Oxford 2000) 11.

[46]   The main discussions of these concepts in antiquity are to be found in Aristotle's *Organon*, but *cf.*, *e.g.*, Plato, *Theaet.* 206D, *Soph.* 262C; P. T. Geach, 'History of the corruptions of logic', in P. T. Geach, *Logic Matters* (Berkeley 1972) 44–61; L. M. de Rijk, *Plato's Sophist: A Philosophical Commentary* (Amsterdam 1986) 133.

[47]   267 / IV. C. Moreschini, *Apulei Platonici Madaurensis* (n. 44, above) 191.18–192.12.

[48]   267 / IV. C. Moreschini, *Apulei Platonici Madaurensis* (n. 44, above) 192–17.

[49]   268 / IV. C. Moreschini, *Apulei Platonici Madaurensis* (n. 44, above) 192.23–193.13.

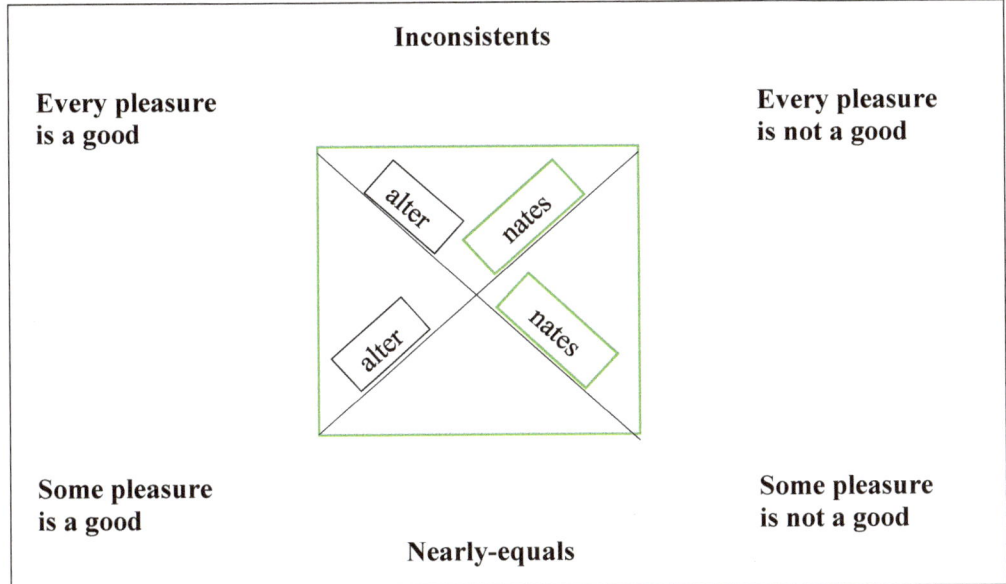

Figure 1. 'The Apuleian square of opposition'

known as the 'Apuleian square of opposition', since its first appearance in the history of Western logic is probably in the *Peri hermeneias* (fig. 1).[50] Capella does not name Apuleius, but he copies the *Peri hermeneias*' paradigmatic examples: A. *Every pleasure* ('*voluptas*') *is good*; B. *Every pleasure is not good*; C. *Some pleasure is good*; D. *Some pleasure is not good* (V). We will not, of course, consider the formalities of the logic here, but must note, first, that these are indeed primarily examples of *formal* logical relations; second, that despite the 'irrelevance' of propositional content to logical form, the content of these examples takes us into the realm of *moral* action; and, finally, that at least something of Apuleius' more salacious reputation resonates in the use of 'voluptas' in these otherwise austere, scientific examples. We must not forget that this is a textbook of logic for princes and well-to-do youths who, when they have completed their education, are likely to become influential members of their cities with the power to make important decisions.[51] Indeed, as Capella himself says in the verse proem to the *Dialectica*, 'speech consists in words which are ambiguous and judges nothing as having a standard meaning unless it be combined with other words'.[52] What is otherwise dry and potentially difficult academic material is thus made *both* more morally relevant and humorous, but, for exactly the same reason, also a little more risqué. Capella replicates useful practice the resonance of which is both potentially productive and potentially transgressive.

Nevertheless, in Apuleius' *Peri hermeneias*, such practice is generally limited to mildly suggestive examples. Furthermore, innuendo seems to fade away when 'Apuleius' considers

[50]   397. See Sullivan, *Apuleian Logic* (n. 44, above) 64–66; Londey and Johanson, *The Logic of Apuleius* (n. 44, above) 108. For the history of logic, see I. M. Bocheński, *A History of Formal Logic* (Notre Dame, IN 1961) esp. 37 n. 14; D. Gabbay and J. Woods, *Handbook of the History of Logic. Volume I. Greek, Indian and Arabic Logic* (Amsterdam 2004).

[51]   See above, n. 30.

[52]   See above, n. 42.

syllogisms ('If A, then B'), the more action-oriented elements of reasoned speech, the greater power of which arguably calls for greater moral and pedagogical responsibility. Thus, for example, section VII of the *Peri hermeneias* highlights the following syllogism (271–2, here arranged graphically for clarity):

> omne honestum bonum est;
> omne bonum utile est;
> omne igitur honestum utile est.

> Every honourable thing is good;
> Every good thing is useful;
> Therefore every honourable thing is useful.

The propositional content of this formal syllogism contains an important moral element, which is also reflected in all of the syllogistic examples in all following sections of Apuleius' *Peri hermeneias*.

Martianus' discussion of syllogisms is, as we stressed, heavily indebted to the *Peri hermeneias*. He relies on Apuleian concepts and method and he is well aware of the moral message underlying logical formalities. Thus, for example, in section 405 of the *Dialectica*, he says 'putemus quaestionem esse, utrum voluptas utilis est?' ('let us consider the question, is pleasure [otherwise 'desire'] useful?'). Like *Peri hermeneias*, the *Dialectica* is not a manual of moral philosophy but merely a technical handbook. The propositional content of the question has no bearing on the formal structure of the logical argument. Yet, clearly, the content of the question and its moral resonance cannot be entirely elided. It is here, however, that Capella illustrates his formal discussion by means of most extraordinary and revealing examples. While copying the logical structure from the *Peri hermeneias*, his examples seem to reach out to the most salacious themes of Apuleius' *Metamorphoses*. Capella's text says (405, again arranged graphically for clarity):

> omnis voluptas bonum est;
> omne bonum utile est;
> omnis igitur voluptas utile est.

> Every pleasure is a good thing;
> Every good thing is useful;
> Therefore every pleasure is useful.

Shortly afterwards, he repeats similar propositional claims in the subsequent discussion of formal logical variation (408):

> omne bonum utile est;
> omnis voluptas bonum est;
> omnis igitur voluptas utile est.

> Every good thing is useful;
> Every pleasure is a good;
> Therefore, every pleasure is useful.

It seems that here the 'formal' character of logic provides a protective mask, behind which all human animals, including young students of logic and their schoolmasters, can exercise their 'voluptas sub rosa', as it were, without sanction.

Adapting Apuleius' tale of curiosity and matrimony as the frame narrative of the *De nuptiis*, Capella takes what is of practical use to him. The rest he hides or silences. 'Cupid and Psyche are', as Shanzer suggests, 'no longer the lovers of the Apuleian tale'.[53] In Martianus, she argues, the soul's descent into the material world is a death-producing 'fall', not productive of life or desire.[54] This is true, inasmuch as Cupid and Psyche's issue, Voluptas, has been written out of the narrative of book I of the *De nuptiis*. Yet, as we have seen, 'Apuleian' 'voluptas', intensified and enhanced, seems to be alive and well in some of the most important lessons of Martianus Capella's pedagogy. Furthermore, Apuleian 'voluptas' is indeed 'utile', as Capella's formal example suggests. It will have helped schoolmasters teach the dry art of dialectic. Capella the pedagogue cannot resist the exuberant charms of 'voluptas'. Yet, in approaching 'voluptas' in this way, Capella also highlights her more dangerous, transgressive nature, which, if given formal license, could undermine society's control over itself. Educators, moralists, parents, and indeed those traditions of reception whose agglomerated effect is responsible for the formation of canon, would not wish, nor could they risk, to have schoolboys praise the virtues of pleasure except through a veil.[55] 'Voluptas', the double-sided essence of Apuleius, has enormous power and, for this exact same reason, like Apuleius himself, constitutes both an allure and a threat. Its exuberant, protean disregard for authority is a life force which is ignorant of social constraint. It is a force that, perhaps a little like the power of horses and asses, must be harnessed, but which, harnessed, has no independence. In literary and literary historical terms, the 'dialectic' status of this force, let me suggest, characterizes something of Apuleius' in the tradition, or at least in his reception in Martianus Capella. Apuleius is always there, yet he is kept *sub rosa*, unacknowledged. Capella is a good witness to such canonical status. He both imitates and enhances the Apuleian habit, and is, for this reason, also himself a variant example of the dialectic of canon. Capella, as we noted at the beginning of this essay, is an immensely popular author whose role in the history of pedagogy is seminal. He is an effective pedagogue, partly because of his exuberant habit, yet, sailing rather close to the wind, he lives largely on the margins of the canon. Martianus Capella's double-sided fate is thus both an incisive critique of Apuleian canonicity and one of its most revealing examples.

Trinity College Dublin

---

[53] Shanzer, *A Philosophical and Literary Commentary* (n. 4, above) 69: 'In the *Metamorphoses* the *unio mystica* of Cupid and Psyche has a positive value. The tale is one of a relationship between a human *mystes* and a divinity [...] Martianus's account, however, owes far more to the Hermetic thought of the *Poimandres*, where sexual union of ἄνθρωπος and φύσις is the metaphor which expresses the soul's fall into the material world. [...] [C]ertainly later mediaeval writers knew that Cupid and Psyche are no longer the lovers of the Apuleian tale'.

[54] Shanzer, *A Philosophical and Literary Commentary* (n. 4, above) 70: 'The Marteanean version is a hybrid: it is heavily allegorized in that there is no description of the downward flight of the soul. Within this allegorical framework there is perhaps intentional narrative confusion: the soul (like Pandora) is nubile [...]'.

[55] Society's fundamental principle is, of course the *Unbehagenheit* it forces upon its members through the imposition of boundaries on behaviour, as Freud had argued in his classic work in 1930: see *The Standard Edition of the Complete Works of Sigmund Freud, Volume XXI (1927–1931)*, ed. J. Stachey (London 2001).

A TRANSLATION OF APULEIUS' *METAMORPHOSES* AND THE DEBATE ABOUT FICTION IN THE SIXTEENTH CENTURY: *L'ASINO D'ORO* BY AGNOLO FIRENZUOLA (1550)

FRANÇOISE LAVOCAT

Any exploration of my long-standing interest in Apuleius' *Metamorphoses* must begin by investigating the history of interpretation as it is related to a changing consciousness of fictionality.[1] This evolving historical consciousness is far from linear (moving from simple unawareness to awareness), but instead uneven, complicated by disconcerting regressions (or what seem to be relapses, based on a teleological view of intellectual history).[2] Sixteenth-century translations of Apuleius' *Metamorphoses* are an excellent case study in a puzzling phenomenon: a shift from literary and allegorical meaning to factual and referential interpretation, along with the rise of demonological knowledge.[3] I, as well as other scholars,[4] have noticed an impoverishment of allegorical interpretations of Apuleius' *Metamorphoses* in the time following Beroaldo's commentary. This de-allegorization can be linked to a new historical and factual reading, according to which Apuleius' Lucius is an actual magician. This reading was based on the belief that real metamorphosis is possible, perhaps due in part to the influence of Jean Bodin. In any case, at the beginning of the seventeenth century Apuleius' tale was broadly considered to be merely autobiographical—as was, for example, by Jean de Montlyard (whose translation of Apuleius' text was published in 1612).

More broadly, from the beginning of the seventeenth century the use of the first person became largely incompatible with fiction. Indeed, the number of first-person narratives began to decrease. According to my research, only 7.5% of fictional texts published in France between 1611 and 1623 were first-person narratives, as opposed to 9% between 1585 and 1610 (thirty-three texts for the whole period). Among this small group of first-person narratives, 25% were republications or translations of older fiction: La *Fiammetta* by Boccacio, *El*

[1] With regard to the affirmation of fiction in the sixteenth century—under the name of 'fable' or 'poetry'—that was allowed by the victory of the Aristotelian current over the supporters of Platonism, see T. Chevrolet, *L'Idée de fable. Théories de la fiction poétique à la Renaissance* (Genève 2007).

[2] With regard to Apuleius in the sixteenth century, see my articles 'Frontières troublées de la fiction à la fin de la Renaissance: Apulée et le débat sur la métamorphose', *Cahiers du dix-septième: An Interdisciplinary Journal* 13.2 (2011) 92–109 [http://se17.bowdoin.edu/2011-volume-xiii-2 (accessed 16 January 2020)], and 'Zirze ist keine Fable: Verworrene Grenzen in der Spätrenaissance', in *Fakt und Fiktion, Text in Kontext*, eds U. Schneider and A. Traninger (Stuttgart 2010) 57–70; on fiction more broadly, see my *Fait et fiction, pour une frontière* (Paris 2016).

[3] This knowledge spread across Europe with the publication of Sprenger and Kramer's *Malleus Maleficarum* in 1487. In France, its peak was certainly between the 1580s (Bodin, *Démonomanie des sorciers*, 1580) and 1620 (Pierre de Lancre, *Tableau de l'inconstance des mauvais anges et démons*, 1612)

[4] See, in particular, O. Pédeflous, 'La traduction de l'âne d'or par Guillaume Michel (1517): une contribution à la poétique du roman au XVIe siècle', *Revue d'histoire littéraire de la France* 3.107 (2007) 515–535.

Lazarillo de Tormes, *El Buscón* by Mateo Aleman, and the *Metamorphoses* by Apuleius.[5] I presume that this was due to an increasing difficulty at the time in grasping the status of a fictional, first-person narrator. Indeed, even today, it is sometimes difficult to comprehend this status and it often becomes the source of competing interpretations. Narratologist Käte Hamburger is right to claim that first-person narratives are a particular kind of fiction, based on simulation. It is therefore especially interesting to examine Apuleius' *Metamorphoses* in relation to the problem of interpretation that is inherent in the use of a first-person narrative.

I will focus on a fascinating case of translation-adaptation by Agnolo Firenzuola. *L'asino d'oro* was written in Rome in 1524–1525, completed around 1532, and published for the first time in Venice in 1550.[6] It was republished three times in the sixteenth and the seventeenth centuries, and then included in several editions (one or two every century) of Firenzuola's complete works in the eighteenth, nineteenth, and twentieth centuries.

This text, far from being the most famous Italian translation of Apuleius' *Metamorphoses*, is seldom cited by current specialists on the topic (such as Julia Haig Gaisser, Olivier Pédeflous, Giuseppina Magnaldi, and Gian Franco Gianotti). Franziska Küenzlen, however, compares translations of Apuleius' *Metamorphoses* by Beroaldo, Sieder, Michel, Lopez de Cortegana, and Firenzuola in her doctoral dissertation.[7] Some of my analysis overlaps with that of Küenzlen, but while she approaches the topic from a linguistic perspective I will focus instead on other aspects, in particular those connected to the history of fiction and the intellectual shift from fiction to fact mentioned above. Since a central feature of Firenzuola's translation-adaptation is the use of a first-person narrator—referencing not Apuleius but himself—we must ask ourselves the following question: what kind of interpretation (allegorical? fictional? factual?) is triggered by the autobiographical appropriation of *L'asino d'oro* by Agnolo Firenzuola?

I. Unproblematic originality

As with all of Firenzuola's works (with the exception of a treatise against the introduction of Greek letters into the Latin alphabet),[8] *L'asino d'oro* was released some years after the author's death, in 1550 (by Giolito de Ferrari in Venice, republished in 1555, 1556, 1557).[9] Firenzuola's brother, Gerolamo, along with his friends, took charge of preparing this first edition. *L'asino d'oro* was also republished by Filippo Giunta in an expurgated edition in 1598 and 1603 (after the censorship of Apuleius' *Metamorphoses*).[10] Born in 1498,

---

[5]   I have developed this inquiry in 'Fictions en prose à la première personne (1585–1623)', *Études de langue et littérature françaises*, Société d'Études de langue et littératures françaises de l'Université de Kyoto, 14 (2014) 69–87.

[6]   *Apuleio dell'asino d'oro, tradotto per messer Agnolo Firenzuola fiorentino* (Venice, Gabriel Giolito de Ferrari, 1550). The work was probably written in 1525 (D. Maestro, *Opere di Agnolo Firenzuola* (Turin 1977) 45).

[7]   F. Küenzlen, *Verwandlungen eines Esels: Apuleius' 'Metamorphoses' im frühen 16. Jahrhundert* (Heidelberg 2005).

[8]   Agnolo Firenzuola, *Discacciamento de le nuoue lettere, inutilmente aggiunte ne la lingua toscana* (Rome, Lodovico Vincentino and Lautitio Perugino, 1524). As Riviello has shown, Firenzuola, along with Bembo and in opposition to Trissino, rejects the introduction of the Greek letters epsilon and omega, because the Italian language would have lost the clarity and simplicity it had inherited from Latin.

[9]   *Apuleio dell'asino d'oro* (n. 6, above); as Küenzlen notes, *L'asino d'oro* was the last Firenzuola work prepared and funded by Gerolamo. Does this mean he did not consider it to be his brother's most important work? Did he fear censorship? See Küenzlen, *Verwandlungen* (n. 7, above) ch. 7.

[10]   *Apuleio dell'asino d'oro. Tradotto per Agnolo Firenzuola* (Florence, Filippo Giunta, 1598); *Apuleio dell'asino*

Firenzuola wrote this translation in his youth, during a stay in Rome as a priest in the court of pope Clement VII (Giulio de' Medici) between 1523 and 1526. Afterwards, freed from his monastic vows and seemingly infected by syphilis or malaria, he spent the remainder of his life in Prato, where he created and developed an academic and intellectual circle. He died in 1543 at the age of 50.[11]

The most remarkable feature of his translation of Apuleius' *Metamorphoses* is his replacement of Lucius' name and biography by his own. Lorenzo Scala underlines this choice in his dedicatory letter to Lorenzo Pucci (dated 15 May 1549). But he does not in the least emphasize its originality. He argues that *L'asino d'oro* was probably dear to its author, because Firenzuola never revealed anything about his own life except in this translation.[12]

> Questa è adunque la presente traduttione d'Apuleio da lui fatta con quei debiti modi, che convengono a simili imprese; cio è, benissimo intesa, e propriamente trasportata co'veri, e puri, e significanti vocaboli nella lingua nostra, con le figure del dire, e in somma con tutto ciò ch'a lui si richiedeva, per acquistarne onore, et per sodisfarne altrui. E ben mostrò egli d'haverla approvata, poi chè, quello che in nessuno altro suo componimento non havea più fatto, volle nel principio di questa sua fatica, fare brevemente memoria della vita sua: la quella fu sempre virtuosa et honorata, benche poco lieta et infelice.
>
> (Al molto magnifico signor Lorenzo Pucci, *Apuleio dell'Asino d'Oro*, 1550, f. 2v–3r)

> So here is the translation of Apuleius that he [Firenzuola] wrote, with all that is suitable for a similar undertaking; that is to say, [a translation] that is clearly understandable, presented in an appropriate manner, with pure, correct words, full of meaning in our language, with properly executed stylistic devices—in short, all that was needed to gain honour and satisfy others. And [Firenzuola] clearly showed that he had approved it, because, unlike in any of his other works, at the beginning of this one, he wrote a short tale of his life, which was always virtuous and honourable, though sad and miserable.[13]

We find a second example of the unproblematic reception of this most interesting aspect of Firenzuola's adaptation in the same letter. Lorenzo Scala explains that Lodovico Domenichi, another author and friend of Firenzuola's, replaced missing pages in *L'asino d'oro* with passages of his own:

> Vero è, che in questa traduttione s'è trovato mancare alcune carte in diversi luoghi, ne si sa à per cui difetto; lequali dallo eccellente e mio molto virtuoso et carissimo amico Messer Lodovico Domenichi vi sono state supplite, per la grande affettione, che la virtù sua porta al valor di lui. Dove s'è talmente adoperato, che havendo egli molta pratica delle cose del Firenzuola, l'ha cosi bene imitato, che lo stile dell'uno non è

---

d'oro. Tradotto per m. Agnolo Firenzuola fiorentino, Di nuouo ricorretto, e ristampato (Firenze, nella stamperia de' Giunti, 1603; the colophon carries 1607, a date difference for which I have no explanation).

[11] See T. C. Riviello, ch. 1, 'Agnolo Firenzuola and the intellectual life (early sixteenth century)', in *Agnolo Firenzuola: The Androgynous Vision* (Rome 1986).

[12] This is not entirely true: Firenzuola also mentions his own life events—in particular the death of his beloved Costanza Amaretta—at the beginning of another book, written at the same time as *L'asino d'oro: I Ragionamenti* (1525, printed in 1548): *Opere*, ed. A. Seroni (Florence 1958) 37–184.

[13] All translations are my own unless otherwise indicated.

punto differente dall' altro.

(Al molto magnifico signor Lorenzo Pucci, *Apuleio dell'Asino d'Oro*, 1550, p. 3)

It is true that a few pages were found to be missing from this translation, we don't know how, and that they were replaced by the excellent Lodovico Domenichi, my very virtuous friend, due to the great affection that his virtue brings to the value [of Firenzuola]. And he did it so well, having had much practice with the works of Firenzuola, that one cannot distinguish the style of one from the other.

Indeed, as contemporary critics have shown, Domenichini borrowed several passages from Boiardo's translation to complete gaps in *L'asino d'oro* (mainly in book 10).[14] But he also added something of his own to the first book: praise of Firenzuola's father, Sebastiano, who was a lawyer and humanist scholar. This interpolation suggests that the substitution of Agnolo for Lucius did not raise any questions in Firenzuola's circle. We may assume that contemporary readers interpreted it as a statement of authorship, probably linked to the use of Italian, at a time when the dignity of vulgar language was being reclaimed. Firenzuola, who sees himself as a successor to Boccaccio and Petrarch, and a friend of Pietro Bembo and Pietro Aretino, replaces Lucius because his translation into Italian makes him as worthy as Apuleius. In Scala's view, Firenzuola's linguistic choices (in favour of the purity of the Italian language) and the autobiographical adaptation are probably part of the same agenda. Indeed, Firenzuola's proper name refers to a place and recalls the author's familial roots in Florence, as well as his close relationship with the Tuscan language:

Firenzuola, posta appiè delle Alpi, che sono già tra Fiorenza, e Bologna, è picciolo castello, ma come il nome, e le sue insegne dimostrano nobilitato, e tenuto caro da i suoi signori ; e Fiorenza medesima sono la mia antica patria […] Io principio adunque una Thosca favola.

(*Apuleio dell'Asino d'Oro*, 1550, f. 4r-5r)

Firenzuola, at the foot of the Alps, between Florence and Bologna, is a small castle, but as its name and its titles indicate, noble and popular among its lords; and Florence is the homeland of my ancestors. […] I am therefore beginning a Tuscan fable.

Firenzuola's text indicates a complex identification between high opinions of vulgar language, praise of a city, pride in a lineage, allegiance to the Medicis (repeatedly affirmed), and the metaphorical portrait of a young and promising author who, as we shall see, stages and dramatizes his literary vocation.

For all these reasons, Firenzuola's autobiographical appropriation of the *Metamorphoses* is no mere interpolation. Instead, it entails a deep transformation of the entire text. I shall scrutinize some of the elements of this transformation, akin to a modernization, Italianization, and moderate Christianization. I will also try to pinpoint what is at stake in this translation-adaptation of the *Metamorphoses*.

---

[14] A. D. Scaglione, 'L'asino d'oro e il Firenzuola', *Giornale storico della letteratura italiana* 126 (1949) 230–31.

II. Modalities of modernization

II.1. Places, names, and customs

In the Tuscan fable written by Firenzuola, all the names of people and places are modern and Italian. In contrast to his other works (for instance a pastoral prayer imitating antique religious ceremonies),[15] Firenzuola's *L'asino d'oro* does not in the least try to revive the Latin world; without any care for geographical coherence, Thessaly is replaced by Naples, Corinth by Florence, Athens by Siena, Aetolia by Bologna. According to Küenzlen, the choice of Bologna (and not Naples, which was allegedly a city devoted to sorcery) can be explained by the fact that Bolognese faculties of law were famous, and, as we shall see, Firenzuola equates studying law with being an ass. In Firenzuola's translation-adaptation, Photis is Lucia (translation of the Greek 'Photis'), Phytoas is Francesco, and Byrrhena is Laura, which is also the name of Firenzuola's actual aunt. It therefore seems that Firenzuola does not penetrate the world of the *Metamorphoses* alone; he disguises several historical figures, family, and friends in fictional but unantiquated clothing. Indeed, Firenzuola does not limit the modernization of the antique world to onomastic changes; he accurately transforms all the elements of daily life and customs, leaving no record and almost no trace of antiquity. Among many examples (concerning clothes, dishes, and money),[16] Agnolo and Lucia, unlike Lucius and Photis, no longer mix their wine with warm water (book 2). All mentions of gladiatorial fights are removed. But the best example of this meticulous modernization is the replacement of a pyrrhic dance (in book 10) by a dance described in detailed, technical terms, which seems to have been borrowed from one of the dance treatises of the Renaissance:

> Egli fu ordinato un bellissimo e ornato ballo [...] : Quelle volte preste, quei salti leggeri, quelle capriolette minute, quelle ripresse nette, quelle scempi tardetti, quei doppi fugaci, quelle gravi continenze, quelle humili riverenze, e cosi a tempo; che e pareva, che ogni loro movimento fusse de gli instrumenti medesimi [...]
>
> (*Apuleio dell'Asino d'Oro*, 1550, f. 133r–v)

> A very beautiful ball was organized [...] these rapid spins, these light jumps, these little cabrioles, these clean pick-ups, these slow steps, these quick *pas de deux*, these serious countenances, these humble bows, and all this so much in time, that it seems each movement comes from the instruments themselves.

Firenzuola, who wrote a treatise in 1541 about feminine beauty,[17] expresses a court ideal of gracefulness and decorum in this passage, close to that of Castiglione (whom he probably knew during his stay in Rome).

II.2. Christianization and anti-Semitism

In the Renaissance, the modernization of the customs of the Roman empire necessarily meant their Christianization. Firenzuola, who never expressed any devout thoughts in his writings, seems to have been a moderate Christian, although perhaps at odds with ecclesiastical authorities. He converts the *Metamorphoses* into a modern, but not entirely Catholic, tale;

---

[15] I am referring to the 'Sacrificio pastorale' by Agnolo Firenzuola (1540) in *Opere* (n. 12, above) 789–798.

[16] F. Küenzlen gives many examples of these changes, see *Verwandlungen* (n. 7, above) 349–350.

[17] *Celso o Delle bellezze delle donne* (1541), in *Opere* (n. 12, above) 525–596.

his Christianization of the Pagan world is limited. In Firenzuola's version, for example, a beggar asking for money at a crossroads begs in front of churches. More significantly, the traditional allegory of Isis as the Virgin (by Filippo Beroaldo in 1500 and Guillaume de Tours in 1517) is missing, because Firenzuola almost entirely removes the last chapter of the *Metamorphoses*. The ass returns to human form not with the help of any goddess—pagan or Christian—but instead through the mediation of an earthly woman, Costanza Amaretta. The final metamorphosis and return to human form do, however, involve a priest who purifies and blesses the ass in a church. Costanza Amaretta, who is accompanied by a little boy (sitting astride the ass, perhaps as Christ entered into Jerusalem) may also be a reference to the Virgin. Whatever the case, religious commentary is remarkably understated in this text.

The religious modernization of Apuleius' novel is also noticeable in the anti-Semitic statements found therein. Contemporary critics have never noticed these elements, perhaps because they are unpleasant. They are nevertheless part of the modernization of the text and of its satirical and even referential dimension. The first example involves the transformation of the physician and his wife into a Jewish couple (book 10, the story of the female poisoner). The second and most significant example is a satirical development that is also found in book 10: the ass' target is a certain Martino Spinosa, allegedly one of the author's enemies. The ass alludes to an ecclesiastical condemnation that contemporary critics never clarify (nor understand).[18] He also criticizes the Italian reception of Spanish people banned for religious reasons—that is to say, Jews or descendants of Jewish families:

Ne possò tacere il giudicio di Martino Spinosa nella Romana ruota de i primi avolgitori; il quale, corrotto da alto favore, dandomi contro ad ogni giustitia e equità una sententia e domantado della cagione, non arrossì almeno a dire : perchè mi è piacciuto. Ma sia gli perdonato, poscia che egli è Spagniulo di quelli, a cui per atto di religione e interdetto lo stare in Ispagna, né biasimiamo quel paese, come facciamo, anzi dogliamoci di noi, che come una sentina, o come uno asilo riceviamo la feccia, e la ribalderia del mondo; e gli facciamo sedere nelle catedre, e chiamiangli maestri.

(*Apuleio dell'Asino d'Oro*, 1550, f. 135v)

I cannot remain silent about Martino Spinosa's judgment at the Roman Rota tribunal, a first-rate swindler, who, corrupted by favours from up high, pronounced a sentence against me, contrary to justice and fairness, and when I asked him why, he was unembarrassed to say: 'because it pleased me'. But I forgive him for it, because he is a Spaniard, among those who do not have the right to remain in Spain, for religious reasons; and instead of blaming this country, as we do, let us rather complain about ourselves, who, like a stream or a refuge, receive the litter and scoundrels of the world, whom we allow to sit in professorial chairs and whom we call masters.

Besides this anti-Semitic charge, it would perhaps be of interest to know the consequences of the aforementioned condemnation upon Firenzuola's life and career. Is it linked to the relinquishment of his religious status? Either way, this example demonstrates that the work's autobiographical dimension is not limited to a brief summary of the author's genealogy at the beginning of the work (as Scala claims in his dedicatory letter); autobiography and modernization pervade the whole adaptation, and they are inherent to its intent and meaning.

---

[18]   Delmo Maestri obviously misunderstood this passage in his critical edition of Firenzuola's works in 1977 (*Opere* (n. 6, above) 462).

III. The stakes of autobiographical appropriation

III.1. From Christian to personal allegory

The replacement of Lucius by Agnolo is explicit, steady, and repeated; the other characters, Lucia and Laura (themselves substitutes for Photis and Byrrhena), frequently hail or address him using the name 'Agnolo'. The table of contents in the 1550 edition introduces the third book in these terms: 'Presa del Firenzuola. Accusa contra l'autore. Risposta dell'autore. [...] Il Firenzuola divenuto asino. Il Firenzuola Asino è bastonato dal proprio famiglio' ('Capture of Firenzuola. Accusation of the author. The author's response. [...] Firenzuola turned into an ass. Firenzuola, the Ass, is beaten by his own servant'). The end of the story is summed up as: 'Agnolo ritornato d'Asino nella propria forma' ('Agnolo returns from the Ass to his original form'). The identification between the character and the author (by the author himself, as well as the editor of his work) is complete. Yet this uncanny substitution has never really been interpreted, and, when it has, it has been as a self-affirmation of Firenzuola as the author, rather than simply the translator, as I previously stated. An interpretation of this sort is developed by Teoli, for example, in his late edition of this work from 1863.[19] His interpretation is plausible, because it fits with the status of translation in Renaissance Italy. Moreover, his interpretation can be corroborated by the emphasis Firenzuola places upon aesthetic and auto-referential statements. For instance, he develops (in the second book) an ekphrasis of the statues of Diana and Acteon which is an opportunity to celebrate the genius of the artist who imitates life and movement to perfection, as well as the account of the prophecy that forecasts the literary fame of the narrator.

Moreover, the metamorphosis, as Firenzuola explicitly interprets it, is the story of a literary and amorous education. At the beginning and the end of *L'asino d'oro*, Firenzuola explains that the shape of an ass symbolizes the years spent studying law and practicing the function of a lawyer (as Firenzuola actually did at the tribunal of the Curia). Studying and practicing poetry, however, under the amorous authority of a beloved woman (Costanza Amaretta), is akin to becoming a man from a platonic perspective—that is to say, reaching a superior state of self-consciousness through love and artistic creativity.

> Questa fu quella Costanza, a la quella fattasi Signora dell'anima, svegliò l'ingegno a quelli lodevoli esercitii, che me hanno fatto fra i virtuozi capere. Questa fu quella che trattomi dell'asinino studio delle leggi civili, anzi incivili, mi fece applicare alle humane lettere.
>
> (*Apuleio dell'Asino d'Oro*, 1550, f. 138r)

And it was this Costanza, who, having become mistress of my soul, awoke my mind to these commendable exercises, which allowed me to become part of those who distinguish themselves in them. It was she who pulled me back from idiotic studies of civil, or rather uncivil, law, and made me dedicate myself to letters and humanities.

This change of vocation from law to literature recalls Ovid's biography, as he recounts it in the *Tristia*. But in Firenzuola's text, it is not only a literary reference. Rather, it refers to his own dedication to poetry and to the consequences it has had for him: leaving Rome, the papal court, and later his religious identity (including ecclesiastical benefits at the end of his life).

---

[19]   *L'asino d'oro di Lucio Apuleio volgarizzato da Agnolo Firenzuola, con l'aggiunta della Novella dello sternuto tradotta da Matteo Boiardo* (Milan 1863). The introduction is written by Marco Teoli.

Firenzuola stages his choice of vocation. At the beginning of *I Ragionamenti* (an unfinished work modelled on the *Decameron*, in which Costanza Amaretta is the main character), he explains that he wrote his first works after Costanza's death, following her last wishes. In the last book of *L'asino d'oro*, Firenzuola also mentions Costanza's death, presented as the starting point and incentive for his literary vocation. This woman, real or imagined (one critic expresses doubts about her historical identity[20] despite her being presented as a referential character), is based on the model of Dante's Beatrice or Petrarch's Laura. The metamorphosis through art and love has to be understood as a general and exemplary programme of humanist and courtly education.

Firenzuola also touches upon a more traditional interpretation of the metamorphosis from human to animal form (and vice versa); it can be seen as standing for the passage from a licentious life to a virtuous life, respectively embodied by Lucia and Costanza, sensual and virtuous love, according to Marsilio Ficino's lesson. But the sexual licence symbolized by the donkey also corresponds to the period of Firenzuola's life that was spent in the priesthood. The way in which he applies the Apuleius fable to his own life is therefore potentially scandalous—no wonder that it was never published while the author was living. One may also think that the use of an autobiographical first person, in a narrative talking about a magical operation and a monstrous coupling, is a tricky endeavour. However, the editions of *L'asino d'oro* that were released after Firenzuola's death, even expurgated,[21] demonstrate that the work was not considered to have exceeded the limits of propriety. Indeed, its ultimate interpretation depends on the status of the first person, along with the multiple choices available to the reader between an allegorical and a literal reading.

Following our line of analysis, the suggested and appropriate reading of *L'asino d'oro* is neither allegorical, in the traditional, religious sense of the term, nor literal. In relation to the three traceable positions on the *Metamorphoses* in the sixteenth and seventeenth centuries—religious allegory (Beroaldo), entertainment with poor moral meaning (Louveau, Adlington), and a literal reading based on demonological thinking (Bodin, Montlyard)—Firenzuola's represents a completely original, hermeneutical view. Identifying himself with Lucius makes these three attitudes nonsensical. Since paganism is erased from his modernized world, any metaphorical consistency with Catholicism becomes pointless. Since personal reference is involved, this piece of fiction cannot be reduced to meaningless trifles. Finally, since Firenzuola, unlike Apuleius, cannot be charged with sorcery, the metamorphoses and magical phenomena described in the book are merely fictional.

The status of the first person is, therefore, rather complex. As in many sixteenth-century works, it is partly referential, or, rather, intermittently referential. This is clearly suggested in the table of contents, in which the narrator is called 'The author', 'Agnolo', 'Firenzuola', and sometimes 'l'asino'; under these circumstances, he is probably only, or almost only, a fictional character. The reader is invited to interpret this as a direct reference at certain times (when the narrator talks about his genealogy or Costanza Amaretta) and a loose one at others. The identification of the author with the main character of Apuleius' *Metamorphoses* may also function as a model and exemplification of the act of reading; every reader can imagine himself or herself as the protagonist through a thought experiment that is precisely the point of fiction. The broad symbolism of the ass in the Renaissance (ignorance, sin, sexual licence, concealed wisdom) allows for a multiplicity of applications, lending itself to the diversity of the audience.

---

[20] See Adriano Seroni's claim in his introduction to Firenzuola's works (*Opere*, n. 12, above).

[21] In later editions (1598 and 1603–07), erotic passages are softened.

To conclude, there are different ways, based on varying perspectives, of understanding Firenzuola's highly unique work.[22] First, in the framework of the history of translation (as linked to an affirmation of the Italian language and an appropriation of antiquity), this text emphasizes the status of translator as author. This substitution occurs in a culture dominated by paradoxes and a tradition of comical first-person narrative, as with Erasmus' *Praise of Folly*, Thomas More's *Utopia*, and *Lazarillo de Tormes*: indeed, it is through his comical and bizarre appropriation of the character of Lucius transformed into a donkey that Firenzuola the translator affirms his auctoriality.

Firenzuola's adaptation is thus also part of a history of first-person narrative. The status of the first person is complex in this text, as well as in other texts of the same period, because it is simultaneously referential, inter-textual, and fictional. The same goes for the character of Costanza Amaretta, who belongs to different ontological spaces, both inside and outside of fiction. Such a combination was no longer possible by the seventeenth century.

Lastly, this work can be understood within the context of a general history of fictionality. From a narratological perspective, Firenzuola performs a kind of metalepsis, breaching a narrative sphere in introducing himself, the author-translator, into a work of fiction.[23] But this transgression is mitigated, since Firenzuola completely transforms the antique world into a Renaissance setting. This liberty was characteristic of fiction before the seventeenth century and after the nineteenth century (that is to say at times when likelihood was not a decisive aesthetic criterion). To draw a contemporary parallel, today's internet users and young authors of fan fiction are prone to including a counterpart of themselves in the action. In some ways, Firenzuola's unique gesture bears a resemblance to ancient and modern modes of self-representation, but it goes further, as the translator here assumes the role of author *and* main character.

Firenzuola's translation-adaptation should therefore be understood in the context of the Renaissance affirmation of authorship. Significant elements of this context include a sophisticated (albeit temporary) use of the first person, the free appropriation of antique texts for contemporary and even personal purposes, and, lastly, the development of a consciousness of fictionality and a diversification of the uses of fiction.

Université Sorbonne Nouvelle
Institut Universitaire de France

---

[22] Pompeo Vizzani did publish a translation of the *Metamorphoses* in which he drew a parallel between Lucius' story and his own life, but he did not replace Lucius with a character named Pompeo Vizzani: *L'asino d'oro di Lucio Apuleio filosofo platonico tradotto nuouamente in lingua volgare dal M. illust. sig. Pompeo Vizani nobile bolognese; et da lui con chiari argomenti ornato, & da motti dishonesti purgato* (Bologna, Heredi di Gio. Rossi, 1607). This translation was published several times in Venice (1629, 1644, 1662, and 1704).

[23] For an updated definition of metalepsis, see J. Pier, 'Metalepsis', in *The Living Handbook of Narratology*, eds P. Hühn, J. Pier, W. Schmid, J. Schönert, J. Chr. Meister, and W. Schernus (Hamburg 2016) [http://www.lhn.uni-hamburg.de/article/metalepsis-revised-version-uploaded-13-july-2016 (accessed 17 November 2019)].

APULEIUS' *ASS* AND CERVANTES' *DOGS* IN DIALOGUE[1]

LORETO NÚÑEZ

I. Introduction

Scholars who study Apuleius' *Asinus Aureus* together with Cervantes' *Coloquio de los perros* often focus on questions of influence or filiation, either advocating for such a relationship between the texts or rejecting claims of this sort.[2] González de Amezúa, for instance, denies that Cervantes could have been influenced by Apuleius:

> Aunque tenga por muy probable o casi seguro que Cervantes leyó este libro [*i.e. El asno de oro*] que tan a la mano tenía, esto no quiere decir, empero, que lo tomase por modelo y ejemplar suyo, porque todas la semejanzas que el Coloquio pueda ofrecer con él se reducen a la expresada y escueta cita, sin valor sustancial alguno, y a una exposición de las artes mágicas, tema harto frecuente también en los libros de entonces.

> Although I think it is very probable or almost certain that Cervantes read this book [*i.e. The Golden Ass*], which he had so much in hand, this does not mean, however, that he took it as a model or example, since all the similarities the *Colloquy* can offer with it may be reduced to the explicit and short mention ('escueta cita'), which has no substantial importance, and to the exposition of magical arts, a theme which was very common in the books of that time.[3]

The 'escueta cita' of *The Golden Ass* mentioned by González de Amezúa appears towards the middle of the *Coloquio*. An old witch speaks to the dog Berganza, whom she believes to be a man who has been transformed into a dog, about his potential retransformation:

> Quisiera yo que fuera tan fácil como el que se dice de Apuleyo en El asno de oro, que consistía en sólo comer una rosa.

---

[1] I would like to thank Carole Boidin, Raphaële Mouren, Olivier Pedeflous, and Greg Woolf for organizing a wonderful and inspiring conference on 'The Afterlife of Apuleius', as well as for the subsequent editorial work on our papers.

[2] For Apuleius' text: Apuleius, *Metamorphoses*, eds D. S. Roberston and O. Sers (Paris 2010); Apuleius, *The Golden Ass*, trans. P. G. Walsh (Oxford 1994). For Cervantes' text: M. de Cervantes Saavedra, *Novelas ejemplares*, ed. H. Sieber, 2 vols (Madrid 2001); Cervantes, *Exemplary Stories*, trans. C. A. Jones (London 1972). All other translations are mine, unless otherwise indicated.

[3] A. González de Amezúa y Mayo, *Cervantes, creador de la novela corta española: introducción a la edición crítica y comentada de las 'Novelas ejemplares'*, 2 vols (Madrid 1982) II 421. See also the longer discussion in M. de Cervantes Saavedra, *El casamiento engañoso y el coloquio de los perros*, ed. A. González de Amezúa y Mayo (Madrid 1912) 83–86.

I wish it were as easy as the way they say Apuleius did it in *The Golden Ass*, simply by eating a rose.[4]

For González de Amezúa, this passage does not provide any evidence for a connection between *The Golden Ass* and the *Coloquio*. The scholar's statement is, of course, a defence of Cervantes' unquestionable originality. Yet, over the last decades, various critics, promoting the advantages of an intertextual approach and accepting that connections with other authors do not undermine a writer's singularity, have tried to demonstrate Apuleius' influence on Cervantes.[5] However, the present chapter will not consist of a piece of *Quellenforschung* that seeks to prove that Apuleius influenced Cervantes, although this may ultimately appear more probable as a result of our case study.[6] Instead, I propose to consider 'The afterlife of Apuleius' from a slightly different point of view: I will approach his *Metamorphoses* and Cervantes' *Coloquio de los perros* from a double dialogical perspective. The expression 'in dialogue' in the title of this chapter should be understood in two senses: first, as an act of bringing-into-dialogue in a comparative perspective, and, second, in connection with the notion of 'intertextual dialogue'.

Regarding the comparative point of view, I should add that my approach is not that of classical tradition or reception studies, which concentrate, to put it very schematically, on one of the two poles of the comparison, the ancient or the later, respectively. As García Jurado puts it:

Tradición clásica sigue unida a la idea de 'influencia' e 'historicismo', mientras que la Recepción clásica se sustenta en la idea del lector como creador y de la lectura estética.

Classical tradition is still related to the idea of 'influence' or 'historicism', whereas Classical reception is based on the idea of the reader as creator and of the aesthetical reading.[7]

---

[4]   Cervantes, *Novelas* (n. 2, above) II 339.

[5]   For the *Novelas*, *cf. e.g.* G. Hainsworth, *Les 'Novelas exemplares' de Cervantès en France au XVII*ᵉ *siècle: contribution à l'étude de la nouvelle en France* (Paris 1933); F. Carrasco, 'El coloquio de los perros /v./ El asno de oro: concordancias temáticas y sistemáticas', *Anales cervantinos* 21 (1983) 177–200; E. C. Riley, 'The antecedents of the *Coloquio de los perros*', in *Negotiating Past and Present: Studies in Spanish Literature for Javier Herrero*, ed. D. T. Gies (Charlottesville 1997) 161–75; E. C. Riley, 'Tradición e innovación en la novelística cervantina', *Bulletin of the Cervantes Society of America* 17.1 (1997) 46–61; A. Guarino, 'Las huellas del asno: presencia de Apuleyo en la narrativa española del siglo XVI', in *Modelli, memorie, riscriture*, ed. G. Grilli (Napoli 2001) 43–59; T. Leuker, 'Cervantes zwischen Apuleius, Lukian und dem "spanischen Amyot"—Zu Finale und Prolog der *Novelas ejemplares*', *Romanische Zeitschrift für Literaturgeschichte* 25 (2001) 409–27; M. Guillemont and M.-B. Requejo Carrió, 'De asnos y rebuznos. Ambigüedad y modernidad de un diálogo', *Criticón* 101 (2007) 57–87; C. García Gual, 'The ancient novel and the Spanish novel of the Golden Age', in *Fictional Traces: Receptions of the Ancient Novel*, eds M. P. Futre Pinheiro and S. J. Harrison, 2 vols (Groningen 2011) I 183–201.

[6]   I am not denying the importance of *Quellenforschung*: it is a very useful practice that allows for a deeper understanding of the works analysed. Nevertheless, it conceals certain dangers. See, for example, G. Highet, *The Classical Tradition: Greek and Roman Influences on Western literature* (Oxford 1976) 499 (orig. 1949): 'The false parallel with science caused many more errors and exaggerations in classical study. One odd one was the habit of *Quellenforschung*, the search for sources, which began as a legitimate inquiry into the material used by a poet, historian, or philosopher, and was pushed to the absurd point at which it was assumed that everything in a poem, even such a poem as the *Aeneid*, was derived from earlier writers. It is a typical scientific assumption that everything can be explained by synthesis, but it omits the essential artistic fact of creation'.

[7]   F. García Jurado, 'Tradición frente a recepción clásica: historia frente a estética, autor frente a lector', *Nova Tellus* 33.1 (2015) 1–37 (37), *cf.* also 32 and F. García Jurado, 'La metamorfosis de la tradición clásica, ayer y hoy', in

In the field of Apuleian studies, these approaches have produced such inspiring works as the studies by Carver and Gaisser.[8] In spite of the importance and relevance of such investigations, I propose a comparative analysis in the strong sense of the word, and this according to a specific comparative method: the 'differential comparison' ('comparaison différentielle'), as theorized by Heidmann. According to this method, we not only compare texts on the basis of their similarities but also take into account their differences and specificities. Far too often, the focus is placed on analogies while the particularities of each text are left to one side. Instead, Heidmann's method 'applies comparison in order to differentiate the literary creations' ('recourt à la comparaison avec l'objectif de différencier les créations littéraires'), thus taking into account the fact that literature 'proceeds by differentiation' ('procède par différenciation'), since, at least in our culture, an author wants to distinguish him/herself from his/her predecessors.[9] Furthermore, the differential comparison tries to avoid pre-established hierarchies. Hierarchies of this sort are very frequent when dealing with ancient texts: these texts are either considered to be mere sources of inspiration but of no further interest, or they are put up on a pedestal, with everything that follows them being dismissed as inferior. Heidmann instead suggests constructing an 'axis of comparison' ('axe de comparaison') which puts the texts 'on the same level, *i.e.* in a non-hierarchical and non-hierarchizing relation' ('sur un même plan, c'est-à-dire dans un rapport non hiérarchique et non-hiérarchisant').[10]

One possible level of comparison if we move in this direction is the 'intertextual dialogue', the second facet of the expression 'in dialogue'. Instead of a static conception of intertextuality, in the sense of influence or borrowing, Heidmann proposes a dialogical notion according to which 'a text responds to a proposal of meaning by another text' ('un texte répond à une proposition de sens faite par un autre texte').[11] In this sense, the texts are involved in a dialogue in which the two interlocutors have equal importance. This is very important from the point of view of the differential comparison, since Heidmann proposes to consider not so much the different, but the '*differential* resulting from the process of *differentiation*. The differentiation is a relational notion which, instead of opposing the *same* and the *different*, indicates the process leading from one to the other' ('*différentiel* résultant d'un processus de *différenciation*. La différenciation est une notion relationnelle qui, au lieu d'opposer le même et le différent, désigne le processus qui mène de l'un à l'autre').[12]

Studia classica Caesaraugustana: vigencia y presencia del mundo clásico hoy : XXV años de estudios clásicos en la Universidad de Zaragoza, eds J. Vela Tejada, J. F. Fraile Vicente, and C. Sánchez Mañas (Zaragoza 2015) 69–109.

[8]   R. H. F. Carver, *The Protean Ass: The 'Metamorphoses' of Apuleius from Antiquity to the Renaissance* (Oxford 2007) and J. H. Gaisser, *The Fortunes of Apuleius and the 'Golden Ass': A Study in Transmission and Reception* (Princeton-Oxford 2008). Furthermore, see also the interesting studies by F. Küenzlen, *Verwandlungen eines Esels. Apuleius' 'Metamorphoses' im frühen 16. Jahrhundert* (Heidelberg 2005); M. Acocella, *'L'Asino d'oro' nel Rinascimento: dai volgarizzamenti alle raffigurazioni pittoriche* (Ravenna 2001); and V. Gély, *L'invention d'un mythe: Psyché – Allégorie et fiction du siècle de Platon au temps de La Fontaine* (Paris 2006); as well as K. Heyerick, 'Les sens d'une métamorphose: les traductions françaises de *L'âne d'or* au XVIᵉ siècle', *Revue de littérature comparée* 315 (2005) 273–93; and O. Pédeflous, 'La traduction de *L'âne d'or* par Guillaume Michel (1517): une contribution à la poétique du roman du xviᵉ siècle', *Revue d'histoire littéraire de la France* 107 (2007) 515–25.

[9]   U. Heidmann, 'La comparaison différentielle comme approche littéraire', in *Nouveaux regards sur le texte littéraire*, ed. V. Jouve (Reims 2013) 203–22 (203).

[10]   Heidmann, 'La comparaison' (n. 9, above) 209–10; author's emphasis.

[11]   U. Heidmann, 'Intertextualité et dialogicité des contes', in *Textualité et intertextualité des contes: Perrault, Apulée, La Fontaine, Lhéritier...*, J.–M. Adam and U. Heidmann (Paris 2010) 31–152 (37); author's emphasis.

[12]   U. Heidmann, 'Que veut et que fait une comparaison différentielle? Propos recueillis par Jean-Michel Adam & David Martens', *Interférences littéraires* 21 (2017) 199–226 (200); author's emphasis.

In my opinion, the dialogical elements between Apuleius and Cervantes take various forms. Before taking a closer look at the texts, I will briefly mention two general examples of this dialogue. The first focuses on the content of the texts. If we consider the animal dimension of the protagonists, a general comparison reveals that both authors have chosen to narrate the majority of the events from the perspective of an animal: ass or dog, both character and narrator. Yet in Apuleius we find a man, Lucius, who is transformed into an ass and then retransformed into a human being. In Cervantes, Berganza and Scipio are dogs and remain so, even if the possibility also remains that they might have a human mother. Therefore, we could speak of an animalized man in Apuleius, and of two humanized dogs in Cervantes. Yet, as I have shown elsewhere,[13] a more detailed comparison reveals that the situation is not so clear, and that both authors actually play with the fluctuation between the human and the animal, even if they do so in different manners.

The second general example of intertextual dialogue between our authors concerns a rather formal aspect of their respective tales, namely the distribution of the masters to whom the heroes are subjected during the story:

Lucius' Masters	Berganza's Masters
1. Milo	1. Butcher Nicholas
2. Robbers	2. Shepherds
3. Charite and Tlepolemus	3. Rich merchant
4. Charite's fugitive slaves	4. Police officer
5. Syrian goddess' priests	5. Company's drummer
6. Miller	6. Gypsies
7. Gardener	7. Moor
8. Soldier	8. Poet
9. Two brothers, cooks of a wealthy man	9. Theatrical troupe
10. Isis	10. Good Mahudes

As we can see, the number of masters in each text is the same. Furthermore, there are similarities between cases, in spite of the evident differences. Apuleius' robbers may find an echo in Cervantes' shepherds, who steal their master's animals. The Roman soldier may have been transformed into the corrupt Spanish police officer, a choice which would underline a critical portrayal of authorities. Apuleius' gardener has a double in Cervantes' Moor. The ancient divinity Isis may have been metamorphosed into the pious Mahudes, a historical figure who, after having been cured of a terrible illness, dedicated his life to the Christian God.[14] Thus, the formal analysis soon brings to light interesting points concerning the contents. This is particularly the case in the passages that I intend to consider in the following pages: the beginnings, which will receive more detailed attention, and the endings, as well as episodes towards the middle of each work, which I will mention more briefly.

---

[13] L. Núñez, 'Diálogos animales y humanos entre los perros de Cervantes y el asno de Apuleyo', in *Ficciones animales y animales de ficción en las literaturas hispánicas*, eds G. Cordone and M. Kunz (Wien-Zürich 2015) 101–22.

[14] *Cf.* A. K. Forcione, *Cervantes and the Mystery of Lawlessness: A Study of 'El casamiento engañoso' y 'el Coloquio de los perros'* (Princeton 2014) 140; see also N. Alonso Cortés, 'Los perros de Mahudes', *Revista de filología española* 26 (1942) 298–302; González de Amezúa y Mayo, *Cervantes* (n. 3, above) II 411–13; and González de Amezúa y Mayo's edition of *El casamiento* (n. 3, above) 75–80.

II. Beginnings

Both works start with what we might consider to be a multi-level opening. First, there are the openings of the works proper—the famous prologue in Apuleius and the 'prólogo al lector' in Cervantes—which are peritextual passages the statuses of which oscillate between 'reality' and fiction. Then there are the openings that are already part of the fictional world: the Aristomenes episode in the *Metamorphoses* and, in Cervantes' collection, the 'novela' of the *Casamiento engañoso* (*Deceitful marriage*), a trickster-tricked-story. Coming out of hospital after being treated for syphilis, the *Alférez*/Ensign Campuzano reports to the Licenciate Peralta how, pretending to be a rich man, he had married Doña Estefanía hoping to profit from her wealth. But, as he explains, he had been outwitted by her. This narrative is followed by the reading of the *Coloquio de los perros*, in which Berganza narrates his life to Scipio. In what follows, I would like to present an overview of certain elements in both openings.

Much has been written about Apuleius' famous and complex prologue and it will not be possible to consider all of its features here.[15] I will mention only a few aspects which are relevant for the dialogue between Apuleius and Cervantes. Keeping our focus on the word 'dialogue', we can note that the Latin author begins his work by giving the reader the impression of overhearing a conversation which has already started:

> At ego tibi sermone isto Milesio varias fabulas conseram auresque tuas benivolas lepido susurro permulceam [...] figuras fortunasque hominum in alias imagines conversas et in se rursus mutuo nexu refectas ut mireris.

> But as to me, for you I will connect in this Milesian discourse various stories and caress your benevolent ears with a pleasant murmuring [...] I want you to feel wonder at the transformations of men's shapes and destinies into alien forms, and their reversion by a chain of interconnection to their own.[16]

As though answering an opposition ('at'), an indefinite 'I' ('ego') addresses a 'you' ('tibi'). It promises a variety of stories ('varias fabulas') dealing with transformations ('conversas [...] refectas'). The initial passage anticipates the general topic of the work: Lucius' surprising transformation into an ass, his adventures, and the stories which he hears before his re-transformation into a man. Yet the anticipation is neither explicit nor detailed, being limited, rather, to general and vague indications. What receives more attention is the portrayal we find in the second part of the prologue, introduced by the famous passage 'I begin. "Who's that?" Wait a little bit' ('Exordior. "Quis ille?" Paucis accipe').[17] Then there is a biography in miniature about a person born in Greece who came to Rome and there learnt to speak Latin. The last element may of course also be related to Apuleius himself. The prologue

---

[15] For Apuleius' complex prologue, I only mention the commentaries on book I: A. Scobie, *Apuleius, Metamorphoses. (Asinus Aureus), I. A Commentary* (Meisenheim am Glan 1975), and, more recently, W. H. Keulen, *Lucius Apuleius (Madaurensis), Metamorphoses: Book I, Text, Introd. and Commentary* (Groningen 2003); *cf.* also *A Companion to the Prologue of Apuleius' 'Metamorphoses'*, eds A. Kahane and A. Laird (Oxford 2001); and L. Núñez, *Voix inouïes: étude comparative de l'enchâssement dans 'Leucippé et Clitophon' d'Achille Tatius et les 'Métamorphoses' d'Apulée*, 2 vols (Saarbrücken 2013) I 113–34.

[16] Apul. *Met.* 1.1.1–2. In order to stay as close as possible to Apuleius' text, I have inserted modifications in Walsh's translation at the very beginning of the passage quoted here.

[17] Apul. *Met.* 1.1.3. Again, I modify Walsh's translation in order to stay as close as possible to the original. Walsh identifies the Latin 'ille' with the narrator, whereas the Latin text is less explicit.

is then concluded by the statement: 'We're about to start a Greek story. Reader, look out: you will have fun' ('Fabulam Graecanicam incipimus. Lector intende: laetaberis').[18] The prologue thus ends with the promise that the book will give pleasure to the reader ('laetaberis'), and also arouse his admiration ('mireris').

Various of these elements receive a response in Cervantes' 'prólogo al lector' (prologue to the reader) to his *Novelas ejemplares*. There is the abrupt address to the reader at the start of the prologue: 'I wish it were possible, dearest reader, to avoid writing this prologue' ('quisiera yo, si fuera posible, lector amantísimo, escusarme de escribir este prólogo[…]').[19] Instead of an adversative beginning, as in Apuleius, we have a negative statement about the text we are reading. In addition, and this is rather more interesting, the fictional biographical statements of Apuleius' prologue receive a response through a biographical passage. Cervantes explains that a portrayal of him should have opened the edition of his 'novelas', and then adds that a friend 'would have written under the portrait: "The person you see here […]"' ('poniendo debajo del retrato : "Éste que véis aquí […]"').[20] There then follows a quotation from this imaginary text, which deals with Cervantes' real life and works. There is, therefore, a combination of fiction and reality, as in Apuleius, even if it is somewhat different here. Whereas the fictional biography in the Latin text contains some real information about Apuleius, in the Castilian work, by contrast, the real biography is set into the frame of an imaginary portrayal of the author.

A last point should be mentioned regarding the end of Apuleius' prologue, where he introduces a 'fabula Graecanica'. This statement finds an echo in a famous passage of Cervantes' prologue, where he proudly affirms:

> Yo soy el primero que he novelado en lengua castellana, que las muchas novelas que en ella andan impresas todas son traducidas de lenguas estranjeras, y éstas son mías propias, no imitadas ni hurtadas.

> I am the first to have 'novellated' in the Castilian language, for the many novels printed in this language are all translated from foreign languages, and these are my own, neither imitated nor stolen.[21]

This assertion about his own originality should not be understood as a negation of, but rather as an implied allusion to, his being inspired by other authors, such as Boccaccio[22] or, more importantly for our present purposes, Apuleius. With his 'fabula Graecanica', the latter may hint at other authors as well, perhaps even at the Greek *Metamorphoses*.

After both prologues, we face other beginnings. As is well known, Apuleius gives the reader another start inside Lucius' fiction: the Aristomenes episode. Lucius reports, as narrator

---

[18] Apul. *Met.* 1.1.6. Modification in Walsh's translation in order to avoid talking of specific literary genres such as 'romance' and to leave open the question of whether 'Graecanica' refers to a translation or to an imitation in the sense of 'in Greek fashion'.

[19] Cervantes, 'prólogo' to the *Novelas* (n. 2, above) I 50; all translations of the prologue are my own.

[20] Cervantes, 'prólogo' to the *Novelas* (n. 2, above) I 50.

[21] Cervantes, 'prólogo' to the *Novelas* (n. 2, above) I 52.

[22] For further references to Boccaccio in Spain, see, *e.g.*, T. González Rolán and P. Saquero Suárez-Somonte, 'Un nuevo testimonio sobre la presencia de Giovanni Boccaccio en España', *Revista de filología románica* 1 (1983) 35–50 (35–37), and the whole issue of *Cuadernos de filología italiana* número extraorinario 8 (2001): *La recepción de Boccaccio en España*. *Cf.* also in general C. Brown Bourland, 'Boccaccio and the *Decameron* in Castilian and Catalan Literature', *Revue hispanique* 12 (1905) 1–231.

of the present, how his Lucius-character of the past met two travellers when journeying to Thessaly.[23] One of these was castigating the other one, calling him a liar because of a story he had just narrated: 'Spare me this tissue of crazy and monstrous lies' ('Parce […] in verba ista haec tam absurda tamque immania mentiendo').[24] Lucius the character interferes in the conversation. He criticizes the sceptical traveller, saying:

> Tu vero crassis auribus et obstinato corde respuis quae forsitan vere perhibeantur. Minus hercule calles pravissimis opinionibus ea putari mendacia quae vel auditu nova vel visu rudia vel certe supra captum cogitationis ardua videantur; quae si paulo accuratius exploraris, non modo compertu evidentia verum etiam factu facilia senties.

> Your ears are deadened and your mind is closed, you are contemptuous of reports that may well be true. Heavens, man, you aren't too bright in your quite perverse belief that all that seems unfamiliar to the ear, or unprecedented to the eye, or even too hard for our thoughts to grasp, is to be accounted lies. Investigate such features a little more carefully, and you will find that they are not merely open to discovery but are also easily performed.[25]

The passage is a sort of apology for fiction. As if the preparation of the prologue had not been sufficient, this initial episode too prepares the unbelievable story of the protagonist's transformation into an ass. These elements anticipate a possible censure from the reader, who is asked to believe the unbelievable. The first time, in the prologue, the method is more direct, since the words are explicitly addressed to the reader. In its repetition, the procedure is indirect: this time the apology comes through the dialogue reported by Lucius the narrator, who quotes the words of Lucius the character. Yet neither of the passages is explicit regarding the anticipation of the protagonist's adventures.

Several of these aspects can also be found in Cervantes, albeit with some variations.[26] Here too there is a multi-layered beginning. After the prologue which introduces the whole collection, there is a piece about the *Casamiento engañoso*, which brings in the *Coloquio de los perros*. Yet, rather than a serial or lineal presentation as in Apuleius, there is a system of duplication by insertion, since the *Coloquio de los perros* is embedded in the 'novela' *El Casamiento engañoso*. Just after narrating his trickster-tricked-story, the Ensign Campuzano gives a notebook to the Licentiate Peralta. He says that he has written down the dialogue between Berganza and Scipio that he overheard while in the hospital. There is an immediate difference: the anticipating elements in Apuleius were quite implicit, focusing on the general question of the unbelievable and lacking any explicit preparation for Lucius' transformation into an ass. In Cervantes, on the other hand, the reader is informed in advance that the characters are about to read an exchange between two dogs. However, here too, the reality of the unbelievable is questioned, since Peralta rejects the likelihood of the canine dialogue. Furthermore, he does so without Campuzano giving a complete defence of it in response:

---

[23] The distinction proposed by J. J. Winkler, *Auctor and Actor: A Narratological Reading of Apuleius's 'Golden Ass'* (Berkeley-Los Angeles-London 1985) 135–79 between 'auctor'/'Lucius-*now*' and 'actor'/'Lucius-*then*' is very important for the general understanding of the work and will be observed in this paper.

[24] Apul. *Met.* 1.2.5.

[25] Apul. *Met.* 1.3.2–3.

[26] *Cf.* also Leuker, 'Cervantes zwischen Apuleius' (n. 5, above) 410–12.

[Peralta] '¡Si se nos ha vuelto el tiempo de Maricastaña, cuando hablaban las calabazas, o el de Isopo, cuando departía el gallo con la zorra y unos animales con otros!' […]

[Campazuno] 'Pero puesto caso que me haya engañado, y que mi verdad sea sueño, y el porfiarla disparate, ¿no se holgará vuesa merced, señor Peralta, de ver escritas en un coloquio las cosas que estos perros, o sean quien fueren, hablaron?'

[Peralta] 'We're back to the time of Methuselah, when pumpkins talked; or Aesop's days, when the cock conversed with the fox and animals talked to each other.' […]

[Campuzano] 'But although I may be wrong, and what I think is true may be a dream, and to persist in it may be nonsense, won't it interest you, Mr Peralta, to see written down in the form of a colloquy the things that these dogs, or whatever they were, had to say?'[27]

Peralta's sceptical position echoes the incredulous traveller in Apuleius. However, whereas in the Latin author, the prologue and then Lucius' answer were set against such criticism, the situation is different in Cervantes. As one sees in this passage, Campuzano defends first of all the pleasure of reading the *Coloquio* and not so much its 'reality'. The truthfulness of the canine dialogue is questioned through other elements in the text. First, the transcriber, Campuzano, is characterized just before his narration as a figure who does not hesitate to deceive or mislead other people. Furthermore, he claims to have overheard the dialogue while in the hospital, probably in a febrile condition and in a state of delirium. He therefore admits the possibility that the conversation might have been a dream. Finally, at the opening of the *Coloquio* proper, the dogs are themselves surprised by their capacity to speak:

[Berganza] 'Cipión hermano, óyote hablar y sé que te hablo, y no puedo creerlo, por parecerme que el hablar nosotros pasa de los términos de naturaleza.'

[Cipión] 'Así es la verdad, Berganza, y viene a ser mayor este milagro en que no solamente hablamos, sino en que hablamos con discurso, como si fuéramos capaces de razón, estando tan sin ella que la diferencia que hay del animal bruto al hombre es ser el hombre animal racional, y el bruto, irracional.'

[Berganza] 'Brother Scipio, I hear you speak and I know that I am speaking to you, and I cannot believe it, for it seems to me that our speaking goes beyond the bounds of nature.'

[Scipio] 'That is true, Berganza, and this miracle is greater in that not only are we speaking, but we are speaking coherently, as if we were capable of reason, when in fact we are so devoid of it that the difference between the brute beast and man is that man is a rational animal, and the brute irrational.'[28]

The difficulty of the 'reality' of the dog-speech is neglected in favour of the only possible explanation the dogs themselves give: according to Berganza, it is something which 'goes beyond the bounds of nature' ('pasa de los términos de naturaleza'); for Scipio it is a 'miracle' ('milagro'). Such statements do not increase the 'reality'-aspect of the canine conversation; rather, they intensify its supernatural or preternatural character. More than

---

[27] Cervantes, *Novelas* (n. 2, above) II 294.

[28] Cervantes, *Novelas* (n. 2, above) II 299.

giving a 'reality'-value to the canine dialogue, such statements question it. This is reinforced further through the attraction of opposites which seems to be present between the two dogs: leaving their irrational nature behind, they have now become rational beings. Through the various beginnings, Cervantes' dogs show how extremes meet, mixing the categories of the human and the animal in a way that is very similar to that found in Apuleius, after Lucius' transformation. Starting from different situations—a man who will become an ass in Apuleius, and two dogs who talk and think like human beings in Cervantes—both authors manage to destabilize the frontiers between the animal and the human, between the rational and irrational and, more generally, between 'reality' and fiction. This oscillation is to be found in the endings of the two works as well.

III. The conclusion in Apuleius and the endings in Cervantes

As is well known, *The Golden Ass* ends with Lucius recovering his human shape, thanks to the goddess Isis. However, this does not mean that the protagonist is presented as a rational person. On the contrary, he is characterized as a religious zealot. He mentions the numerous initiations he goes through, the fact that he spends a great deal of money on these activities, and that he even sacrifices his hair for the goddess:

> Rursus denique quam raso capillo collegii vetustissimi et sub illis Syllae temporibus conditi munia, non obumbrato vel obtecto calvitio, sed quoquoversus obvio, gaudens obibam.

> So I had my head completely shaved once more, and gladly performed the duties of that most ancient college, founded as long ago as the days of Sulla. I did not cover or conceal my bald head, but sported it openly wherever I went.[29]

The last sentence of the text offers a portrayal of Lucius not so much as a rational man but, rather, as a fanatic, proud of his baldness ('calvitio') and willing to work in order to increase the money of his congregation ('gaudens obibam'). Scipio and Berganza also end up with religion as a last step, following the 'good Christian Mahudes' ('buen cristiano Mahudes').[30] Yet this lifestyle does not mean that the two dogs do not appreciate the gift of speech and of intelligence. They show that they do throughout their conversation, as well as at its end, when they express their hopes to repeat the dialogue and enjoy the possibility of talking in order to narrate and hear the life of Scipio:

> [Cipión] '[...] esta noche que viene, si no nos ha dejado este grande beneficio de la habla, será la mía, para contarte mi vida.'

> [Scipio] '[...] tomorrow night, if we haven't been deserted by this great blessing of speech, will be mine, so that I can tell you my life story.'[31]

The rational aspect of the text is intensified in the second ending, which turns back to the frame with Campuzano and Peralta. Even if the latter still does not want to fully accept the 'reality' of the canine dialogue, he now does so in a more qualified way:

---

[29] Apul. *Met.* 11.30.5.

[30] Cervantes, *Novelas* (n. 2, above) II 355.

[31] Cervantes, *Novelas* (n. 2, above) II 359.

[Peralta] 'Señor Alférez, no volvamos más a esa disputa. Yo alcanzo el artificio del Coloquio y la invención, y basta. Vámonos al Espolón a recrear los ojos del cuerpo, pues ya he recreado los del entendimiento.'

'Vamos' dijo el Alférez.

Y con esto, se fueron.

[Peralta] 'Ensign, let's not return to this argument. I appreciate the art of the colloquy and the invention you've shown, and that's enough. Let's go off to the Espolón and refresh our eyes, for my mind's been well refreshed.'

'Let's go,' said the ensign.

And with that, off they went.[32]

Peralta accentuates not only the 'art' and the 'invention' of the *Coloquio* ('artificio […] invención'), but also the pleasure it has been to read it, a recreation for the 'mind' ('entendimiento'). This is linked to two dogs, which are animals from the beginning to the end, but are provided with a certain degree of intelligence and reason, indeed even rationality. Compared to these dogs, which remain canine but seem rational, the human ex-ass Lucius, in spite of his re-transformation into a human being, appears to be even less rational. Before looking at the final two passages, I would like to note a possible parallel between the last words of the two texts. In *The Golden Ass*, Lucius says he used to walk around happily with his baldness, 'gaudens obibam';[33] the last expression of the *Casamiento engañoso* is 'off they went' ('se fueron').[34] Another structural similarity, combined with content elements, is to be found in the middle of the two works.

IV. The central embedded narratives and the remarks concluding them

Both texts contain towards the middle an important embedded narrative.[35] In Apuleius, there is the famous story of Cupid and Psyche, narrated by an old servant to Charite, the young woman kidnapped by the same thieves who had stolen Lucius the ass from Milo's house. In Cervantes, it is the speech of the old witch Cañizares, who reports to Berganza that he is the son of the dead witch Montiela and that he has been transformed into a dog at his birth. These are two extremely interesting episodes.[36] It is impossible to analyse the complexity of both passages, either considered individually or in their connection to one another. The intertextual dialogue is accentuated through the explicit mention of Apuleius in Cervantes' scene, in the text mentioned towards the beginning of my paper: the old witch wishes that

---

[32] Cervantes, *Novelas* (n. 2, above) II 359.

[33] Apul. *Met.* 11.30.5.

[34] Cervantes, *Novelas* (n. 2, above) II 359.

[35] On the level of their importance, the centrality of both narratives is unquestionable, yet the situation is rather different concerning their position in the two works. In Apuleius, the narrative about Cupid and Psyche is at the centre of the eleven books (4.28–6.25). The situation is slightly different in Cervantes, since, quantitatively speaking, the Cañizares-episode appears rather in the second half of the *Coloquio de los perros*. However, looked at from the perspective of the masters mentioned by Berganza, the passage is exactly between the first five and the last five. Of course, the situation changes if one considers the *Novelas ejemplares* as a whole: the *Coloquio* is not in the middle of the collection but at its end. Yet this is also an important strategic position and therefore betrays centrality in another sense.

[36] For a detailed analysis of the narrative about Cupid and Psyche, and for further bibliographical references, see Núñez, *Voix* (n. 15, above) II 287–387.

Berganza's retransformation will be 'as easy as the way they say Apuleius did it in *The Golden Ass*' ('fuera tan fácil como el que se dice de Apuleyo en *El asno de oro*').[37] I will confine myself to the concluding part of the episodes, where we return to the frame narrative, *i.e.* the narrative by Lucius and Berganza respectively, and thus to the main narrators. In these passages, one can perceive more precisely what Maingueneau calls the 'scenography' ('scénographie') of the narration: it is the 'narrative scene constructed by the text' ('scène narrative construite par le texte') in which the 'reader is assigned a place' ('le lecteur se voit assigner une place').[38] In Apuleius, the scenography of the narration about Cupid and Psyche is especially alluded to when Lucius concludes the insertion as follows:

> Sic captivae puellae delira et temulenta illa narrabat anicula; sed astans ego non procul dolebam mehercules quod pugillares et stilum non habebam qui tam bellam fabellam praenotarem.

> This was the tale told to the captive maiden by that crazy, drunken old hag. I was standing close by, and God only knows how sorry I was not to have writing-tablets and a stylus to set down such a pretty story![39]

Lucius does not present the secondary narrator, the old servant of the thieves, in a positive manner. On the contrary, he characterizes her negatively and ridicules her by saying that she is a 'crazy, drunken old hag' ('delira et temulenta […] anicula'). However, he accentuates the beauty of the narrative she has just been narrating ('tam bellam fabellam'). Lucius explains how much he regretted not having been able to write down the story ('dolebam […] quod pugillares et stilum non habebam qui […] praenotarem'). This sentence recalls the asinine status of his character in the past. It was impossible for him to write anything down with a stylus, since he had not hands but hooves. As Heidmann has shown, precisely by reference to this sentence, Lucius the narrator, again a human being, accentuates the fact that what has just been read is not the old woman's oral narrative heard by an ass, but the text written down by a man after having recovered his human shape.[40]

The scenography in Cervantes also plays with the status of the communicative partners and with the tension between human and animal, but in a different manner. The possible human nature of Berganza and Scipio which Cañizares explains to Berganza is not presented as the version that the two dogs would prefer. On the contrary, if they could choose, they would prefer to be dogs and not the sons of a witch. Furthermore, Cañizares' speech is characterized as especially artificial through the deployment of a complex embedded structure

[37]   Cervantes, *Novelas* (n. 2, above) II 339.

[38]   D. Maingueneau, *Le discours littéraire: paratopie et scène d'énonciation* (Paris 2004) 192. The first to relate the concept of scenography to Apuleius was Heidmann: see, *e.g.*, U. Heidmann, 'La (re)configuration des genres dans les littératures européennes: l'exemple des contes', *Colloquium Helveticum* 40 (2009) 91–104; 'Intertextualité' (n. 11, above) 57–65; 'Zur poetologischen und intertextuellen Bedeutung der *Metamorphosen* des Apuleius für Jean de La Fontaine und Charles Perrault', *Würzburger Jahrbücher für Altertumswissenschaft, Neue Folge* 37 (2013) 157–90; and 'L'efficacité heuristique du concept de scénographie pour l'étude comparative des contes', in *Analyse du discours et dispositifs d'énonciation: autour des travaux de Dominique Maingueneau*, eds J. Angermuller and G. Philippe (Limoges 2015) 147–56.

[39]   Apul. *Met.* 6.25.1.

[40]   *Cf.* Heidmann, 'Intertextualité' (n. 11, above) 56; *cf.* also 'Comment faire un conte *moderne* avec un conte *ancien*? Perrault en dialogue avec Apulée et La Fontaine', *Littérature* 153 (2009) 19–35 (21) and 'La (re)configuration' (n. 37, above) 94–95.

which cannot be analysed here.[41] Moreover, what she says is explicitly called into question. In reference to Camacha's words, quoted by Cañizares in her narrative, and anticipating a possible re-transformation of the two dogs into human beings, Scipio says in a very negative way:

> Todas estas cosas y las semejantes son embelecos, mentiras o apariencias del demonio; y si a nosotros nos parece ahora que tenemos algún entendimiento y razón, pues hablamos siendo verdaderamente perros, o estando en su figura, ya hemos dicho que éste es caso portentoso y jamás visto […] no son sino palabras de consejas o cuentos de viejas.

> All these things and others like them are frauds, lies, or manifestations of the devil. And if we seem now to have some understanding and power of reason, since we are speaking when we are in fact dogs, or have the form of dogs, we have already said that this is something marvellous and never seen before […] [and] these are nothing but fairy stories or old wives' tales.[42]

In Cervantes, the canine presence is used in order to insist on the ridiculous aspect of the human explanation for the existence of speaking dogs. In Apuleius, the allusion to the asinine status of Lucius the character accentuates the fact that it is the human narrator Lucius who has just been reporting the story about Cupid and Psyche, and not the old woman. Notice that the aged feminine figure is used by both authors. In Cervantes, as if accentuating the dialogue, the figure even appears twice: through the character of the old Cañizares and through Scipio's expression 'old wives' tales' ('cuentos de viejas'). The motif of the old women's tale is an element which has had a huge success in literature, with its reuse in the tradition of fairy tales, such as in Perrault's *contes* or the Grimms' *Märchen*, continuing a game of variations which is already present in our authors.[43] To this generic tendency, Scipio here adds another, in reference to the novel, or rather to the 'novella' à la Boccaccio, when he says that his speech is something new and 'never seen before' ('jamás visto'). This is, of course, also a hint at the 'novela ejemplar' which includes the Cañizares-episode, and at the collection of the *Novelas ejemplares* as a whole. This element invites us to relate Apuleius' old woman's tale not only to Cañizares' narration but also to its frame, the *Coloquio de los perros*. I think that Cervantes responds in a twofold manner to the scenography of the narration of Cupid and Psyche: through Cañizares' narration, on the one hand, and through the narrative setting of the *Coloquio* as a whole, on the other. In order to clarify this point, it will be useful to refer to a series of images. I will not argue that these representations are genetically related, at least not all of them, but I do think that they illustrate very well the respective scenographies, which may in fact be connected.

---

[41]   The complex embedded structure of the passage distances and artificializes the speech about the human origin of the two dogs. It can be summarized as follows (Cervantes >) Campuzano > Berganza > Cañizares > Camacha (the witch quoted by Cañizares).

[42]   Cervantes, *Novelas* (n. 2, above) II 346. Slight modification of Jones' translation, which renders 'jamás visto' as 'unprecedented'.

[43]   For Perrault, *inter alia* see especially Heidmann, 'Intertextualité' (n. 11, above) 55–63, and for the Grimms, who quote Cervantes' passage and use the Spanish term *conseja* as equivalent of their *Märchen*, see L. Núñez, 'Les commentaires paratextuels des *Kinder- und Hausmärchen, gesammelt durch die Brüder Grimm*', *Féeries* 9 (2012) 197–247 (216–17 and 245).

Figure 1. Boiardo, *Apulegio volgare* (Venise 1537) 31 recto, © Bayerische Staatsbibliothek München: 1228692 A.lat.b. 34, p. 31 recto, urn:nbn:de:bvb:12-bsb10171417-6.

Figure 2. Bernardo Daddi, *Story of the Love of Psyche and Cupido* © Paris BnF Richelieu - Estampes et photographies, location: TA-39-4.

I will start with a representation (fig. 1), in Boiardo's translation, of the context of the narration of Cupid and Psyche's story by the old servant of the brigands. One can see on this image the servant speaking to the young Charite and Lucius the ass looking at and listening to this communicative exchange. Under the image, we read 'novella of Amor and Psyche's falling in love' ('novella dello innamoramento di Amore & di Psiche'). Note the use of 'novella' for the Cupid-Psyche narrative.

On the famous illustration (fig. 2) by the Master of the Die and Agostino Veneziano, the position of Lucius the ass is a little different. Lucius the ass is no longer on the same level as Charite and the old woman. Instead, he is hidden behind the scene between the two women. It is from this marginal and hidden position that our protagonist is listening to the narrative and he does so very attentively, with his ears pricked up.[44] The text under the image comments on the narrative situation. As has often been done, the text identifies the ass with Apuleius himself: 'Apuleius narrates that (while he was transformed into an ass [...])' ('narra Apuleo che (mentr'egli cangiato /In Asino [...])'). Furthermore, the text explains that the old woman 'in a nice fable tells her Psyche's novella' ('con grata favella / Le racconta di Psiche la novella'). As in Boiardo's translation, we have again the term 'novella' for the narrative about Cupid and Psyche.

The same designation of 'novella' also appears in other texts, for instance in Diego López de Cortegana's Castilian translation of Apuleius, which Cervantes might have read. Cortegana translates the passage, concluding the embedded narrative as follows:

> En esta manera aquella vejezuela loca y liviana contaba esta conseja a la doncella cautiva; pero yo, como estaba allí cerca, oíalo todo y dolíame que no tenía tinta y papel para escribir y notar tan hermosa novela.[45]

> Thus was the tale the mad and inconstant little old woman told to the captive maiden; but for me, I was there, close, I heard everything and was sorry not to have ink nor paper to write and note down such a beautiful 'novella'.

The generic label 'novella' accompanies the narrative about Cupid and Psyche along its *Nachleben*, perhaps also in Cervantes' *Novelas ejemplares* in general and in the scenography of the *Casamiento-Coloquio* in particular. The image (fig. 3 on p.150) from the Antonio Sancha edition illustrates the narrative situation in Cervantes very well.[46] In the foreground are the talking dogs Berganza and Scipio, whereas the background is occupied by the patients and the nursing staff of the hospital. Campuzano is one of the patients, perhaps the first figure on the right: the man is in a very difficult position, yet he is looking in the direction of the two dogs.[47] Now, when set beside an image representing the scenography of the narration of Cupid and Psyche, the two illustrations of course shows differences, but we can also see a number of very interesting similarities. The foreground is occupied by the figures involved in a communicative exchange: a pair of women or two dogs. In the background, we see another character listening to the narrative exchange, an ass in the one case and an ill man in the other. This strange listening figure is to be situated in the past of the narration. Yet, being in the past, this character was not in a position to transcribe what he was hearing. The record or, to put it more precisely, the re-writing, or writing *tout court*, must, then, have been effectuated after the represented scene. Thus, the text is marked as re-creation or full creation, first by Lucius the man or Campuzano the sane character, and then, ultimately, by the author, be it Apuleius or Cervantes. Hence, our authors insist on the artificial aspect of the transcription of the narratives and simultaneously accentuate their own creative act.

---

[44] From the perspective of the dialogue between Apuleius and Cervantes, note also the presence of a dog in front of the two feminine figures; *cf.* Heidmann, 'Zur poetologischen' (n. 38, above) 163, n. 11.

[45] D. López de Cortegana, *Apuleyo. 'El asno de oro'. Traducción*, ed. C. García Gual (Madrid 2010) 201.

[46] For a general study of the illustration of Cervantes' text, see P. W. Manning, 'Present dogs, absent witches: illustration and interpretation of "El coloquio de los perros"', *Cervantes: Bulletin of the Cervantes Society of America* 27.2 (Fall 2007 [2008]) 125–54.

[47] Of course, the figure on the right side behind the first group might also represent Campuzano, as the man seems to look to the dogs as well. However, since the first figure is nearer and even leans over in order to see, and especially to hear, the two talking dogs, it seems to be he who corresponds to Campuzano.

V. Conclusion

This act also leads, of course, to the creation of the collection as a whole, in the case of both the *Novelas ejemplares* and the *Metamorphoses*. A more detailed comparison between the two works, taking into account other pieces of Cervantes' collection, would doubtless constitute an invaluable complementary research topic. Alternatively, one might consider extending the literary comparison to an intermedial approach, including other representations, such as, for instance, *Las Meninas* by Velázquez (fig. 4), with which the image in the 1783 edition (fig. 3) might very well be related (the figures follow on pp. 150–51).[48] We might even expand the reflection back to Apuleius' *Golden Ass* and perhaps discover other incredible 'metamorphoses' of its *Nachleben*. Kahane, for instance, has offered an inspiring comparison between Apuleius and *Las Meninas*, explaining that,

> in Velazquez's *Las Meninas* we find paradoxes of pictorial representation, *i.e.* of the relation between three-dimensional and two-dimensional objects. In the *Metamorphoses* we find comparable paradoxes, but ones based on the relation between vocalized discourse and written text.[49]

This statement establishes a parallel with the *Metamorphoses* as a whole. But a similar connection could be made concerning the image staged in *Las Meninas* and the scene of the narration of Cupid and Psyche in Apuleius, as represented in Boiardo's translation or on the engraving by the Master of the Die mentioned above. We can also go further and explore the relation with Cervantes' *Coloquio* as well.

The images by the Master of the Die and Velázquez are probably not related to each other, at least not in the same way as that of the Antonio de Sancha edition is to *Las Meninas*. Yet even a comparison which does not pursue the agenda of attempting to prove a genetic connection might well bring to light an unexpected relationship. This is the case in our short study of Apuleius' *Metamorphoses* and Cervantes' *Coloquio de los perros*. The various elements that have been observed in this chapter in the light of the differential comparison pursued here serve, both individually and collectively, to highlight the dialogue between Apuleius' *Ass* and Cervantes' *Dogs*.

Université de Lausanne, CLE-Centre de recherche 'Comparer les Littératures en langues Européennes'

---

[48]   There are various parallels between the engraving by Ximeno and Barranco on the *Coloquio* and Velázquez' *Las Meninas*: Velázquez's dog in the foreground is transformed into two dogs by Ximeno/Barranco, there are different levels behind or above the dogs, one of which has a man standing in the door frame in a similar position on both images, or the two ceiling lamps; on the right, there are windows in both images.

[49]   A. Kahane, 'Antiquity's future: writing, speech, and representation in the Prologue to Apuleius' *Metamorphoses*', in *A Companion to the Prologue of Apuleius' 'Metamorphoses'*, eds A. Kahane and A. Laird (Oxford 2001) 231–41 (239).

Figure 3. Engraving by José Ximeno and Bernardo Barranco in the following edition: Cérvantes, *Novelas exemplares*, Madrid, Antonio Sancha, 1783 © Bayerische Staatsbibliothek München, 10816628 P.o.hisp. 45–2, vol. 2, p. 340, urn:nbn:de:bvb:12-bsb10607094-7..

Figure 4. Velázquez, *Las Meninas*, 1656 © Museo Nacional del Prado, catalogue number P001174. Reproduced with permission. Accessible online at https://www.museodelprado.es (accessed on 22.03.20).

'HE DOES NOT SPEAK GOLDEN WORDS: HE BRAYS.' APULEIUS' STYLE AND HUMANISTIC LEXICOGRAPHY[*]

CLEMENTINA MARSICO

It is well known that Filippo Beroaldo was not the only Italian Humanist scholar with a passion for Apuleius. Between the fourteenth and fifteenth centuries, the *Metamorphoses* were imitated in vernacular literature on a number of occasions. Moreover, Apuleius' fame as a *philosophus platonicus*, which was already consolidated in the Middle Ages, brought about a widespread dissemination of both authentic philosophical writings and numerous pseudo-epigraphic Apuleian works on various themes.[1] With respect to language, Antonio Stramaglia has convincingly demonstrated that the use of Apuleius as an authoritative linguistic model rests on a long tradition stretching back to late antiquity which, while limited in terms of quantity, was extremely significant.[2] According to Stramaglia, this tradition may be linked to the subsequent presence of Apuleian texts in several masterpieces of fifteenth-century scholarship which generations of humanists used in perfecting their Latin: Giovanni Tortelli's *Orthographia* and Niccolò Perotti's *Cornu copiae*. This would clearly mean that Apuleius also played an important role in the Latin revival of the fifteenth century.[3]

In this chapter, I intend to assess this assumption, delving further into certain aspects of Apuleian reusage in the works of Tortelli and Perotti, and comparing them to the different attitude towards the Madaurensis' Latin found in Lorenzo Valla's writings. The goal is to identify the moment in the fifteenth century at which Apuleius started to be considered as an example of linguistic authority by evaluating his presence in several fundamental instruments for the study of Latin: Valla's linguistic writings and the previously cited texts by Tortelli and Perotti.[4]

---

[*] I am grateful to Mariangela Regoliosi for her useful suggestions.

[1] For Apuleius' *Nachleben*, see especially R. H. F. Carver, *The Protean Ass: The 'Metamorphoses' of Apuleius from Antiquity to the Renaissance* (Oxford 2007); J. H. Gaisser, *The Fortune of Apuleius and the 'Golden Ass'. A Study in Transmission and Reception* (Princeton-Oxford 2008). From a linguistic point of view that is relevant for this article, see also: S. Prete, 'La questione della lingua latina nel Quattrocento e l'importanza dell'opera di Apuleio', in *Groningen Colloquia on the Novel*, eds H. Hofmann and M. Zimmerman (Groningen 1988) I 123–40; J. F. D'Amico, 'The progress of Renaissance Latin prose: the case of Apuleianism', *Renaissance Quarterly* 37 (1984) 351–92; H. E. Elsom, 'Apuleius in Erasmus' Lingua', *Res Publica Litterarum* 11 (1988) 125–40.

[2] *Cf.* A. Stramaglia, 'Apuleio come *auctor*: premesse tardoantiche di un uso umanistico', *Studi umanistici piceni* 16 (1996) 137–61 (later in O. Pecere and A. Stramaglia, *Studi apuleiani. Note di aggiornamento di L. Graverini* (Cassino 2003) 119–52, from which I quote).

[3] See Stramaglia, 'Apuleio' (n. 2, above) 119–20 with references to R. Sabbadini, *Storia del ciceronianismo e di altre questioni letterarie nell'età della Rinascenza* (Turin 1885) 42–45, to Prete 'La questione' (n. 1, above), and to D'Amico 'The Progress' (n. 1, above). However, the reuse of Apuleius in Tortelli's work plays a very marginal role in these last two papers (see, respectively, 137 and 369).

[4] For Apuleius' reuse in another lexicographical work of that time, Nestore Dionigi's dictionary, see J.-L. Charlet, 'Nestor Denys de Novare, moine et lexicographe latin du Quattrocento', *Res publica litterarum* 15 (1991) 19–47 (26–31).

To anticipate the results, I argue here that Apuleius was not a linguistic model for Valla, and nor was he for Tortelli. While it is true that Beroaldo was not the only writer responsible for Apuleius' success as *auctor* in the linguistic arena, it is important to provide evidence for the change of direction in humanistic lexicography that occurred between the first and the second halves of the fifteenth century. That is to say, amongst the multitude of models that Valla and Tortelli offered to their contemporaries for learning Latin, Apuleius only actually held a marginal position. The same cannot, however, be said in the case of Perotti.

Valla, Tortelli, and Perotti were bound by both friendship and intellectual affinity. To the first, the most famous of the triad, can be attributed the most important work for the restoration of Latin, the *Elegantie lingue latine*. The second, Giovanni Tortelli, was the author of an imposing encyclopaedic work, the *Commentariorum grammaticorum de orthographia dictionum e Graecis tractarum libri* (better known as the *Orthographia*), in which the most disparate themes were treated, starting from orthography. Finally, Niccolò Perotti, younger than both Valla and Tortelli, composed at the end of his life (and therefore almost thirty years after the dissemination of the writings of Valla and Tortelli) a commentary on Martial entitled the *Cornu copiae*, which is, in reality, a vast encyclopaedic dictionary of Latin.

The debts of Tortelli and Perotti to the *Elegantie* are numerous:[5] it has already been established that many lexical, morphological, and syntactic definitions, in addition to a significant number of sources, pass from the *Elegantie* to the *Orthographia* and to the *Cornu copiae*. The shared ambitions of the writings and their underlying conception of the language, as well as the quantity of materials that are repeated throughout the three works, have led scholars to define them as kindred and even complementary.[6] This does not mean, however, that there are no differences, nor that the differences that can be identified are insignificant. We shall examine the way in which Apuleius is used in the texts of our three humanists in order to illustrate some of these differences more clearly.[7]

Lorenzo Valla and Apuleius' Latin

First disseminated in 1449, together with the *Raudensiane note* and the *Antidotum in Facium*, the six books that made up the *Elegantie* sought to restore the Latin language, which had, by Valla's time, become quite different from the language of Cicero and Quintilian.[8] As

---

[5] For the relations between the three works, see O. Besomi, 'Dai 'Gesta Ferdinandi regis Aragonum' del Valla al 'De orthographia' del Tortelli', *Italia medioevale e umanistica* 9 (1966) 75–121; M. Regoliosi, 'Nuove ricerche intorno a Giovanni Tortelli. 2. La vita di Giovanni Tortelli', *Italia medioevale e umanistica* 12 (1969) 129–96 (137–38); M. Furno, 'Du *De orthographia* de G. Tortelli au *Cornu copiae* de N. Perotti: points communs et divergences', *Res publica litterarum* 12 (1989) 59–68; M. Pade, 'Valla e Perotti', *Studi umanistici piceni* 20 (2000) 72–85; J.-L. Charlet, 'Tortelli, Perotti et les Élégances de L. Valla', *Res publica litterarum* 24 (2001) 94–105; J.-L. Charlet, 'Les instruments de lexicographie latine de l'époque humaniste', in *Il latino nell'età dell'Umanesimo. Atti del Convegno Mantova, 26–27 ottobre 2001*, ed. G. Bernardi Perini (Florence 2004) 167–96; G. Donati, 'L'Orthographia' di Giovanni Tortelli (Messina 2006), 13–14, 29–53, 69; J.-L. Charlet, *La restauration du latin au quattrocento: Valla, Tortelli, Perotti*, in *Giovanni Tortelli primo bibliotecario della Vaticana*, eds A. Manfredi, C. Marsico, and M. Regoliosi (Vatican City 2016) 249–64; C. Marsico, 'Dal Valla al Tortelli. Il V libro delle *Elegantie* e l'*Orthographia*', in *Giovanni Tortelli primo bibliotecario*, eds Manfredi, Marsico, and Regoliosi (see this note, above) 209–47.

[6] See J.-L. Charlet, 'L'encyclopédisme latin humaniste: de la lexicographie à l'encyclopédie (XVe-début XVI s.)', *Moderni e Antichi. Quaderni del Centro di Studi sul Classicismo* 2–3 (2004–2005) 285–306 (286, 290).

[7] To be clear, all of the testimonies presented here involve explicit mentions of Apuleius; I will not venture into the sphere of the less-defined allusions.

[8] The bibliography on the *Elegantie* is large; I will only refer to a number of recent works from which it is possible to obtain further bibliography: *Lorenzo Valla. La riforma della lingua e della logica. Atti del convegno del comitato*

medieval barbarisms had polluted communication right down to its core, it was thought necessary to begin the process of recovery by returning to a basic quality of the language, its 'elegantia', made up of 'latinitas' (correctness) and 'explanatio' (clarity of the language).[9] To bring the 'elegantia' of the language to light, proponents of this programme believed, there was only one, laborious path: the meticulous study of the language of the great writers of the past. The *Elegantie*'s Latin is thus based on the way these writers used language, and, consequently, on the *exempla* of an enormous number of *auctores* from all periods and disciplines. The catalogued authors range from comic writers to historians, poets, orators, rhetoricians, grammarians, polygraphs, jurists, and the Fathers of the Church.[10] From these elements, a grand fresco unfolds that testifies to the variety and the richness of Latin. This fresco, however, has many shades.

First of all, although the sources cited are numerous, the most central reference models are only two in number: Cicero and Quintilian. As Valla writes in chapter I, XIII, 'here above all we will analyse that which is worthy of the ears of the scholars of the perfect Latinity and 'elegantia', observed especially by M. T. Cicero and M. F. Quintilian, the two luminaries and jewels of not only all knowledge, but also of the eloquence of Latin'.[11]

Second, in the *Elegantie* the humanist demonstrates a refined perception of the historical evolutions of Latin. He clarifies, for example, the difference between the forms used in Cicero's time and those used in Quintilian's; the archaic forms of the Plautine lexicon, despite being included, are characterized as 'vetustissimae' and are not always accepted. The employment of such an abundant range of sources did not mean that all of the catalogued forms in the *Elegantie* had to be judged as equal. The preferred forms are the 'usitatae'; majority rules in the most complicated cases.[12]

---

nazionale VI centenario della nascita di Lorenzo Valla (Prato, 4–7 giugno 2008), ed. M. Regoliosi (Florence 2010); *La diffusione europea del pensiero del Valla. Atti del convegno del comitato nazionale VI centenario della nascita di Lorenzo Valla (Prato, 3–6 dicembre 2008)*, eds M. Regoliosi and C. Marsico (Florence 2013). For the editorial work for the critical edition of the *Elegantie*, see: M. Regoliosi, *Nel cantiere del Valla. Elaborazione e montaggio delle 'Elegantie'* (Rome 1993); M. Regoliosi, *Per l'edizione delle* Elegantie, in *Pubblicare il Valla*, ed. M. Regoliosi (Florence 2008) 297–304; C. Marsico, *Per l'edizione delle 'Elegantie'. Studio sul V libro* (Florence 2013). For the *Raudensiane note* and the *Antidotum in Facium*, see: L. Valle, *Raudensiane note*, ed. G. M. Corrias (Florence 2007); L. Valle, *Antidotum in Facium*, ed. M. Regoliosi (Padua 1981).

[9] For the 'elegantia' in Valla's works, see D. Marsh, 'Grammar, method and polemic in Lorenzo Valla's 'Elegantiae'', *Rinascimento* 19 (1979) 91–116; V. De Caprio, 'L'idea di *elegantia* nelle *Elegantiae* di Lorenzo Valla, in *Le parole 'giudiziose'. Indagine sul lessico della critica umanistico-rinascimentale*, eds R. Alhaique Pettinelli, S. Benedetti, and P. Petteruti Pellegrino (Rome 2008) 99–115.

[10] For a general (but not complete) overview of the authors quoted in the *Elegantie*, see V. De Caprio, 'Appunti sul classicismo delle *Eleganze*', *F.M. Annali dell'Istituto di Filologia moderna dell'Università di Roma* 1–2 (1981) 59–80; V. De Caprio, 'La rinascita della cultura di Roma: la tradizione latina nelle "Eleganze" di Lorenzo Valla', in *Umanesimo a Roma nel Quattrocento. Atti del Convegno (New York, 1–4 dicembre 1981)*, eds P. Brezzi and M. De Panizza Lorch (New York 1984) 163–90.

[11] '[...] in hoc potissimum loco exequemur rem dignam auribus studiosorum de exactissima antiquorum latinitate et elegantia a Marco Cicerone Marcoque Fabio Quintiliano precipue observata, duobus luminibus atque oculis quum omnis sapientie, tum vero eloquentie Latine' (*Elegantie*, p. 19). In the absence of a critical edition, I cite the *Elegantie* from the vulgate, the version found in the *Opera* published in Basel in 1540 in the anastatic reprint L. Vallae, *Elegantiarum libri*, in L. Valla, *Opera omnia*, ed. E. Garin (Turin 1962), indicating the number of the book, the chapter, and the page number, with the exception of the citations of book V which are taken from Marsico, *Per l'edizione* (n. 8, above). Hereafter when reproducing Valla's texts, I have normalized them to the orthographic uses of the author, particularly regarding the lack of indications of diphthongs, and I have modified the punctuation where necessary. All translations are my own unless otherwise indicated.

[12] For Valla's ideas on the language, see M. Regoliosi, 'Le Elegantie del Valla come "grammatica" antinormativa', *Studi di grammatica italiana* 19 (2000) 315–36.

Notwithstanding these points, it will not be surprising that there are only two Apuleian quotes in the *Elegantie*, both taken from the *Apologia*. The first passage is in chapter I, V of the *Elegantie*, where Valla concentrates on diminutives formed with the suffix -ulus; amongst the many entries, the humanist inserts 'pulvisculum' (dust, powder), considered a regular diminutive in terms of meaning and suffixation, but not with respect to its gender.[13] Valla knows two passages, in fact, in which the word has two different genders: one is taken from Hieronymus' work, in which 'pulvisculum' is neutral, while the other is taken from the *Apologia*, where 'pulvisculus' is masculine.[14]

> *Pulvis* et significatione et formatione legitima diminutivum facit, sed genus mutat apud Hieronymum: 'ut vile pulvisculum' [Jerome, *c. Vigil.* VIII 1, 3]. Masculine tamen posuit Apuleius in quodam suo carmine de quo meminit in *Apologia de Magia*: 'misi, ut petisti, munditias dentium, / nitelas oris ex Arabicis frugibus, / tenuem, candificum, nobilem pulvisculum, / complanatorem tumidule gingivule, / sarritorem [*sic*] pridiane reliquie, / ne qua visatur tetra labes sordium, / restrictis si forte labellis riseris' [Apul. *Apol.* 6].[15]

> 'Pulvis' regularly forms the diminutive regarding the meaning and the form, but changes gender in Hieronymus 'as worthless speck of dust ('pulvisculum')'. Apuleius instead used it in the masculine form in one of his poems mentioned in the *Apologia de Magia*: 'I've sent, as you required, the dentifrice, Arabian produce, brightener of the mouth, a fine choice powder ('pulvisculum'), a rare whitener, a soother of the swollen tender gums, a cleaner-out of scraps of yesterday; that no unsightly blemish may be seen, if you should chance with opened lips to laugh'.[16]

This is one of the many open chapters of the *Elegantie*: the author does not propose unequivocal solutions, limiting himself instead to presenting the reader with the various possibilities found in ancient texts. One of these is offered by Apuleius.

More interesting, however, is the second passage, taken from chapter V, XLII. Despite softening his position at the end of the chapter, Valla claims that Apuleius does not know the correct meaning of the verb 'gratulor' and that he used it incorrectly in the *Apologia*:

> *Gratulari* est verbo testari te gaudere fortuna ac felicitate alterius apud eum ipsum qui affectus est felicitate [...]. Ideoque fere postulat dativum, ut 'gratulor tibi ob preturam adeptam'. [...] Poete nonnunquam pretereunt dativum, utique cum fuerit pronomen, que fuit causa ut quidam existimarent, quorum est Apuleius, hoc verbum idem significare quod *gaudeo* [...]. Verba autem Apuleii hec sunt in *Apologia de magia*:

---

[13] See *Thesaurus linguae Latinae* X.II, 2633, *s.v.* pulvisculus (-um).

[14] It is interesting to note that one of the two chapters in which Apuleius is quoted in the *Elegantie* is devoted to the diminutive, which is a peculiar aspect of his language; see L. Pasetti, *Plauto in Apuleio* (Bologna 2007) 11–60 (with further bibliography) and for 'pulvisculus / -m', 21–22.

[15] *Elegantie*, 8. 'Sarritorem' is in the Basel print; the *Elegantie*'s manuscripts (including the Escorial, M III 13, corrected by Valla) have 'surritorem' instead of 'converritorem' ('one who sweeps together') as in the critical edition. 'Surritorem' or 'sarritorem' are not even registered in Apuleius' modern editions. 'Surritor' seems to be a mistake, probably caused by the difficulty of the correct 'converritor'; it could be a deformation of 'sarritor' or 'saritor', from 'sarrio' or 'sario' ('to hoe'). Many manuscripts, probably because of the meaning of 'sarritor', read 'ne qua visatur terra [...]' instead of 'tetra'.

[16] The translation of Apuleius is by S. Harrison, J. Hilton, and V. Hunink (Apuleius, *Rhetorical Works* (Oxford 2001)), with appropriate changes.

'eo in tempore, quod non negabunt in Getulie mediterraneis montibus fuisse, nisi pisces per Deucalionis diluvia reperirentur. Quod ego gratulor nescisse istos legisse me' [Apul. *Apol.* 41]. Pretermisit dativum quia *gratulor* pro *gaudeo* accepit, quod tantum abest ut approbem, ut possit gratulari quis cum minime gaudeat atque adeo doleat (quod frequenter usu venit utique inter falsos amicos, cum alter invidus atque emulus tacite quidem dolens quod alter honoribus auctus sit, tamen illi gratulatur). Forte et Apuleius subintellexit *mihi*.[17]

'Gratulari' means: to declare in words that you rejoice for the good fortune and happiness of another person with the same person that is happy [...]. And for this it generally postulates the dative, like 'I congratulate you ('gratulor tibi') on your appointment as praetor' [...]. Sometimes the poets leave out the dative, especially when it is a pronoun; this was the reason for which some thought, including Apuleius, that this verb meant the same thing as 'gaudeo' [...]. These are the words, instead, of Apuleius in the *Apologia de magia*: 'They will not deny I was in the inland mountains of Gaetulia, a region where fish can be found only as a result of Deucalion's flood. I am so glad they did not know I also read [...]'. He left out the dative as he meant 'gratulor' as 'gaudeo', something that is far from my approval, in that one can congratulate ('gratulari') not just those who are barely rejoicing ('gaudeat'), but even one who is grieving (this happens frequently, especially amongst false friends, when one who is invidious and jealous grieves in silence that another received important honours, but still congratulates him). Perhaps Apuleius also implied 'mihi'.

According to Valla the verb 'gratulor' means 'give thanks', 'congratulate', and not, instead, 'be glad', 'enjoy', and requires, for its meaning, a dative that indicates the beneficiary of the verb. However, poets often imply the dative, and perhaps it is precisely this that is to blame for the misunderstanding that Valla finds in Apuleius' text, namely the mix-up of meaning between 'gratulor' and 'gaudeo'. For Valla, the passage of the *Apologia* can be understood only by interpreting 'gratulor' as 'I rejoice, I am glad' (Apuleius, accused of preparing spells using fish, rejoices in the fact that his enemies do not know some of his readings, from which he could have learned to prepare poisons even without fish). This interpretation of the verb, however, is incorrect because 'gratulor' defines a behaviour that does not always indicate an authentic internal joy. Often, the humanist writes, false friends hypocritically congratulate ('gratulari') someone without feeling any sort of happiness (without 'gaudere', therefore), but rather envying their success. To soften the criticism Valla, concludes this part by affirming that, perhaps, despite being in prose and not in verse, a 'mihi' in Apuleius' text could have also been implied (to be understood thus as 'I rejoice with myself').[18] In the *Elegantie*, therefore, while Apuleius is a quotable *auctor*, it is only for the very rare cases in which the examined usages are not entirely trustworthy.

Let us move on to the *Raudensiane note*, which, in the Vallian project to publish a vast linguistic *summa*, make up the seventh and eight books of the *Elegantie*.[19] In this case as well, the citations from Apuleius can be counted on a single hand. Of the three, one is the reuse of

---

[17]   Marsico, *Per l'edizione* (n. 8, above) 292–93.

[18]   It is interesting to note that, in the *Cornu copiae*, Perotti rewrites Valla's entire chapter, in doing so eliminating the criticism of Apuleius: see Nicolai Perotti, *Cornu Copiae seu linguae Latinae commentarii*, ed. J.-L. Charlet, 8 vols (Sassoferrato 1989–2001) III (1993) 116, 46–47 (with a reference to the *Elegantie*). Hereafter I cite this work using the abbreviation *CC*, along with the number of the volume, lemma, and page.

[19]   *Cf.* Regoliosi, *Nel cantiere* (n. 8, above) 1–35.

a citation present in the *Imitationes rhetoricae* by Antonio da Rho, the work that Valla takes apart point by point in the *Raudensiane*.[20] In the second, Valla gives a positive evaluation of Apuleius, even if it appears to be almost incidental:

> *Deficio* cum tempore ponitur similibusque, non cum persona, iunctum accusativo. 'Dies—enim—me deficiet' [Apul. *Apol.* 54] idem est, quod 'dies mihi deficiet', sed illo modo (per accusativum) apud eruditos frequentius.[21]

> 'Deficio' is used with time and similar things, not with a person, and it is used with the accusative. 'Dies', in fact, 'me deficiet' is the same as saying 'dies mihi deficiet', but that way (with the accusative) is used more frequently by learned scholars.

In this case, the Apuleian example is valid and is even defined as specific to 'eruditi' (directly after Apuleius' text, in fact, Valla proposes a Ciceronian example).

Nevertheless, to gain a more precise idea of Valla's opinion of Apuleius' style, another passage from the *Raudensiane* must be considered—a passage which, as has been written, 'machte Schule' (the play on words can be found in Giovanni Pontano, Philipp Melanchthon, Gilbert Cousin, Juan Luis Vives, and others).[22]

> Ra.: A. Gellius dixit 'villatice pastionis' [Gel. 2.20.2].

> La.: Quasi non Terentius Varro de villaticis pastionibus. Neque vero Raudensi faciendum fuit, ut tam sepe Aulum Gellium pro teste afferret, hominem sepe curiose nimis ac superstitiose loquentem. Quid dicam de Apuleio in eo presertim opere, cuius nomen est *De asino aureo*, cuius sermonem siquis imitetur, non tam auree loqui, quam nonnihil rudere [sed asinine *I redaction*] videatur?[23]

> Raudense: A. Gellius said 'farm feeding' ('villatice pastionis').

> Lorenzo: As if it had not been Varro to speak of farm feeding. Raudense truly should not have cited Gellius as a witness so often, a man who often speaks with excessive curiosity and in a pedantic way. What will I say about Apuleius, especially in the work by the title *The Golden Ass*, of which, if one imitated the language, he would not speak golden words but would rather seem to bray [but he would speak like a donkey *I red.*]?

Valla calls Varro into question because Raudense cites a passage from the *Attic Nights* in which Gellius, in turn, is quoting Varro. The humanist does not dispute the linguistic expression in itself, but rather the sources on which Antonio da Rho founds his argument, here and elsewhere. In the *Imitationes rhetoricae*, in fact, Gellius' name, like that of Apuleius, appears multiple times. However, they alone do not provide an adequate guide in the search for 'latinitas'. One of them, Gellius, is an excessively curious and pedantic author. For the other, Apuleius, the same holds true, especially with respect to the *Metamorphoses* (in which the protagonist Lucius is characterized by an exceptional 'curiositas'):[24] he who proposes

---

[20] See Valle, *Raudensiane note* (n. 8, above) I XV 32–33 (on Apul. *Met.* 5.20 and the expression 'gradus pensiles').

[21] Valle, *Raudensiane note* (n. 8, above) II II 15–16.

[22] *Cf.* K. Krautter, *Philologische Methode und Humanistiche Existenz. Filippo Beroaldo und sei Kommentar zum 'Goldenen Esel' des Apuleius* (München 1971) 97; E. Norden, *Die antike Kunstprosa: vom VI Jahrhundert bis in die Zeit der Renaissance*, 2 vols (Stuttgart 1958) II 590–91, 778–79; Elsom, *Apuleius* (n. 1, above) 126–27.

[23] Valle, *Raudensiane note* (n. 8, above) I XV 16.

[24] For 'curiositas' in Apuleius, see C. Moreschini, 'Ancora sulla *curiositas* in Apuleio', in *Studi classici in onore*

the *Metamorphoses* as a stylistic model will be followed by braying donkeys like Lucius. The evaluation is one of the most severe critiques in Valla's work (similar expressions can be found only with respect to later authors, such as Isidore, Alexander de Villedieu, and Giovanni Balbi).

Nevertheless, we have seen that some examples from Apuleian works (although not his novel) are cited in Valla's writings. Apuleius is even considered in one passage to be a learned writer. How must one then interpret this violent attack? Despite not wanting to define Valla as an admirer of Apuleius, it must be noted that the negative evaluation of the Madaurensis' style is framed in a polemical work written against Raudense's *Imitationes*. The humanist here attempts to undermine the very foundations of that work, forcefully emphasizing that even the models chosen by Antonio are altogether inadequate. Raudense looks to identify the precise meaning of the words, their 'elegantia', but he does so using Apuleius' Latin as a model, a Latin full of audacious neologisms, archaic and popular forms, *hapax*, refined expressions, and Greek calques. In Valla's view, which is substantiated by Quintilian's analysis of the language, the only guide towards the 'elegantia' is the 'consuetudo', the 'certissima loquendi magistra', to which the humanist frequently refers.[25] Choosing Apuleius as a reference is, essentially, a step in the opposite direction.[26]

Apuleius' function in Tortelli's 'Orthographia'

The *Orthographia* is a vast encyclopaedic work, the principal goal of which is the restoration of the orthography of true or presumed Greek words transposed into Latin.[27] In the alphabetic section, more than three thousand four hundred lemmas are analysed.[28] Starting from the orthography of the selected words (terms related to technical languages, names of real or legendary figures, or toponyms, for example), Tortelli studies various themes which often distance him from the original orthographical goal.

The arsenal of ancient Greek and Latin sources used to explain the entries and to enrich the discourse is impressive. Amongst the numerous *auctores* explicitly cited by Tortelli, the name of Apuleius can also be found. However, I do not believe it is correct to affirm, as Stramaglia has proposed, that a 'conspicuous presence of Apuleius' can be noted in the *Orthographia*.[29] In the approximately 380 pages of the *Vat. Lat.* 1478 (one of the most authoritative witnesses of the *Orthographia*),[30] Tortelli mentions Apuleius on only a small number of occasions: as far as I have been able to tell, his name appears only ten times in all. It is important to clarify

---

di Quintino Cataudella, 3 vols (Catania 1972) III 517–24; D'Amico, *Progress* (n. 1, above) 388–89; F. Bertini, 'The *Golden Ass* and its *Nachleben* in the Middle Ages and in the Renaissance', in *Fictional Traces: Receptions of the Ancient Novel*, eds M. P. Futre Pinheiro and S. J. Harrison, 2 vols (Groningen 2011) II 61–82 (61–63).

[25] The fundamental work on Valla and Quintilian is S. I. Camporeale, *Lorenzo Valla. Umanesimo e teologia* (Florence 1972); see also M. Regoliosi, 'Valla e Quintiliano', in *Quintilien ancien et moderne. Etudes réunies* eds P. Galand, F. Hallyn, C. Lévy, and W. Verbaal (Turnhout 2009) 233–78, from which it is possible to obtain further bibliography.

[26] To complete the list of explicit quotations of Apuleius in Valla's linguistic writings, I mention the three short references to the author in the *Antidotum in Facium* (n. 8, above): I II 15; I XIV 20; II VI 24.

[27] An introduction to the *Orthographia* can be found in M. Regoliosi, 'Ritratto di Giovanni Tortelli Aretino' and in G. Donati, 'Per l'edizione critica dell'*Orthographia*', both in *Giovanni Tortelli primo bibliotecario* (n. 5, above) 17–57, 135–69.

[28] For the list of the words analysed, see Donati, *L'Orthographia* (n. 5, above) 354–83.

[29] Stramaglia, 'Apuleio' (n. 2, above) 119.

[30] See Donati, 'Per l'edizione' (n. 27, above) 143–55.

that I do not include in this count citations from Apuleius the grammarian—author of a *De nota aspirationis* and a *De diphthongis*, probably composed in the medieval period, and almost always referred to by Tortelli as *Apuleius* or *Apulegius grammaticus*—as these are not pertinent to our discussion.[31]

Let us turn now to the texts to clarify the methods and aims of the reuse of Apuleius in Tortelli's masterpiece. The first reference to Apuleius can be found at the entry for *Archimedes*. Tortelli uses the *Apologia* here (without, however, citing it word for word) as the source for a brief historical report on Archimedes, defined as one of the most clever men in the field of geometric science:

> *Archimedes* cum *ch* aspirato et *i* latino scribitur; fuit Syracusanus in omni geometria ante alios mira subtilitate laudatus, ut testatur Apulegius libro primo *de magia* [*cf.* Apul. *Apol.* 16] (*Orth.* f. 75r).[32]

> *Archimedes* is written in Latin with *ch* and *i*; he was originally from Syracuse and was the most highly praised for his extraordinary acuity in every branch of geometry, as Apuleius testifies in the first book *de magia*.

In the entry for *crocodilus*, Apuleius' text is used to describe a characteristic of the exotic animal:

> *Crocodilus* [...] detinetque dentes magnos ad corporis proportionem quos ut ait Apulegius libro primo *de magia* 'innoxio hiatu ad purgandum praebet' [*cf.* Apul. *Apol.* 8] (*Orth.* f. 129r).

> *Crocodilus* [...] and it has large teeth with respect to the rest of its body, that as Apuleius says in the first book *de magia* 'harmlessly opens his mouth to have his teeth cleaned'.

In the entry devoted to *Epimenides*, Apuleius is introduced to testify to the philosopher's Cretan origin:

> *Epimenides* cum *i* latino utrobique et unico *n* scribitur. Fuit philosophus Cretensis contemporaneus Pythagorae ut scripsit Apuleius libro secundo *Floridorum* [*cf.* Apul. *Fl.* 15] (*Orth.* f. 159r).

> *Epimenides* is written with *i* on both parts and with one *n*. He was a Cretan philosopher contemporary with Pythagoras, as Apuleius wrote in the second book of *Florida*.

In the quoted passages, Apuleius' text is not used to document the correct spelling of *Archimedes*, *crocodilus*, and *Epimenides*. This is also the case in the other seven citations of Apuleius in the *Orthographia*: in the entries for *Hippocrates*, *Magus*, *Pythagora*, *Protagora*, and *Samothracia*, the *Apologia* and the *Florida* are used to provide information on doctors, philosophers, and distant locations. Of Asclepiades, for example, Apuleius recalls a miraculous recovery; of Thessaly he recounts its ill fame as a land home to sorcerers; of

---

[31]   For Apuleius the grammarian, see L. Biondi, 'Mai, Osann e Apuleius grammaticus. Un testis antiquior del «de nota aspirationis» e del «de diphthongis»', *Acme* 50 (1997) 65–108; Charlet, 'Nestor' (n. 4, above) 26–31; L. Biondi, *Recta scriptura. Ortografia ed etimologia nei trattati mediolatini del grammatico Apuleio* (Milan 2011).

[32]   Hereafter I cite the *Orthographia* from the codex *Vaticanus latinus* 1478, introducing punctuation and italics for the words analysed by Tortelli.

Pythagoras he speaks of an extraordinary beauty, and of Protagoras an exceptional linguistic fluency.[33]

The analysis of the passages in which Tortelli explicitly cites Apuleius' works allows for some considerations concerning the ways in which the humanist uses the ancient source. Besides the novel, which is practically never cited,[34] the *Apologia* and the *Florida* are used as sources of information on little-known figures or locations, to confer greater authority to the accounts, and to justify affirmations made, all in the spirit of the historical-antiquarian research specific to the *Orthographia*. Apuleius' texts, rarely cited in any case, are never used to support the underlying linguistic discussion.[35]

A new role: Apuleius in Perotti's 'Cornu copiae'

The *Cornu copiae* is the work to which Niccolò Perotti dedicated his efforts after retiring from the political arena in 1477. The humanist never actually saw the publication of his work, as it was only printed in 1489.[36] Much like the *Orthographia*, the work is encyclopaedic in nature. Starting from the lemmas of Martial (of which the *Liber Spectaculorum* and the first book of epigrams are commented upon), Perotti examines entire series of terms, more or less linked either etymologically or semantically, discussing their meaning and proposing citations of authors to provide examples of usage. A single Martial lemma thus offers the starting point for the examination of hundreds of other lemmas, based on an infinite number of models. The evident preference for authors from Archaic literature has already been noted. Among the principal sources, there are—as the studies by the research team led by J.-L. Charlet have shown—many pre-existent lexicographical collections, including medieval ones, and, above all, the *Elegantie* and the *Orthographia*.

Perotti's re-usage of Apuleius—which has been framed within the complex question of the presence in the *Cornu copiae* of otherwise unknown fragments of classical authors—was first studied in detail by Sesto Prete and then in greater depth by Francesca Brancaleone.[37] I refer the reader to these studies for significant clarifications. Here, I will only present a summary of Perotti's Apuleian readings, highlighting the purposes to which Apuleius' texts are bent.

---

[33] See *Orth.* f. 188r (on *Hippocrates* with reference to Apul. *Fl.* 19); f. 221r (on *Magus* with a general reference to the *Apologia*); f. 282v (on *Pythagoras* with reference to *Apol.* 4 and *Fl.* 15); f. 308r (on *Protagoras* with reference to *Fl.* 18); f. 330r (on *Samothracia* with reference to *Fl.* 15). To complete the list of the explicit citations of Apuleius in the *Orthographia*, in the entry *Magus* Tortelli partially cites and partially paraphrases the famous extract of book 18 of the *De civitate Dei* in which Augustine declares he is aware of the fantastical tales linked to the transformation of men into animals, similar to those of Apuleius (see *Orth.* f. 221v).

[34] The novel is only quoted by Augustine: see n. 33, above.

[35] For the copies of Apuleius' texts in the Vatican Library when Tortelli worked there, see A. Manfredi, *I codici latini di Niccolò V. Edizione degli inventari e identificazione dei manoscritti* (Vatican City 1994), numbers 610, 663, 688.

[36] For a profile of Perotti, see J.-L. Charlet, 'Perotti (Niccolò)', in *Centuriae latinae. Cent une figures humanistes de la Renaissance aux Lumières offertes à Jacques Chomarat*, ed. C. Nativel (Genève 1997) 601–05. For the *Cornu copiae*, see the introduction of Perotti, *Cornu copiae* (n. 18, above) (1989) I. In volume VIII, eds J. -L. Charlet, M. Pade, J. Ramminger, and F. Stok (2001) 304–05 the reader can find a complete list of Apuleius' quotations in the *Cornu copiae*.

[37] See Prete, 'La questione' (n. 1, above) 133–38; S. Prete, 'Frammenti di Apuleio e pseudo-apuleiani nel Cornu copiae di Niccolò Perotti', *Nuovi Studi Fanesi* 2 (1987) 39–63, and especially F. Brancaleone, 'Considerazioni sulle citazioni apuleiane e pseudo-apuleiane nel *Cornu copiae* di Perotti', *Studi umanistici piceni* 14 (1994) 49–54; F. Brancaleone, *Citazioni 'apuleiane' nel 'Cornu copiae' di Niccolò Perotti* (Genoa 2000).

Approximately fifty citations of authentic Apuleian works have been identified in the *Cornu copiae* (from the *Metamorphoses*, *De mundo*, *De deo Socratis*, and *De Platone*). Perotti was probably able to consult them in the *editio princeps*, given his easy access to the library of Cardinal Bessarion, who was very interested, as is well known, in the valorization of Latin Platonism. Indeed, he was even the inspiration behind Bussi's printed edition, of which he possessed two copies (in addition to two Apuleian manuscripts).[38]

Beyond the unquestionably authentic citations, various scholars have identified 161 further references to Apuleius. However, it has not been possible to find the material attributed to Apuleius in these cases in any modern edition of his works. These references have been carefully studied, both because of their significant quantity and for the affinities that the lexicon of these pericopes shares with the Apuleian idiolect. There has not, as yet, been any universalized explanation for all of the fragments taken collectively. In some cases, scholars have considered them to be the result of lapses in Perotti's memory and imprecise recollections of Apuleian material. In other cases, it is not possible either to conclusively assert that these passages do not have an Apuleian origin, or to affirm that they do by reference to a possible lost work or version, or even to show with confidence that they at least derived from a source that Perotti *believed* to be Apuleian. The hypothesis that the unidentified fragments are from other works attributed to Apuleius between the Middle Ages and the Renaissance has been proposed by some scholars but has not yet been demonstrated conclusively. The situation is rendered even more complex both by Perotti's usage of the *De nota aspirationis* and the *De dipthongis* of Apuleius the grammarian, and by the possibility that sections of the work by Lucius Caecilius Minutianus Apuleius, often confused with the Madaurensis, were already in circulation in Perotti's time.[39]

In any case, what is important to note in terms of the present research is that Perotti uses Apuleius' work (both the authentic texts and those of more dubious paternity) in a much more ample fashion than do Valla and Tortelli, and he does so in order to reach different goals. In some rare cases, the texts of Apuleius (and above all his novel) are cited to illustrate the meaning of common words. See, for example, the following passage:

Capulum etiam manubrium ensis appellatur, sed hoc quia manu capiatur. Apuleius: 'ensem que capulo tenus infixit' [*cf.* Apul. *Met.* 1.13.4].[40]

'Capulum' is also called the handle of a sword, but because it is taken with the hand. Apuleius: 'plunged the sword right down to the handle ('capulum')'.

Much more frequently, Perotti uses the texts in order to focus on peculiarities in Apuleius' language, such as diminutives, archaisms, rare terms, or late terms:

Ab *opera* fit *operula* diminutivum. Apuleius: 'operulas etiam in eam contuli, quas adhuc vegetus saccariam faciens merebam' [*cf.* Apul. *Met.* 1.7].[41]

[38]   For this theme and the role of Bessarion in Bussi's print, see Gaisser, *Fortunes of Apuleius* (n. 1, above) 158–61.

[39]   For the moment we only know about a circulation of Minutianus' works starting from 1516. For his work, see H. D. Jocelyn, 'L. Caecilius Minutianus Apuleius', in *Homo sapiens. Homo humanus. I. La cultura italiana tra il passato ed il presente in un disegno di pace universale. Atti del XXVII convegno internazionale del centro di studi umanistici, Montepulciano - Palazzo Tarugi, 1986*, ed. G. Tarugi (Florence 1990), 207–18; A. S. Hollis, '"Apuleius" de Orthographia, Callimachus fr. [815] Pf. and Euphorion 166 Meineke', *Zeitschrift für Papyrologie und Epigraphik* 92 (1992) 109–14.

[40]   *CC* IV 88, p. 36. As in the case of Tortelli, the quotations of Apuleius are not literal.

[41]   *CC* I 455, p. 161.

From 'opera' derives the diminutive 'operula'. Apuleius: 'I gave her even the scant wages ('operulas') I earned as a porter, as long as I was still vigorous'.

Invenitur tamen aliquando *exodus* sive *exodium* pro *exitu* sive *fini* alicuius rei. Apuleius: 'nullum ego eius rei exodium inveniebat' [*cf.* Apul. *Plat.* 1.8].[42]

Nevertheless, sometimes 'exodus' or 'exodium' is found for 'exitus' or 'finis' of something. Apuleius: 'I could not find the end ('exodium') of his thing'.

Item *divinitas*, sicut a *deo deitas*, et adverbium *divinitus* et *divinipotens*. Apuleius: 'Saga, inquit, et divinipotens caelum deponere, terram suspendere, fontes durare, montes diluere, manes sublimare, deos infimare, sydera extinguere, Tartarum illuminare' (*cf.* Apul. *Met.* 1.8).[43]

Similarly, 'divinitas', as from 'deus deitas', and the adverb 'divinitus' and 'divinipotens'. Apuleius: 'A witch, he replies, and with supernatural power, she can lower the sky, suspend the earth, solidify fountains, dissolve mountains, raise up ghosts, bring down gods, darken the stars, light up Tartarus'.

At other times, in a way that is very similar to Tortelli, Perotti also cites Apuleius, although not as a linguistic authority but, rather, in order to extract information, especially that of a philosophical nature:

Homo diffinitur animal rationis capax. [...] utinam non tam vere ab Apuleio describitur: 'homines rationem callentes, oratione pollentes, immortalibus animis, moribundis membris, brutis et obnoxiis corporibus, dissimilibus moribus, similibus erroribus, pervicaci audacia, pertinaci spe, casso labore, fortuna caduca, singillatim mortales, vicissim sufficienda prole mutabiles, volucri tempore, tarda sapientia, citata morte, querula vita' [*cf.* Apul. *Socr.* 4].[44]

Man is defined as an animal able of reasoning. [...] How I wish that Apuleius had not described him so truly: 'men knowing well the reason, being powerful because of the word, provided of immortal souls, of moribund limbs, of ugly and submissive bodies, with different customs, subject to similar errors, with obstinate audacity, stubborn hope, vain efforts, fleeting fortune, individually mortal, in turn fickle thanks to the procreation of the species, for a fugitive time, being wise rather late, with a very quick death, with a lamentable life'.

Daemones [...]. Apuleius irritari eos iniuriis scribit, obsequiis donisque placari, gaudere honoribus, diversis sacrorum ritibus oblectari [*cf.* Apul. *Socr.* 12, 14].[45]

Daemones [...]. Apuleius writes that they are irritated by the offenses, they are appeased by services and gifts, they enjoy the honours, they are delighted by the various sacred rites.

---

[42]   *CC* X 102, p. 59.

[43]   *CC* I 88, p. 44.

[44]   *CC* X 117, pp. 63–64.

[45]   *CC* XIX 13, p. 180.

It is clear that, despite the fact that the Ciceronian lexicon constitutes the primary reference for Perotti in his *Cornu copiae* as well, Apuleius ascends to the status of *auctor* worthy of scholarly attention. His texts are just as valid as are those of Cicero or Virgil for illustrating some of the peculiarities of Latin, despite Perotti's deep knowledge of Valla's linguistic works, and therefore of his opinions on Apuleius' bad Latin. It has been authoritatively shown, in fact, that Valla represents for Perotti 'l'autorité la plus sûre et le garant de la latinité' and that the *Cornu copiae* can be read, largely, as a lexicographical and encyclopaedical complement to the *Elegantie*.[46] The *distinguo*, nevertheless, are still important to point out.

As has been said, Valla knew of Apuleius' work (at least of his novel, the *Apologia*, and the *Florida*) and, albeit rarely, he put it to use. This was because the humanist showed an unmistakable interest in the language of all of the epochs that preceded the fall of Rome. However, his use of Apuleius always evidenced the nuances, praises, disagreements, and various underlying degrees of the historical evolution of the language. Plautus, Pliny the Elder, Apuleius, Gellius—authors loved by Perotti and increasingly well-studied in the second half of the fifteenth century, when Perotti worked on the *Cornu copiae*, and when the work of Valla and Tortelli had been in wide circulation for around thirty years—are also present in the *Elegantie*, although not overwhelmingly so. Rather, they are often used only to advance doubts or as springboards for pungent critiques. In the thirty years that divide the *Elegantie* and the *Orthographia* from the *Cornu copiae*, the revival of the ancient tradition had progressed. The 'arduous frontiers of *latinitas*' (the Archaic and Silver Ages of Latinity),[47] to which Valla had conceded very little space, became better known and increasingly appreciated: archaisms, rare terms, neologisms—carefully avoided by Valla— aroused the interests of young, combative humanists and, consequently, found ample space in the new lexicographical studies, of which Perotti is one of the best representatives.

Ludwig Boltzmann Institut für Neulateinische Studien, Innsbruck

---

[46]   Charlet, 'Tortelli, Perotti' (n. 5, above) 104–05.

[47]   I translate from C. Dionisotti, *Gli umanisti e il volgare fra Quattro e Cinquecento*, ed. V. Fera (Milan 2003) 74 (orig. Florence 1968).

THE GOLDEN ASS UNDER THE LENS
OF THE 'BOLOGNESE COMMENTATOR':
LUCIUS APULEIUS AND FILIPPO BEROALDO

ANDREA SEVERI

As everyone who is familiar with the topic is aware, Julia Haig Gaisser and Robert Carver have written many very interesting things about the reception of Apuleius' *Golden Ass* in general, and about its first great commentator, Filippo Beroaldo, in particular. Indeed, so comprehensive are their volumes that proposing something original in the wake of these impressive works is no easy task.[1] This is why I will not discuss one of the most beautiful and exciting aspects of Beroaldo's commentary, the peculiar digressions that are able to 'bring antiquity to life', for Gaisser has already addressed this dimension of his work in the most brilliant fashion. However, Beroaldo's commentary on *The Golden Ass*, the most important work by the 'Bolognese Commentator', is truly immense: in it you can find (almost) whatever you seek. Consequently, by bravely rowing across the ocean that is Beroaldo's scholarship in their own little boat, every scholar is able to find something new. Or at least that is my hope.

Anyone who has crossed paths with the writings of the Bolognese humanist and professor Filippo Beroaldo the Elder remembers at least one passage of his seemingly endless commentary on Apuleius' *Golden Ass*, that found at the beginning of the tale of Cupid and Psyche (*Met.* 4.28). After reporting the rhetorical difference between *fabula*, *argumentum*, and *historia*, and then reviewing the most famous interpretations of this myth,[2] Beroaldo closes his long didactic digression as follows:

> Sed nos non tam allegorias in explicatione huiusce fabulae sectabimur quam historicum sensum, et rerum reconditarum verborumque interpretationem explicabimus, ne philosophaster magis videar quam commentator.[3]

> But, explaining this myth, I will not chase after the allegories but rather the historical significance, and I will explain the meaning of ancient things and words, in order to appear not a *philosophaster* but a commentator.

[1] R. H. F. Carver, *The Protean Ass: The 'Metamorphoses' of Apuleius from Antiquity to the Renaissance* (Oxford 2007) 174–182; J. H. Gaisser, *The Fortunes of Apuleius and the 'Golden Ass': A Study in Transmission and Reception* (Princeton-Oxford 2008) 197–242. But see also: K. Krautter, *Philologische Methode und humanistische Existenz: Filippo Beroaldo und sein Kommentar zum 'Goldenen Esel' des Apuleius* (München 1971); J. Robert, 'Apuleius, Beroaldus and Celtis', in J. Robert, *Konrad Celtis und das Project der deutschen Dichtung: Studien zur humanistischen Konstitution von Poetik, Philosophie, Nation und Ich* (Tübingen 2003) 211–218; B. Plank, *Johann Sieders Übersetzung des 'Goldenen Esels' und die frühe deutschsprachige Metamorphosen-Rezeption: ein Beitrag zur Wirkungsgeschichte von Apuleius' Roman* (Tubingen 2004) 34–43; S. Chaudhuri, 'Lucius, thou art translated: Adlington's Apuleius', *Renaissance Studies* 22.5 (2008) 669–704 (681–85); G. M. Anselmi, 'Codro e il mito classico: Bologna crocevia', in G. M. Anselmi, *Letteratura e civiltà tra Medioevo e Umanesimo* (Roma 2011) 173–196.

[2] *Cf.* C. Moreschini, *Il mito di Amore e Psiche in Apuleio* (Napoli 1999) 7–67.

[3] Filippo Beroaldo, *Commentarii in Asinum aureum Lucii Apuleii* (Bologna, 1500 GW2305), 95v. All translations from Beroaldo's commentary are my own.

This is, without doubt, the single most significant passage in the text for arriving at an understanding of Beroaldo's approach to Apuleius' masterpiece. It is not by chance that this passage has been quoted in almost all modern writings devoted to the Bolognese Commentator.[4] None, however, highlight the term *philosophaster*, which here is so crucial to the meaning of the sentence that I have decided not to translate it. *Philosophaster* is a neologism coined by Augustine to define Cicero. It originates in a muchdebated passage of the *De civitate Dei* (2.27.1: 'Vir gravis et philosophaster Tullius' some manuscripts read, while others give 'Vir gravis et philosophus Tertullius'), recovered by humanistic scholarship during the fifteenth century. Valla was the first to reuse it in his *Elegantie latine lingue* (I 7), assigning it the non-pejorative meaning of 'imitatorem philosophorum'. Niccolò Perotti inserted the term with the same meaning into his *Cornu copiae* (III 167) and Poliziano used it at the end of his *Lamia*.[5] The *Elegantie* and the *Cornu copiae* were the two most important lexicographical works of the fifteenth century, while Poliziano was a friend and correspondent of Beroaldo. As such, it is very likely that Beroaldo took the term over from these predecessors. Hence, Beroaldo's *philosophaster* is better translated as 'would-be philosopher' than 'bad philosopher'. However, what is more important is that this rather uninteresting linguistic caveat alerts us to the cultural tradition to which Beroaldo alludes in his main work: philological scholarship, 'l'umanesimo della parola', to use the title of one of Vittore Branca's famous books.[6]

Before moving on to consider further the significance of this term, I must confess that this passage had always sounded rather strange to me. In the final years of his life and career, Beroaldo seems to have changed the direction of his studies from the literary to the philosophical arena: in 1496 he published his commentary on Cicero's *Tusculan Disputations* (a great *summa* of key ethical doctrines of the Greek philosophical schools);[7] in 1498, he gave his academic prolusion on the *Seven Sages of Greece*;[8] in 1501, he published Alamanno Rinuccini's Latin translation of the *Life of Apollonius of Tyana* (without commentary), a biography of an individual considered to be a holy man, a second Christ, and a miracle worker;[9] finally, in 1503, less than two years before dying, he gave the last prolusion of his academic career on the *Symbola Pythagorae*.[10] It is useful to remember that Beroaldo seems to have already shown an interest in Platonism in 1487, in the preface to his commentary on Propertius, in which he claims for the role of the commentator the same divine *furor* that Plato's *Phaedrus* and *Ion* bestow upon the figure of the poet. Beroaldo had felt the influence of the Florentine circle since 1486, in the wake of an Easter trip to Florence with his friend

[4]   Carver, *Protean Ass* (n. 1, above) 181–82; Gaisser, *Fortunes of Apuleius* (n. 1, above) 231; Krautter, *Philologische Methode* (n. 1, above) 149 n. 1; M. Acocella, '*L'Asino d'oro' nel Rinascimento: dai volgarizzamenti alle raffigurazioni pittoriche* (Ravenna 2001) 57.

[5]   Angelo Poliziano, *Lamia: praelectio in priora Aristotelis analytica*, ed. A. Wesseling (Leiden 1986) 18: 'Me enim vel grammaticum vocatote, vel, si hoc magis placet, philosophastrum, vel ne hoc ipsum quidem' (112 for the linguistic commentary on this word). See also J. Ramminger, 'philosophaster', in J. Ramminger, *Neulateinische Wortliste: ein Wörterbuch des Lateinischen von Petrarca bis 1700* [www.neulatein.de/words/0/003348.htm (accessed 14.08.20)].

[6]   V. Branca, *Poliziano e l'umanesimo della parola* (Torino 1983).

[7]   Cicero, *Tusculanae disputationes*, ed. and comm. F. Beroaldo (Bologna 1496, ISTC ic00640000).

[8]   F. Beroaldo, *Heptalogos sive septem sapientes* (Bologna 1498, ISTC ib00487000).

[9]   Philostratus, *De vita Apollonii Tyanei scriptor luculentus a Philippo Beroaldo castigatus* (Bologna 1501 Edit16 CNCE 36020).

[10]   F. Beroaldo, *Symbola Pythagorae moraliter explicata* (Bologna 1503).

Mino de' Rossi during which he met Pico, Poliziano, and perhaps Ficino and Lorenzo the Magnificent. However, if we move beyond simply flipping through the catalogue of his works to actually reading them, we come to realize that Beroaldo, despite changing the subjects of his academic courses and prolusions, does not change his own method and approach towards literary texts over time: his focus remains on their grammatical, lexicographical, and philological aspects.

Nine years before Beroaldo's Apuleius was published, Poliziano decided to teach an academic course on Aristotle's *Prior Analytics*. By opening that course with his famous oration, the *Lamia*, he gave himself, as a grammarian, the power to comment on the philosopher Aristotle. I think that, in the passage quoted above, Beroaldo wished to claim a similar power for himself: he, as a professor of Grammar and Rhetoric, assigns to himself the power to comment on Apuleius, an author who was, in Augustine's opinion, considered to be a Platonic philosopher. The importance of this decision (the decision to provide, as a grammarian, a commentary on Apuleius' *Golden Ass*) becomes increasingly significant if we recall that Apuleius' masterpiece was printed for the first time, together with his other rhetorical and philosophical works, in Rome in 1469 by Giovanni Andrea Bussi. Moreover, this occurred against the backdrop of the general cultural framework of the promotion of Platonism that took place during the famous controversy between supporters of Aristotelianism and Platonism, led by George of Trebizond and Johannes Bessarion respectively. However, the provocation that Beroaldo directed against the philosophers by setting up his own discipline as in some sense superior was stronger than that of Poliziano, as the Bolognese professor is the first author of a complete commentary—a word-by-word commentary—on *The Golden Ass*. Furthermore, he endeavoured to print his commentary in two thousand copies, so that his wealthy students could follow his lessons with their own copy at hand and then, upon their return home, spread it all over Europe.[11]

However, despite this very important difference, it is also necessary to underline the similarities between the bishop working in Rome and the Bolognese commentator: 1) both Bussi and Beroaldo greatly appreciated Apuleius' luxuriant prose, and they both considered the Madaurensis to be an *arbiter elegantiarum*; 2) they were both attracted to the narrative flow and the inclination towards realism of the *Asinus*. Let us examine these two points carefully, beginning with the stylistic features.

Perhaps, as Sesto Prete and Francesca Brancaleone have argued,[12] Beroaldo was not the first scholar to have been fond of Apuleius' prose, since a humanistic interest in his work can be traced back to Niccolò Perotti and his *Cornu copiae* (printed in 1489 but composed between 1450 and 1480). Nevertheless, it is difficult to deprive Beroaldo of the prize of 'alter Apuleius', for it is hard to deny that in his orations, prolusions, and letters he was the first to have used—and abundantly so—puns (anaphors, polyptotons, etymological figures, chiasmus, and so on) and the ornate and elaborate *copia verborum* that is so peculiar to Apuleius' Silver Latin. Against the supporters of Cicero, and by distancing himself from

---

[11] 'Et sane impressor optimus operam dedit ut volumina commentariorum circiter duo milia formis excussa divulgarentur', *cf.* Beroaldo, *Commentarii* (n. 3, above) f. a4v, dedication letter to Peter Varadi, Archbishop of Calocsa. For Beroaldo's dedication letters to very important lords, see M. Menna, 'Epistole prefatorie di Filippo Beroaldo il Vecchio (1453–1505): esempi illustri di *ars scribendi* nelle lettere ai vescovi mitteleuropei', *Esperienze letterarie* 40.1 (2015) 95–108.

[12] S. Prete, 'La questione della lingua latina nel Quattrocento e l'importanza dell'opera di Apuleio', in *Groningen Colloquia on the Novel*, ed. H. Hofmann, 9 vols (Groningen 1988–98) I (1988) 123–40; F. Brancaleone, *Citazioni 'apuleiane' nel 'Cornu copiae' di Niccolò Perotti* (Genova 2000).

the so-called 'eclectics' as well, Beroaldo and his 'Asian' fellows filled their prose with words and phrases taken from Plautus, Pliny the Elder, Aulus Gellius, and, obviously, from Apuleius. Was it only an affectation, a charm, a grace? I do not think so. Yes, it was also a peculiar seal of the Bolognese school,[13] useful for distinguishing the professors of the *Studio Bolognese* from those teaching in other Universities (let us recall that Antonio Urceo Codro, who was praised by Beroaldo in one of the digressions typical to his comments, also used the *sermo cotidianus*).[14] However, I think that this stylistic choice also had both pedagogical and political causes. First, Apuleius' rich prose—'florulenta' and 'bracteata', as Beroaldo describes it—was very useful for young pupils studying Latin and aiming to build their own Latin vocabulary. Second, although this is a more personal opinion of mine, Apuleius, who was born in Africa, was a significant example, useful to the hundreds of foreign students following Beroaldo's courses, of the fact that good Latin was not necessarily a prerogative of the Italian population; everybody, irrespective of their place of birth, could become a good Latinist.

With regard to our second point in particular—the narrative flow and the inclination towards realism of the *Asinus*—it is necessary to keep in mind that our contemporary perspective on this subject is influenced by Erich Auerbach's *Mimesis* (even if this book does not have a chapter dedicated to Apuleius' novel).[15] Beroaldo, like Bussi, held the belief that the Latin used by Apuleius was the natural language of the street, and he was particularly fascinated by this aspect of Apuleius' writing. In his commentary, he often tries to link the supposed popular words he found in *The Golden Ass* with the vernacular language of his own days, a particularly interesting aspect of his work for later Italian scholars studying the history of Italian language.[16] From this specific point of view, we can say that Beroaldo's *opus magnum* on Apuleius is also, or above all, a strangely shaped dictionary of the Latin language, a dictionary that the Bolognese Professor considered to be a living one. However, as Gaisser has pointed out, the belief shared by both Bussi and Beroaldo that the so-called 'Realien' used by Apuleius in his masterpiece were part of the *Umgangsprache*, the everyday language of common people, is a great blunder. Gaisser writes very pointedly that: 'The language he admires is not that of 'cookshops or lodging houses' but rather of a highly educated man writing for a sophisticated audience about cookshops or lodging houses, which is a very different matter'.[17] So the stylistic realism used by Apuleius does not transport us

---

[13]   For this aspect, see J. D'Amico, 'The progress of Renaissance Latin prose: the case of Apuleianism', *Renaissance Quarterly* 37.3 (1984) 351–92.

[14]   See A. Urceo Codro, *Sermones I–IV : filologia e maschera nel Quattrocento*, eds L. Chines and A. Severi, intro. E. Raimondi (Rome 2013) 60: 'Accipite laetis animis, viri clarissimi, sermonem meum, si modo meus est qui sit a virorum doctissimorum sententiis concinatus [...] Praeterea ego quoque quotidie fere Luciani et Apuleii asinos in manibus habeo, unius brevitatem et inventum, alterius copiam admirans atque elegantiam' (*Sermo* I, 1–4); and *cf.* Beroaldo, *Commentarii* (n. 3, above) f. 94: 'Codrus collega meus in professione litteraria homo impense doctus et utriusque linguae callens, qui plus habet in recessu quam ostentet in fronte, qui in pensitandis tam priscorum quam recentiorum libris iudicio est praecellenti praeditus'.

[15]   E. Auerbach, *Mimesis: Dargestellte Wirklichkeit in der abendländischen Literatur* (Bern 1946).

[16]   See the following examples (Beroaldo, *Commentarii*, n. 3, above, 28, f. 78v): 'Utendum enim est vulgaribus verbis et vernaculis dictionibus ad rem dilucidandam'; 'Verba non pauca sunt vernacula ac plebeia atque in opificum sermonibus usitata quae cum dehonesta deculpataque videantur, tamen latina sunt et in usu quoque eruditorum frequentantur, quo ex genere est istud 'rumigare' quod et rustici et foeminae usurpant quod ferme idem significat'. For a provisional catalogue of vernacular words accepted in Beroaldo's Latin, see M. T. Casella, 'Il metodo dei commentatori umanistici esemplato sul Beroaldo', *Studi medievali* s. 3.16 (1975) 627–701 (658–59).

[17]   Gaisser, *Fortunes of Apuleius* (n. 1, above) 169.

back to the road of a Roman province in the second century AD, or to the inside of a tavern or pub, since it is a literary experiment for educated people.

One aspect of his interest that Beroaldo did not declare—and this is why it is also the most interesting—was his fascination for what we nowadays call 'storytelling'. Beroaldo is a rare bird among his fellow humanists, who, as is well known, were not great lovers of prose fiction because it was not considered to reside amongst the noble literary genres according to the rules of classical rhetoric.[18] It is emblematic, for instance, that the father of Humanism, Francesco Petrarch, disliked Boccaccio's *Decameron*: when his pupil Boccaccio sent him a copy of his masterpiece, Petrarch hid with difficulty his contempt for all the novellas, with the exception of the last about Griselda. On the contrary, Beroaldo held Boccaccio's *Decameron* in such high esteem that he translated three of its novellas into Latin. Moreover, in commenting on book 9 of *The Golden Ass*, he praised Boccaccio as the author of the *Decameron*, not as the author of the *Genealogia deorum gentilium* or any of the other scholarly works appreciated and usually cited by humanists.[19] We can say that here the *Decameron* provides some sort of 'mise en abyme' of *The Golden Ass* and Boccaccio is like an 'alter Apuleius': Apuleius is a great storyteller because he succeeds in showing the reader the images he is talking about (rhetorically speaking, the name of this ability is 'hypotyposis', *cf.* Quint. *Inst.* 9.2.40). Beroaldo insists more than once on this capacity of Apuleius. Commenting on the phrase 'Erat in proxima' (*Met.* 8.1), he writes: 'narratio secundum paerceptiones rhetoricas, lucida brevis probabilis, qua singula ita decenter ita graphice describuntur ut non legere te putes sed cernere'.[20] Commenting on 'aper immanis' (*Met.* 8.4), he then explains:

> Magna virtus est res de quibus loquimur clare atque ut cerni videantur enunciare [Quint. *Inst.* 8.3.62]. Hoc cum pluribus locis tum in hac descriptione decenter facit Lucius noster, qui describit, immo depingit aprum tam graphice, tam scite, tam eleganter, ut eum oculis repraesentet, per illam exornationem rhetoricam, quam Graeci enargian, nostri repraesentationem atque evidentiam [Quint. *Inst.* 8.3.61] appellant.[21]

> It is a great virtue to succeed in describing the things we are talking about clearly and as if we could see it. As in many other passages, in this description our Lucius does it very well: he describes, or rather depicts so well, cleverly, and tastefully the boar that he represents it to the eyes, thanks to that figure of speech which Greek scholars call 'enargia' and Romans 'repraesentatio' and 'evidentia'.

In commenting on 'recalcans vestigias' (*Met.* 9.11), the *Commentator bononiensis* finally repeats: 'Per quandam evidentiam et illustrationem totum hoc negocium graphice depictum

---

[18]   F. Rico, 'Classicismo e realtà', in *Letteratura europea e tradizione latina*, eds G. M. Anselmi and F. Florimbii (Bologna 2009) 37–45; F. Rico, *Il romanzo, ovvero le cose della vita* (Torino 2012).

[19]   In his comment on 'gracili pauperie' in *Met.* 9.5, the beginning of the story of the smith and his unfaithful wife, Beroaldo writes: 'Iohannes Boccacius eloquio vernaculo disertissimus condidit centum fabulas argumento et stilo lepidissimo festivissimoque inter quas Apuleianam hanc inseruit transposuitque commodissime, non ut interpres, sed ut conditor, quam foeminae nostrates non surdis auribus audiunt neque invitae legunt. Nos quoque mythopoion, hoc est opificem fabellae Lucium nostrum latialiter personantem et graphice lepidissimeque explicantem inaudiamus, legamus pensitemus auribus oculis animis lubentibus, cum talibus egressionum amoenitatibus non solum lectores, verum etiam commentatores reficiantur. Inter paupertatem et pauperiem differentia haec est [...]'. *Cf.* Beroaldo, *Commentarii* (n. 3, above) f. 193v.

[20]   Beroaldo, *Commentarii* (n. 3, above) f. 166.

[21]   Beroaldo, *Commentarii* (n. 3, above) f. 168; *cf.* also Krautter, *Philologische Methode* (n. 1, above) 63.

subiicitur oculis lectorum, ut non tam legere quam videre videantur'.[22] It is, thus, clear that Beroaldo is very attracted to the figurative force of Apuleius' prose.

What, however, did Beroaldo think about the literary genre of *The Golden Ass*? There are at least two places where Beroaldo addresses this issue: on the first page of his work, by trying to explain 'fabula milesia', and in book IV, when he introduces the story of Cupid and Psyche. In both cases Beroaldo cites many *auctoritates*, but we struggle to understand what Beroaldo really thinks about it. For example: is 'fabula milesia' a licit, good, adequate literary genre according to him? How does Beroaldo reply to the detractors of the 'fabula milesia' who think that it has no beginning or end, and is thereby useless because it lacks a moral teaching ('epimythion')? Unfortunately, he does not give us an answer. His gloss to Apuleius' novel often consists of quotations of a large quantity of *auctoritates* regarding lexicographical or philological problems, but only occasionally does he take sides. Hence, we can say that, above all on hermeneutical or exegetical issues, Beroaldo reveals himself very little. As an example, we can take the brief history of 'fabula milesia' presented by Beroaldo at the beginning of his comment.

> *Sermone milesio* (I 1): idest fabuloso, lepido, iocoso, delicato, ludicro hoc enim significat sermo Milesius a Milesiorum Ioniae populis dictus, qui deliciis luxuque notabiles fuere, quorum est illud memoratissimum 'Nemo nostrum frugi esto, alioqui cum aliis eiiciatur' [Strab. 14.25].[23] Hinc Milesias prisci appellaverunt poemata et fabulas lascivientes sive, ut quidam putant, Milesiae dicuntur fabulae aniles et vanidicae in quibus nec pes nec caput [Hor. *Ars* 8] appareat, nec instat apologorum epimythion ullum morale continens. Iulius Capitolinus in Clodio Albino [Hist. Aug. *Alb.* 11.8] sic ait: 'Agricolendi peritissimus, ita ut etiam Georgica conscripserit, Milesias nonnulli eiusdem esse dicunt quarum fama non ignobilis habetur, quamvis quanti mediocriter scriptae sint'. Extat epistola Severi imperatoris ad senatum missa, in qua id quod ad hanc rem maxime pertinet scriptum legimus; sic enim ait: 'Maior fuit dolor quod illum pro litterato laudandum plerique duxistis, cum ille neniis quibusdam anilibus occupatus inter Milesias Punicas Apuleii sui et ludicra letteraria consenescoeret' [Hist. Aug. *Alb.* 12.12]. [...] Marcianus quoque Capella in libro de nuptiis philologiae [II, 100] "poeticae, inquit, diversitatis delicias Milesias". Aristides poeta Graecus composuit Milesias, hoc est poema milesiacon perquam impudicum, cuius rei Plutarcus [*Crass.* 32.4] et Appianus meminerunt, quod et Ovidius libro Tristium secundo [2.413–14] aperte docet sic scribens: 'iunxit Aristides Milesia carmina secum, / pulsus Aristides nec tamen urbe sua est'. Emaculandus est hoc loco maculosus divi Hieronymi codex, ubi de Milesiis hisce fit mentio, et in sinceram lectionem restituendus. Namque in libris contra Ruffinum [I, 17] sic passim legitur, 'quasi non curatorum turba Milesiorum in scholis figmenta decantent', ubi non 'curatorum' sed 'cirratorum' legendum est, hoc est comatulorum puerorum.[24]

Sermone milesio (I 1): that is fabulous, amusing, playful, entertaining, this is the meaning of 'Milesian speech', called in this manner because it comes from the Ionic people living in Milesia, who were famous for their luxury and riches and whose sentence is very worthy of remembrance, 'None of us has to be useful, otherwise he

---

[22] Beroaldo, *Commentarii* (n. 3, above) f. 197v; *cf.* also Krautter, *Philologische Methode* (n. 1, above) 63.

[23] Probably read in the Latin translation by Gregorius Tiphernas.

[24] Beroaldo, *Commentarii* (n. 3, above) f. 3.

must be ejected with others' [Strab. 14.25]. Hence ancient people called 'Milesia' licentious poems and tales or, as some people think, Milesias are those tales told by old women and full of emptiness where you can find no rhyme or reason, and where there is no final 'epimythion' containing a moral teaching. Julius Capitolinus reports in the life of Clodius Albinus: 'In the cultivation of land he was thoroughly versed, and he even composed Georgics. Some say, too, that he wrote Milesian tales, which are not unknown to fame though written in but a mediocre style' [Hist. Aug. *Alb.* 11.8].[25] We have a letter sent to the Senate by the emperor Severus where we can find the peculiar features of this literary genre; we read: 'It is even a greater source of chagrin, that some of you thought he should be praised for his knowledge of letters, when in fact he is busy with old wives' songs, and grows senile amid the Milesian stories from Carthage that his friend Apuleius wrote and such other learned nonsense' [Hist. Aug. *Alb.* 12.12][26] [...] Marcianus Capella too in the book of the Wedding of Philology says [II, 100]: 'Milesian delights of poetical diversity'. The Greek poet Aristides wrote *Milesias*, that is an extremely dirty Milesian poem: Plutarch [*Crass.* 32.4] and Appianus remembered this, and Ovid too, in the second book of his *Tristia* where he reveals this by writing: 'Aristides connected the vices of Miletus with himself, yet Aristides was not driven from his own city' [2.413–14].[27] We must correct the manuscript of Saint Jerome on that page where he makes mention of Milesian tales, and give back the authentic lesson. In fact, in the books against Ruffinum we read [I, 17]: 'quasi non curatorum turba Milesiorum in scholis figmenta decantent' where we should not read 'curatorum' but 'cirratorum', which means 'of the children having thick hair'.

As Robert Carver has pointed out with regard to Beroaldo's style of commentary, 'in general the accretion of glosses seems rather undiscriminating, particularly to anyone of a narratological bent', and, more generally, 'Renaissance collations are generally philological rather than hermeneutic'.[28] This is why an unidentified hand in this until now unknown copy of the *editio princeps* of Beroaldo's comment reports an annotation taken from Johannes Baptista Pio's *Annotamenta* (n. 40, ed. 1505, f. G3v) in order to examine in depth the phrase 'papyrum Aegyptiam' at the beginning of *The Golden Ass*. When Beroaldo explains it with the words 'est enim papyrum sive papyrus, utroque enim modo dicitur, frutex nascens in palustribus Egypti, aut quiescentibus Nili aquis. Unde Niliacas papyros appellavit epigrammarius poeta etc',[29] the anonymous reader writes in the lower margin of the page:

Existimo *papyrum Aegyptiam* genus dicendi molle et lascivum significare, qua mollitate male audiebant Aegyptii: quam ob rem Varroni Canopitici libidinosi sunt.

---

[25] Translation by D. Magie in *The scriptores Historiae Augustae* (Cambridge, MA-London 1960) I 483.

[26] Trans. D. Magie (n. 25, above) 487.

[27] Translation by A. Leslie Wheeler in Ovid, *Tristia, ex Ponto* (Cambridge, MA-London 1953) 85.

[28] R. H. F. Carver, '*Quis ille?* The role of the prologue in Apuleius' *Nachleben*', in *A Companion to the Prologue of Apuleius' 'Metamorphoses'*, eds A. Kahane and A. Laird (Oxford 2001) 163–174 (165). Carver continues by offering an example: 'in glossing *Taenaros* Beroaldus notes that "there is also a breathing vent with the same name from which the descent to the underworld lies revealed" ('est et spiraculum eodem nomine ex quo descensus ad inferos patet') but gives no indication that he has made an interpretive link between the Prologue and Psyche's *katabasis* at *Met*. 6. 18–20'.

[29] Beroaldo, *Commentarii* (n. 3, above) f. 3.

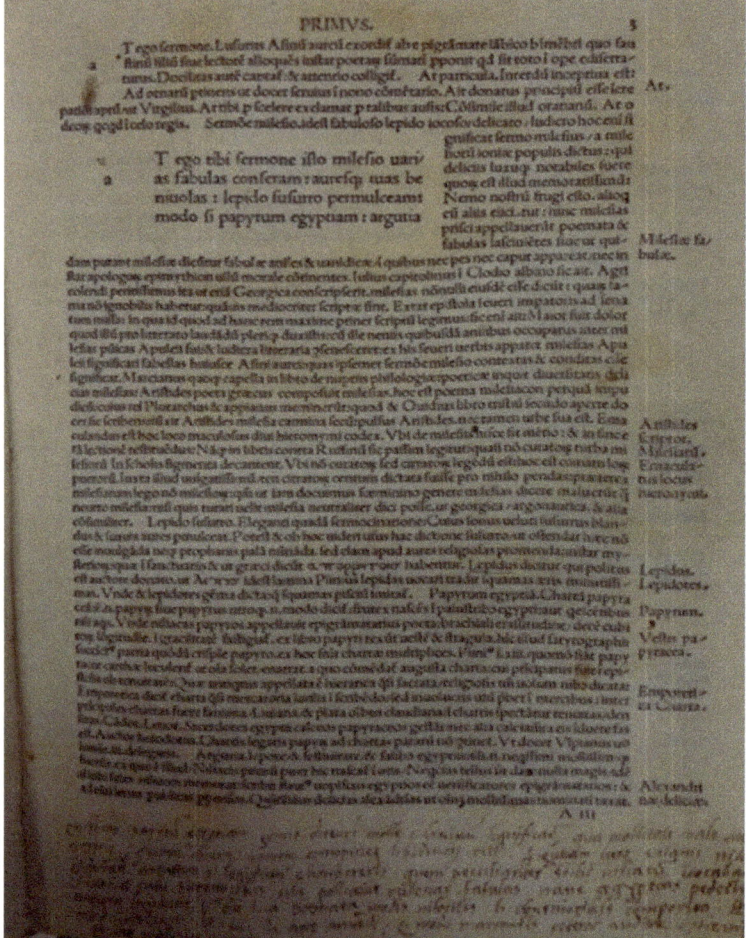

Figure 1. P. Beroaldo, *Commentarii in Lucii Apuleii Asinum aureum* (Bologna 1500), p. 5 (University of Bologna, Department of Classical and Italian Studies: Camporesi W I 001).

Argutiam vero calami nilotici elegantiam argutam et lepidam […][30]

I think that 'papyrum Aegyptiam' means a flabby and lascivious literary genre, and for this licentiousness the Egyptians did not approve it: this is why, according to Varro, Canopitics are lustful. 'Argutiam vero calami nilotici' is a witty and humorous politeness […]

This comment evidently reflects the fact that the unidentified reader was dissatisfied with Beroaldo's gloss on the passage, which is a digression focused on the material support ('papyrum') and not, as in the case of Pio, on the literary genre to which 'papyrum' might refer. It is clear that this reader required a less encyclopedic and a more hermeneutic contribution from the commentator. This copy of the *editio princeps* belonged to the scholar and professor Piero Camporesi (1926–1997) and is now kept in the Library of the Department of Classical Philology and Italian Studies of the University of Bologna (shelfmark Camporesi W I 001).

It is true that Beroaldo leaves the modern reader, particularly those more interested in Apuleius' masterpiece than in Renaissance culture, largely empty-handed. The word or the

---

[30]   G. B. Pio, *Annotamenta* (Bologna 1505) f. G3v (chapter 40, but 'Puto ego papyrum […]').

phrase from *The Golden Ass* that Beroaldo analyses in his commentary is often (almost always) used as a starting-point for a lexicographical tour of the grounds of Latin Literature, or to brilliantly emend a passage of Apuleius, or even of other authors. So, if we may put the point in the form of a joke, Beroaldo's *Asinus* seems more like a text formed of thousands of beautiful words or phrases than a work full of deep meanings. Beroaldo, as a diligent commentator, explains in the *Scriptoris intentio atque consilium* that the story of *The Golden Ass* has an allegorical and moral meaning (and, as Walsh and Schlam have pointed out, the echo of Beroaldo's words reverberated perhaps as far as the first German translator of *The Golden Ass*, Johan Sieder, and the first English translator, William Adlington).[31] However, this allegorical interpretation is not where his attention is focused. In contrast to Bussi, Beroaldo is not interested in a complete interpretation of Apuleius and his major work.

On the one hand, this is because Beroaldo wants to exhibit his classical knowledge with his humanist colleagues in mind. On the other hand, it is a consequence of the fact that his great work is not only, and not chiefly, a commentary on *The Golden Ass* but also a dictionary or, better, an encyclopedia,[32] of the Latin world that each of Beroaldo's pupils, upon returning home, brought with him and kept for life. This is why, in the second half of the sixteenth century, the Bolognese naturalist Ulisse Aldrovandi (1522–1605) compiled a very detailed manuscript index (running to 80 pages!) of names and subjects taken from Beroaldo's commentary and bound it to the end of his own copy,[33] a copy that is now preserved in the University Library of Bologna (shelfmark A.V.KK.VII.38).

Ultimately, I think Beroaldo would have approved of this use of his *Commentarii* since, at the end of the prologue (*praefatio*), he speaks to his reader and encourages them to become familiar with Apuleius' masterpiece and to consider it (of course with his own commentary) as a handbook, a textbook:

> Te, lector, oro, moneo, hortor ut familiaris tibi fiat hic scriptor sitque tuum manual et enchiridion in quo si quid durum videbitur id nostrorum commentariorum expolitione emollietur ac levigabitur.[34]

> Reader, I pray, I encourage, I urge you in order for this author to become familiar to you and a sort of a handbook and a manual, where, if you find something difficult, it will be smoothed over by the polish of my comment.

The use of the classical text as a pretext for showing off the scholar's culture was a very widespread custom during the Humanistic period. Rather less widely diffused was Beroaldo's peculiar custom of acting as *interpres* to provide a gloss we can often define as 'politically correct', namely a gloss in which the Bolognese professor tries to account for the various positions on a given subject, sometimes without making his own position clear. This could

---

[31]   P. G. Walsh, 'Petronius and Apuleius', in *Aspects of Apuleius' 'Golden Ass': A Collection of Original Papers*, eds B. L. Jijmans Jr and R. Th. van der Paardt (Groningen 1978) 17–24 (32); C. C. Schlam, *The 'Metamorphoses' of Apuleius: On Making an Ass of Oneself* (London 1992) 1. According to Schlam, Beroaldo and Adlington 'saw the work as edifying and having religious depth'.

[32]   Cf. *Renaissance Encyclopedism: Studies in Curiosity and Ambition*, eds S. W. Blanchard and A. Severi (Toronto 2018).

[33]   It is worth recalling that the *Tabula Apulei* ('Habes lector humanissime L. Apulei de Asino aureo tabulam vocabulorum et historiarum') mentioned by Carver is present only in some copies of the *editio princeps*: *Protean Ass* (n. 1, above) 190.

[34]   Beroaldo, *Commentarii* (n. 3, above) f. 1v.

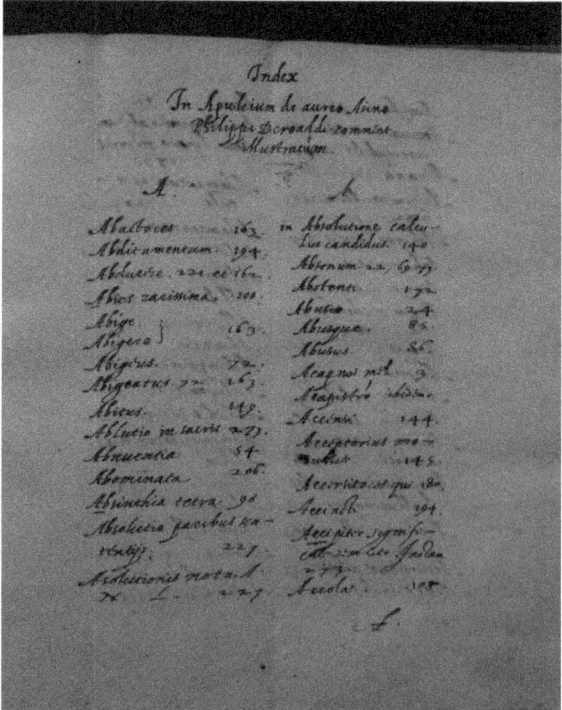

Figures 2. and 3. Beroaldo's *Commentarii in Lucii Apuleii Asinum aureum* (Bologna 1500), copy belonged to Ulisse Aldrovandi (Bologna, University Library of Bologna, A.V.KK.VII.38). Note of ownership at the beginning 'Ulissis Aldrovandi et amicorum' (f. a1r) and manuscript index of remarkable things at the end (f. 1r). Modern numbering in pencil at the bottom right.

also be due to the fact that, in contrast to many of his colleagues, he had a peaceful nature and did not like to engage in controversy. When Beroaldo tries to explain what 'crepitaculum' in *Met.* 11.4 means, he reports the version of the story given by Lucian, the use of the term in Livy and Pliny, and the conflicting opinions of the Platonists and the Aristotelians on celestial harmony:

> *Dextra ferebet crepitaculum* (11.4): Lucianus simulacrum deae describens [...] cuius rei praeter poetas Livius [26.5.9] quoque et Plinius [2.54] meminere [...] De musico mundi concentu et syderum tinnitu Plato et platonici omnes scribunt [...] Quod Aristoteles et aristotelici alacriter inficiantur [...].

> *Dextra ferebet crepitaculum* (11.4): Lucian by describing the statue of the goddess [...] besides the poets also Livy [26.5.9] and Pliny [2.54] remember it [...] About the harmonious concert of the world and the hum of the stars, Plato and all Platonists write [...] This is clearly denied by Aristotle and the Aristotelians [...]

He then concludes this review as follows:

> Caeterum cum commentatoris officium sit varias interpretationes afferre et non solum quid sibi sed quid et aliis videatur ostendere, dixi opiniones aliorum super hac re mysticas, quas qui volet sequi possit. Ego vero existimo per crepitaculum hoc significari sistrum, quod Isis dea Egyptiorum gestat in dextra.[35]

> After all, since the duty of the commentator is to report different interpretations and to show not only his own opinion, but also those of others, I report the mystical opinions of others on this matter, so that (he) who wants to follow them can do so. However, I think that this 'crepitaculum' means 'sistrum', which Isis, Egyptian goddess, wears on her right hand.

This programmatic statement about the task of the commentator is the same as we find at the end of the Prolusion of Beroaldo's first great commentary to Propertius (1487), where he clearly cites the source of the idea of writing commentaries on texts, that is Jerome's *Contra Rufinum* (I 17).[36] It is, thus, not surprising that Beroaldo's glosses grow year after year, eventually drowning out Apuleius' text. This is why Beroaldo's commentary also represents today a *summa* of fifteenth-century Humanism and a kind of ideal index of Beroaldo's previous works, which he often refers to for further information about the meaning of a word or the amendment of a passage.[37]

---

[35]   Beroaldo, *Commentarii* (n. 3, above) f. 255v.

[36]   F. Lo Monaco, 'Alcune osservazioni sui commenti umanistici ai classici nel secondo Quattrocento', in *Il commento ai testi : atti del Seminario di Ascona 2–9 ottobre 1989*, eds O. Besomi and C. Caruso (Basel-Boston-Berlin 1992) 103–39. Beroaldo often lets the reader decide on the correctness of a reading or interpretation, with formulas such as the following: 'Habes, o lector, utramque sententiam ut si haec nostra curiosius pensitata sordescit sequaris alteram vulgatiorem nec ob id me arguas inscientiae aut superstitiose curiositatis'; 'sive haec sive illa lectio magis placet habe utriusque interpraetamentum'; 'Hoc ego sentio, ita interpraetor cum primis hoc meum commentum est, heac mea interpraetatio quae si cui non probatur is habet alteram'; 'Haec lectio, haec distinctio, haec interpretatio magis placere magisque quadrare videtur quam illa superior sed hoc totum diiudicandum pensitandumque lectoris relinquo'; *cf.* Casella, *Il metodo* (n. 16, above) 650.

[37]   See the following two examples taken from Beroaldo, *Commentari* (n. 3, above) f. 6, 252v: 'non quidem Curio sum' [*Met.* 1.2, but today: 'curiosum']: 'in libro annotationum nostrarum [*cf.* F. Beroaldo, *Annotationes centum*, ed. L. Ciapponi (Binghamton NY 1995) 112, § 51.4] hic locus copiose satis opinor explicatus est, ex quo poteris siquid amplius desideraveris mutuari, ubi docuimus Curionem pro ministro atque praeconem usurpari'; septies submerse

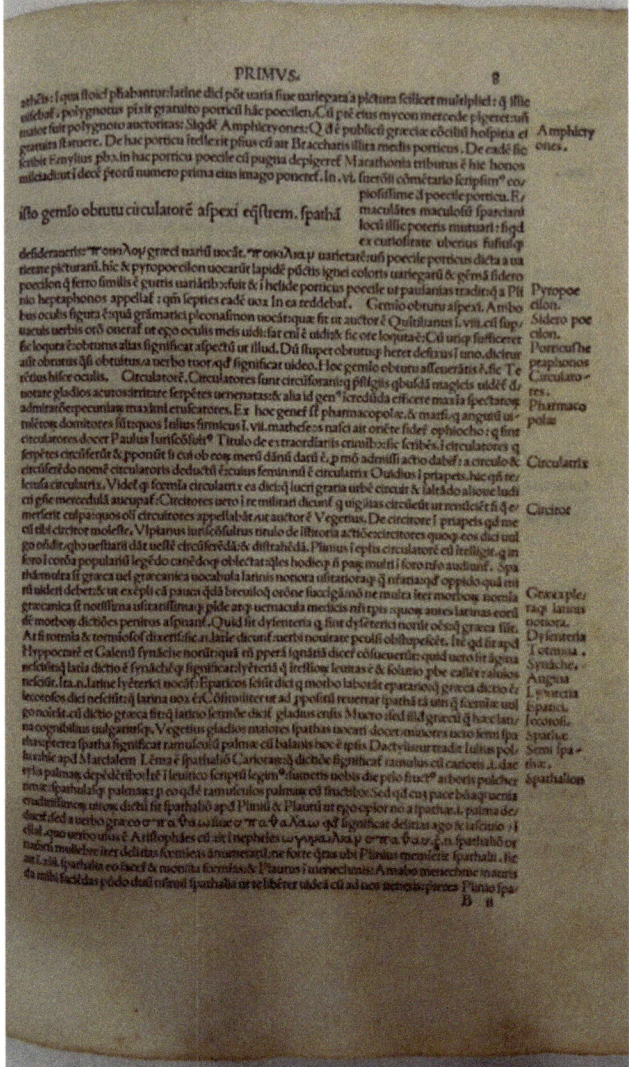

Figure 4. P. Beroaldo, *Commentarii in Lucii Apuleii Asinum aureum* (Bologna 1500), f. Bii.

I use the phrase 'grow year after year' because Apuleius is, like Pliny the Elder, one of the loves of Beroaldo's life. However, in contrast to his love for Pliny (his personal copy of which, full of marginal annotations, was lost by Beroaldo), that for the Madaurensis was consolidated in an edition. In one of his glosses, Beroaldo tells the reader that for many years he had taught Apuleius to his more familiar pupils in private lessons, from which statement we learn that the course held in 1500 was not his first on Apuleius but, rather, his first *public* course. As we read at f. 77:

Causae remissionem: Corrigo causae remissionem in causariam missionem et ita aliquot ab hinc annis corrigendum docui, cum privatim intra cubiculum discipulis familiarioribus Apuleium enarrarem.

capite [*Met.* 11.1]: '[...] de vi et potentia septenarii numeri scripsi copiose in libello qui inscribitur heptalogos sive septem sapientes [*cf.* n. 8] de septenario numero, qui graece dicitur heptas sic scribit Martianus in arithmetica [...]'.

Causae remissionem: I amend 'Causae remissionem' into 'causariam missionem' and so I have warned for some years that this reading has to be amended, since I taught Apuleius to the closest students of mine who frequent my home for private lessons.

Why did Beroaldo love Apuleius so much? So much so, in fact, that we can call him, in addition to the Bolognese Commentator par excellence, an 'alter Apuleius', a 'second Apuleius'? This is not an easy question to answer. Apuleius and Beroaldo certainly had many things in common. First of all, they were both wonderful rhetoricians, whose verbal performances were followed by large crowds. For both of them, variety ('varietas') and the pleasantness of literary forms were, as Lara Nicolini has pointed out with reference to Apuleius, a sort of 'religion'.[38] Both Apuleius and Beroaldo liked to play with masks and, like Apuleius, Beroaldo chiefly presented his image and life through his orations and commentaries[39] (in doing so, Beroaldo believed himself to be legitimized by Apuleius' *Golden Ass*, since, like his contemporaries, he takes for granted the identity of the *Metamorphoses*' author with the main character of the work).[40] Furthermore, they both have an artisanal idea of literature, according to which writing a literary work means, as Apuleius says in his *Florida* (9.24 sqq.), 'reficere poemata omnigenus', that is, reviving the different forms of literary expression,[41] or, in short, taking already-used stories and phrases and using them to create something new. Last but not least, Apuleius and Beroaldo share the belief that speaking well means living well, and that the highest form of philosophy is moral; the *studia humanitatis* teaches nothing of heavenly things or the afterlife of men (one of Beroaldo's favourite mottos is from Socrates: 'quod supra nos, nihil ad nos', 'What is above us, is nothing to us'), but it can teach the best way of living in this earthly life (*cf.* Apul. *Flor.* 7.10: 'disciplinam regale tam bene dicendum quam ad bene vivendum repertam').

Unfortunately, Beroaldo never wrote any narrative texts, in contrast to another important Apuleian fan and Italian Renaissance genius, Leon Battista Alberti, who wrote the masterpiece *Momus sive de principe*. In spite of everything, Beroaldo's prose is generally full of humour and jokes, undoubtedly reaching the apex of his humoristic writing in 1499 with the *Declamatio lepidissima ebriosi, scortatoris, aleatoris de vitiositate disceptantium* ('Very funny declamation of a drunkard, a womanizer, and a gambler talking about debauchery').[42] This declamation was very popular in Europe (it was translated three times into German, then into French and English), although it was generally perceived by religious scholars to be a satirical piece directed against the vices of men, such as priests, and thus as valuable for teaching purposes (typical of the medieval manner). Very few scholars noted and appreciated

---

[38]   L. Nicolini, 'Introduzione', in Apuleio, *Le metamorfosi o 'l'asino d'oro'* (Milano 2013) 5–57 (52).

[39]   Gaisser, *Fortunes of Apuleius* (n. 1, above) 5.

[40]   Gaisser, *Fortunes of Apuleius* (n. 1, above) 30. The famous 'Quis ille' in the prologue of Apuleius' novel is annotated as follows by Beroaldo: 'significatur autem ipsemet Apuleius', *cf.* Beroaldo, *Commentarii* (n. 3, above) f. 3v. For the hermeneutical and theoretical problems of the 'Quis ille' see: S. J. Harrison, 'The speaking book: the prologue to Apuleius' *Metamorphoses*', *Classical Quarterly* 40.2 (1990) 507–13; R. Nicolai, '*Quis ille*? Il proemio delle *Metamorfosi* di Apuleio e il problema del lettore ideale', *Materiali e discussioni per l'analisi dei testi classici* 42 (1999) 143–64.

[41]   G. De Trane, *Scrittura e intertestualità nelle 'Metamorfosi' di Apuleio* (Lecce 2009) 9. Beroaldo's colleague, Antonio Urceo Codro, expressed very clearly this idea at the beginning of his *Sermo* I, through words to which Beroaldo would certainly have subscribed: 'Accipite laetis animis, viri clarissimi, sermonem meum, si modo meus est qui sit a virorum doctissimorum sententiis concinatus [...] Praeterea ego quoque quotidie fere Luciani et Apuleii asinos in manibus habeo, unius brevitatem et inventum, alterius copiam admirans atque elegantiam'. *Cf.* Urceo Codro, *Sermones* (n. 12, above) 60.

[42]   F. Beroaldo, *Declamatio ebriosi, scortatoris et aleatoris* (Bologna: Benedictus Hectoris, 1499 ISTC ib00471000).

the Apuleian wit and humour that permeate the text. Among them we can count the German humanist Wolfgang Schenk, who, in 1501 in Erfurt, decided to publish a new edition of Beroaldo's *Very funny declamation*.[43] From the dedication letter of the editor Maternus Pistoriensis to Andrea Delicensis we understand that Beroaldo's humour and style delighted them. It is not by chance that the publisher, the above-mentioned Wolfgang Schenk, chose to translate his own name from German into Latin with the term 'Pocillator' ('cupbearer'), a rare Apuleian word used three times in *The Golden Ass* (6.15; 6.24; 10.17). While this is only a small example, I suggest that this love for precious and rare Apuleian words is, much more than Platonic or Neoplatonic allegories, the real bequest that Beroaldo passed down to European scholars through his commentary.

University of Bologna

---

[43]   A. Severi, *Filippo Beroaldo il vecchio un maestro per l'Europa : da commentatore di classici a classico moderno (1481–1550)* (Bologna 2015) 121–33.

INDEX

Lightning Source UK Ltd.
Milton Keynes UK
UKHW052026030221
378216UK00002B/4